COUP D'ÉTAT IN AMERICA

COUP D'ÉTAT
IN AMERICA

THE CIA AND THE

ASSASSINATION

OF JOHN F. KENNEDY

ALAN J. WEBERMAN

MICHAEL CANFIELD

FOREWORD BY HENRY B. GONZALEZ
CHAIRMAN, HOUSE BANKING COMMITTEE

QUICK AMERICAN ARCHIVES
P. O. BOX 429477
SAN FRANCISCO, CA 94142-9477

Revised edition published by Quick American Archives, a division of Quick
Trading Company.

Revised edition ISBN # 0-932551-10-6
Library of Congress Catalog Card Number: 92-60517

First Printing, revised edition 1992

First edition published by The Third Press
Two printings, 1975

First edition ISBN # 0-89388-204-6
First edition Library of Congress Card Catalog Number: 75-4360

Editors: Ed Rosenthal
              Deborah Zippel
Continuity: Jane Klein

Printed in the United States of America

Distributed by: Quick Trading Company
                P.O. Box 429477
                San Francisco, CA 94142-9477
                (510) 533-0605

                Publishers Group West

Contents

For

Sara Weberman

and

Henry E. Canfield

The authors wish to give special thanks to the following:

Tom Forcade, Max Zetscher, Michael Leahy of National Archives, Marion Johnson, Gail Beagle, Klaus Liedke of Stern, Rex Weiner, Bill Briggs, Ellen Ginsberg and Abbie Hoffman.

ACRONYMS

AFLID-American Federation of Free Labor Department-CIA front group headed by Peter Grace which funnels money to non-communist labor unions and aids in the destabilization of Latin American governments.

AID-Agency for International Development.

Alpha 66/SNFE-Second National Front of Escambray (in coalition with MRP).

BOP-Bay of Pigs Invasion.

CD-Commission Document.

CDM-Christian Democratic Movement.

CIA-Central Intelligence Agency.

CIC-Counter Intelligence Corps (obsolete).

CID-Criminal Investigations Department-Army Intelligence.

Co-Intell-Domestic intelligence program probably implemented by the Nixon Administration.

CRC-Cuban Revolutionary Council.

CRF-Cuban Revolutionary Front.

CTIA-Committee To Investigate Assassinations (reputed CIA front group which has co-opted assassination research field).

DRE-Student Revolutionary Directorate (CIA-controlled student exile group).

Ex-Combatientes-Veterans of BOP trained by U.S. Army in South Carolina.

FBI-Federal Bureau of Investigation.

G-2-Army Intelligence.

HSCA-House Select Committee on Assassinations.

INCA-Information Council of Americas (CIA-influenced anti-Castro propaganda organization).

ICA-International Cooperation Administration.

Interpen/IAB-Intercontinental Penetration Force/International Anti-communist Brigade (anti-Castro group made up of Cubans and Americans led by Frank Sturgis).

IRS-Internal Revenue Service.

JURE/JUNTA-Junta Revolutionaria (leftist exile group led by Manolo Ray).

MIRR or MRR-People's Revolutionary Movement ("liberal" exile group).

MRP-People's Revolutionary Movement

Operation Forty-Top secret exile group trained in assassination by U.S. Army.

ONI-Office of Naval Intelligence.

OSI-Office of Special Investigations (Air Force Intelligence).

OSS-Office of Strategic Services (the predecessor to the CIA).

Permindex/CMC-Permindex-Commercial Mondale Credit-CIA front group in Italy that has funneled money to opponents of the Italian Communist Party.

PRS memo-Memorandum issued by Secret Service regarding potential threats to the President.

SS-Secret Service.

TSBD-Texas School Book Depository.

YAF-Young Americans for Freedom (conservative youth group).

Present Publisher's Note

When A.J. first started researching the Kennedy assassination more than 20 years ago, I used to visit him in his study. He was a thorough, determined and detail minded scholar, sort of a Talmudic researcher. As he pieced together the puzzle, the enthusiasm among his friends grew. We knew he was solving the crime of the century, which would result in major changes in government policies.

In hindsight, we were just a little naive. The junta which plotted control of U.S. policy is in firmer control than ever. Its objectives are greater, and its influence permeates virtually all aspects of American media and government.

Until recently, Weberman believed that the coup took place the day Kennedy was shot. Now we see that it began much earlier. I think that it began in 1949, when Congress authorized the formation of the CIA. This was the first time the U.S. sponsored a covert action agency during peacetime.

During WWII the government set up a temporary spy and covert action group called the OSS, Office of Strategic Services. Influential members included Alan Dulles, William Casey, Richard Helms, James Angleton and E. Howard Hunt. After the war, instead of disbanding, the organization was converted into a permanent part of the government.

From the beginning it had a secret budget and a secret agenda that was not under the purview of Congress. It started as a rogue organization run by a hard-line reactionaries who thought that they, not the American people, should control American foreign policy.

The CIA's first big project was in Greece in 1948 and 1949. It carried out dis-information campaigns, funded extreme right-wing groups and assassinated left-wing politicians, labor leaders, and troublesome American journalists.

By 1952, Arbenz, a democratically elected Guatemalan leader was overthrown in a CIA coup. This was a major departure in American foreign policy. Previously, the army and marines were used to quell uprisings in Central America.

Until 1963 the CIA and the elected government had similar objectives. They diverged for the first time over Cuban policy. The CIA was heavily involved with the Cubans. While Eisenhower was in power, the Agency funded anti-Castro right-wing paramilitary organizations which were preparing for an invasion of the island. These organizations used the Florida Keys to launch raids aimed at destroying the Cuban infrastructure.

Kennedy had a different vision. His Soviet counterpart, Kruschev was also a radical reformer. They were both trying to cool off the cold war and warm up relations. A nuclear arms treaty was signed, joint scientific research programs initiated, strategic accommodations were made by both parties and a new era was upon us.

There were a few problems. The hardliners in both countries could not countenance the new policies which did not meet the ideological objectives of the warriors. To thwart the peace process, the CIA sent Oswald to the Soviet Union where he informed the Soviets of the U2 overflights. The Soviets knocked the spy plane out of the sky and ended the first tentative feelers at detente.

Kennedy's attitudes were anathema to the hardliners. They felt he was a Communist sympathizer or close to it. Even worse, he had expressed dissatisfaction with the Agency and was planning to either eliminate or revamp it. The CIA solution – eliminate the obstacle.

After the assassination, the CIA's budget grew and it gained more power. It took over various parts of the U.S. foreign policy. Policies regarding Vietnam, Iran and Central America were under the CIA's purview, often in direct conflict with the objectives of the State Department. During the late sixties and early seventies the CIA sponsored a "secret army" of 50,000 in Laos and Cambodia.

Starting with the Nixon administration, the CIA began trying to take control of the government, not just foreign policy. The Watergate affair was a joint project between the Nixon Administration and key Agency players. The objectives were to destroy the Democratic party, call off the election and declare a state of emergency.

Although it is part of the public record, most Americans have little idea of the nefarious plans of the Watergate conspiracy. When they were arrested, it was the second time the burglars were visiting Democratic headquarters. The first time they placed dis-information in the files which indicated that the Democratic Party was being funded in part by the Soviet Communist Party. Upon further consideration, the Administration decided that the accusations would not fly, and could backfire on the Republicans. The Nixon administration sent the burglars back to retrieve the information.

Nixon moved some key CIA players such as George Bush and William Casey into the political arena, where they were able to use their skills and dirty tricks to influence American politics. Bush's election was a CIA trumph. Forty-one years after it was formed, the CIA had one of their own elected to the Presidency.

Ed Rosenthal
March, 1992

First Publisher's Note

One afternoon in December last year I received a call from a friend in Washington, D.C. An acquaintance had shown him some unusual photographs. "Frankly, I was scared," he said, "but I told this man that I had a good friend who was a publisher who might be interested in taking a look at the pictures."

"Thanks a lot," I said. "How awfully thoughtful of you!" Jim explained that the material could prove to be quite important but cautioned that he was not in any position to vouch for its authenticity. Since I was due to be in Washington, D.C. that weekend, I agreed after some persuasion, to meet his man and take a look at this material, provided that I would do so in the presence of a third party. Since Watergate one has come to be cautious about meeting with strangers, especially those with "hot" information. That Saturday Michael Canfield walked into the apartment where I was staying and showed me two sets of pictures, one which he claimed were photos taken within minutes of the assassination of President John F. Kennedy, and the other, photos of known and easily identifiable figures from the Watergate episode. Without being discouraging, I was generally skeptical.

As is the case with all publishers, hardly a week goes by without someone approaching me with a manuscript or a book idea concerning revelations of conspiracy or some similar intrigue. Such material runs the gamut from the "they are after me" autobiographies of paranoids, through revelations of international conspiracies, to potentially serious and significant discoveries and insights on matters of major importance resulting from either accidental acquaintance with important documents or from years of persistent research. A good publisher must exercise skepticism at such material lest he find himself sponsoring material that is either simply sensational, or of such tenuous validity as to provoke controversy without substance. He can do damage to the reputation or careers of people who are either completely innocent or so peripherally related to the issue as to be, for all practical purposes, equally blameless. On the other hand, many books of importance have originated simply from phone calls or mailed manuscripts that may have appeared to be unjustifiably sensational, rumor-mongering or simply self-serving. Some have seemed at the outset to be the works of disturbed minds. Leaving aside those publishers who thrive on "muckraking" books, the serious publisher, by the simple act of publishing a manuscript, can create insights or controversies overnight that could have consequences both of a local and global nature, if the subject matter is of grave import.

What made the potential substance of Canfield's material problematic for us was precisely what might have made some other publisher jump at it: A story tying the Watergate burglars with the Kennedy assassination, coming at a time of overwhelming, and largely justified public skepticism over government credibility, could easily be a best seller whether or not the material was founded in truth or fact. The legal problems need not be that severe, since one could easily convert such a manuscript to fiction, with a perfunctory declaration of "all characters in this book are fictitious, and any similarity to real persons is purely accidental." But that would have been to beg the question. The Third Press has in the last few years built for itself a reputation for credibility and integrity; our ability to publish material of significance, no matter how potentially controversial, has always depended on the fact that we go to extreme lengths to convince ourselves that claims and assertions made in such material are verified beyond all reasonable doubt, at least within the limitations of our ability to make such a determination.

Convinced that a series of six to eight pictures did not make a book, I put Canfield through a barrage of questions that would have made the doubting Thomas of biblical legend look like the epitome of credulity. The more I was inclined to take him seriously, the more intense was my probing of his facts and information. There may have been many things going through my head at the time. Perhaps I was scared. Perhaps I felt instinctively that he might be on to something and wanted very much to convince myself that he had left no stone unturned in his efforts to make a case for his theory. But above all, I was concerned about the vulnerability of individuals involved in the story.

It has always been my position that, on matters dealing with the public's right to information, the person most in need of protection is the ordinary individual, who has a right to his anonymity and relative peace of mind, even if, at times, this has meant modifying the extent of public knowledge or curtailed the not infrequently excessive enthusiasm of a zealous journalist or publisher. It is not sufficient to be on the right side of the libel laws. Insofar as part of the commitment of the publisher is to make this world a better place as much for the individual as for society, a good publisher, I believe, can never justify losing sight of the vulnerability of the individual to the power of the published word. This is particularly important because, in most cases, the individual does not have the power to effectively refute that which may have tarnished him or her through publication. And even when he has such power, it is impossible to disseminate a rebuttal to an audience identical to that to which the initial damaging presentation has been made.

With all of this running through my mind, the first decision I had to make was to establish, very much like a grand jury, that there was a *prima facie* case. And although Canfield marshalled his information with such spontaneity and dexterity as to impress not just myself, but others who were present, I still felt a need to stretch my skepticism beyond what one might consider reasonable lengths. The first order of business was to establish, to my satisfaction, the potential consequences that release of his material might have on those concerned should the theory prove to be true. On the legal side, I tried to find out whether or not the rights and guarantees of the statute of limitations would cover anyone who might now be found to have been involved in an assassination that took place twelve years ago. In other words, could anyone be prosecuted as a result of revelations that would come out of such a book? The next order of business was to determine how many of those allegedly implicated by Canfield's theory, were private citizens, those without the power or position to defend or protect themselves against any potentially incriminating charges.

The third question was a strategic one: Assuming that Canfield's theory was correct, who would believe the story? In a slightly different context, who would buy the book? Although it was true that since Watergate, Americans had been shaken out of what most non-Americans have regarded for decades as a certain political naivete, the fact still remained that there was a limit to what they could be persuaded to consider.

It became clear that two things had to be done. One, Canfield had to provide answers to the thousand and one questions I and others in the room had raised against his theory. To do this he had to follow all possible leads and question all people alive who might be in a position to shed some light on the issue. All of these had to be fully documented and presented to me before I would consider publishing his material. Secondly, assuming that there was a plausible case, an audience had to be found. It might be necessary for us to team up with another publisher, preferably a magazine, so that our joint credibility and audience as well as our separate abilities to independently check substantial portions of the alleged facts, would create the best proof of thoroughness and sound publishing homework. So after cross-examining Canfield for what must have been the tenth time, we bade each other goodbye that Saturday afternoon and promised to get in touch with each other during the week, after I had a chance to interest some magazine publisher in looking at the material. To further emphasize the fact that I had made no commitments whatsoever, I declined taking any of the pictures back with me to New York, preferring to set up a meeting between any interested magazine editor and Canfield directly.

An hour or so later something happened that was to change the picture on the entire affair. I was still mulling Canfield's proposal over when the evening news came on. The lead story was a summary of the front page article that was to appear in the Sunday New York *Times* of the following day in which Seymour Hersh revealed that the CIA had engaged for years in widespread and far-reaching domestic espionage activities in open contravention of its charter. It had to be a godsend. In a matter of an hour or two following my conversations with Canfield, it seemed that our problem of finding an audience for such a book, asuming we published it, had been solved. If Americans believed Seymour Hersh's story, as they very well might, then we had an audience for Canfield's book!

But first we had to see just what Seymour Hersh had to say. It seemed like a long wait for the early edition of the *Times*. When I finally read the story, I looked carefully between the lines to determine the manner in which it was being presented. It appeared as if the New York *Times* was also concerned about overcoming the incredulity of its readers. The Hersh style indicated that the information the *Times* had gathered was being disseminated in little doses at a time. That Sunday I also remembered that Canfield had said he had shown some of his material to some reporters from several papers, including the New York *Times*. This posed a serious question, namely, how far-reaching was the material the *Times* had in their possession? Would they go as far as the Kennedy assassination? If so, had their researchers come up with what Canfield and his associates had come up with? Besides the problem of being beaten to the punch by the *Times*, what was serious was that we had no intention of rushing publication of a book on such a sensitive subject. Prior to the Hersh revelation we had assumed that we had several weeks during which Canfield and his associates could double-check their information.

The American public is one that, unfortunately, responds to books as if their content were the same as that of news magazines or television. As a result the "timeliness" of books has always created pressures on publishers that often lead to premature publication of material that might have been of superior quality had the authors and the publisher taken the time necessary to double-check their facts. This problem is not minor, because the timeliness of publication could make the difference between a best seller and a book nobody hears of. That Sunday, I decided to encourage Canfield to pursue his research as best he could without any commitment on my part to publish. Although I was convinced by now that the story, if published immediately, would do well no matter what its quality was, I decided to stick to our original plan for a thorough rerun of the research. I was only too aware of the fact that this decision on my part, while promising substantial moral satisfaction, might prove to be a commercial disaster. I was to worry about this continuously as every day thereafter the New York *Times* and other sources made new revelations about the CIA, while I sat on important information, awaiting double proof. Almost every day, something new came out which corroborated what Canfield had said that Saturday.

The following day in New York, I gave Canfield a small advance and he took off for what must have been one of the most nerve-racking and uncertain trips in his life. Canfield's assignment was to head for Miami and talk to Frank Sturgis, Bernard Barker, and all those involved in the Watergate burglary. He was to find out, one way or the other, if any of them had been involved in the Kennedy assassination or knew who might have been. For a few days thereafter we kept in touch with Canfield on a daily basis. One afternoon Canfield called in excitement to say he had made contact with Frank Sturgis, had gotten along very well with him, and had taped extremely important material. In fact, he said Sturgis was interested in doing a book and was looking forward to a huge advance for it. Sturgis, he claimed, had said that he could tell a good story about CIA domestic operations but only if granted immunity by Congress. Nobody else could protect him, Sturgis said; even the President of the U.S. had been unable to protect him in the Watergate affair. Much as the possibility of a book by Sturgis was exciting,

I had to concede that it would not make sense for him to put himself in legal jeopardy by writing a manuscript which could put him back in jail for violation of his security or CIA obligations regarding disclosure of information.

Next, Canfield headed for New Orleans and Dallas. In Dallas he spoke to, amongst others, the mother of Lee Harvey Oswald, Marguerite. Those conversations, both in their import and in their sheer drama, must be one of the most unusual conversations between two strangers. They revealed among other things, Mrs. Oswald's conviction that her son was framed and her bitterness over the seeming readiness of the book industry and the public to listen to anyone but herself on the question of who was behind the assassination of President John F. Kennedy. After Dallas, Canfield went on to Chicago, promptly ran out of money, and, thanks to my TWA Getaway card, we were finally able to get him back to New York.

A week later a friend of mine privy to my conversations with Canfield, invited me to co-host an interview of Dick Gregory on a radio program. Gregory had obtained copies of photographs identical to those I had seen, from another researcher, A.J. Weberman. Gregory had written to President Ford on Christmas day, requesting the reopening of the inquiry into the Kennedy assassination, on the grounds of new evidence. The following day I learned from Gregory that A.J. Weberman was in fact the researcher with whom Canfield had worked on the material.

A few days later, I met with Weberman and told him once again the thousand and one questions that had to be answered independent of the photographs, as I considered the photographs of relatively minor importance. There were issues of fact, theory and motive that had to be settled. After doing what I thought was a good job of expressing my continuing skepticism, Weberman promptly informed me that he had done precisely that and proceeded to show me several hundred pages of just such documentation. With Canfield having come up with the important interview with Sturgis, and with Weberman having put together the basic documents, I decided the best thing to do was to get the two researchers together to do the book. As soon as Canfield returned from his trip, I met with both authors. On that occasion I laid the ground rules and the conditions under which we would consider publishing this book.

1) Absolutely everything had to be substantiated and referenced even at the risk of over documentation. I wanted every sentence that in any way appeared to be an assertion properly referenced.

2) In all cases involving individuals, they had to be given the benefit of the doubt. In other words, the authors had to bend over backwards in order to protect individuals whom they had to mention in the book.

3) Nobody who had any burning reason to even scores with society (or with the U.S. government in particular) would be allowed to work on the book. In fact, no passions or intensities deriving from any previous political activity could be allowed to rear their heads in this manuscript. (As a result, a potential third co-author had to be dropped from the project.)

4) The book would have to be able to stand on its own, independent of the photographs.

5) The authors had to agree that even in the last stages of their research, any evidence they came upon that was likely to contradict their basic theory would have to be put in the book and identified as such. We agreed that it was not important that the book prove an airtight theory or that it point fingers or engage in any witch hunt, but rather it should offer the best theory so far on the assassination, laying out *all* the facts supporting or contradicting the theory. As a result, we decided to establish a complete section on open or unanswered questions (see Chapter 12). I was convinced that the public would be more satisfied with a book so designed and would not consider it a disadvantage that the authors did not provide a list of scapegoats. We decided that in spite of the pressure of the news that was breaking every day we would still carry out a long, thorough process of careful documentation and preparation, and publish on a schedule that took into account all the time we needed to insure that the final manuscript was meticulously accurate. Not even the obvious appeal of taking advantage of the tremendous press coverage accorded Dick Gregory's release of the tramp photos he obtained from Weberman and Canfield, could make us change our strategy.

Coup d'etat In America: The CIA and the Assassination of John F. Kennedy is a result of what must be one of the most thorough research efforts in recent times. It is also the product of three months of continuous rewriting, editing, legal vetting and more rewriting. A few comments about what the book is and how to read it might be appropriate:

(1) The book is a presentation of as much of all the facts on the assassination of John F. Kennedy as is within the grasp of private researchers. While making a strong case for what logically emerges from the evidence gathered, the authors have not tried to force the issue.

(2) The authors have meticulously avoided any appearance of witch-hunting. In fact, at our insistence, they have left out material which although highly plausible, could not be conclusively documented.

(3) In pursuit of the preceding policy, the authors, in their handling of the material from the exclusive interview with CIA operative Frank Sturgis, honored his request not to be identified by name. Although they had this extremely newsworthy material in hand at the beginning of the year, they held on to it as news items broke around them. When the first interviews took place, Sturgis had not requested anonymity. His request came only during a telephone conversation with co-author Michael Canfield following press reports of allegations linking Sturgis and E. Howard Hunt to "tramps" picked up in Dallas on the day of the assassination. By this time, our catalogues identifying the source of the interview had been printed. In spite of this, in a major sacrifice to honor Sturgis' request, the catalogues (which included books other than this one), were held back. Then, to our surprise, Jack Anderson published reports on Sturgis' secret testimony before the Rockefeller Commission. This was followed shortly by the extensive interviews of Sturgis published in the New York *Daily News*. Since there was so much similarity between these articles and portions of the Canfield interview, it would have been extremely easy for any reader to identify Canfield's source. It would simply have been futile to use "a reliable source" in place of "Sturgis." The authors have, therefore, identified the source appropriately here and we have

only just released our catalogues, two months late. Without a doubt, the decision to allow himself to be identified in the two articles mentioned above released the authors of any obligation to honor Sturgis' request. As for the authors, they did miss the opportunity to create another "Deep Throat."

(4) In his State of the World address to the joint session of Congress a few weeks ago, President Ford, referring to the impending investigation of the CIA, implored Congress not to destroy it. The CIA is important to me, he said, I need it and many of you sitting in this hall who hope to become President someday need the CIA.* Although there are strong arguments for and against the need for organizations such as the CIA, a strong case can be made (for those so inclined) for the need of all governments to gather adequate advance information on plans and activities potentially threatening to their national security. This, however, is a passive stance and cannot be confused with the aggressive action of interfering either in the affairs of other sovereign states or in the dynamics of American domestic politics and social life. The issue is not so much whether or not the President needs the CIA, but what kind of CIA would legitimately serve his needs as Head of State. In fact, in the specific issue raised in this book, namely that of the assassination of one of President Ford's predecessors, it would seem to be of extreme personal and national interest to the President to clearly determine whether or not suggestions of possible CIA involvement in John F. Kennedy's death (directly or by default) have any substance. Furthermore, there is a Frankenstein in all of us, hence we must be careful about creating monsters that may eventually destroy us. The authors and millions of Americans, like the President, will be more than relieved to see the CIA cleared of these suggested allegations.

(5) *Coup d'etat In America* is heavily documented. The seriousness of the subject matter demands this. The preponderance of unproven and sometimes irresponsible or outright false allegations against the CIA doubly compels this documentation. Fortunately, the book mades very easy reading. In preparing the

---

* paraphrase.

final material for publication, we tested the book out on many average readers, most of whom found it difficult to put down. For the detail-oriented reader, we have included over 600 references throughout the text. The reference numbers appear in such small type as to be absolutely unobtrusive to the less ambitious reader. As of the time of going to press, the authors intend to include acetate overlays in each copy of this book for the reader to compare the "tramp" shots with known pictures of E. Howard Hunt and Frank Sturgis. It is important to emphasize that the authors still cannot state for sure that these men are identical to the "tramps." Nor do they care to do so. It is up to the appropriate Congressional investigating committee to clarify this issue.

All has not been dead serious about this book. There have been humorous moments. Against the background of the currently popular "image" of a cloak and dagger CIA, innocent situations sometimes take on an importance of bizarre dimensions, as happened late one night when Weberman was working at his typewriter. A friend shouted something across to him that included the word "cover." In a split second, Weberman had disappeared under the table, his telltale typewriter still running. It turned out that the friend was only talking about the cover of the book. On another occasion, while waiting to be picked up, I found myself killing time by reading the manuscript. I looked up and found a security guard politely walking by. It was nowhere else but the lobby of the Watergate hotel.

After all is said and done, the concept of a possible coup d'etat in America should not be one that people find particularly shocking. Everywhere else people are used to changes in government by means other than the Constitution. This is not only in Africa, and Latin America, but in such citadels of democracy as Greece. In many of these countries, the military is not as non-political as in the United States. They are therefore the most obvious power group for overthrowing the government. Furthermore, the American Presidency is unique in that it concentrates so much power in itself that the government becomes essentially synonymous with the Presidency. Therefore, unlike the case of most other countries, changing the American President is tantamount to changing the government: And to the extent that this is brought about violently or by any means other than through elections (or by way of the Twenty-fifth Amendment, through which Ford became President) such a process of change is essentially a coup d'etat. Given the non-political nature of the American military and the confirmed role of the CIA in surreptitiously changing governments in foreign countries (not to mention the extensive power the CIA has come to develop over the years), it is not unreasonable to suggest that the most logical power to bring about a non-constitutional change in American government would be the CIA.

Americans are not too different from Europeans and what can happen in Greece and Portugal could happen anywhere, even in the U.S. The Watergate example is a case in point.

Furthermore, the CIA for years was involved in overthrowing foreign governments which its directors or immediate superiors did not approve of. It would not require a substantial psychological transformation to transfer the arena for exercising their expertise closer to home. Although plausibility should not be confused with culpability, the possibilities of a *coup d'etat in America* make as much sense as night following day.

Finally, although as publishers we cannot deny having persuaded the authors not to state more than they can absolutely document, this is not to suggest that we have absolute power over these two authors. If, after two months of worn blue jeans and frazzled hair, Michael Canfield and Alan J. Weberman appear at press conferences, on television, or at book promotion parties wearing red and white polka-dot ties (not to talk of complete suits) my editor and I shall have succeeded beyond our wildest dreams! If, however, they remain their old selves, we shall still be grateful for the enrichment we have derived from working closely with two of the most congenial and hard-working authors in our experience—and, believe me, congenial authors are not easy to come by!

Joseph Okpaku
Publisher

June '75

Foreword

On November 21, 1963 I accompanied my good friend President John F. Kennedy to my home city of San Antonio where he was very warmly and enthusiastically received. I had wanted, and the people of my congressional district had wanted him to stay longer in San Antonio and to dedicate the new John F. Kennedy High School there. The high school is in the poorest of the ten San Antonio school districts, and overwhelmingly Hispanic. The President promised me he would come back to San Antonio to dedicate the school.

I had tried to dissuade the White House schedulers from including Dallas on the itinerary because of the climate of hate which prevailed there at the time against the President. But then Democratic Governor John Connally told us in the Democratic Congressional delegation the purpose of the trip was to raise funds for the 1964 Presidential election. So, after San Antonio, I continued with the Presidential party to Houston and then to Dallas where the President died.

I wound up at Parkland Hospital and spent what seemed interminable hours in the confusion there, at one point finding Jacqueline Kennedy in a hall, sitting alone as in a trance. I happened to be in front of the room where the President's body lay.

I suppose I really had questions from the start as to why he died, who killed him, and from what directions had the bullets come? I was in car number four of the motorcade, and distinctly heard three shots.

However, I wanted very much, as did most Americans, to accept the official findings, especially those of the Warren Commission, despite the fact that there were many questions being raised, among them rumors and speculations which I thought were too fantastic to believe.

It was not until the matter involving Vice President Spiro Agnew in September 1973, and then the 1974 Watergate impeachment hearings that my suspicions became sufficiently aroused regarding the death of President Kennedy. Some of the Watergate witnesses testified to the effect that at the time there was great animosity against the President among those involved in the Bay of Pigs fiasco–to the point that some were interested in taking the greatest retaliation possible against him.

Also, I couldn't understand how an "expert gunman" like Oswald could miss his target when he had a clear shot at General Edwin Walker shortly before November 22, 1963.

At the time of the publication of the first edition of *Coup d'Etat in America* (1975) I was urging the enactment of my House Resolution (H. Res. 204) calling for the establishment of a select committee for the purpose of studying the assassinations of President Kennedy, U.S. Senator Robert Kennedy, and Dr. Martin Luther King, Jr., and the attempted assassination of Governor George Wallace. The purpose of such a study was, of course, to determine if we could prevent further national decisions by bullets, rather than by ballots, and the detrimental impact on our democratic and governmental processes.

Subsequently, in late 1976 a select committee was formed in the U.S. House for the purpose of studying President Kennedy's and Dr. King's deaths with the House Speaker naming a colleague of ours as chairman. The new chairman, as well as the Speaker himself, planned to leave Congress at the end of 1976–just three months away! This is the only time in the House's history a "lame duck" was appointed the chairman of a committee.

In January of 1977 I was faced with the challenge of having to defend the need to reestablish the select committee in the new Congress. (Select committees die at the end of each Congress and have to be legislated back into existence if they continue their work.) Unfortunately, the former chairman and former colleague had placed a staff director in charge who had taken some actions which left the chances for reconstitution of the committee shakey. After getting the committee reestablished, but with a limited initial budget, the new Speaker named me as Assassinations Committee Chairman. I resigned shortly thereafter when the House leadership failed to support me in the firing of the staff director.

Later, under another chairman, within a few days of assuming the chair, the staff director was finally fired. The committee spent $6 million and issued reports which were inconclusive about what happened in respect to the assassinations of President Kennedy and Dr. King.

Since the mid-1970's, people from throughout the country–pathologists, writers, social scientists–have shared with me their own private investigations.

Among the writers who I have gotten to know and who have shared with me their investigation of the John F. Kennedy assassination are Michael Canfield and A.J. Weberman.

In this new edition of *Coup d'Etat in America*, Canfield and Weberman continue to offer important research in our important quest, as a people, to learn the truth regarding the death of President Kennedy.

Our quest has been a long one, and hopefully we are coming to the end of it soon. Murder will out.

Henry B. Gonzalez

Henry B. Gonzalez
U.S. Representative
Washington, D.C.

Highlights

The following are a few of the highlights of this book. Each one is thoroughly discussed in the main body of the work.

* Contrary to the Warren Commission Report, independent research and the study of declassified FBI and Secret Service documents clearly lead to the conclusion that there must have been a conspiracy in the assassination of President John F. Kennedy. Although researchers have, in the past, challenged the conclusions of the Warren Report, most have failed to provide the one element crucially needed for proving a conspiracy, namely a motive. This book does just that.

* Evidence would suggest overwhelmingly that Lee Harvey Oswald was clearly a deep-cover CIA operative. His apparent "defection" to the Soviet Union was, in fact, a CIA assignment to gather low-level economic data. According to Yuri Nosenko, a former Soviet Secret Police Officer who defected to the United States shortly after the Kennedy assassination, the Soviets were "so leery of Oswald, who they considered mentally unstable and a possible 'sleeper'* American agent, that they tried to get him out of the country and vetoed his return when he applied in Mexico City in September 1963."

---

* "sleeper"—the Soviet term for a deep-cover agent.

* There is overwhelming evidence to suggest a link between convicted Watergate burglary mastermind, Everette Howard Hunt and Lee Harvey Oswald. (See Chapter 2)

* There is substantial evidence to suggest that claims in the press which link Howard Hunt and Frank A. Sturgis to the "tramps" who were picked up in the vicinity of the Texas School Book Depository after the assassination, have a strong basis in fact. A photo analysis of the now famous tramp photos, including an acetate overlay of known pictures of Hunt and Sturgis appears in Chapter 11 of this book.

In late April 1975, co-author Michael Canfield, in an effort to settle the controversy raging in the national media regarding the "height discrepancy" between the tramps who were photographed in Dealy Plaza and Hunt and Sturgis, took photos of the section of the Texas School Book Depository wall, in front of which the tramps stood when they were photographed in 1963. He located this area by finding the imperfections of the wall that had shown up in the photographs. He set up three yardsticks and a graduated scale with which to make measurements and working with the angles of visibility of identifiable locations on the brickwork, duplicated the angle and distance of the camera in the original photos. With these he computed the heights of the tramps (see chapter 11). Less than a week after Canfield arrived in Dallas, the following report appeared in the New York *Times*;

Photographs of three shabbily dressed men being led by police from the scene of the assassination of President Kennedy are being re-examined by a photographic expert for the Federal Bureau of Investigation. The expert was sent here from Washington on orders from the Rockefeller Commission (to) reconstruct the manner in which the pictures were taken on November 22, 1963, even down to the distance from the ground the person who took the pictures held his camera...By duplicating the distances and angles and by locating the reference points that appear on both the 1963 photographs and the new pictures, he will be able to compute the heights and weights of the three men.

Their procedure happened to be identical to ours.

* Contrary to published statements that Hunt denies having known Frank Sturgis prior to 1972, the truth is that they probably knew each other as far back as 1949.

(a) The name "Sturgis," which the convicted Watergate burglar (whose real name is Fiorini) adopted in 1964, is, in fact, a character in *Bimini Run*, a novel by E. Howard Hunt first published in 1949. The description of the book's major character, Hank Sturgis, as a gambler/soldier-of-fortune, is a fair description of Frank Fiorini, even as he describes himself in an interview in *True* magazine in 1974.

(b) In an exclusive interview with Canfield, Sturgis implied that he worked with Hunt in the 1950's.

(c) In an interview in *True* magazine Sturgis states he knew Hunt in the early 1960's.

(d) In a recent article in the New York *Daily News* an ex-CIA contract employee stated that she met with Hunt and Sturgis in the early 1960's in a Miami safehouse.

* There is evidence to strongly suggest possible links between the CIA, Oswald, Ruby, Meyer Lansky and the Syndicate, all of whom had reasons to hate John and Robert Kennedy because of Cuba and the Bay of Pigs invasion.

* Sturgis admits in an exclusive interview for this book, the existence of an assassination squad within the CIA. Its purpose was to carry out both foreign *and domestic* assassinations of political and military leaders as well as suspected double agents. Says Sturgis, "Operation Forty was formed before the Bay of Pigs invasion, it was a top secret government operation...there was also a group formed in which was the assassination section, which I was part of, that if necessary, this assassination group would upon orders, naturally, assassinate either members of the military in the foreign country, members of the political parties of the foreign country that you were going to infiltrate, and if necessary some of your own members, who were suspected of being foreign agents."

* In the same interview Sturgis says he was approached to carry out a *domestic* assassination: "And I told him well, if it was going to be domestic, well, I could do it in several ways. I could do it either in the Everglades, I could do it by boat, or I could do it by air. But, that if it was going to be done, I did not want nobody to be part of this, I would do it by myself, but I definitely wanted to meet the officer who wanted this done, and I wanted to see him and get it right from him, so I would be sure it would be from someone with authority, and not just a lower-level agent such as he." Sturgis does not say whether or not this "domestic assassination" was ever carried out.

* As a CIA operative Frank Sturgis joined Castro right from his early days in the Sierra Maestre mountains and rose to become his Chief of Air Force Security. In that position he offered to his superiors in the CIA the assassination of Castro and his top military officers: "I told my CIA contacts...pass the word upstairs. You want to kill Fidel...I'll kill him...I can kill him in two minutes."

* Loran Eugene Hall, a member of an anti-Castro group headed by Sturgis, and a possible CIA agent, was reported to have taken a rifle out of pawn "identical to the one used by Lee Harvey Oswald" about a month before the assassination. Hall paid for the gun with a check drawn on the Free Cuba Committee, a reputed CIA front group set up by Mullen & Company.

CHAPTER ONE

How It All Began

On November 22, 1973, the tenth anniversary of the assassination of John F. Kennedy, the Committee to Declassify the Warren Commission Documents held a demonstration in front of the National Archives in Washington D.C., the building in which the withheld evidence about the Kennedy assassination is cached.

About thirty people were addressed by *Executive Action* co-author, Don Freed, who told them that Warren Commission member Gerald Ford should be prosecuted for using classified documents in his book about Lee Harvey Oswald—*Portrait of the Assassin*. He also said that when Dr. Cyril Wecht was given permission to see some previously withheld pathological evidence, he found that Kennedy's brain, preserved in formaldehyde and allegedly turned over to the Archives, was missing!

While this madness was being exposed in front of the Archives, many people at a conference sponsored by the Committee to Investigate Assassinations (CTIA) were eating lunch, unaware of it. This was because earlier that morning, three policemen had ejected two Open-the-Archives Committee members when they tried to distribute leaflets about the event. The officers were acting on orders from Bernard Fensterwald (Watergater James McCord's lawyer) and Richard Sprague, the principals of CTIA.

The next day Phil Ochs persuaded me to go to the CTIA conference with him. When we arrived, Sherman Skolnick was in the midst of haranguing Fensterwald:

> We know all about CTIA—all you want to do is pick our brains—see where the current state of research is at. Come on. Come on. We know about how the Georgetown School of Foreign Affairs is subsidized by the CIA. Georgetown is a CIA training school. Why would they let us have a conference like this, here? We heard about the money the CIA gave CTIA through Lou Russell when McCord's first lawyer, Alch, testified on TV! You guys must think we're stupid—well I've got a petition here signed by 200 people demanding you allow us to have an alternative panel! We know that when a CIA agent gets sick he gets a CIA doctor, when he needs insurance he goes to a CIA insurance agent—when he gets arrested he gets a CIA lawyer!

Skolnick, who sometimes discredits himself by mixing pure fantasy with important facts,* got his 'alternative panel' but it was disrupted by a man named Amos Hickock, who began reading long lists of figures which were supposed to link the KGB with the Kennedy killing. Hickock also raved about how three tramps, picked up after the Kennedy assassination, were really Hunt, Barker, and Sturgis of Watergate fame.

At the end of the conference I met a woman who worked for Fensterwald, but who thought there was something funny about him. She said she had a friend who had some interesting pictures and tapes. We went back to her dormitory room where we were joined by a professor of radio astronomy who was also an assassination buff. The professor said I should take a look at four photos he had of three tramps being picked up after the assassination and compare them with pictures of Frank Sturgis.

"Which of the tramps looks like Sturgis?" he asked.

"Come on, man, you don't believe that nut Amos Hickock, do you?"

"Well, I didn't get the idea from Hickock, but you might be right, it could be nothing.... When I first came to this conference I was sure one of them was Sturgis, but I talked to Richard

---

* His research led to the incarceration of a federal judge.

Sprague and he told me to forget it. He measured the wall they were standing up against and one of the tramps was six foot four inches—Frank is only six feet! Sprague's the one who printed the pictures—but he does think the cops are phoney—he's been unable to identify them."

I took the pictures from the professor's hand and examined them. Not only did one of the tramps look like Sturgis but another one looked like Howard Hunt and the third looked rather like Oswald. It seemed that there could be more to all this than coincidence.

I asked the professor how he had come to make this startling comparison.

"Actually a student of mine discovered it. He happened to have been reading Sprague's article in *Computers and Automation*—that's where you can find the four tramp pictures—on the same day the Watergate story broke. He put the *Computers and Automation* magazine down next to the New York *Times* and..."

In a few weeks I had a copy of *Computers and Automation* and juxtaposed the tramp pictures with pictures of Hunt and Sturgis taken at approximately the same angles and under similar lighting conditions. My article about this—entitled "Wake Up America"— was printed in every major underground newspaper in America and England, but was largely ignored by the establishment press.

A few weeks before the article came out I talked about my discovery on an FM radio show. The next day I received a call from Jed Horne of *Time* magazine who said he wanted to interview me about my theories concerning rock star Bob Dylan. This seemed rather odd since *Time* had quite recently run a long article on him and I had already been quoted in *Newsweek*.

When he arrived at my home, he was more interested in looking at the tramp shots than anything else. I assured him that all my shots came from the May 1970 issue of *Computers and Automation*.

"That's a fine magazine," he said. "Its editor lost a lot of subscribers and advertisers because of all the space he allots to assassination theory." Ninety per cent of the material they print is written by members of CTIA. After Jed left I wondered if I had just had a visit from the CIA.

That night I had someone call Sprague and ask him if he saw any similarity between the Watergaters and the tramps. He said there wasn't any resemblance and Weberman and his friends were agents spreading misinformation. When the caller asked Sprague for negatives of the tramp shots (he had given them to many other researchers) he said he had lost them. I tried calling the papers where the photographers who took the photos were employed; two of them refused to deal with me and when I called the third, I was told the negatives had been missing since December 1973. We finally got a set of glossies from a researcher on the West Coast, and two additional shots originally photographed by Jack Beers of the Dallas *Morning News*.

A few weeks after the comparison shots appeared in the underground press, the headline of the *National Tattler* read, "Key Watergate Figure Placed At The Scene When JFK Was Killed." But instead of printing the tramp pictures, the *Tattler* printed one of a series of shots of a man bending down and said *he* was Hunt. If they had checked almost any of the other shots of the man in the series they would have seen that it wasn't Howard Hunt.

In the spring of 1974 Mike Canfield, a former McGovern campaign art director, was shown the comparison shots. Mike and I began to work together and we opened up an 'office' in Washington, D.C.

I did the research. I looked through *every* piece of paper in the National Archives regarding the Kennedy assassination that was not withheld by the Government. I began by speedreading every one of the 1,555 Warren Commission documents (about 10% of them were still classified); some of them were five hundred pages long! I also went through ten feet of news clippings, two feet of internal memoranda, four feet of the proceedings of the hearings, nine feet of depositions, five feet of Presidential Commission administrative records, eighteen feet of office files of staff members and one foot of records relating to the interrogation and trial of Jack Ruby. I read ten volumes of exhibits and the Warren Report. All this adds up to over one hundred feet of paper!

While I was doing this Mike was meeting with Rep. Henry Gonzalez (D-Tex) who had publicly stated his belief that the Watergaters may have been involved in the JFK assassination. When Mike showed the Congressman a photo of the tramp that looked like Hunt, he recognized the close similarity with the ex-CIA man immediately without even seeing the comparison shot. (Hunt biographer, Tad Szulc, had the same reaction.) Gonzalez had the official congressional photographer make copies for him because he was trying to get an investigation of assassinations started in the House.

Mike volunteered to help him and took the photos to twenty-two members of Congress he felt might be sympathetic, including John Conyers, Jerome Waldie, Ron Dellums, Robert Kastenmeyer and others. Twenty-one of them expressed an interest in the investigation

Encouraged by this response Mike took the pictures to the media where he received a very cold reception. The only journalist who even mentioned the fact that the pictures existed was Jack Anderson. But Mike did manage to meet Sam Jaffee, former ABC-TV correspondent to Moscow who convinced him that what our effort lacked was a carefully documented photo-analyst's report. Jaffee introduced Mike to Richard Pearl, who turned him over to Don Donahue, Sen. Jackson's chief investigator. Donahue arranged to have a photo report done because he believed that the matter was worth investigating.

Shortly after we tried to interest Congress in the tramp shots the FBI showed up at Rep. Gonzalez' office and said they were investigating Canfield. Gail Beagle, the Congressman's administrative assistant, set up a meeting between Mike and the Federal investigators and showed them the comparison shots.

Then, the agents went to Sen. Jackson's office and questioned Donahue. They found out who the photo-analyst was (Donahue had told us that the man wanted to remain anonymous so no pressure could be put on him one way or the other while he was making his decision), and they paid him a visit.

The next day Donahue called Mike and told him to come to his office. When he got there, Don gave Mike back the photos and told him the analyst had abandoned the project because he was afraid of losing his job.

Mike took it to several other photoanalysts but they all either dismissed our theories on the photos on the basis of an alleged 'height discrepancy,' or simply denied our suspicions. They all refused to document their findings.

Around this time (August 1974) I received a letter from Professor J. David Truby, an author of rightwing books on assassination techniques, stating that Hunt "was angry about (our) work in the Dallas/Watergate connection."

Despite the implications of Hunt's anger we continued our work. I made numerous long distance telephone calls while Mike tracked down Howard Hunt in a Washington, D.C. courtroom.

"Mr. Hunt, I'm a freelance writer and would like to ask you a few questions," he said. Hunt smiled and said he'd like to answer his questions but was under a gag rule because of the Watergate case.

"But this has nothing to do with that case...Where were you the day Kennedy was killed?"

Hunt's mouth dropped open and his lawyer, who was standing next to him exclaimed, "Oh my God!" Hunt yelled, "Get away from me, you creep," then both of them ran down the hall and disappeared!

Mike was willing to settle for an interview with Sturgis and he headed down to Miami where he got three hours of Frank Sturgis on tape. This was far from an easy task. Mike reports: "I went over to Frank's house and waited there three days until he finally returned home. I told him I was interested in doing a book with him and we decided we should make some tapes. The next day we spent about five hours together. I recorded him as we drove around downtown Miami looking for a bank he had business in, and we soon ended up in a fashionable restaurant where I bought Frank lunch. I tried to contact Martinez and Barker but they wouldn't speak to me at length since they were under contract with *Harper's*. From there I traveled to New Orleans to speak with Jim Garrison, then I headed to Dallas where I interviewed the ex-chief of homicide, Will Fritz, and the photographers who took the tramp shots. I next measured the wall the tramps were standing up against. I also looked through the Dallas police yearbook for 1963 and found out the names of the officers who brought the tramps in. Because this was so easy to do I wondered why Sprague had been unable to identify them for years."

* * * * *

During the winter of 1974 I was contacted by Dick Gregory, who was interested in the tramp photographs. I gave Gregory copies of the photos and he immediately held a press conference which received considerable national attention. About a month later Gregory testified before the Rockefeller CIA Domestic Activities Panel. He also did numerous interviews and television shows.

Hunt threatened to sue Gregory. While Gregory was giving the tramp photos media exposure, Mike and I continued to process the data we uncovered in the Archives and elsewhere—the tramp shots were but a small part of the overall picture. They had to be put in the context of all the available information on the assassination if they were to have any meaning and validity.

It might have been more profitable to release the book concurrent with Gregory's publicity, but, as our publisher kept reminding us, we were putting together a book of enormous import and of potentially far-reaching implications. "This is a sober undertaking," he would say, "every detail must be checked and rechecked so that when the book comes out every reader will agree that it is as exhaustive a study of this sensitive subject as the resources of mind and body could produce."

Now that we have completed our work we completely agree with our publisher, and believe that we have put forward a book which we hope that, no matter how controversial, many people will agree reflects the sobriety, restraint and good judgment that our publisher calls "the hallmark of responsible writing."

* * * * *

Hunt threatened to sue Gregory but never went through with it. When I spoke with Hunt's lawyer he told me it was because Gregory had no property—actually he owns a large farm outside of Boston.

While Mike was in Dallas he called Lee Harvey Oswald's cantankerous mother, Marguerite. Marguerite hung up on Mike at least three times and wouldn't speak to him unless he paid her in advance. But Mike persisted and explained he was working with Congressman Gonzalez. Marguerite told him, "If Mr. Gonzalez wants to know anything from me, or wants to open the case, let him do so and call me as a witness." Mike then told her about the Watergaters' alleged involvement. "I am not interested in the things you are speaking about," she responded, "I haven't gone into that. My interest is in the framing of my son and who framed him. You know Jack Ruby pulled the trigger, but Jack Ruby didn't have my son killed. He just pulled the trigger. And that's the phase that I'm interested in, which is the natural phase. I really don't care who killed President Kennedy. What I care is that my son didn't kill President Kennedy...well I mean I really listened to your story about Hunt and all but I haven't gone into it to know if you're accurate, or if—" Mike offered to show her the tramp comparison shots—"Now I've read about that. I don't know what you have, but I would assume that you're telling me what you already read in the *Tattler*....the pictures of the man picking up the bullet?"

Marguerite Oswald kept on: "I'm not the President of the United States. But I have tried to make it plain to everybody for the last eleven years I am the only mother of Lee Harvey Oswald. There's nobody else that knows his life like his mother...Just my name alone and something worthwhile to be published is gonna make money for the publishers. And if they can't see that then they're not worthy of Marguerite Oswald. I don't know how else to say it, Mr. Canfield. Look, the *New Yorker* magazine bought an article from Jacqueline Kennedy that was in the paper this week. Just because she's Jacqueline Kennedy? Don't give me that. I'm just as important as Nixon—to the assassination of Kennedy. I may not be a former First Lady, I may not be a former President, but I'm just as important. Now you've got a lot

of information for free, I'll probably never hear from you again."
And she hung up.

Mike Canfield says: "Marguerite Oswald has been abused by
the media and the Federal government. She's grown cynical and
bitter and is convinced her son was framed."

When Canfield returned from Dallas we began editing the information we had gathered trying to document the strong suggestion, engendered by our research, of CIA involvement in President Kennedy's assassination. We firmly believe, as does our
publisher, that the evidence we have gathered in the following
chapters speaks for itself.

In the rest of this book we shall be marshalling an overwhelming amount of well documented information. The importance of
this book demands this kind of thoroughness. Although it will
require of the reader more concentration on details than the
average general interest book of nonfiction, what follows should
be quite easy reading. To doubly guarantee this, we have decided
to start by laying out, in the next chapter, our basic theory on
the assassination of John F. Kennedy as we have deduced from
the evidence. Chapter two is therefore the conclusion that we
have drawn from the arguments we shall present from chapters
three to ten.

The Theory or Why Would Anyone Want to Kill Kennedy?

During the 1950's 'détente' was not exactly a household word. America was in the middle of a cold war with international communism. Domestic communists were required to register as agents of a foreign power under the Smith Act, and many were imprisoned for refusing to do so. It was alleged that Nikita Khruschev had threatened to "bury" America and many people were trying to beat him to the punch by building subterranean fallout shelters. Civil Defense authorities tested the air-raid sirens every month and psychologists speculated on the debilitating effects of living under the constant threat of nuclear holocaust.

Yet all the while, the American economy was chugging along, producing the highest standard of living ever witnessed by many people in this country. What was good for General Motors seemed to be good for America.

The CIA's programs to prevent the spread of communism appeared to be working and at least Americans had the consolation that their hemisphere was still untouched by the "red menace."

At the close of the 1950's there was a mild recession, an upcoming election and a bearded, long-haired Cuban who came down from the Sierra Maestre Mountains of Cuba and threw out the despot, Fulgencio Batista Zaldivar.

But suddenly the man who *Newsweek* had called "a hero" became the new Public Enemy Number One. Even though Castro's revolution was sponsored by the ex-President of Cuba, Carlos Prio, opportunistic hoodlums like Jack Ruby, and Cuban nationalists who believed Castro worked with leftists only for the sake of political expediency, the bearded insurgent suddenly announced he was a Marxist.

If Castro's supporters had known this earlier, they would not have had anything to do with him. In fact, if counter-insurgency experts like Bernard Barker had found this out a little earlier, Castro would have probably been executed by the CIA.

America could not let Castro get away with this sort of thing—Cuba had been our "private preserve" for decades and not only that, it might set a precedent for other Latin American countries. Eisenhower gave the 'okay' to have the exiles establish a beachhead in Cuba and then call for help from the Organization of American States (which would mean the Marines along with some token troops from various rightwing South American banana republics). The soldiers would shoot their way into the Presidential Palace and execute Castro. The leader of the exile brigade, Manuel Artime, would then become Cuba's new "El Presidente," or perhaps pave the way for Batista's return.

But the well-laid plans of the anti-communist establishment were thwarted by the election of John Kennedy as the new American President, rather than Richard Nixon. The men planning what would become known as "The Bay of Pigs" knew Nixon supported their effort; Kennedy, on the other hand, was still largely an unknown quantity—despite his campaign pledge to invade Cuba.

Kennedy fancied himself as an economic reformer in the tradition of Franklin D. Roosevelt: Instead of the New Deal, he offered the New Frontier and the Alliance for Progress. When the moment of truth arrived regarding Cuba, Kennedy reversed the traditional American foreign policy of "sending in the Marines" to any Latin American country where things had gotten out of hand. He refused to launch a second airstrike against Castro's Air Force. The invading exiles were bombed and strafed on the beaches, and the Bay of Pigs invasion turned into a fiasco.

Many conservatives, who had suspected that "liberal" was merely a euphemism for "crypto-communist," wondered if Kennedy was really working for the "international communist conspiracy." "Kennedy could have cancelled the invasion so that all the Cuban exile soldiers would be safe and sound in their training base in Guatemala," the argument went. "Instead, he let them land in Cuba, then refused to wipe out Castro's Air Force, leaving the invaders at the mercy of the Cuban dictator." Kennedy had done the worst thing he could have done to the anti-communists, some of whom believed, with varying degrees of conviction, that he had deliberately aided the communist cause.

It now appears that John Kennedy was doomed. He had alienated the most reactionary and powerful elements in American society—the CIA, the Foreign Policy Establishment, the Joint Chiefs of Staff, the gangsters whose Cuban holdings had been nationalized by Castro and the dispossessed exiles.

Fearing an invasion, Russia sent missiles to Cuba which were aimed at America. Kennedy gave Khruschev an ultimatum—remove the missiles or face an atomic war! Fortunately for all concerned, the USSR agreed to take the missiles back if Kennedy would promise to curtail the anti-Castro operations of the Cuban exiles. The young President agreed to this compromise and greatly angered the exile Cuban community by doing so. This episode was later to be televised nationwide by the ABC network in a factual drama, "The Missiles of October" in November 1974. The enthusiastic controversy with which it was received, rekindled in the minds of many Americans, vivid memories of those few tense dramatic days in October 1962. But this time with a difference—it was against the background of Watergate and the stunning revelations of numerous other covert government activities which a decade earlier few Americans would have considered even vaguely plausible. Our research and the evidence we will present in the succeeding chapters, suggest, overwhelmingly, the following as the most plausible theory of the assassination of John F. Kennedy, the thirty-fifth President of the United States of America. Only a court of law or the U.S. Congress can conclusively determine the truth of the assassination and prove or disprove the theory we give below. Such a task requires resources and powers far beyond the grasp, competence or authority of the average citizen or the private researcher. In what follows, we only make deductions and draw inferences from the evidence which, we believe, we have exhaustively documented. We make no assertions, and any impression to the contrary is accidental.

The Theory

By 1963 Kennedy's murder was being planned by assassination experts within the Central Intelligence Agency. Orders had come down from upstairs that Kennedy must die and the then recently formed Domestic Operations Division was assigned the task. The leader of its covert operations department had it in for Kennedy even before the Bay of Pigs and he recruited some of the Agency's most dangerous operatives who would be part of an elaborate plot to assassinate the President and blame it on an agent of Castro.

In innocuous "public relations" offices in Washington and Mexico City; in exile hangouts and safehouses in New Orleans, Miami and Dallas, members of a specially trained assassination squad called Operation Forty, were briefed on their roles in the conspiracy.

A CIA agent named Lee Harvey Oswald, who had a high "expendability rating," was chosen to play the role of "patsy" in the killing. A covert action team was sent to the city where Oswald lived. Their mission was to create the impression that a leftist assassin was running loose there by staging a phoney assassination attempt on General Edwin Walker, a rightwing hero.

In the summer of 1963 a strange charade took place on a street corner in New Orleans. Lee Harvey Oswald was giving out pro-Castro pamphlets with the CIA's New Orlean's address stamped on them when several CIA contract employees pretended to attack him. In a few weeks Oswald would use the newspaper clippings about the incident (along with the fact that he had defected to Russia for several years) in an attempt to gain a visa ostensibly to enter Cuba. Oswald was led to believe he was part of a plot to assassinate Castro when in reality he was being set up as a pro-Castro scapegoat for the John Kennedy assassination.

But the officials at the Cuban Consulate in Mexico City refused to issue Oswald a visa. If they had acted differently, and the visa had been found on Oswald's person after the assassination, most Americans would have been convinced that the assassin of President Kennedy was an agent of Fidel Castro. Castro would have been doomed.

Oswald returned to Dallas after his abortive attempt to get a Cuban visa and a woman with close ties to the CIA got him a job at the Texas School Book Depository. His CIA case officer ordered him to bring a rifle to the depository on the same day Kennedy was visiting Dallas and told him that there would be a message waiting for him somewhere in the building around 12:30 that day.

Oswald had to be kept off the sixth floor of the depository while the shooting was taking place. The plan would be worthless if he saw the CIA agent he spoke with in Mexico City standing next to a gunman who closely resembled himself because he would then catch on immediately that he was being framed.

Before the execution, the "Oswald double" had been visiting shooting ranges, appearing in gun shops, saying he was coming into money—in other words, doing the kinds of things one might do before trying to kill the President, if one were a Castro agent.

The rest of the assassination squad was located behind the infamous grassy knoll and consisted of two close friends of the former Mexico City CIA station chief. One of them would fire the shot that blew a good deal of Kennedy's head away (the one that causes Kennedy to be thrown backwards in the Zapruder film) and the other would pretend to be a Secret Serviceman (with CIA-furnished credentials) and tell police and onlookers that he had everything under control in the area. There were also two phoney Secret Servicemen behind the book depository to help cover the assassin's tracks.

Meanwhile, the killers, disguised as tramps, hid in some nearby boxcars, which appeared to be locked from the outside. All different kinds of Federal agents appeared on the scene and some of them knew which boxcars the police had to be dissuaded from searching. The assassins would have gone free if not for a sharp-eyed railroadman named Lee Bowers, who saw one of them jump from one car to the next as the freight they were hidden in left the yards. The tramps were brought in for questioning but were released on the FBI's word that they were guiltless.

The tramps' apprehension was not the only thing to go wrong with the plan—Oswald suddenly realized he was a patsy after a policeman stuck a gun in his ribs and told him that the Texas School Book Depository was under suspicion. He took a bus and a cab back home and got his gun.

When a policeman who might have been moonlighting for the Syndicate tried to execute Oswald (dead patsys don't talk), the latter turned the tables on him. Then, smoking gun in hand, Oswald headed for a nearby movie house where he hoped all the people watching the film would be witnesses to his arrest—thus forcing the police to take him alive.

After the initial attempt on Oswald's life failed, the Syndicate boss who arranged it was given the "contract." Jack Rubenstein had to kill Oswald or the mob would have killed him. Ruby had other motives—he had run guns to Castro and had been granted part of a gambling concession in return, only to have it all taken away from him when Castro closed down Cuba's casinos. Ruby had been part of a plot to assassinate the Cuban Premier which was sponsored by the CIA and he no doubt hated Kennedy. Ruby also had reason to hate Robert Kennedy because the Attorney General was determined to nail his former boss, Jimmy Hoffa.

Within forty-eight hours after Kennedy's murder, Oswald was shot to death in the Dallas County Jail while being paraded past dozens of reporters.

With Oswald out of the way, the only thing the assassins had to deal with were a lot of unanswered questions.

The new President, Lyndon B. Johnson, solved this problem for them when, rather than having a Congressional investigation, he asked Justice Warren to chair a commission of inquiry that would answer all the questions posed by Oswald's untimely death. Many of the Commission members chosen by Johnson and

Warren had close ties with Nixon (who had been the White House action officer during the early phases of Bay of Pigs), Nelson Rockefeller (the top family in the Foreign Policy Establishment), and with the CIA. Others were relatively independent.

These men in turn appointed the Warren Commission counsels. J. Edgar Hoover made sure the honest ones did not get to see the important documents by burying them or by having his agents prematurely close an investigation that touched on the CIA. Some Commission counsels were also taken in by their less candid colleagues and some of them now feel the investigation should be re-opened. The report itself was written largely by the Warren Commission staff members led by an Air Force historian, and differs greatly from the evidence found in the documents and exhibits.

With Kennedy out of the way, plans could be formulated for the elimination of Castro—but for some reason a second invasion never occurred. Perhaps the military felt that stopping communism in Southeast Asia was now of more pressing importance because of the "domino theory" and the large concentration of people there.

Shortly after Kennedy died, America began the costliest and longest war in her brief history—a war that Kennedy's close advisors claim he was trying to scale down.

The Kennedy assassination was thus really the first take-over of government by organized violence, the first coup d'etat in America, because after it happened there was a radical change in policy. It differed from most coup d'etats in that the man who replaced the slain leader, namely Lyndon B. Johnson, was not part of the conspiracy to assassinate his predecessor. The roots of the coup could be traced back to the Bay of Pigs as could the personnel who participated in it.

By 1972 there were two governments existing side by side in America, one visible, the other invisible. As the power structure became more arrogant and sure of itself, the invisible government became more clear and overt. Watergate gave us a glimpse into how invisible government agents go about their daily work: One could compare the *modus operandis* of the covert team caught in Watergate with that of the Kennedy killers. It also told us who were some of the people in Operation Forty and Domestic Operations and it became possible to trace these people's movements after the Bay of Pigs.

It also gave us a series of White House tapes in which Nixon expresses fear about Watergate "blowing the Bay of Pigs," something that would be bad for the CIA and American foreign policy. Since there was nothing left to reveal about the fiasco, "Bay of Pigs" might have been a code name for another CIA covert operation.

If the preceding is proven to be true, then Americans have been living under an Administration installed by the intelligence community for over ten years. Its history has been ignominious. In the mid-60's America abandoned her committment to the poor, and money that was needed for social programs went down the drain in Vietnam. Blacks were drafted in disproportionate numbers and used as cannon fodder in Southeast Asia. Riots erupted in the ghettos after which they were flooded with heroin. Democracy fell in Greece and soon after in the Philippines. Ruthless dictators came to power thanks to sponsorship from the CIA. CIA puppets also took power in Cambodia and Vietnam.

On the homefront our domestic civil liberties began to be curtailed—Army intelligence agencies spied on Congressmen and private citizens, the CIA opened mail going to communist countries, spied on anti-war groups—all in violation of their charter. The "Co-intell" program was signed into law by President Nixon (he claims he rescinded the order a few days before it was to go into effect because of strenuous opposition from J. Edgar Hoover) and covert operations, mail covers, wiretapping, disruption and provocation became acceptable tactics for the FBI to use in their "war" on radical and anti-Vietnam groups.

The FBI also launched an all-out campaign to stop the rise of a "black messiah" who would lead the former slaves out of the economic and social wasteland of the ghetto. Martin Luther King was made the subject of one of the most intensive surveillance campaigns in the history of the FBI and was probably the victim of the same covert action team that killed John F. Kennedy.

The Nixon Administration hired many of the Warren Commission counsels and the only politician to question the veracity of the Warren Report was a maverick District Attorney from New Orleans named Jim Garrison. Garrison's investigation was leading in productive directions but appears to have been 'Watergated' by the Federal government and the CIA.

Nixon began a campaign to bring the media into line and Spiro Agnew became a household name. The bombs continued to fall, Americans continued to die in Vietnam and Nixon continued to make further cuts in important social programs. His Supreme Court appointee, Warren Burger, was part of an effort to re-write the Constitution and the "destabilization" of Chile became part of America's foreign policy.

This was only the tip of the iceberg: According to an ex-Los Angeles Police Department political informant, Louis Tackwood, a faction of Nixon's secret police may have been planning to turn America into an outright military dictatorship. Tackwood claims that he was supposed to help provoke a bloodbath outside the Republican Convention while bombs exploded inside the convention hall, killing some of the delegates. A state of emergency would have been declared, the media and the mails would have been censored and the elections cancelled.

Then came Watergate, which temporarily forestalled the final phase of the November 22, 1963 coup d'etat. If not for the Watergaters' errors combined with Watergate guard Frank Wills' keen powers of observation, or if McCord had not been a double-agent, whatever, we might now be living under an overt military and/or intelligence dictatorship.

Despite Watergate, Nixon was re-elected and began to assume the proportions of a dictator by usurping Congress' power, impounding funds earmarked for social programs. It was not until McCord began to point to higher-ups that Nixon began to weaken. When the Senate Watergate hearings began, Nixon called on a lot of Warren Commission people to defend and "prosecute" him.

Suddenly Spiro Agnew was discredited and America got its first unelected Vice-President, former Warren Commissioner, Gerald Ford. Significantly (or perhaps ironically), the law that allowed Nixon to appoint the Vice-President had been passed as a reaction to the Warren Commission Report.

White House aide Alexander Butterfield administered the *coup de gráce* when he testified that Nixon routinely recorded everything that took place in the White House for "historical purposes." Interestingly enough, one of the most devastating tapes was the one that concerned "blowing the Bay of Pigs."

Nixon resigned and Ford became President. In the fall of 1974, Ford appointed Nelson Rockefeller Vice-President. Although Rockefeller was not on the Warren Commission, his top deputy, John J. McCloy, was.

Unless the forces responsible for the death of John Kennedy are ultimately exposed they will probably try to subvert American democracy all over again. It is up to Congress—only a full-scale Congressional investigation utilizing its enormous resources can finally present the American people with the true story of what was behind the Kennedy assassination. The evidence and arguments which we present in what follows, although substantial, constitute perhaps the best that can be expected of private researchers, even at their most diligent. The rest must come from Congress.

Will Gerald Ford expose the full Kennedy assassination story? Will a Democrat, if elected President in 1976, do so? The Rockefeller Commission could not have been expected to expose the CIA domestic assassination program. The ill advised appointment of former Warren Commission counsel, David Belin, (who had already staked his reputation in a vested position in his book, *You Are The Jury*), as counsel to the Rockefeller Commission, as well the background of some of the Commission members, doomed from the onset the Commission's investigation reports to open distrust and disbelief by most Americans, including many members of Congress.

CHAPTER THREE

Was Oswald a CIA Agent?

Lee Harvey Oswald's family had close ties to the military. His first stepfather was represented in a divorce suit by a former Secretary of the Navy, Fred Korth. His halfbrother was a career Air Force officer and his brother, Robert, served with the Marine Corps.

Evidence exists that Oswald's cousin, Dorothy Murret, was an agent of the CIA. This evidence is contained in Warren Commission Document 1080 which is a classified, withheld file open only to the Federal government and the Warren Commission and which probably would have been unavailable to researchers for at least fifty more years had it not been misfiled.

The first page of CD1080 is reprinted on page 269; the rest of the document is a biography of Harold R. Isaacs compiled from FBI interviews with him in the early 1950's. Isaacs was a disillusioned leftist intellectual who had become a professional anti-communist on a very high "think-tank" level.

Why is CD1080 classified? One reason could stem from the fact that the government agency that endows the Center For International Studies, with which Isaacs was associated, is the CIA. But this had already been exposed in a book by Ross and Wise, called *The Invisible Government*. Another possible reason could be its relation to another FBI document, CD942, which tells us that it had been alleged that "Murret was linked in some manner with the...apparatus of Professor Harold Isaacs" and that she traveled extensively in the Far East and spent long periods of time in India. CD1080 reveals that Isaacs was interested in Far Eastern affairs and his work "takes him away from MIT and consists of international travel and concentration on study in India."

The document (CD1080) does not say one way or another whether a connection definitely exists between Murret and Isaacs. However, the existence of this document, entitled "Marilyn Dorothea Murret," that does not even mention her but is entirely about a different party, certainly leaves room for speculation.

Was Murret really just a traveling "teacher" or was she using this as a cover for spying activities she was performing for Harold R. Isaacs, a professor at a notorious CIA think-tank? The FBI investigation stopped before they got a chance to interview Issacs.

Some speculation has been made regarding Isaacs' role in the actual assassination. In CD645 and CD866 a man reported overhearing two men speaking about the Kennedy assassination while at a Canadian airport. Richard Giesbrecht told the FBI that when the first man asked the second how much Oswald knew, the second one said, "We have a film that I have seen where Issacs is near Kennedy after the landing." The first man then mentioned something about Issacs, ending with the query, "Why should a person with such a good record such as Isaacs, become mixed up with a psycho?" In a November 1967 article in *McCleans Magazine,* Giesbrecht stated that the "psycho" referred to was Oswald.

An independent researcher at the Massachusetts Institute of Technology discovered that Isaacs taught the course,"Changing Outlook and Identities in the World,"every year throughout the sixties except for 1963 to 1964.

* * * * *

Oswald was a member of the Civil Air Patrol as a youth and when he became a Marine, he was stationed at Atsugi, a Japanese base devoted to training intelligence agents. A recently declassified CIA document entitled "Oswald's Access to Information Regarding the U-2" reveals that the ultra-secret CIA spy plane was kept on this base.[1] Oswald was taught Russian as part of his military training: Lieutenant Colonel Allison G. Folsom, in the course of his testimony concerning Oswald's military record, read out loud one of Oswald's grades in a Russian examination given him the same year he left for the USSR.[2] He also had security clearance.[3] According to ex-CIA official Victor Marchetti, the Agency was having a difficult time penetrating the totalitarian Soviet society of the 1950's. Oswald may have been part of an operation to put an agent behind the Iron Curtain who would pretend to be an average American soldier, disillusioned with capitalism. Oswald's hardship discharge from the Marines in September 1959 was probably part of the plan because it would indicate to the Russians that Oswald was no longer working for the United States Government and that his family had been victimized by capitalism, thereby giving him a motive to defect. In order to make his defection seem more genuine, Oswald waited until December before leaving for Russia and when he arrived there he said the only reason he had joined the Marines was to "watch U.S. imperialism in action."[4]

Just before Oswald left for the Soviet Union, the CIA may have sent another phoney defector there. Robert Edward Webster, a "plastics technician" from Pennsylvania, decided to remain in the USSR after participating in a trade exhibition in Moscow. Webster was working for the Rand Development Corporation, which might have been a front for the Rand Corporation, a notorious CIA-funded think-tank. Daniel Ellsberg worked for Rand when he copied the Pentagon Papers.[5]

* * * * *

Is the Rand Development Corporation a front for Rand and the CIA? When we called the Rand Development Corporation in New York City (it is listed in the phone book) it turned out to be the "crushed foam" division of Martin-Marietta, a conglomerate that also has a large aerospace division. Even though the phone numbers for Rand Development and Martin-Marietta are the same, no one at Martin-Marietta ever heard of Rand. We called their main office in Rockville, Maryland and got another categorical denial—"Martin-Marietta has a lot of things going on but Rand Development isn't one of them."

We went to the address of Rand Development listed in the New York City phone book and looked at the building's register—nothing. We questioned one of the doormen. "I've been here for thirty-three years and there's never been a Rand Development Company in this building," he insisted; then he added, "maybe you want the Rand Corporation—it's right across the street at 405 Lexington Avenue." We went to the library and searched through microfilms of old telephone directories: Rand Development's first appearance in the New York City telephone book was in 1958. At that time there was no listing for the Rand Corporation. By 1960 both organizations were listed. It remained this way until 1971 when "Rand Development" disappeared. By 1973 both corporations were listed again.

Several "coincidences" link the Rand Corporation with the Rand Development Corporation. When Webster defected to Russia, the Rand Corporation was in the midst of conducting detailed studies of the Soviet economy in order to find out what proportion of the Russian GNP went into National Defense. These studies entailed careful analysis of the average Russian's purchasing power. Webster was connected with the Carnegie Institute as was a director of Rand. The father of the president of Rand Development was vice-chairman of the board of Sperry-Rand which worked closely with the United States Air Force. Sperry-Rand had initially funded the Rand Corporation. During the course of a House Expense Inquiry it was revealed that Rand Development held several CIA contracts. Though initially formed by the Air Force, RAND received most of its money from the CIA. *

Extensive research has uncovered the fact that the Rand Development Corporation's president, Dr. H.J. Rand, was one of

* New York **Times**: April 25, 1955; June 15, 1959; October 20, 1959; April 16, 1967; March 7, 1968.

the first to undertake private negotiations with the USSR for purchase of technical devices and information. During the late 1950's CIA agent Christopher Bird [6] was Rand Development's Washington representative.

Dr. Peter Dale Scott, a history professor at the University of California, Berkeley, discovered that Webster's admission back into the United States was facilitated by "affidavits from Rand." [7] Dr. Scott, probably America's number one assassination researcher, already suspected that Sturgis was implicated in the Kennedy assassination about a year before Watergate broke.

It is noteworthy that Webster became "disillusioned" with Russia and returned to America a month before Oswald did. [8]

* * * * *

When Oswald reached Russia he denounced his citizenship at the United States Embassy in Moscow. The man he spoke with, Richard E. Snyder, has been identified by East German Intelligence as a CIA agent. [9]

Even the reporter who interviewed Oswald in his Moscow hotel room may have been working for the Agency. Consider the following:

When the daughter of Russian Communist Party leader Joseph Stalin defected, she stayed at the home of the Stuart H. Johnsons of Locust Valley, New York. [10] Because they would be in the position to undertake the first debriefing sessions undergone by a defector, it is not far-fetched to assume that the Johnsons had connections with the U.S. intelligence community. They are the parents of Priscilla Johnson, the "journalist" who interviewed Oswald the defector. Ms. Johnson had attended the Russian Research Center at Harvard University, which is part of the CIA-funded Center For International Affairs. Soon after interviewing Oswald, Ms. Johnson spoke with Richard E. Snyder of the U.S. Embassy. [11] In the 1970's the CIA admitted that many of its spies used the cover of "journalist" while working abroad.

Despite the help given to Oswald by his CIA contacts the Russians did not trust him. In spite of the classified radar codes he gave them, they would not issue him a visa. It was only after he staged a fake suicide attempt that they decided it would be more trouble *not* to let him in.

He was then given a job in a radio plant where he could be carefully watched. He made extensive notes about economic conditions in the USSR for the CIA. Even this kind of lowgrade information was valuable to the Agency because they were hardpressed for intelligence regarding life in Russia at the time.

While he was in Russia, Oswald's mother contacted the State Department and asked for financial help because she believed her son was on a CIA mission overseas.[12]

Soon the information Oswald was gathering became redundant and he received orders to return to the USA with his Russian bride, Marina. He visited his old friend Richard E. Snyder who said that because he had not filled in the special forms denouncing his citizenship, but had only denounced it orally and in a handwritten note, he was eligible to return to the United States. Snyder also conveniently forgot about the anti-U.S. broadcast Oswald made which he mentions in his diary.[13] This fact alone could have provided Snyder with grounds for holding up Oswald's return for years. Snyder was aided by other CIA agents at the State Department. For example, the official at the passport division, who was instrumental in getting Oswald re-admitted,[14] worked for Robert C. Johnson. Johnson, like Snyder, is listed as a CIA agent by East German Intelligence. Despite Oswald's obviously traitorous behavior the State Department granted Marina and him a loan. They took a ship back to America.

When Oswald returned, the authorities were not waiting to arrest him despite the fact that he had violated his Security Termination Statement in which he swore not to reveal "or divulge to any person any information affecting the national defense" and acknowledged that doing so would make him liable to "severe penalties" under the Internal Security Act of 1950. On the contrary, he was greeted in the port of New York City by another member of the intelligence community, Professor Spas T. Raiken.

Aside from working with Travelers Aid, Raiken was Secretary-General of the American Friends of the Anti-Bolshevik Block, an emigré group that worked with the CIA. Raiken surfaced in 1973 as a member of the Fairness to the President Committee, formed to defend Nixon against charges of involvement in the Watergate affair. [15]

The Oswalds then headed straight for Dallas where they were befriended by members of the White Russian emigré community, who had close ties to American intelligence agencies. One of the members of this community who befriended Oswald, Paul M. Raigorodsky, worked for the Special Representative to Europe—a NATO office—and testified that he had to destroy his credentials after he quit. Raigorodsky also admitted being on the Board of Directors of the Tolstoy Foundation which many researchers believe to be CIA-sponsored: "Now, anybody who comes to the Tolstoy Foundation—you know right off the bat they have been checked, re-checked and double-checked. There is no question about them. I mean, that's the number one stamp." Raigorodsky was questioned by Warren Commission counsel Albert Jenner, who asked, "That's the number one stamp of an approval or of their genuineness?" Raigorodsky replied, "Of approval—in fact the U.S. Government recognized that and has been, up until about a year or two ago, giving the Tolstoy Foundation as much as $400,000 year." [16]

Another one of Oswald's acquaintances in Dallas was the founder of the Dallas chapter of the Greek Orthodox Church which *Newsweek* reported was used as a CIA conduit. He also worked with the American Relief Committee, also known as The American Committee for Russian Relief, which "made a five-thousand-mile uncensored tour of Russia" assessing war damage. [17]

Oswald also knew the head of security at Convair, a giant war contractor. Convair employed former German scientists at its facilities.

There were many more. But the most important one of all was George DeMohrenschildt because he was most closely associated with Oswald.

DeMohrenschildt is a descendant of Russian nobility: his father was the representative of the landed classes to the Czar and was a director of Nobel Oil. After the Bolshevik Revolution he was jailed, but was soon released and became head of the Soviet Department of Agriculture. After a while he was re-arrested for opposing the campaign against religion, managed to escape, and spent the World War II years in Germany.

His family suffered under communist rule. George was forced to beg for crusts of bread while his brother, who was "a ferocious anti-communist," was jailed by the Russians, then exchanged for another prisoner. The two came to America where George's brother was first a foreign language examiner with the Bureau of Censorship, then soon became a director of the Tolstoy Foundation. He was also "affiliated with the War Department in an unknown manner." [19]

At the time of the Kennedy assassination, DeMohrenschildt was married to a woman whose father was the pre-revolutionary director of the Chinese National Railroad. One of her brothers was a CIA agent. Another worked for Howard Hughes. Charles Colson has said, "You can't tell where the Hughes Corporation begins and the CIA leaves off" [20] and documents released because of Watergate tend to back this up. DeMohrenschildt's daughter is married to the son of a vice-president of Lockheed Aircraft. [21] Lockheed is another corporation that employed former German scientists and it had worked closely with the CIA on the U-2 project. Lockheed's international representative became head of Nixon's security team in 1968. [22]

Albert Jenner* tries to make us believe that DeMohrenschildt had no ulterior motive when he asked his daughter to house Oswald [23] and allowed the self-proclaimed Marxist to use him as a reference on job applications.

Jenner continually asks him if he is or was ever a spy, because he had been accused of being one so many times in the past: In 1941 he was suspected of being a German spy; a few years later

---

* A Warren Commission counsel who eventually became Nixon's minority counsel on the Judiciary Committee.

he was accused of collecting data regarding the operation of a uranium plant; in 1957 he was suspected of spying in Yugoslavia.[24]

DeMohrenschildt denied he was ever a spy except for a stint with French intelligence during World War II. But in a moment of candidness he told Jenner that if he was one, he could take the Fifth Amendment if anyone questioned him about it.

In fact, DeMohrenschildt had a career that paralleled that of master spy Howard Hunt. Both men were connected with the Office of Strategic Service (OSS) during World War II. Hunt was in the 202 Detachment of OSS in China while DeMohrenschildt says he applied for a job with OSS, but does not say if he was accepted or rejected. There is reason to believe he was accepted because he was going to be used as a witness against a possible enemy alien *and*, when he was stopped for alleged spying in 1941, he had a letter regarding how to get references from Nelson Rockefeller on his person. (See document on page 269.) When he was stopped, DeMohrenschildt was on his way to Mexico where he would be deported for engaging in espionage with General Douglas MacArthur's nephew.[25]

Both Hunt and DeMohrenschildt were close to people directly connected to Pantipec Oil. In 1945 DeMohrenschildt worked under Warren Smith, who was then the president of Pantipec. Soon Smith and DeMohrenschildt quit and formed the Cuban-Venezuelan Oil Trust Company, "a land development company to promote eventually a large oil drilling campaign in Cuba...(We) almost owned about one half of the whole country under lease." When Castro took over, all of this was forfeited.

Howard Hunt worked closely with William F. Buckley on a deep-cover operation in Mexico in the early 1950's. Buckley's parents owned Pantipec Oil.

Both Hunt and DeMohrenschildt worked for the Agency for International Development, which, among other things, funded the construction of "tiger cage" prison cells in South Vietnam.

DeMohrenschildt was sent to Yugoslavia by a subsidiary of AID—the International Cooperation Administration (ICA)—to help the country discover oil so they would not have to rely on the Russians for it. (See document on page 270.) Hunt worked for the predecessor of ICA—the Economic Cooperation Administration (ECA), also a subsidiary of AID. [26]

Cuba in 1956 was a scene once again common to both men. Hunt was in Havana to attend a meeting of CIA station chiefs from the Caribbean and Central America, while DeMohrenschildt claims he was there in connection with the oil business. Yet DeMohrenschildt may very well have attended this meeting as a consultant—he earned his Ph.D. by writing a thesis on the "U.S. Economic Influence in Latin America." [27]

Both men were in Guatemala when troops were being trained there for the Bay of Pigs invasion; DeMohrenschildt ended up there after an alleged walk he claimed to have made from Dallas to Guatemala in 1960. He admits seeing the troops but claims he had no idea of their purpose. Hunt was frequently in Guatemala around this time. As the liaison between the CIA and the exile Cuban groups, he was there trying to straighten out differences between the troops and their leadership.

In retrospect, we see the connections between Oswald, De-Mohrenschildt and the man who's now a heartbeat away from the Presidency, Nelson Rockefeller. Aside from the fact that De-Mohrenschildt had a letter mentioning references from Rockefeller on his person, he also worked for Humble Oil and for oil interests in Venezuela—two areas dominated by the Rockefellers.

DeMohrenschildt was also acquainted with the Shah of Iran, [28] who is a close friend of Richard Helms, former Director of the CIA. Helms helped engineer the coup that put the Shah in power. He was in charge of reporting on Oswald's activities while he was out of the country and worked closely with Howard Hunt in the CIA. [29]

Another one of DeMohrenschildt's friends was William R. Grace of Grace Lines. An executive of Grace Lines suffered a concussion after coming into contact with an Army Intelligence agent. While in delirium he said, "The President is in danger..." [30]

It is obvious that a man of DeMohrenschildt's background and connections had to have an ulterior motive for associating with Oswald. Perhaps he hoped to be rewarded for his work; the Warren Commission found that DeMohrenschildt was in the middle of implementing a business deal that would have made him economic czar of Haiti. As a personal friend of Duvalier, he was able to convince the dictator to allow him to do a mineral survey of Haiti for $300,000. This money was going into a trust company and DeMohrenschildt hoped he could get other intelligence-oriented corporations to invest in it. He approached the Shlumburger Corporation—which Raigorodsky described as "a worldwide organization that deals with every country in the world—you know what I'm trying to say..." the Inter-American Development Bank, and George Brown of Brown and Root, the largest U.S. contractors in Vietnam. When he had amassed enough capital, DeMohrenschildt was going to build food processing plants, hydroelectric plants, a casino, a hotel, and much more. Note that Meyer Lansky, kingpin of organized crime, had also tried to get a casino franchise from Duvalier. [31]

DeMohrenschildt brought Oswald to a party where he met Michael and Ruth Paine. The Paines were closely associated with the intelligence community: Mr. Paine worked for Bell Helicopter and had a security clearance. He was worth at least a third of a million dollars. Copies of a highly censored document about him were sent to Navy, Air Force and Army intelligence. Bell Helicopter also happened to employ General Dorhenberger, [32] an officer under Hitler, and has recently been training Saudi Arabian pilots. Ruth Paine's father worked for AID as did her brother-in-law whom she visited in Washington, D.C. in September 1963. [33]

Around this time the Oswalds were living in a small apartment in Dallas. Lee was working for Jagger-Chiles-Stovall which was "cleared through the Navy Bureau of Materiale" to do classified work and was rumored to print maps of Cuba. [34]

In April 1963 Oswald allegedly took a pot shot at General Edwin Walker, who was regarded as a martyr by the anti-Kennedy forces in the country because he had been accused of leading a riot at Oxford, Mississippi, adjudged "insane" and sent to the Federal medical facility at Springfield, Missouri—by Robert Kennedy. The attempt on Walker's life and the burglarizing of Dr. Fielding's office at Watergate had the same *modus operandi.* Oswald allegedly studied photographs he had taken of Walker's home. Howard Hunt photographed the outside of the psychiatrist's office before entering then—". . . rented a car and scouted Dr. Fielding's residence which [they] also photographed from all three sides." Walker's assailant(s) waited for a church gathering to provide cover; the Watergaters acted similarly: "While renting the Continental Room from the Watergate Hotel, we learned that a large convention would be occupying most of the hotel's other rooms. . . the presence of a large crowd would be helpful in giving anonymity to our group." [35]

The fact that one of Walker's neighbors said her dog was drugged coupled with testimonies of other neighbors that there were suspicious cars near the Walker house that left right after the shooting also makes it seem like an organized covert operation rather than an amateur's job. Walker stated that he believed that the assassins deliberately missed. [36]

A few days after this assassination attempt DeMohrenschildt asked Oswald if he took a shot at Walker, and he ". . . sort of shriveled and made a peculiar face." Marina also held Oswald responsible but produced little tangible evidence. She told the Warren Commission that Oswald kept detailed notes of the preparations for his attack on Walker, but burned them all; she said that he admitted the act to her and promised not to do it again. Marina did submit a note regarding what she should do in the event Oswald was arrested, but it did not specifically refer to the Walker shooting. [37]

Marina was questioned about the Walker incident by a man asked to act as an interpreter for her by Army Intelligence shortly after the Kennedy assassination. By her statements *through* him, Marina seemed anxious to establish a past history of violence for her husband: She said that about two weeks after the Walker incident Oswald told her, "Nixon is coming and I'm going to take a look"; she said that with the Walker shooting fresh in her mind, she locked her husband in the bathroom and made him promise he would not do it. (See document on page 270.) There was nothing in the newspapers about Nixon visiting Dallas at this time.

The only person the FBI questioned who remembered an article about a proposed Nixon trip to Dallas at that time was Rosemary Woods, Nixon's personal secretary. Questioned about the article by Issac Don Levine,* Woods told him that the girl who was bringing the Nixon papers was still in California. However, she believed that a certain Tad or Ted Smith, an influential Republican, had sent an invitation sometime before for Nixon to attend a Republican fund-raising dinner; that she thought there was one clipping in the press announcing the fact of Nixon's being invited and his acceptance. "There may have been a radio announcement—maybe a Walter Winchell column." When the Nixon papers finally arrived, Woods told Levine that there were too many "immense cartons" and that she was too short-handed to check on the invitation. [38]

Nixon also remembered it, but "could not observe the circumstances surrounding the invitation." He did observe that conceivably there could have been some publicity indicating that he had been invited to come to Dallas. Woods' credibility was questioned in the Watergate affair when she took responsibility for some gaps in the Presidential tapes, and nothing need be said about Nixon's. An FBI interview about the "Nixon Incident" is still classified. [39]

Even the Warren Commission could not lend credence to Marina's story: "The credibility of Marina Oswald's story is subject to some question since Nixon was neither in or reported to have been in Dallas at the appropriate time," and the incident "was of no probative value" in determining who shot Kennedy. Warren himself stated that the story was somehow tied up with Marina's financial interests. [40] The only one in the Commission who seemed to believe it was Representative Gerald Ford, whom

---

* Levine was instrumental in convincing Whittaker Chambers to testify that a high State Department official, named Alger Hiss, was in his Communist Party Cell, paving the way for Nixon's victory in the "Hiss Case."

President Johnson had put in the Commission at the request of Richard Nixon.

Ford, dissenting with the majority said that "additional proof was hardly needed," and her story "would seem to add considerable weight to the strong evidence that Lee Oswald's mind turned to murder whenever he wanted to impress Marina."[41]

In retrospect, it seems odd that so many assassins initially go after Nixon but end up shooting one of his enemies. Artie Bremer, like Oswald, first set out to shoot "Nixy boy"[42] but ended up going after Nixon's opponent George Wallace. Wallace believes the attempt on his life was part of the overall pattern of Watergate dirty tricks involving many things: Nixon funneled about $400,000 to Wallace's political rivals, initiated an Internal Revenue Service investigation on Wallace and his brother,[43] and helped the American Nazi Party to register members of Wallace's American Independent Party so that the latter couldn't vote for Wallace in the primaries.[44] About an hour after the Bremer incident, Nixon's attorney, Charles Colson, ordered Howard Hunt to fly to Milwaukee and burglarize Bremer's apartment. Nixon was so concerned about Bremer being linked to the Republicans that he ordered the FBI to give him briefings every thirty minutes on the progress of the case.[45]

A few weeks after the Walker and Nixon incidents, Oswald moved to New Orleans, leaving Marina and his child in Irving, at the home of the Paines. When he first arrived there he stayed with his cousin Dorothy Murret, but soon found his own apartment and a job at the William Reily Company which was located close to the hub of anti-Castro activity in New Orleans—a three-story building known as 544 Camp Street. Oswald's boss at Reily informed the FBI that Oswald would disappear for about an hour almost every day.[46]

It was around this time that Oswald began to form a New Orleans chapter of the Fair Play For Cuba Committee. Oswald was the chairman and only member of the committee which never held meetings. To stage a demonstration, Oswald hired people from a local employment agency to distribute leaflets.[47] Ten years later Don Segretti would be hiring demonstrators to perform at the campaign rallies of Nixon's opponents.

Obviously the "New Orleans chapter" of the FPCC was a totally fictitious organization designed to re-establish Oswald's credentials as a leftist.

But the strangest thing about Oswald's FPCC was the fact that some of its literature was stamped with the address "544 Camp St." (See page 271.) As mentioned earlier this was the address of the Cuban Revolutionary Council, an alliance of anti-Castro groups put together by the CIA. (See pages 271, 272.) It was also the New Orleans address of Howard Hunt, who worked closely with the Cuban Revolutionary Council. Hunt remained friends with members of this organization over the years and Bernard Barker testified that when Hunt came to Miami to recruit him for a job with the White House Plumbers, "...we did speak in Spanish to two or three members that were in the old Cuban Revolutionary Council." [48]

In fact, almost everyone who had an office in or was associated with 544 Camp Street, could be traced to Howard Hunt.

Guy Bannister, a former FBI and Military Intelligence agent had an office there. In 1954 Bannister started the Anti-communist League of the Caribbean which helped overthrow the leftist Arbenez regime in Guatemala. [49] Howard Hunt was in charge of this operation and he writes about his experiences in *Give Us This Day* and *Undercover*. Hunt said that he had wanted to get rid of Arbenez the minute he was elected, but it was not until a lobbying effort in behalf of Rockefeller's United Fruit was begun that action was taken. Hunt was summoned to the office of Tracy Barnes, who was "related through marriage to the Rockefeller clan" and was told that Eisenhower, Nixon, and the National Security Council had ordered the overthrow of "Arbenez's communist regime." [50] Hunt arranged for troops to begin training in Honduras and eventually Arbenez was deposed. Che Guevara, who worked for Arbenez at the time, had to flee to Mexico as a result of the coup.

When Hunt was assigned to the overthrow of Castro in 1960 he recruited many of the same personnel he had used in the Guatemalan operation: The same propaganda chief, finance officer and many of the same operatives. [51] It seems likely that he also used Bannister; why? When Hunt's original group, the

Cuban Revolutionary Front, was located in the Balter Building, Bannister had an office there as well. When the Cuban Revolutionary Front became known as the Cuban Revolutionary Council and moved to 544 Camp Street, Bannister also moved to the same address. The FBI questioned Bannister after the Kennedy assassination and he gave his address as 531 Lafayette Street, the side entrance to 544 Camp. The Bannister interview is exceedingly short and the only thing Bannister admits to knowing about 544 Camp is that Arcacha Smith of the Cuban Revolutionary Council once told him he had an office there. [52]

Yet after Bannister's death in 1964, his wife found hundreds of "Hands Off Cuba" leaflets in his office along with the index cards to his files—the FBI had seized everything else. One of the cards was entitled, "Italy, U.S. Bases Dismantled in General Assembly of the United Nations." When Hunt worked in the Office of Policy Coordination, the predecessor of the CIA, one of his main interests was to "reverse Italy's leftward political trend and defeat the communists at the polls." Another card read—"American Central Intelligence Agency—Latin America."[53]

Jim Garrison reported that on November 22, 1963 Bannister allegedly was so tense that he struck an employee, Jack Martin. A few hours later Martin called the authorities and reported that David Ferrie, an associate of Bannister, was involved in the killing. [54]

Another resident of 544 Camp, Sergio Arcacha Smith, was the head of the Cuban Democratic Revolutionary Front, also known as the Cuban Revolutionary Front. Howard Hunt was the liaison between this organization and the CIA. After the Front folded, Smith became the New Orleans delegate to the Cuban Revolutionary Council, which was also connected with Hunt. [55] It is likely that Hunt and Smith worked together because Smith was a diplomat under Batista, and Hunt favored the inclusion of Batista's people in the Front and in the Council. [56]

Smith was involved in training anti-Castro Cubans in the New Orleans area and was accused by Jim Garrison of taking part in the burglary of a munitions bunker along with Gordon Novel, a CIA agent who *must* have been acquainted with Howard Hunt.

Novel ran an electronics firm in New Orleans which specialized in selling equipment used for bugging. [57] His lawyer claimed he held a position identical to that of Hunt, an intermediary between the Cuban exiles and the CIA. [58] After initially denying that he had had any part in the burglary, he stated that "It was one of the most patriotic burglaries in history," and that it was done under the direction of the CIA as part of the Bay of Pigs operation. Novel confessed he had been given a key to the bunker and that the people he had met there, Arcacha Smith and David Ferrie were also working for the CIA. [59]

Note the fact that the munitions bunker that was burglarized was owned by the Shlumberger Corporation, the same people DeMohrenschildt approached for help in his Haitian venture. The New Orleans States Item reported that a reliable source informed them that there were crates marked "Shlumburger" in Guy Bannister's office soon after the burglary. [60]

Novel also worked with the propaganda end of the invasion. As a director of a CIA front called the Evergreen Advertising Agency, he was responsible for transmitting cryptographic messages to alert the exiles to the invasion date. Hunt was in charge of domestic propaganda for the Bay of Pigs operation [61] and was probably Novel's superior.

After Garrison indicted him, Novel eventually ended up in McLean, Virginia, where he took a lie-detector test from a retired Army Intelligence agent, which, of course, proved he was innocent. [62] While he was away from New Orleans, two women who had taken over Novel's apartment discovered a note written in his hand which was seemingly addressed to his CIA contact.

"Dear Mr. Weiss:

"This letter is to inform you that District (sic) Jim Garrison has subpoenaed myself and an associate to testify before his Grand Jury on matters which may be classified TOP SECRET. Actions of individuals connected with DOUBLE-CHEK CORPORATION in Miami in first quarter of 1961.

"We have no current contact available to inform of this situation. So I took the liberty of writing you direct and apprising you of current situation. Expecting you to forward this through appropriate channels.

"Our connection and activity of that period involves individuals presently...about to be indicted as conspirators in Mr. Garrison's investigation.

"We have temporarily avoided one subpoena not to reveal Double-Chek activities or associate them with this mess. We want out of this thing before Thursday 3/67. Our attorneys have been told to expect another subpoena to appear and testify on this matter. The fifth amendment and/or immunity (and) legal tactics will not suffice.

"Mr. Garrison is in possession of *unsworn* portions of this testimony. He is unaware of Double-Chek's involvement in this matter but has strong suspicions. I have been questioned extensively by local FBI recently as to whether or not I was involved with Double-Chek's parent-holding corporation during that time. My reply on five queries was negative. Bureau unaware of Double-Chek association in this matter. Our attorneys and others are in possession of complete sealed files containing all information concerning matter. In the event of our sudden departure, either accidental or otherwise, they are instructed to simultaneously release same for public scrutiny in different areas simultaneously.

"Appropriate counteraction relative to Garrison's inquisition concerning us may best handled through military channels vis (a) vis D.I.A. man. Garrison is presently colonel in Louisiana Army National Guard and has ready reserve status. Contact may be had through our attorneys of current record, Plotkin, Alverez, Sapir."

During the planning of the Bay of Pigs invasion, Howard Hunt also worked for Double-Chek, a dummy electronics firm located just outside Miami. "Headquarters proved to be an office building converted for our use and disguised as an electronics firm," Hunt stated. Novel's lawyer said his client's work at Double-Chek had "little or nothing to do with the assassination of President Kennedy," although he admitted that "...everything in the letter as far as Novel is concerned is actually the truth."[63]

After the U.S. District Attorney refused to honor Garrison's request to extradite Novel from the District of Columbia, Novel went to Columbus, Ohio where he was finally arrested and held on a ten-thousand-dollar bond. During the hearing he said, "I did not intend to do that (return to New Orleans) because of this Cuban..." Before he could finish his sentence he was interrupted by his lawyer. Governor Rhodes, the same man who ordered the National Guard on the Kent State campus, also blocked Novel's extradition from Ohio. [64]

In 1974 Jack Anderson reported that Charles Colson asked Gordon Novel to help him build a "degaussing gun" to erase tapes stored at the CIA and White House that would incriminate Nixon. Novel consulted with other experts on the matter but they "mutually decided not to pursue the plan because of its danger to national security tapes and computers near the target tapes." [65]

Novel's former lawyer, Dean Andrews, testified that Oswald came into his office in the summer of 1963 accompanied by some "gay mexicanos." When asked by the FBI to produce documents relating to this visit, Andrews could not because his office had been burglarized shortly after the assassination. [66]

This is a typical CIA maneuver—when Jill Vollner was prosecuting ex-CIA agents involved in Watergate her apartment was broken into. Little was stolen and her papers were rifled. Recently the home of Senator Howard Baker of Tennessee, a member of the Church Committee and outspoken critic of the CIA, had a similar experience.

A man named Clay Betrand called Andrews on November 22, 1963 and asked him to represent Oswald. Jim Garrison, the former District Attorney of New Orleans, contends that Clay Betrand was really Clay Shaw, an alleged CIA agent. Although Garrison couldn't prove his charge in a court of law, recent revelations by ex-CIA agent Victor Marchetti seem to substantiate Garrison's charges: Marchetti stated that during the time of the Garrison investigation he attended morning briefing sessions with high officials of the Agency who often voiced serious concern that Shaw's CIA contacts might be uncovered by the maverick D.A. Marchetti and Richard Helms decided that Shaw's ties to the

Agency had to be kept secret along with the fact that Shaw was connected with the Bay of Pigs. [68]

If in fact Shaw did work on the Kennedy assassination his role had to be that of paymaster because he was connected with CMC-Permindex, a proprietary of the CIA that was expelled from Italy for meddling in its internal affairs by funneling money to political parties that opposed the communists. CMC-Permindex was made up of people like Mussolini's Secretary of Agriculture and a director of the Agency for Provocative Information from and for Socialist Countries. Another important member of Permindex was a former intelligence agent with vast holdings in Canada and Israel. An official of the National Committee for Labor Israel handled the liquidation of Permindex in New York City. Ex-CIA agent Philip Agee has stated that the Committee for Labor Israel is often used as a CIA cover. [69]

While in New Orleans, Oswald also associated with a man named Carlos Bringuier, a fanatical anti-Castroite. Bringuier was a leader of the Student Revolutionary Directorate (DRE) which established a force in Cuba's Escambray Mountains in order to help Castro overthrow Batista. During the revolution they took over the presidential palace for Castro but were given no power in the post-revolutionary government and so began to oppose it militarily. Agee reports that they were CIA-controlled.

In August 1962, the Miami-based DRE was shelling Havana from boats positioned offshore, which brought them into conflict with the Kennedy Administration's policy of détente with Russia. After a warning from the Justice Department, the DRE distributed leaflets accusing President Kennedy of abandoning the exiles and publicly announced that they would continue to make raids on Cuba because the United States' efforts to overthrow Castro "always culminated in treachery." [70]

About a month before the assassination, they stated that they were being forced to curtail the raids, because of threats from the Kennedy Administration. [71]

Bringuier had worked with Batista's police, as Secretary at the Criminal Court in Havana and was also a member of the Cuban Revolutionary Council. Watergater Bernard Barker also worked for the Cuban police as a consultant on counter-insurgency—he was a CIA agent at the time—and was also on the Cuban Revolutionary Council. It seems probable that the two men knew each other. [72]

Oswald came into Bringuer's store in the summer of 1963 and asked to join the DRE but was refused. A few days later Bringuier spotted Oswald giving out pro-Castro leaflets on a street corner in New Orleans and allegedly punched him. Oswald, Bringuier's and two other Cubans were arrested for disturbing the peace; but a week later Oswald was back handing out his propaganda again. [73]

Oswald's arrest provides us with more information about the nature of his activities on behalf of Castro. He threw away the leaflets after the press showed up and photographed him and he requested to see an FBI agent when he was in jail. On another occasion, Oswald was questioned by the police while distributing leaflets in front of an aircraft carrier, but the Office of Naval Intelligence had no record of his subversive activities. In fact, after the assassination, ONI had no derogatory material *at all* in their files on Oswald. [74]

Oswald sent clippings about the incident to the chairman of the Fair Play for Cuba Committee, to enhance his credibility with them. [75]

After the assassination, an informer for the Secret Service and the FBI who had infiltrated a Cuban exile group and was in the process of selling them machine guns, reported that on November 21, 1963 he was told, "We now have plenty of money—our new backers are the Jews—as soon as they take care of JFK." This man had furnished reliable information in the past. In a recently declassified memo written by Warren Commission counsel, Leon Hubert, we find that one of these men was from the DRE and the other was from the 30th of November Movement, which operated in the Escambray Mountains of Las Villas Province in Cuba. Hubert also quotes a Chicago newspaper reporter who had "learned from Chicago police and various other sources that an anti-Castro Cuban Committee was active in Chicago, attempting to obtain arms for use against Castro"; and that these anti-Castro Cubans had underworld ties and might have been involved in the assassination of President Kennedy. [76]

The fact that in 1972 Carlos Bringuier was head of "Cuban-Americans For Nixon-Agnew"[77] also casts doubt on the authenticity of Oswald's leafletting operations. After all, it's quite a jump from street-brawler to Nixon's main contact in the exile community. A recently declassified document reveals that White House secret policeman, John Caufield, formerly of the New York City Red Squad, just happened to be in charge of keeping an eye on the DRE in New York City. (See page 272) In the White House tapes John Dean expresses consternation over whether Herbert Kalmbach's records would be subpoenaed because they would expose the fact that Caufield was working for Nixon around the time of Chappaquidick: "If they get to it—that is going to come out and this whole thing can turn around on that. If Kennedy knew the bear trap he was walking into. . ."[78]

In the Nixon tapes transcribed and released by the House of Representatives the following exchange was reported between Nixon and Dean:

> Dean: Not being in this business I turned to somebody who had been in this business. Jack Caufield, who is, I don't know if you remember Jack or not. He was your original bodyguard before. . .
> Nixon: Yeah.
> Dean: candidate, candidate. . .
> Nixon: Yeah.
> Dean: protection* an old New York City policeman.
> Nixon: Right. I know, I know him.

Bringuier shared many similar ideas with Howard Hunt. Both men were afraid that Kennedy was going to replace Castro with another leftist. Bringuier called this Operation Judas.[79] Hunt felt that the leftist who was going to replace Castro was Manolo Ray whose program ". . .was soon known among the exiles as *Fidelismo sin Fidel*—Castroism without Castro." Hunt reasoned that since Ray's intimates were all "inhabitants of the extreme

---

* The Secret Service extended protection to candidates since Robert Kennedy was assassinated in 1968. Actually Caufield knew Nixon since 1960.

socialist left" they would receive the "sympathetic attention of...Kennedy's advisors."[80]

With the help of the intelligence community, Oswald managed to get on two radio programs in New Orleans, which helped to further establish his identity as a leftist. Both shows were moderated by William Stuckey, a "Latin-American affairs expert" who was in close contact with the Cuban exile community. Stuckey was also a close friend of Edward Butler of the Information Council of the Americas. One of the directors of INCA, Manuel Gil, was also a member of the Cuban Revolutionary Council.[81] Hunt worked on domestic propaganda for the Council and it is likely that he knew Gil.

Butler and Bringuier both took part in one of the Stuckey-Oswald radio programs and capitalized on this fact after the assassination. Bringuier wrote a book called *Red Friday* which defended the findings of the Warren Commission, and Butler moved to California where he got his own TV program. Butler was also instrumental in organizing pro-Nixon demonstrations, working very closely with Young Americans for Freedom[82] (Hunt's attorney, Douglas Caddy, was a co-founder of YAF as was his friend, William F. Buckley.)

* * * * *

The oddest of Oswald's alleged associates in New Orleans was William David Ferrie. Although he was raised as a strict Roman Catholic and had studied for the priesthood, Ferrie was a devout homosexual who was forced to wear a wig and pencil in eyebrows because he had lost all his hair.

Ferrie was a gay version of Watergater Frank Sturgis; like Sturgis he allegedly smuggled guns to Castro in the late 1950's and attempted to raise funds for him. A New Orleans businessman recalled that Ferrie carried a loaded gun with him while soliciting funds for Castro's campaign.[83] But by 1960 both men were working to overthrow Castro by training pilots in Guatemala for the Bay of Pigs invasion,[84] and were both flying air strikes and underground support missions into Cuba.[85] Ferrie worked closely with Eladio del Valle, a former Cuban congressman who fled with most of his wealth before Castro took over. In Miami, del Valle set up a grocery store as a front for his anti-Castro activities, and was seen with Ferrie every day for a six-month period. The pair made many airborne penetrations into Cuba but Federal agents put a stop to the raids in 1961 by confiscating the plane. (Around this time, Federal agents revoked the registration on Frank Sturgis' B-25.) When Ferrie was arrested on a morals charge in the early 1960's the police found three blank, stamped United States passports in his possession.[86]

Ferrie was linked to Arcacha Smith in a 1961 New Orleans police report[87] and claimed to have made some of his flights from Swan Island, a CIA-controlled area. Marchetti has confirmed the fact that Ferrie worked for the CIA.[88]

After the abortive Bay of Pigs invasion, Ferrie was invited to speak about its failure before the New Orleans chapter of the Military Order of World Wars. Ferrie was introduced as a pilot in the invasion "who couldn't land in Cuba due to heavy ground fire" and spoke emotionally about Kennedy's "double-cross."

Aside from his CIA ties, Ferrie was connected with organized crime: he worked for Carlos Marchello's lawyer and flew to Guatemala twice in the fall of 1963.[89] Robert Kennedy had Carlos Marchello deported to Guatemala around this time and many people believe it was Ferrie who flew the New Orleans crime boss back to the States. Marchello's lawyer provided Ferrie with an alibi for November 22, 1963.

From 1962-1963 Ferrie reportedly drilled anti-Castroites in a training camp sponsored by dispossessed Havana gaming house owners[90] and was questioned by the FBI immediately after the President's assassination, because Guy Bannister's employee, Jack Martin, had phoned in a tip implicating him. Ferrie told the FBI that he had been in Galveston, Texas just after the assassination, looking at a skating rink. According to the rink's owner Ferrie was there, making numerous calls from a public phone booth.

Jim Garrison discovered that in the fall of 1963 Ferrie made quite a few calls to Mexico City. Howard Hunt was station chief there around this time.[91]

The FBI asked Ferrie if he lent his library card to Oswald.[92] The hairless pilot was also identified as one of the men Giesbrecht overheard discussing the assassination at a Canadian airport (see page 22). Initially Giesbrecht described one of the men as having "the oddest hair and eyebrows I'd ever seen"[93] and on February 23, 1967 he saw Ferrie's picture on TV and identified him as the mysterious man at the airport. In a taped conversation he said he was "one hundred per cent" sure it was Ferrie.[94] Giesbrecht also recalled that one of the men made a reference to a "sales meeting," the reservations for which would be made in the name of a textile firm. The Watergaters were allegedly attending a sales meeting of a dummy corporation the night they were caught trying to break into the offices of the Democratic Party National Committee.

Ferrie reportedly came into money before and after the assassination. Everything was going fine for him until Jim Garrison indicted him for conspiracy to kill the President of the United States. Ferrie was dead four days later, the victim of a massive brain hemorrhage. He supposedly left a typed death note—even the signature was typewritten. How he died of a brain hemorrhage, yet was able to leave a note, still remains a mystery. Carlos Bringuier was one of the last people to see him alive.[95]

Ferrie's friend and employer, E. del Valle, was found dead in a parking lot on *the same day* that Ferrie died. Someone had shot him in the heart and split his head open with a hatchet.[96]

Professor Scott reports that an A. del Valle was once an executive in the Eversharp Corporation. Eversharp was a client of one of Nixon's law firms[97] but Scott is not sure if it is the same man.

* * * * *

One of the last things Oswald did in New Orleans was apply for a passport. Even though the State Department had issued a "lookout card" on Oswald after he defected,[98] he still got his papers within 24 hours because the lookout card suddenly disappeared.[99] By a strange twist of fate, Orest Pena, the owner of a bar that was a center of exile intrigue, and a member of The Cuban Revolutionary Front and Council, applied for a passport on that same day. Orest was reportedly a follower of Orlando Piedra, one of the top men in Batista's secret police and a friend of Bernard Barker. Pena was an FBI informer, had a long record of arrests with many dismissals, lifted weights, bounced customers from his bar, and constantly offered to take a lie-detector test to "prove" he was telling the truth. This description fits Jack Ruby perfectly.[100]

After the assassination, Pena's brother told the FBI that two men entered his bar and had a pro-Castro conversation. A waiter at the bar was certain that one of the men was Lee Harvey Oswald.[101] The FBI questioned him and he confirmed the story. They then interrogated Orest, who at first said Oswald was in his bar, then refused to talk with the FBI, then finally denied seeing Oswald in his bar at all, claiming that he was away at the time. When he testified before the Commission he went back to his original story.[102]

Because of his vacillating testimony, it is hard to believe Pena. Although he says he was in Mexico in May 1963, he may very well have been there in August of the same year when Hunt was reportedly station chief. When it comes to accounting for his whereabouts that particular summer he says he was in Brazil, Puerto Rico and the Dominican Republic *all at the same time.*
Even though he told Bringuier about the Oswald incident he claims to hate the man. A pattern of deliberate disassociation appears between people who probably worked very closely together on the assassination operation.[103]

Pena was questioned by FBI agent Warren C. deBrueys who served as "legal assistant" for U.S. embassies in Brazil, Mexico and Argentina, and was recently made chief of the FBI in Puerto Rico, following a series of bombings there.[104] DeBrueys is a Latin America counter-insurgency expert and has close ties to the CIA.

On September 25, 1963, after "losing" his job at the Reily firm, Oswald left for Mexico City. Many of the men who had worked with him at Reily were eventually hired by big defense contractors.[105]

Traveling by bus, Oswald arrived in Mexico on September 27, 1963 and checked into the Hotel Commercio. According to former *Times* reporter Tad Szulc, Howard Hunt just happened to be CIA station chief in Mexico City in August—September 1963.

Oswald probably thought he was part of a plot to kill Castro because he seemed to be using his credentials as a defector and as a leader of the Fair Play For Cuba Committee in New Orleans, to enter Cuba.

The first thing he did in Mexico City was to go to the Cuban Consulate and show the clippings and letters he had received from the Communist Party and FPCC to an official there. While he was waiting for the official, Oswald borrowed a pen from someone and made a notation in his address book—the name of the person he had initially spoken with, Silvia Duran. He also drew a floor plan, presumably of the embassy, in the same ink. The page from Oswald's notebook with the diagram is reprinted on page 273.

Howard Hunt specialized in burglarizing communist embassies in Mexico City and elsewhere with the help of floor plans. In *Undercover* Hunt admits to breaking into, "one communist embassy in Mexico City located two blocks from the American Embassy" with the help of "a floor plan of the offices." While planning a covert entry operation into the offices of Las Vegas newspaperman Hank Greenspun, Hunt says in his book that he was promised a "floor diagram"; he also states that he actually received one to facilitate his team's entry into Senator McGovern's suite. [106]

The Cubans told Oswald that if he could get a visa from the Russians they would let him in.

Oswald had applied for a Russian visa around July 8, 1963 and he called the Russian Embassy from the Cuban Consulate in Mexico City to see if it had arrived. When Oswald was told there would be a delay of four months, he became furious and began to yell at the Cuban consul who told him that as far as he was concerned people like Oswald were harming the Cuban revolution and if it was up to him, he would deny the visa. Still steaming mad, Oswald went over to the Russian Embassy and spoke with the Soviet consul who described their encounter this way: "He stormed into my office and wanted me to recommend and introduce him to the Cubans. I told him I would have to check before I could recommend him. He was nervous and his hands trembled..." [107]

Oswald's activities after his trip to the Cuban and Russian embassies were a mystery to the Warren Commission: "We have a very limited report from the hotel keeper that he knew nothing about him..." The FBI was able to come up with very little, although they interviewed all the guests at the hotel who were there around the same time as Oswald. The only suspicious thing they found was that a group of "Cubans," one of whom was allegedly from Florida, were registered at the hotel.

One of these "Cubans" was described as being a "white male, 55-58 years old, 5 feet 8 inches in height, slender build, fair complexion and grey hair" (See document DC1243 on page 274). Although this description fits Howard Hunt to a "T", in all fairness it must be stated that in his suit against the *National Tattler*, the former CIA agent denies having had any conversations with Oswald in Mexico City. On the other hand there is ample evidence that Hunt had extensive connections in the Mexican capital because he had served there for several years as a spy and had rented "safehouses" (secret havens for CIA agents) there in the past. He had also been known to "work independently" of the Mexico City CIA station. [108]

There is some evidence that certain Warren Commission staff members thought that Oswald may have made contact with anti-Castro agents while visiting Mexico City. A recently declassified memo reveals that the CIA was asked to question "all pro-Castro and anti-Castro organizations in the Mexico City area..." [109]

The investigation into Oswald's Mexican activities by the CIA was a classic case of cover-up. First of all, the photograph of Oswald entering the Cuban Consulate, allegedly taken by their hidden camera, did not look like Oswald. After receiving the photograph, J. Lee Rankin, General Counsel of the Warren Commission, sent the CIA a letter asking who the man was. This question has yet to be properly resolved. [110]

When the CIA learned from their "sensitive and reliable source" that Oswald had visited the Russian Embassy in Mexico

City, they sent a message about it to the State Department, the FBI and the Department of the Navy. But when the Agency turned over their "Oswald file" to the Commission this message was missing from it. CIA official Richard Helms excused it because "internal messages utilized confidential communications techniques and revealed confidential sources." After some discussion, it was agreed that the CIA would supply the Commission with "a paraphrase of any message or any other writing requested by the Commission, the original version of which would reveal a confidential source or a confidential communications technique."[111]

The document reprinted in appendix page 276 is the CIA's "paraphrase" of the message alerting the Government that Oswald was having dealings with the Russians again. Notice how Oswald's middle name is "Henry" rather than "Harvey." His wife's maiden name is misspelled. It is odd that they know about his defection yet do not know his exact full name. Also notice how the name of the station chief is missing.

Warren Commission counsel William T. Coleman, who had been granted access to all top secret documents of the Warren Commission because he already had security clearance from the Arms Control and Disarmament Agency and the Atomic Energy Commission, did not feel the paraphrase was good enough and sent the memorandum reprinted on page 276 to the Agency. Notice how parts of it have been cut out with a razor blade. In some of the other documents white correction fluid was used to do the same thing, but held up to a strong light the forbidden words could be read. Usually ail they said was "Mexico City CIA Station." Notice how Coleman is moving in the direction of asking, "Who was the CIA official in charge in Mexico City?" For some unknown reason, Coleman did not press the matter any further.

While the Warren Commission was in session, Coleman was on leave from the Dilworth law firm, which represents Nelson Rockefeller's financial interests. After the Commission finished its work, he became a director of the Rand Corporation (See page 23), and was eventually appointed to the Federal Wage and Price Control Commission by Nixon.[112]

Nixon also considered him for the job of Special Prosecutor in the Watergate affair[113] and President Ford appointed him Secretary of Transportation, the only Black in his cabinet.

The man in charge of conducting the investigation of Oswald's activities abroad was Richard Helms. This seems odd since rather than being in charge of gathering intelligence, Helms was Deputy Director of Plans, a euphemism for head of the "dirty tricks" division, at the time. Helms was promoted to Director of the CIA by President Johnson and was serving in that capacity when Hunt obtained assistance from the Agency in conducting domestic operations including Watergate. Helms was eventually "kicked upstairs" by Nixon and is now the Ambassador to Iran. Before he left the Agency he ordered the destruction of all the tapes of his phone conversations dating back several years, including those with Nixon. He has been implicated in the recently exposed CIA domestic spying scandal.[114]

When evaluating the CIA reports on Oswald's activities in Mexico City, one must remember that Helms and his deputies Rocca and Karamessines put together the reports.[115] During the Watergate hearings Senator Baker asked Helms how well he knew Howard Hunt. Helms replied, "I knew him relatively well because he and I over many years worked for the same general section of the Agency."

On October 1, 1963 Oswald left Mexico City. According to the Warren Report he took a bus back to Dallas. Yet when this mater was discussed by the Warren Commission a different matter unfolded:

> Rankin: He went one way on a bus...
> Warren: One way on a bus...
> Russell: I thought he went down in a bus and came back in a car?
> Rankin: That is right.[116]

To this day no one knows how and with whom he returned.

When Oswald returned to Dallas, he rented a room from Earline Roberts, the sister of Bertha Cheeks, who was a friend of Jack Ruby's. A former employee of Cheeks stated to the FBI that there were two Cubans who were residents in Bertha Cheeks' boarding house during 1959. Both Bertha and Earline had no recollection of these Cuban male residents even though Cheeks checked her records for the year in question. Jack Ruby also reportedly asked Cheeks to invest money in a nightclub in the late 1950's. [117]

Leon Hubert, the man in charge of the Ruby aspect of the investigation, felt these events were "significant, in the light of Jack Ruby's admission that in 1959 he was interested in selling jeeps to Cuba and other reports that persons interested in Cuban arms sales were responsible for the assassination of President Kennedy."[118]

About two weeks after his return from Mexico, and three weeks before Kennedy's visit to Dallas was publicly announced (it had been planned in June 1963), Oswald got a menial job at the Texas School Book Depository (TSBD).

Dr. Werner Teuter, Jack Ruby's last psychiatrist who is now a professor at Loyola University in Chicago, said he was told by Ruby that if he wanted to get a good idea of what really happened in regard to the Kennedy assassination he should "read Buchanan's book."[119] One of the books major contentions is that Oswald was a patsy who thought his job was to bring the rifle. This was why Frazier, the man who drove Oswald to the Depository—he had no connection with the intelligence community—swore Oswald had gone out to the Paines (where Marina was still staying) to pick up some curtain rods the night before the assassination. Before they drove to work on the morning of November 22, 1963, Oswald put a long paper bag in the back of the car. [120]

But Oswald was not carrying his *Mannlicher Carcano*, the rifle established as the murder weapon by the Warren Commission. He was carrying a rifle which couldn't be traced back to him, somewhat shorter than the *Mannlicher*. Mr. Frazier and his mother, Ms. Randle, both said that the long and bulky package was *shorter* than the disassembled *Mannlicher* and stuck to this story despite constant re-questioning by the FBI and the Warren Commission. Oswald may not necessarily have brought the weapon *inside* the Depository. Frazier testified that Oswald walked far ahead of him after they reached the TSBD's parking lot that morning, and the only employee to see Oswald enter that morning "did not see anything in his hands at the time." [121]

Meanwhile, Oswald's *Mannlicher Carcano* had been stolen from his garage. There is evidence that at least one apartment Oswald lived in had been surreptitiously entered. Oswald's former landlord, reported that "someone who had a key to the padlock has been going into the apartment" Oswald once inhabited. [122]

Nobody in the Texas School Book Depository saw Oswald during the time of the assassination, either on the sixth floor, from where the assassin's bullet allegedly struck home, or anywhere else.

CHAPTER FOUR

The Tramps

Lee Bowers was railroad towerman for the Union Terminal Company. He was perched on a fourteen-foot tower behind the Texas School Book Depository and had an excellent view of that area and the space behind the fence that faced Elm Street. This was the spot on top of the famous "grassy knoll" from which many eyewitnesses and researchers believe the fatal shots were fired. He knew every square inch of the railroad yard and since the police had cut off traffic into the area at 10 a.m. and there was little to draw his attention, he had to be distracted. At 11:55 a car with out-of-state license plates, covered with red mud and Goldwater-for-President stickers circled in front of the tower, catching Bower's attention. About twenty minutes later another car entered. Bowers believed "the occupant of this second car was a police officer" as he observed him "talking into a radio telephone or transmitter".[1]

Walkie-talkies were used extensively throughout the Watergate affair. Hunt and his cohorts communicated through them when they burglarized Ellsberg's psychiatrist's office: "We adjusted and ran tests on the four walkie-talkies, finding, to our consternation, that the frequency was also utilized by radio cabs..." They were used in both Watergate break-ins and Hunt quotes Sturgis as saying, "Without a walkie-talkie I feel real naked..."[2]

At 12:22 p.m. a car very similar to the first (muddied, with stickers and non-Texan plates) "circled the area and probed one spot at the tower." There is other evidence of diversionary maneuvering—just before the assassination a man had an epileptic fit. He later disappeared from the hospital before he could be questioned.*³

Just after the last car left, Bowers observed two men standing behind the fence on top of the knoll. "These were the only two strangers in the area. The others were workers whom I knew. They were standing within ten or fifteen feet of each other and gave no appearance of being together...They were following the caravan (the motorcade) as it came down the street." One of them was "hard to distinguish from the trees."⁴

Around the same time the second car arrived, people began to see figures in the eastern corner windows of the TSBD. Arnold Rowland saw two men, one of whom was holding a rifle.⁵ Carolyn Walthers saw the exact same thing: two men, one rifle. The other man was standing erect and his head was above a dirty window so it could not be seen.⁶ Bob Edwards and Roland Fisher noticed a man in the window about a half minute before the motorcade passed in front of the TSBD. Fisher reported "...he was looking down toward the triple underpass toward the end of Elm Street...(the fence/knoll area)...I watched him—he never moved his head...he was there transfixed."⁷

Just after the fatal shots were fired at the President, several railroad men on the triple overpass said they saw smoke coming from the same area the assassin in the TSBD was reportedly staring at. S.M. Holland saw "a puff of smoke (that) came out about six or eight feet above the ground right out from under those trees." At least five other railroad men also saw it. Two policemen reported smelling smoke: Patrolman J.M. Smith, the second policeman to scale the fence "smell(ed) gunpowder...in the parking lot near the TSBD,"⁸ and so did another patrolman. Bowers also noticed "...something out of the ordinary, a

---

* In his book **Counterplot** Warren Commission defender Edward Epstein claims this man was Jerry Boyd Belknap, a Dallas **Morning News** employee who fainted about a half hour before the assassination. The Dallas Police radio transcripts reveal that the man we're interested in passed out at about 12:20 p.m., ten minutes before the motorcade arrived.

sort of 'milling around' but something occurred in this particular spot...Nothing I can pinpoint..."[9] When asked to amplify on his testimony by Mark Lane he said, "At the time of the shooting—in the vicinity of where the two men I have described were, there was a flash of light...or smoke...."

Seymour Weitzman was the first police officer to scale the fence. He was questioned by Warren Commission counsel Joe Ball: "What did you notice in the railroad yards?" Weitzman: "We noticed numerous kinds of footprints..."[10] Railroadman S.M. Holland, who had run to the area where he saw the puff of smoke, noticed footprints between a station wagon and the picket fence: "It was muddy...a hundred tracks in one location. There was mud on the bumper as if someone had cleaned their foot...the spot was three foot by two foot [*sic.*] and it looked to me like somebody had been standing there for a long period." Holland told Mark Lane, "...it looked like a lion pacing a cage...." Two other railroadmen also saw footprints behind the fence.[11]

Although Weitzman scaled the fence first, the officer who was right behind him, Patrolman J.M. Smith, was the first to encounter a Secret Service agent there: "...I wasn't alone. There was some Deputy Sheriff and I believe one Secret Serviceman when I got there...I pulled my pistol from my holster, and I thought 'this is silly, I don't know who I am looking for'...Just as I did he showed me he was a Secret Service agent...he saw me coming with my pistol and right away he showed me who he was."[12]

Weitzman also saw the agent. Ball questioned, "Were there other people there (behind the fence) besides you?" Weitzman answered, "Yes sir, other officers, Secret Service as well."[13] Because the Warren Commission questioned every Secret Service man and they all stated that they either went to Parkland Hospital or stayed at the Trade Center where Kennedy was scheduled to speak,[14] there is reason to believe that Weitzman and Smith encountered one of the assassins' accomplices who possessed false Secret Service credentials.

As far back as 1954 Howard Hunt was able to obtain false identification papers from the CIA: "On joining the Guatemalan project, I was turned over to Central Cover Division, which provided me with documentation in an alias name, authentic but non-functional credit cards, bank references and the like..."[15] In the 1970's Hunt obtained any kind of false ID from General Cushman, a former Nixon aide who had been promoted to Deputy Director of the CIA by Nixon. Cushman had shared an office with Hunt in the 1950's.[16]

When he was caught at the Watergate hotel, Sturgis had a birth certificate, two driver's licenses and a Social Security card in the name of Joseph Hamilton; he also had a Mexican passport prepared by the CIA. The other Watergaters also had credentials issued by the CIA.

Note the fact that Joe Ball, the Commission counsel who questioned Bowers and Weitzman, became the number one defense attorney for John Ehrlichman in the Ellsberg break-in case.[17] And Wesley Leibler, the Commission counsel who questioned Patrolman Smith, was appointed to the Federal Trade Commission by Nixon.[18]

We have a suspicion that the fake Secret Serviceman encountered by Weitzman was a Watergater, and we are attempting to obtain photographs, taken immediately after the shooting, of the area in question. Our suspicions were strengthened when we discovered that Seymour Weitzman has been in at least three Federal "rest homes" since he had a nervous breakdown in June 1972. If the reader remembers it was at that time that the Watergaters were apprehended and their pictures disseminated.

In April 1975 Michael Canfield visited with Weitzman in a home for aged war veterans. Weitzman requested that his doctor, Charles Laburda, be present at the interview. Canfield explained that he was writing a book on the Kennedy assassination and because Weitzman was an eyewitness, his testimony would be very useful for us. Weitzman's memory seemed clear and sharp and he indicated that he would tell Canfield the same thing he had told the FBI, the Warren Commission and the Dallas authorities. We compared his statement with his testimony and found them to be identical.

Weitzman said he encountered a Secret Service agent in the parking lot who produced credentials and told him everything was under control. He described the man as being of medium height, dark hair and wearing a light windbreaker. Canfield showed him a photo of Sturgis and Barker. He immediately stated, "Yes, that's him," pointing to Bernard Barker. Canfield asked, "Was this the man who produced the Secret Service credentials?" Weitzman responded, "Yes, that's the same man."

Unfortunately Weitzman refused to make a tape-recorded statement but said he would be willing to do it for official investigators. Doctor Laburda suggested a notarized affidavit; Weitzman agreed, but later changed his mind. "So many witnesses have been killed," he explained, "and two Cubans forced their way into my house and were waiting for me when I came home. I had to chase them out with my Service revolver. I fear for my life." The next day Canfield made a poor quality tape recording of a telephone conversation with Weitzman in which he reaffirms the Barker identification.

J.C. Price may have seen the fake Secret Serviceman's partner run from behind the fence towards the railroad yards carrying the murder weapon. Price, who was watching the motorcade from the roof of the Terminal Annex Building saw someone run from behind the fence "...towards the passenger cars on the railroad siding after the volley of shots."[19] Price told Mark Lane he "was running very fast, which gave me the suspicion that he did the shooting...(he)...was carrying something in his right hand which could have been a gun..." Price saw this man run at about the same time Bowers' "darker dressed man" may have disappeared. Bowers wasn't sure of this because, like all professional snipers, the man was hard to distinguish from the foliage.

One of the bystanders, Jean Hill, was almost hit by a police motorcycle as she attempted to chase a man in a brown overcoat who was running from the direction of the TSBD "to the railroad tracks to the West; I kept running toward the train tracks and looked all around but I couldn't see him...some policemen...turned us back."[20] By the time S.M. Holland arrived at the scene, "there were twelve or fifteen policemen or plainclothesmen and we looked for empty shells..." These officers were soon joined by others who were responding to an order sent out by Sheriff Decker moments after the assassination—"Move all available men out of my department back into railroad yards and try to determine what happened..."[21] Two officers tried to "clear the area and get all civilians out"[22] while another said that the police did not know "who they were checking" because "there was so much milling around."[23] Inspector Sawyer did organize a detail to methodically check "...all persons and automobiles in the parking lot surrounding the TSBD, taking names, telephone numbers..."[24] A Deputy Sheriff set up a command post behind the fence and ordered a thorough search of all the railroad cars. Several U.S. Alcohol, Tobacco and Firearms agents assisted in the search.[25] The police also received help from Army Intelligence agent James Powell, who just happened to be taking pictures of the Texas Book Depository Building about the time of the shooting. Powell told the FBI that he searched the railroad cars with the police for about ten minutes but found nothing.[26]

Even the people in the TSBD standing underneath the "assassin's window" ran to the other side of the building and looked at the railroad tracks. One of them saw a "policeman" on top of a freight car.[27] Could this have been one of the assassins going into hiding? Most of the other TSBD employees ran to the tracks until the reports of eyewitnesses cast suspicion on the TSBD.

James Worrell said he saw a man "run like a bat out of hell" from the rear exit of the TSBD.[28] He told Arlen Spector, a Warren Commission assistant counsel who would eventually be asked by Nixon to coordinate his Watergate defense,[29] that the man was "flat moving on." He also furnished Spector with a description.

In a letter dated January 14, 1964 addressed to the Warren Commission, J. Edgar Hoover admitted that the original description of Kennedy's assassin broadcast by the police was "initiated on the basis of a description furnished by an unidentified citizen who had observed an individual approximating Oswald's description running from the TSBD immediately after the assassination."[30] (This description could not have been furnished by Worrell because he did not report to the police until the next day.) Oswald was still in the TSBD at the time of this sighting.[31] Who was this man?

James Romack contradicted Worrell's and the "unidentified citizen's" statements. He told the FBI that he started watching the back door of the building seconds after the shots were fired and saw no one except a policeman who had run there to check the fire escapes.[32] But TSBD employee Vicki Adams testified she ran out the back door soon after the shooting. Why didn't Romack see her?

Although a patrolman says he sealed off the building within three minutes of the shooting,[33] this is doubtful because Oswald and other employees were able to leave.[34] The TSBD was not sealed off until Sergeant D.V. Harkness decided to act after receiving a report from Amos Euins of a gunman in the sixth floor corner window. He went to the back of the building and found that "there were some Secret Service agents there. I didn't get them identified. They told me they were Secret Service."[35] James Romack also saw them: "There was two other gentlemen which I never said anything about that taken over. They were FBI or something standing right here at the very (back) entrance and just stood there."[36]

After the TSBD became the focal point of suspicion the railroad yard behind it got searched again. F.M. Turner shook down a "caboose of a boxcar" in back of the building but found nothing. He may have had help from an unidentified Army major who accompanied him.[37] Six men were sent into the yards to check tracks, shake down freights, and interview witnesses. Orders went out on the police radio to go about ten blocks behind the TSBD and check all the tracks.[38] Inspector Sawyer assigned Harkness and some other officers "to some freight cars that were leaving the yard." Harkness shook down a long string of boxcars but found nothing and soon the "clearall" sounded and the trains were allowed to leave the yards.[39] Several minutes later (about 2 p.m.) a message went out over the police radio, (see CD1420 on page 277) followed by "Pat. Whitman, contact Sawyer and notify him they are holding up a northbound freight train in the yard and want to shake it down before they go."

The only man who could "stop the trains" and was "behind the TSBD" was the sharp-eyed Lee Bowers who was still on duty. Bowers told Mark Lane: "Since there was the possibility that someone could...have climbed aboard this freight primarily, I pulled the train up immediately opposite the tower after alerting the police that I intended to do so, and I stopped the train and gave them a chance to examine it and to be sure that there was no one on it. As a matter of fact there were three people on it who appeared to be winos and perhaps were the most frightened winos I've ever seen in my life since there were possibly fifty policemen with shotguns and tommy guns and various other weapons shaking them out of these boxcars..."[40] During his testimony to the Warren Commission, Bowers was going to elaborate on the tramps but was cut short by Joe Ball (see page 112 of the Bowers Deposition reprinted on page 277). The session ended immediately after this exchange.

D.V. Harkness was one of the policemen who discovered the tramps. But when they came up in his deposition, David Belin tried to change the subject (see reprints of the Harkness Deposition on page 278). In 1968 David Belin became head of Lawyers For Nixon-Agnew[41] and in 1975 he was appointed General Counsel on the Rockefeller committee "investigating" the CIA.

While the tramps were being marched over to the Sheriff's office by Officers Bass and Wise,[42] several newspaper photographers took pictures of them and there is at least one movie in which they appear briefly.[43] George Smith of the Fort Worth *Star Telegram* took two pictures: one was a frontal shot as they marched past the cyclone fence which is actually part of the TSBD loading dock (P1), and the other was a profile shot snapped as they passed in front of the masonry facade of the TSBD (P2). Jack Beers of the *Dallas Morning News* also took two photographs: one had the entrance to the TSBD as a background (P3), the other was shot as they walked by the intersection of Houston and Elm Streets (P4). William Allen of the Dallas *Times Herald* got three photographs: one in front of the TSBD (P5), one as they crossed Houston and Elm (P6), and the third as they neared the Sheriff's office (P7). Officers Bass and

Wise brought them to the Sheriff's office where Will Fritz had set up temporary headquarters. As you can see from the document reprinted on page 279 Sheriff Elkins turned them over to Fritz. Michael Canfield questioned the ex-chief of the Dallas Police Department's Homicide Bureau about why there were no records of the "tramps'" detainment.

Canfield: The case in point is three hobos that were brought in...
Fritz: Yes, I know it. I know it. If you talk to the FBI they might help you with it...The FBI would be the only place that you could get that...that's the only ones who'd have it...I don't know anything about them at all.
Canfield: They were turned over to you, weren't they?
Fritz: No...The only one who could help you were the FBI. I've told you where you can find out. [44]

From the gist of Fritz's statement it seems as if the FBI questioned the tramps, cleared them, and let them go. (See photographs)

Many other suspects were picked up that day, and records exist on almost all of them. The anti-Kennedy demonstrators outside the Trade Mart were arrested; two men were picked up on false tips; [45] a drunk near the railroad tracks was brought in along with a man carrying a rifle. [46] The police also questioned a man inside the Daltex building because he tried to give them a credit card as identification—Jim Braden told them he was in Dallas on oil business, was staying at the Cabana Motel, and lived in Beverly Hills. [47] FBI agent John K. Anderson eventually visited him at his office in Beverly Hills and Braden gave him a story which was very similar to the one he gave the Dallas Police Department. [48] It was not until 1969 that Peter Noyes, producer for CBS-TV in Los Angeles, discovered, by simply checking on his driver's license number, that Jim Braden was really a gangster named Eugene Hale Brading. Brading had a long arrest record, a long history of association with organized crime, and was a charter member of the La Costa Club, located twenty miles south of San Clemente. Financed by the Teamsters and owned by Meyer Lansky's "front man" Moe Dalitz, La Costa was frequented by many organized crime figures as well as Nixon's close friend Murray Chotiner.[49] La Costa Club was also where Nixon's aides John Dean, John Ehrlichman and H.R. Haldeman met to get their stories about the Watergate cover-up synchronized. Peter Noyes reports that Brading had an office next door to Ferrie's in New Orleans and that he was in Los Angeles the night Robert Kennedy was shot.

The only suspects, questioned that infamous day, who were not accounted for in one way or another appear in unpublished newsphotos—and none of the ones we have seen look a fraction as suspicious as the tramps do.

First of all they did not look like tramps: they were clean-shaven and two of them had recently had haircuts. Although they smelled (a woman reporter is seen holding her nose in P3), there was no visual evidence of physical degeneration. All of them looked well-fed and their shoes were not worn. One of them seemed to be trying to avoid being photographed. In P1 and P2 the older tramp is standing behind the tramp who looks like Oswald; in P1 you can't see him at all and in P2 you can see half a profile. In P3 you get a good look at him, and in P4 he's making a face so he won't be recognized. In P5 you can just see his face in the shadows and in P6 and P7 he's hiding behind the tallest tramp. The fact that one of them looks a little like Oswald is suspicious in itself.

But what is most suspicious about the tramps is the fact that they were picked up after about three different searches of the railroad yard by literally hundreds of policemen. In a private tape-recorded conversation with D.V. Harkness, we asked him, "About how long after the assassination did you search that train?" Harkness said, "Oh, it was quite awhile—quite a time after that—they just didn't have anything leaving...the freight yards till after they gave the allclear." Thinking that the train they were on was parked in a faroff corner of the yards, we asked Harkness where the train was parked. "It was in the railroad yards, right adjacent to the railroad yards when it happened. It was within rifle range," he answered.

An assassination eyewitness said that "a train that looked like a circus train" was on the railroad track that ran near the triple underpass. And Sheriff Boone told Senator Cooper that "there were four railroad cars down approximately one hundred yards from the retaining wall.'' [50]

A little detective work reveals that the tramps fit quite closely the description of President Kennedy's assailants given by key eyewitnesses. The chart following juxtaposes our descriptions of the tramps with eyewitness accounts of the Kennedy assassins:

Description of tramps:

Oswald-like tramp	*Oldman-tramp*
1. slender build	1. very thin build
2. white/male	2. white/male/some wrinkles
3. brown hair/close cut/full in back	3. wearing hat
4. light shirt/dark pants/shirt could open at collar/herring bone sports jacket	4. plaid shirt/light pants
5. 25-30	5. 50

Tramps fit descriptions of suspected assassins seen in the upper windows of the TSBD:

The man Rowland saw in the sixth-floor window of the TSBD had: [51]	*Oswald-like tramp*
1. slender build	1. slender build
2. dark hair/close cut	2. brown hair/close cut/full in back
3. light shirt/dark pants/open at collar	3. light shirt/dark pants/shirt can be opened at collar

The older man Rowland saw near the man in the sixth-floor window of the TSBD [52]	*Oldman-tramp*
1. Negro/fairly dark/face was marked or wrinkled	1. white/male/some wrinkles
2. very thin build	2. very thin build
3. thin hair if not bald	3. wearing hat
4. plaid shirt—red and green/very bright color	4. plaid shirt
5. 50—possibly 55 or 60	5. 50

The man with the strange gun seen by Carolyn Walthers in the fifth-floor window had:	*Oswald-like tramp*
1. light brown hair	1. brown hair/close cut/full in back
2. white shirt	2. light shirt

The man standing next to the man with the strange gun was described by Walthers: 53	*Oldman-tramp*
1. brown suit/coat	1. not wearing jacket

Edward's and Fisher's combined descriptions of man they saw in sixth-floor TSBD window 54	*Oswald-like tramp*
1. slender face and neck	1. slender build
2. brown hair/short	2. brown hair/close cut/full in back
3. light-colored sport shirt/short-sleeved, open-necked	3. light shirt/could be opened at collar
4. 22-25	4. 25-30

(These comparisons assume that the tramp who looked like Oswald took off his jacket before firing.)

The similarity is definitely there, and the discrepancies become minor if you examine them further. The fact that Rowland describes the gunman's partner as "negro" is insignificant; the top floors of the TSBD are shaded at around noon because the light is coming from directly overhead. D.V. Harkness sealed off the TSBD after Amos Lee Euins told him he saw a "colored man" firing a rifle from the southeast window. [55] The fact that Carolyn Walthers says she saw the men on the fifth floor also becomes insignificant under closer scrutiny: Three police officers called in after the shooting with reports of witnesses who had seen the rifleman on the second, the fourth, and fifth floors. [56]

The tramps also fit the descriptions of the men seen running from the TSBD immediately after the assassination

The man Jean Hill saw running toward the railroad tracks from the TSBD [57]	*Oldman-tramp*
1. shorter than Ruby/stocky	1. very thin build
2. Brown overcoat	2. no coat

The man Worrell saw running from the back door of the TSBD after the shooting [58]	*Oswald-like tramp*
1. white/male	1. white/male
2. 5 feet 7 inches to 5 feet 10 inches tall/155-165 pounds	2. slender build
3. black/brunette/full in back	3. brown hair/close cut/full in back
4. sports jacket/dark in color, blue, black or brown/light pants	4. light shirt/dark pants/herring bone sports jacket
5. late 20's or early 30's	5. 25-30

Worrell also said that the man's coat was "opened and kind of flapping back in the breeze when he was running." The Oswald-like tramp's coat is flapping in P7. Worrell's testimony is backed up by an officer who said that when he reached the back of the TSBD minutes after the shooting the door was wide open. [59] Worrell died in a motorcycle accident in Dallas on November 9, 1966. He was 23 years old.

Tall tramp fits witnesses' descriptions of one of the men behind the fence

The man Price saw run from the fence to some railroad cars in the yard was: [60]	*Tallest tramp*
1. 145 lbs.—5 feet 6 or 7 inches—not too tall	1. 175-200 lbs./six feet tall
2. bareheaded, sandy-hair and long	2. sandy hair/long

3. white shirt/khaki trousers	3. white shirt/brown trousers
4. about 25 years old	4. about 30 years old

The man Bowers saw hanging around behind the fence who disappeared after the shooting [61]	*Tallest tramp*
1. plaid shirt or plaid coat or jacket	1. white shirt/brown trousers
2. mid-20's	2. about 30

Neither of these witnesses got a good look at the people in question. Price was on the roof of the Terminal Annex Building at least three blocks away and Bowers stressed the difficulty he had in distinguishing the man from the foliage. In fact the foliage could very well have made a white shirt look plaid.

Some of the inconsistencies in the eyewitness testimonies disappears if one allows for an exchange of a brown suit jacket between the older tramp and the tallest one. After all, if the plan was for the assassins to escape undetected on the freight train, they must have become very frightened when Lee Bowers had their train stopped and brought back into the yards for another search. No doubt they would try and alter their appearance as best they could.

If one looks closely at the tall tramp's shoes in P3 page 220, traces of mud on the sides of the shoes can be distinguished. This is consistent with the reports of Weitzman, Holland, etc. of footprints in the mud behind the fence. The fact that the mud is only on the sides of the shoes and not on the bottom dovetails with the reports that it looked like someone had scraped their shoes clean on a nearby automobile bumper.

From the preceding testimony it appears that the death squad was composed of two men in the TSBD and two men behind the fence on the knoll. They were supported by at least two other conspirators who assured the police and bystanders that they had everything under control behind the TSBD.

It also appears that the men inside the TSBD exited through the back door seconds after the shooting. The FBI estimated that it takes one minute and forty-five seconds to get out of the TSBD from the sixth floor *at a fast walk.*⁶² One of these men ran towards the railroad yard and the other went the opposite way joining the crowds on Elm Street who were rushing to the knoll area. Once inside the railroad yard, the first assassin was able to disappear by hiding in a freight car, just as his partners had done.

Judging from the fact that the tramps escaped detection for so long, and that it was not until Lee Bowers spotted one of them that they were apprehended, it is safe to say that the search of the railroad yards had been set up so that the tramps would *not* be found.

Perhaps the large number of Federal agents who converged on the scene had something to do with it. James Powell, the mysteryman of Army Intelligence, helped "search" for the tramps. During Detective Brian's testimony before the Commission, he was asked by Representative Ford:

Ford: As you drove from the TSBD building after making a check of the facilities who was in the car?

Brian: Our car?

Ford: Yes.

Brian: Let me see, Lt. Revill, myself, Westphal, Tarver, and we gave a man a lift, and I don't remember whether he was a CID, I don't know the man. I don't remember whether he was a CIC agent or a CID or OSI, he was some type of, as I recall, Army Intelligence man.

Dulles: Army, Air Force or something?

Brian: ...he was connected with the service and we let him out a couple of blocks, if I recall, up about Field Street...Lt. Revill knew who he was... ⁶³

Except for Brian, none of the other men who drove back with Powell mentioned him in their testimony. After they dropped off Powell, Revill and Brian, who pretty much comprised the Dallas Red Squad, met with FBI agent Hosty at Police Headquarters. These were the men who were supposed to keep track of radicals and their activities in Dallas. It was their job to warn the Secret Service about "characters like Oswald."

Powell was not the only intelligence agent to appear on the scene. There were Treasury agents and at least one Army major who helped search for the tramps. Jack Crichton, another Army Intelligence agent, may also have been there. A few hours later he would call upon one of the members of the Dallas White Russian Community to act as an interpreter for Marina Oswald. [64]

A massive influx of Federal agents has its analogue in Watergate. After the plane carrying Hunt's wife Dorothy crashed under mysterious circumstances in December 1973, the chairman of the National Transportation Safety Board told the House Government Activities Subcommittee that he had sent a letter to the FBI which stated that over fifty agents came into the crash zone. [65] The FBI denied everything until William Ruckleshaus became temporary Director, at which time they admitted that their agents were on the scene. [66] Independent researcher Sherman Skolnick believes that Dorothy Hunt was carrying documents that linked Nixon to the Kennedy assassination. According to Skolnick these papers, which were being used to blackmail Nixon, were seized by the FBI. Skolnick's theory is corroborated by a conversation that allegedly took place between Charles Colson and Jack Caufield.

According to Caufield, Colson told him that there were many important papers the Administration needed in the Brookings Institution and that the FBI had recently adopted a policy of coming to the scene of any suspicious fires in Washington D.C. Caufield believed that Colson was subtly telling him to start a fire at Brookings and the FBI would then steal the desired documents. [67]

Note at this point that *one day* after the plane crash, White House aide Egil Krogh was appointed Undersecretary of Transportation. This gave him direct control over the National Transportation Safety Board and the Federal Aviation Administration—the two agencies that would be in charge of investigating the crash. Soon Dwight Chapin, Nixon's Appointment Secretary, became a top executive at United Airlines. Dorothy Hunt was on a United carrier when she made her ill-fated journey.

Another victim of sudden death in an accident was Lee Bowers, if not for whom we would never have gotten a look at the tramps. Lee Bowers was killed in a one-car accident in Midloathean, Texas on August 9, 1966. The sharp-eyed Bowers plowed into a concrete bridge abutment. His physician told independent researcher Penn Jones that he "...never saw a case like this—that man was in some sort of strange shock." Bowers was dead in three hours and was cremated the next day. No autopsy was performed. [68]

CHAPTER FIVE

The Tramps and the Watergate Burglars

Make-up, costumes and other paraphernalia are part of any self-respecting spy's bag of tricks. Howard Hunt used a variety of disguises in the course of his undercover activities. When he visited Dita Beard in regard to the ITT scandal, he disguised himself in his famous "red wig and voice modulator." Whatever he said then and however he said it must have worked, because shortly after his visit, Beard recanted her damaging statements about the Nixon Administration. On another assignment, before meeting with an "informer" within the Kennedy clan Hunt met with a man from the CIA Technical Services Division who "...outfitted me with dark, non-refractive glasses and a brown wig, which he showed me how to don and adjust." The agent also gave Hunt a device which fitted into his mouth and produced a lisping effect. [1]

Hunt always seemed to go through a lot of trouble to disguise himself. He must also have consistently avoided cameras because there were no pictures of him available anywhere until he was implicated in the Watergate affair.

His operatives also made extensive use of disguises. Eugenio Martinez (one of the Watergaters) claims Hunt had his team dress up as deliverymen during the Ellsberg caper [2] although the janitor reported they were disguised as mailmen. [3] Martinez also said that Hunt instructed them to pretend to be "junkies looking for dope," should they be caught in the midst of their operation.

Hunt has also been known to hide in the same fashion that the Oldman-tramp did. When he was in the White House visiting Arthur Schlesinger he "...saw Ambassador Ellis Briggs waiting to pay his respects to the President. Having known the Ambassador in the Far East and Latin America I was not anxious to have him see me in the White House, so I turned my head as we passed."[4] While Hunt was in Havana shortly after Castro came to power he saw the wife of a man he had known in the CIA reflected in the window of a street-level radio station:* "For a moment I feared the lady would recognize me...but I...kept my face turned toward the broadcaster."[5]

But why, after all his painstaking precautions, would the CIA let pictures of Howard Hunt, disguised as a tramp on the scene of the Kennedy assassination, circulate? The answer lies in the fact that the photographs have been doctored. In P7 page 216 there is a brush stroke covering the small part of the Old-man-tramp's face that would have been visible in the picture. The brush stroke extends onto the tallest tramp's face. In P5 two blocks of light appear in front of what is showing of the Old-man-tramp's face. P3 is also doctored—a new ear has been spliced on. If you look at page 216 you can see a minute art-knife notch. The shadow is too deep around the edges of the ear. This ear is identical with the ear of the tallest bum shown in P6. The probable reason that they used it was that it was taken under the same lighting conditions. The ear shown in this picture does not correspond to the tip of a fox-like ear, which sticks out behind the Oswald-like tramp, under a hat and some thin hair in P1. The CIA forgot to take this minute detail out. The only man who could tell us if this picture was altered is photographer Jack

---

* Part of Hunt's formula for overthrowing Castro was to "destroy the Cuban radio and television transmitters before or coincident with the invasion." On the local scene, Watergater James McCord served with a special sixteen-man unit whose job was the "censorship of news media and U.S. mail" in time of national emergency.[6] If Hunt's plans for a coup were ever implemented in the United States, McCord would have been in a key position to help him.

Beers, and he died of a "heart attack" on February 16, 1975, about a week after the tramp pictures got published in many newspapers.

In P6 we finally get a look at the Oldman-tramp and he is a dead ringer for Everette Howard Hunt. We went down to Dallas and measured the wall he was standing up against and discovered that the Oldman-tramp is five feet eight inches tall. Hunt is exactly the same height. (see page 208) The open-mouthed expression on his face is also very significant. We have studied hundreds of photographs of Howard Hunt, all taken as a result of the Watergate affair, and that open-mouthed expression is characteristic of him when he is being photographed by newsmen–whom he despises. Notice how the shadows fall in the same places in page 217. This shot was taken around the same time the tramp pictures were taken. Notice the flatness on the tip of Hunt's nose in P6 and page 217. In P2 look at the lines on the side of Hunt's face and compare them with the lines of page 217. Also notice the slope of the nose. Finally, we've included an acetate overlay of Hunt which can be placed on top of a photograph of the tramp.

But why the amazing resemblance when there's an age discrepancy of ten years? Were the tramps made-up to look older than they actually were in the course of being transformed into tramps? We would have liked to use contemporary pictures but the only one available of Hunt from 1961-63 appears in his book *Give Us This Day* and just happens to be blurred. Another of Hunt's books, *Undercover*, has plenty of pictures of him, but they end abruptly in 1959 and don't resume until June 1972.

The reactionary Hunt had plenty of reasons to hate the liberal Kennedy, but what especially irked him was Kennedy's actions in the Bay of Pigs invasion (BOP), because Hunt himself had a strong personal involvement in it. He believed that "No event since the communization of China in 1949 has had such a profound effect on the United States and its allies..."; he holds the BOP responsible for the Berlin Wall, the Cuban Missile Crisis and more, terming it a "Pandora's box" of troubles.[7]

On March 17, 1960 President Eisenhower approved a National Security Council recommendation to arm and train Cuban exiles in an effort to overthrow the Fidel Castro regime in Cuba. Allen Dulles, Director of the CIA at that time, ordered Deputy Director Charles Cabell, Tracy Barnes, who had worked with Hunt on the overthrow of Arbenez, and others, to rid the United States of its "Dagger in the Heart."

Howard Hunt was in charge of forming a government-in-exile that would take over Cuba after Castro was deposed. Initially he tried to locate this government-in-exile in Costa Rica and Mexico but the political climate was not right, so he was forced to set up "The Cuban Revolutionary Front" (also known as the Cuban Democratic Revolutionary Front) in Miami. Hunt then visited Guatemala where he was able to secure the use of a large plantation, which was immediately turned into a training base.[8]

The members of the Cuban Revolutionary Front included two hardline anti-communists: Manuel Artime of the Movement of Revolutionary Recovery (MRR) and Jose Ignacio of the Christian Democratic Movement. Artime's father was an ex-communist who had turned against the party and had his son trained by the Jesuits to be a doctor. Artime ran a student group that opposed Batista and joined Castro in the Sierra Maestres three days before Batista was deposed. Castro put him in charge of collective farming, but he had an argument with Che Guevara and had to go underground. Artime was exfiltrated from Cuba by Bernard Barker, one of the men caught in Watergate. Ignacio's Christian Democratic Movement and the MRR shared common members[9] just as they shared a conservative political orientation.

The Cuban Revolutionary Front also had three members who were representatives of the old Prio* government: Justo Carrillo, President of the Bank for Industrial Development under Prio; Aureliano Sanchez Arango, Foreign Minister under Prio; and Tony Varona, the titular leader of the CRF, and former Prime Minister of Prio's government.

After the CRF and its allies failed to foment an internal uprising in Cuba, they decided on a full-scale invasion.

---

* Carlos Prio was a President of Cuba who had been overthrown by Batista, had come to America and set up a government-in-exile while supplying Batista's enemies with arms. Prio had funded Castro only to be double-crossed by him after the revolution. He was thus determined to overthrow him.

Everything was going according to plan until the elections appeared on the political horizon. Suddenly the Coast Guard began interfering with exile operations against Cuba. [10] But most members of the CRF, and most Cuban exiles for that matter, thought that after Kennedy was elected, all Federal police actions against them would end. After all, Kennedy had taken a harder line regarding an invasion than Nixon had, during their famous televised debate. Insiders like Hunt and his friend Artime knew that the Vice-President's lips were sealed because he was one of the planners of the operation, and he did not want to tip off Castro's people about the government's intentions.

After Kennedy won the election, the exile community was jubilant only to find that recruitment for the training base in Guatemala was suddenly stopped, paralyzing project activity. Hunt's superior told him not to worry, "...after Dick (Nixon) and Dulles have briefed Kennedy it will be full speed ahead... Kennedy campaigned on a promise to back them." [11]

After making the CIA draft a new Cuban Constitution, Kennedy gave a tentative go-ahead for the invasion. He also demanded that the CRF be expanded to include leftist elements of the exile community such as Manolo Ray. The Cuban Revolutionary Council was formed and a new CIA liaison appointed, because Howard Hunt refused to work with leftists. Kennedy also insisted that no American could be involved in the actual invasion. [12]

The invasion's scenario called for the assassination of Castro followed by air strikes flown against Cuba by planes with Cuban markings and prefabricated bullet holes—to give the world the impression that elements of Castro's Air Force were turning against him. This was to be followed by a second air strike in order to make certain that Castro's air power was neutralized completely before the massive ground invasion was launched. The invasion, which was to occur coincident with an internal uprising, was supposed to establish a beachhead, after which help from the Organization of American States would be called for.

Everything went wrong. Hans Tanner of the Christian Democratic Movement reported that "...twenty-seven terrorists had been arrested in Havana and charged with a plot to kill Castro."

Even though a New York advertising agency, at Hunt's instigation, put out a press release stating that the pilots of the planes that had attacked the Cuban Air Force were "defecting members of Castro's Air Force with whom the Cuban Revolutionary Council was in touch," many reporters did not believe the story. One of the planes was forced to land in Miami and its bullet holes did not look real enough. The coup de grâce was administered by Kennedy when he refused to authorize a second air strike, after the cover story regarding the first had become transparent. General Cabell got Secretary of State Dean Rusk to plead with Kennedy at least twice and even spoke directly with the President, but his efforts were of no avail. On the second night of the invasion, Kennedy met with Rusk, Lemnitzer, and others. They got a minor concession out of him, but still no second air strike.

The CIA's troops, commanded by Artime, were promptly dispatched by Castro's army and the remnants of his Air Force. Artime was taken prisoner.

This was a tremendous blow to Hunt, who had hoped Artime would replace Castro as the leader of Cuba. He felt so bad about Artime languishing in a Cuban prison that he made him a godfather of one of his children.

Hunt had mistrusted the Kennedy Administration from the very beginning and told his assistant Bernard Barker, several months before the invasion that "...it was becomingly increasingly hard to identify the enemy." Hunt stated that the second air strike was "basic to the success of the entire invasion. The fact that it was not honored resulted in the brigade's defeat."

Hunt laid the blame for the Bay of Pigs fiasco almost entirely on Kennedy, and there is reason to believe that he suspected the President of being part of the "international communist conspiracy." In *Give Us This Day* Hunt links Kennedy advisor Arthur Schlesinger with a member of the Fair Play for Cuba Committee, and calls Schlesinger's decisions "the ultimate in folly." He also criticized the Administration for deriding "any talk of international communist conspiracy" and believed that Kennedy made a deal with the Russians regarding Cuba. [13] Hunt was especially bitter about Kennedy's campaign promises which won over the exile community, and largely exempts the CIA from any blame. [14] The only one in the CIA that Hunt finds fault with is General Cabell, who was in charge of the operation because Dulles was in Puerto Rico that day. According to Hunt it was Cabell who decided to ask Kennedy for a go-signal on the second air strike instead of just doing it. "If only Cabell hadn't come mousing around..." he writes. But there is no reason to blame Cabell. Shortly after Castro came to power, he deplored—before the Senate Internal Security Subcommittee—the tremendous communist influence in Castro's government. Obviously, with regard to the Bay of Pigs operation, he was "just following orders."

Hunt is the only conservative historian to put any of the blame for the failure of the invasion on Cabell. In Ralph DeToledano's book on Robert Kennedy he writes about an article in *Fortune* about the Bay of Pigs and points out how it says that Cabell pleaded with Kennedy for air cover many times and did the best he could. In *Give Us This Day* Hunt says that Dulles assigned him to the task of finding out who leaked the highly accurate facts in this article to its author. He traced it to a high official of the Kennedy Administration, but Kennedy himself believed it was Dulles.

There is reason to believe that Hunt is deliberately disassociating himself from Cabell, just as Pena disassociated himself from Bringuier. General Cabell's brother, Earl, was Mayor of Dallas when Kennedy was assassinated. He was instrumental in arranging the motorcade route and admitted knowing Jack Ruby. [15]

General Cabell was "fired" from the CIA as a result of the Bay of Pigs and went to work for the Pacific Corporation as a member of its Board of Directors. The Pacific Corporation is the parent company of Air America, the CIA-run carrier that has been heavily involved in opium traffic in Southeast Asia. Dulles was also forced to retire. [16]

At the end of 1961 Richard Helms became Deputy Director of Plans and "after a considerable bureaucratic struggle Barnes established the Domestic Operations Division and appointed (Hunt) its chief of covert action. The new division accepted both

personnel and projects unwanted elsewhere in the CIA...
Many men connected with that failure (BOP) were shunted into
the new domestic unit..." [17]

Around this time Tad Szulc, a former New York *Times*
newsman, reports that Kennedy told him that he was under great
pressure from advisors in the intelligence community (whom he
did not name) to have Castro killed. Kennedy refused. [18] Because
almost all of the future attempts against Castro can be traced
back to Hunt, there is sufficient reason to believe that he was
one of these advisors. Szulc also reports that Hunt was on the
Inter-Agency Committee on Cuba which studied various possible
actions against Castro. [19]

Very little is known about Hunt's activities during 1962-63.
This period is totally omitted from his autobiography [20] and all
that is known about it is that he was the CIA Chief of Station in
Mexico City during August and September 1963.

It is likely that Hunt's attitude toward Kennedy did not
change much during this period. After the Cuban Missile Crisis,
Kennedy made a deal with Khrushchev not to invade Cuba in
return for the removal of Soviet missiles from the island. In April
1963 Miro Cardona, head of the Cuban Revolutionary Council
resigned because, under Kennedy, "the struggle for Cuba was in
the process of being liquidated by the government." [21] The CRC
was disbanded and the Cuban Committee of Liberation, a purely
propagandistic group, was formed. [22] As we shall see, many of
Hunt's friends were restrained by the Federal government from
attacking Castro and the sincerity of the advertisement eulogizing
the late President, which Hunt's close friend, Manuel Artime,
placed in the major exile newspapers, is questionable.

After the assassination there was talk of making Hunt the
station chief in Madrid; perhaps they wanted to get him out of
the country.* Although Hunt did not receive the appointment,
there is reason to believe he went to Madrid anyway—to work on
a secret plan that combined Castro's assassination with another
invasion. Tad Szulc reports that this plan had to be canceled (or

* After Hunt was implicated in the Watergate break-in, John Dean advised him to go
abroad. [23]

postponed) after President Johnson sent troops into the Dominican Republic in 1965. He also says that James McCord was associated with this activity. In early 1966 a man named Cubela was arrested in Havana for attempting to assassinate Castro. Dr. Scott reports that this man admitted to Castro's interrogators that Hunt's protege, Artime, was one of his co-conspirators. Hunt has also been linked to earlier attempts on Castro's life by the CIA and the Syndicate, as we shall learn later on in this book. *Newsweek* reported that while working in the White House in July 1971, Hunt had an assassination team in Mexico ready to kill the ruler of Panama. [24]

Kennedy dug his own grave by trying to stop the Howard Hunts of the CIA from killing Castro. As Frank Sturgis put it "...Howard tried to assassinate Castro, and Castro is still around, bigger than ever. Alright, but hey, listen, Howard was in charge of other CIA operations that involved 'disposal' and I can tell you, some of them worked." [25]

One gains insight into Hunt's feelings about Kennedy by looking at his activities exposed as a result of Watergate. There is Howard Hunt, a CIA agent who also wrote books. One of these books is a blatant anti-Kennedy allegory. When John Dean opened Howard Hunt's safe he found bogus telegrams linking Kennedy with the assassination of Ngo Dinh Diem. Hunt had shown General Charles Conein copies of these forged telegrams because the General had served under Kennedy in Vietnam in 1963. After speaking with Hunt, Conein began to shift the blame for Diem's assassination to Kennedy. Soon after, Conein got a job in the Drug Enforcement Administration. While he was with the DEA, Conein was in contact with a private company that produced sophisticated assassination weapons. The New York *Times* printed part of a memo written on the letterhead of this company which read, "Enclosed is a catalogue which was put together only after we started working with Lou Conein." There is no evidence that Conein helped forge the telegrams.

Hunt's safe also contained material relating to an investigation of Chappaquidick. He cultivated informers within the Kennedy clan [26] and may have forged documents blaming the failure of the Bay of Pigs invasion on a secret agreement between Kennedy and

Castro. Colson recorded a telephone conversation with Hunt about this:

> Hunt: I would particularly like to see the Bay of Pigs stuff declassified including the alleged agreement that Castro made with JFK.
> Colson: Because you were part of that and knew it was a phoney?
> Hunt: Sure. [27]

Many people involved in the Bay of Pigs operation turn up in the Watergate investigation. Manuel Artime was called before the Watergate Grand Jury because his telephone number appeared in Hunt's phone book; he visited Hunt in jail on several occasions and organized a defense fund for him. Bernard Barker* turned up as a Watergater and money-launderer. Barker had worked with the Cuban Revolutionary Council and admitted that "the methods utilized in the operation were the same methods utilized when I worked for Mr. Hunt in the Bay of Pigs invasion. This training I received with the rest of the Cubans..." Barker is referring to the training he received as part of Operation Forty, which he elaborated about in the course of talking about Felipe Dediego, who had worked on the Ellsberg mission. "Mr. Dediego had been a member of Operation Forty, which had been specially trained to capture documents of the Castro government and the operation was successful. He had received further training as an intelligence officer in the Army of the United States." Sturgis throws a different light on Operation Forty: "...it was a top secret government operation, it consisted of many Cuban intelligence officers, who worked for the CIA and this organization...the assassination section, which I was part of...would, upon orders, naturally, assassinate either members of the military in the foreign country, members of the political parties of the foreign country you were going to infiltrate, and, if necessary, some of your own members..." [28] The training these men received from the CIA could have been used against President Kennedy.

---

* A CIA agent who helped train the Cuban Secret Police under Batista, then worked as a finance officer during the Bay of Pigs operation, arranging funding of the exiles through foreign banks.

If Barker had a role in the Kennedy assassination, other former members of Batista's police force might have been aware of the plot. A nurse at a Philadelphia hospital advised the FBI, after the President's death, that a woman named Christina Suarez had told her that her brother Miguel "had said that President John F. Kennedy would be killed by Castroites" long before the assassination. Miguel Suarez's father was Chief of Police under the Batista regime and Miguel was a member of Ex-Combatientes, a group of anti-Castro veterans who trained at Fort Jackson in South Carolina.[29]Angel Ferrer, who happened to have been registered at the Watergate hotel at the time of the burglary, trained the exile troops at Fort Jackson. Tad Szulc reports that the Ex-Combatientes maintained contact with Hunt and McCord.[30]

When the Watergaters registered they did so under the name of Ameritus, a dummy corporation headed by Miguel Suarez. We called Suarez at his law office in Miami and he said that he had no sister but he was director of Ameritus.

The FBI interviewed a man, who sounded insane, yet made a reference to "Ferry" in his rantings. His wife was a fingerprint expert with the Cuban Police under Batista.[31]

In Martinsburg, Pennsylvania a housewife named Margaret Hoover found a piece of paper with the words "Ruby," "Rubenstein" and "Oswald" written on it in October 1963. She suspected it came from one of her neighbors, a Cuban exile named Dr. Julio Fernandez. We have reprinted the interview with Dr. Fernandez on page 279. Notice his relationship with Batista's police and what a big publisher he was. In the other pages of the interview he tells the FBI agents how he had lost "all of his worldly possessions" and how he had "great sympathy for the American people in their loss of President Kennedy." He denied knowing anything about the piece of paper that Margaret Hoover had found.

Hoover lost the piece of paper with the names written on it, but while she still had it in her possession, she exhibited it to her daughter, who verified the story to the FBI. Despite constant pressure from her husband, Hoover's daughter stuck to her story.[32]

One of Dr. Fernandez's newspapers was published in Las Villas, Cuba, a center of anti-Castro activity. Hoover also found a railroad ticket from Miami to Washington dated September 25, 1963. It was around this time that members of the anti-Castro DRE were traveling from Miami to Washington to testify before a Congressional Committee. [33]

The people connected with the Bay of Pigs operation and Watergate certainly had a motive for killing Kennedy: they felt he was standing in the way of the "liberation of Cuba."

In *Give Us This Day* Hunt named Richard Milhous Nixon as the "secret action officer" in the White House for BOP. Hunt and Nixon may have first become acquainted with one another when Nixon, Vernon Walters and Robert Cushman (the latter two men became Deputy Directors of the CIA during the time Hunt worked with the CIA in conjunction with his Watergate activities) visited Uruguay in 1958. Hunt was a CIA agent there at the time.

In *My Six Crises*, Nixon takes credit for starting Operation Forty: "The covert training of Cuban exiles by the CIA was due in substantial part, at least, to my efforts." A reliable source reports that, as Action Officer, Nixon "approved dirty tricks and terror."

Hunt and Nixon both tended to side with the "Batistaites." In *Give Us This Day* Hunt writes, "True, Batista had been a corrupt dictator, but under him and his predecessors the Cuban standard of living was far above the Latin American average." William Pawley, the organizer of the Flying Tigers, an early intelligence-oriented airline, and the pre-revolutionary owner of the Havana Bus Company, had the ear of Richard Nixon. [34] Pawley had urged Eisenhower to support Batista against Castro in the late 1950's and continually pointed this out to then Vice-President Nixon. [35]

Hunt was also connected to Nixon through Robert Cushman, Nixon's military liaison. Cushman met with Hunt and assured his old friend (they had shared an office together in the 1950's—see page 56) that his boss wanted nothing to go wrong with the invasion. [36]

General Alexander Haig, another Watergate-linked figure, was probably involved with Hunt and Nixon because he was in the Caribbean section of the Planning Division of the Department of the Army at the time of Bay of Pigs. [37] Professor Trowbridge Ford reports Haig became the liaison between the Pentagon and the White House after Kennedy was killed.

Haig was alleged to have had a key role in forcing Nixon to resign by playing damaging excerpts from the White House tapes for the ex-President. He is now in charge of NATO in Europe.

In April 1959 Nixon had a meeting with Castro after which he announced that the Cuban strong man was a communist. [38] There is little doubt that if Nixon had been elected Castro would have been overthrown. Nixon told the Miami *Herald* in 1967 that he would have "advocated to President Eisenhower that it be done before (his) inauguration..." and explained that the only reason he protested a 1960 Kennedy proposal of aid for Cuban exiles was because "the covert operation had to be protected at all costs." In this interview Nixon refers to the assassination as "the supreme tragedy"; later, many other suspicious persons use this same phrasing. [39]

Like Hunt, Nixon may have also believed that the failure of the Bay of Pigs invasion had its roots in a sinister international conspiracy. In the White House tapes he is quoted as saying, "...Chester Bowles had learned about it and he deliberately leaked it. Deliberately, because he wanted the operation to fail. And he admitted it. Admitted it."

Nixon had always had Cuba on his mind. Just after he married Patricia Ryan in 1940, he went to Cuba to "explore the possibilities of establishing law or business connections in Havana." [40] In 1952 he visited there again accompanied by ex-FBI agent Richard Danner.

As the former City Manager of Miami, Danner knew many of the gangsters operating in that area, including Meyer Lansky. In the late 1960's Danner was employed by Howard Hughes and was exposed in the Watergate affair as the courier who delivered a hundred thousand dollars from Hughes to Bebe Rebozo, as contribution to the Nixon campaign. Rebozo kept this money until 1973 at which time he returned it to Hughes. Charles Colson has stated, "...I think that Hughes paid Bebe that dough. I think that Bebe used that one hundred grand for himself and for the President, his family and the girls. Hughes can blow the whistle on him..." [41]

Rebozo lived next door to Nixon at Key Biscayne and participated in numerous real estate deals with the ex-President. He was Nixon's closest Cuban friend. Many people believe that they first became acquainted with one another when Nixon was on the Automobile Tire Price Board during World War II. By a strange twist of fate, Rebozo made his fortune recapping tires during this period. Nixon was a big depositor in Rebozo's bank and after he became President, Rebozo got a loan from the Small Business Administration which was soon funneled to the rightwing elements in the Cuban community in the form of shopping center concessions. Note the fact that Rebozo's business partner Edgardo Buttari, is also a partner in the meat business of Manuel Artime, Howard Hunt's best friend. [42]

Nixon was in Dallas until 11:00 on the morning of November 22, 1963. Keeping Nixon's Cuban connections in mind, a pertinent question arises: "What was Nixon doing in Dallas and why did he lie to the FBI about being there?" In the Warren Commission exhibit, prophetically numbered "1973" and reprinted on page 280 Nixon told the FBI that "...the only time he was in Dallas, Texas during 1963 was two days prior to the assassination of John F. Kennedy."

Ostensibly, Nixon was in Dallas attending the American Bottlers of Carbonated Beverages Convention as a representative of Pepsi-Cola. The Pepsico company has long been associated with rightwing politics—Senator Joseph McCarthy earned the nickname "Pepsi-Cola Kid" after it was revealed that soon after he helped end sugar rationing a Pepsi-Cola bottler named Arundel paid off some bank loans for him. [43] Nixon also helped establish a Pepsi-Cola factory in Laos—with the help of AID funds—that never produced a single bottle of Pepsi. Instead it became one of the largest heroin factories in Southeast Asia. [44] Professor Scott reports that Nixon was also in Dallas to purchase land for a new

Pepsi syrup plant from the Great Southwestern Corporation, a company partially controlled by the Rockefellers. Marina Oswald's attorney was a partner in the law firm handling the Great Southwestern Corporation in Dallas.[45] Immediately after the assassination he took Marina to the Inn of the Six Flags (owned by Great Southwestern) where she was questioned by select Federal and local enforcement personnel.[46]

Donald Kendell, President of Pepsi-Cola in 1963, became head of the U.S.-U.S.S.R. Trade and Economic Council, an organization established to increase Soviet-American trade. Pepsico also received a lucrative franchise to bottle Pepsi in Russia during the Nixon Administration.

Jack Ruby was indirectly connected with the Pepsi-Cola Corporation. He was a friend of a man named Lawrence Meyers whose brother Ed was one of the owners of a Pepsico bottling company in Queens, New York controlled by Arundel, the same man who worked closely with Joseph McCarthy. (In the Kefauver hearings Meyer Lansky testified that he once worked with a man named Ed Meyers.[47]) Ed Meyers visited Mexico during November 1963 and was also in Dallas attending the bottlers' convention when Nixon was there.[48]

The Meyers brothers had dinner with Ruby at the Bon Vivant Room of the Cabana Hotel the night before the assassination. Did Eugene Hale Brading, who was also staying at the Cabana at the time, have dinner with them? Jim Garrison reports that a check of the records of the Cabana Hotel for November 1963 revealed that Meyers' son, Ralph, was also there. Ralph Meyers was an Army Intelligence agent with a crypto-clearance, who had been stationed at a top-secret base in Turkey.[49] This may have been one of the bases where the U-2 spy plane was kept. Meyers spoke with Ruby for thirty minutes on the night before Ruby shot Oswald; he has also been linked to David Ferrie through the long distance telephone records of the automotive supply house he worked for.[50] Meyers also refers to the assassination as the "tragedy."

Professor Trowbridge Ford unearthed the fact that before Nixon came to Dallas in November "threats" were allegedly made against him. On October 20, 1963 the Dallas *Morning*

News carried the following story:

> The FBI and postal inspectors are on the trail of a man in the Dallas area who has been mailing postcards with obscene charges against Representative Bruce Alger and former Vice-President Richard M. Nixon. All bear the same handwriting. Most of them carry Dallas postmarks but some have been mailed at Irving and Fort Worth. The sender is believed to be a possible social deviate.

Oswald frequently visited Irving, Texas, because his wife lived there at the time, and Rep. Bruce Alger often frequented Ruby's Carousel Club. Dallas Postal Inspector Holmes was one of the few government officials who got a chance to quesion Lee Harvey Oswald during his brief period of incarceration. He also claimed to have watched the railroads through binoculars from a building two blocks away immediately following the assassination hoping "I would see somebody running across the railroad tracks..." He said he saw nothing. [51]

Dr. Ford reports that despite these threats Nixon told the Dallas Police Department that he felt safe in their city. The *Morning News* carried an article entitled "Guard Not for Nixon" which said that the police stationed at the hotel where Nixon was staying were there to protect Pepsi heiress Joan Crawford. Dr. Ford wonders if Nixon's laxity rubbed off on Kennedy's advance man in Dallas, Wayne Hawks, who was a former press aide of Nixon's.

When, in November 1973, *Esquire* questioned him on his whereabouts on November 22, 1963, Nixon finally admitted to being in Dallas, but said that he left before noon, possibly implying that because he was not there when it happened, he had nothing to do with the assassination. The pro-Nixon introduction to the White House tapes contains the following line: "When the break-in at the Watergate occurred and the participants were arrested the President was in Florida." Nixon is also quoted as having said, "Last June 17, while I was in Florida...I first learned from news reports of the Watergate break-in." [52]

Another unsolved Watergate mystery exposed by the Ervin Committee is why Hunt could blackmail Nixon for a million dollars. Perhaps Hunt knew that Nixon was involved in the Kennedy assassination, whose code name has become, aptly enough, "Bay of Pigs." Maybe this is what Nixon was referring to on June 23, 1972, when he told his Chief of Staff, H.R. Haldeman:

Nixon: O.K., just postpone (scratching noises) (unintelligible) Just say (unintelligible) very bad to have this fellow Hunt, ah, he know that? If it gets out that this is all involved, the Cuba thing would be a fiasco. It would make the CIA look bad it's going to make Hunt look bad, and it is likely to blow the whole Bay of Pigs thing which we think would be very unfortunate—both for CIA, and for the country, at this time, and for American foreign policy. Just tell him to lay off. Don't you?

Haldeman: Yep. That's the basis to do it on. Just leave it at that.

Nixon: I don't know if he'll get any ideas for doing it because our concern political (unintelligible). Helms is not one to (unintelligible; —I would just say, lookit, because of the Hunt involvement, basically this...

Haldeman: Yep. Good move. [53]

What is there about the Bay of Pigs that could be blown at this late date and why would it be "very unfortunate for the CIA...the country" and Howard Hunt? Nixon wanted Helms to tell Patrick Grey, Director of the FBI, to "lay off" the Watergate investigation regarding Hunt. Was he afraid that if Hunt was thoroughly investigated or even put in the limelight someone might realize that Howard Hunt was the key to the John F. Kennedy assassination?

When Nixon says "I don't know if he'll get any ideas for doing it because our concern political (unintelligible)" and Helms is not one to (unintelligible)—I would just say, lookit, because of the Hunt involvement..." is he really saying: "Helms may not want to do it because our concern is politically motivated and Helms isn't one to play politics. So tell him Hunt is involved and domestic assassinations may be exposed"?

Later that afternoon Haldeman reported back to the President after speaking with Helms and CIA Deputy Director Walters:

> Haldeman: . . . (unintelligible—perhaps "I told Helms") the problem is it tracks back to the Bay of Pigs and it tracks back to some other leads run out to people who had no involvement in this, except by contacts and connection, but it gets to areas that are liable to be raised? The whole problem (unintelligible—perhaps "revolves around") Hunt. So at that point he kind of got the picture. . . Walters is going to make a call to Grey. . .

In another conversation later that day Nixon told Haldeman:

> Nixon: When you get in—when you get in (unintelligible) people, say, "Look the problem is that this will open the whole, the whole Bay of Pigs thing, and the President just feels that ah, without going into the details—don't, don't lie to them to the extent to say there is no involvement, but just say this is a comedy of errors, without getting into it, the President believes that it is going to open the whole Bay of Pigs thing up again.

When Haldeman was questioned about this meeting by the Senate Appropriations Subcommittee on Intelligence Operations he told them:

> I neither asked the CIA to participate in any Watergate cover-up nor did I ever suggest that the CIA take responsibility for the Watergate break-in. . . General Walters was asked to meet with Director Grey of the FBI to insure that any unrelated covert operations of the CIA of any unrelated national security activities which had been previously undertaken by some of the Watergate principals, not be compromised in the process of the Watergate investigation. . .

According to Senator McClellan, the former Presidential aide told the committee that CIA activities relating to the Bay of Pigs might be affected, but had not made clear how the FBI investigation could have been related to the CIA-sponsored invasion of Cuba in 1962. Senator Pastore found the Bay of Pigs connection to the Watergate investigation "a little far-fetched."

Haldeman was also questioned about this meeting by the Ervin committee. He stated that he had told Walters and Helms that Nixon was concerned about "the Bay of Pigs question being re-raised" and "the possibility of the investigation of Watergate being extended beyond Watergate itself into matters unrelated to Watergate...Mr. Helms said there was no CIA involvement in the Watergate at all and he had so informed Patrick Grey." Fred Thompson, the Ervin committee's chief minority counsel, asked Haldeman if the two CIA officials had responded to his question about other unrelated CIA activities being exposed:

> Haldeman: Not in any detail, no. The only area where there was a response to that, and it was in my interpretation sort of a curious response, was on the CIA problem, question of whether there was a CIA problem with relation to the Bay of Pigs, and on that one Mr. Helms jumped very rapidly and very defensively to say, 'That is of no concern at all. We don't want to get into that at all.' It was a sort of little different reaction than the flat and calm reaction that there had been no CIA involvement in the Watergate. There was—well, it's not germane.

Haldeman went on to say that Walters agreed to meet with Grey for national security purposes, not to cover up Nixon's involvement in Watergate. Former FBI Director L. Patrick Grey said that Walters told him that the FBI might very well uncover a CIA operation in the course of their Watergate investigation; on the other hand, Helms told him that there was no CIA involvement in the Watergate affair. Grey attributed this discrepancy to "the compartmentalization which is alleged to exist within the CIA." Walters testified that he told Haldeman and Grey that there was no CIA involvement in the Watergate operation. Somebody is obviously lying.

Richard Helms, the CIA's expert on Oswald's movements in Mexico City, told the Watergate Committee that he was approached by Haldeman who—

> made some, what to me was an incoherent reference to an investigation in Mexico, or an FBI investigation, running into the Bay of Pigs. I do not know what the reference was alleged to be, but in any event, I assured him that I had no interest in the Bay of Pigs that many years later, that everything in connection with that had been dealt with and liquidated as far as I was aware and I did not care what they ran into in connection with that.

During his testimony later that afternoon Helms was questioned about his meeting with Haldeman once again:

> I recall, as I said earlier this morning, that Mr. Haldeman made some reference to the Bay of Pigs; I referred to it as an incoherent reference because it was frankly, in my recollection, I don't know exactly what he, what point he had in mind but I reacted to that question very firmly. Now, the Bay of Pigs is the rubric for a very unhappy event in the life of the CIA. A dead cat that has been thrown at us over the years ever since and, therefore, it is one to which I am likely to react and react rather quickly, for the simple reason that the Bay of Pigs was long since over, the problems arising from it had been liquidated. I was well aware of this, and I didn't care what any investigation had to do with the Bay of Pigs that could have gotten into anybody involved with it, about it, below it or above it, I didn't care, and was trying to make it clear to Mr. Haldeman on that occasion. [54]

Helms does not explain what problems arising from the Bay of Pigs "had been liquidated." Nor does he explain the mysterious deaths of Lee Bowers, James Worrell, and other witnesses who died under suspicious circumstances. All Helms does is blanket the entire question with a transparently evasive "I-don't-care attitude.

The following is excerpted from the Presidential tapes:

> Nixon: Let me put it this way; let us suppose that you get the million bucks, and you get the proper way to handle it. You could hold that side?
> Dean: Uh-huh.
> Nixon: It would seem to be worthwhile. ...my point is, do you ever have any choice on Hunt?...I don't think we need to go into every (adjective deleted) thing Hunt has done. ...There is nothing in it for Hunt. Let me ask you this (unintelligible but probably "will the Watergate Grand Jury") go back over everything he's done prior to that time? There might be something?... You open that scab there's a hell of a lot of things and we just feel that it would be very detrimental to have this thing go any

further. This involves these Cubans, Hunt, and a lot of hanky-panky that we have nothing to do with ourselves...Yeah, but the point that I make is this—is really, of course, you know, it's the limits of his testimony...If he testifies just on Watergate that's fine. Your major guy to keep under control is Hunt...I think. Because he knows...about a lot of other things.
[The preceding line was transcribed in the White House version as "Your major guy to keep under control is Hunt?...I think—Does he know a lot?]...But at the moment, don't you agree that you better get the Hunt thing?...Hunt, of course, who is most vulnerable in my opinion, might, uh, blow the whistle,...and his price is pretty high, but at least uh, we should buy the time on that... [55] [this segment is also altered on the White House version of the tapes]

When Hunt called Colson to demand the million dollars he said, "The stakes are very high" and "we've set a deadline for the close of business on the twenty-fifth of November." [56]

Two other major Watergate documents may shed some light on the shadowy netherworld of the November twenty-second coup d'etat in America. On July 1, 1971 Charles Colson recorded a telephone conversation he had with Howard Hunt at the end of which Colson asked, "Weren't you the guy who told me, maybe the last time we were up to your house for dinner, that if the truth ever came out about Kennedy and the Bay of Pigs, that it would destroy them?" [57] The next day Colson sent the memo we have reprinted on page 280 to H.R. Haldeman recommending Hunt for a position with the "plumbers." Colson points out that Hunt was "the CIA mastermind on Bay of Pigs." That is, of course, hardly a recommendation—the Bay of Pigs was an abysmal failure. Colson then goes on to contradict his recorded conversation of the day before when he says that Hunt told him *"a long time ago"* that "Kennedy would be destroyed."

Perhaps a memo, released by the partner of Hunt's lawyer at the end of the Watergate trial, written by Hunt five months after the break-in, best sums up the Nixon-Hunt relationship:

"The Watergate bugging is only one of a number of highly illegal conspiracies engaged in by one or more of the defendants at the request of White House officials. These as yet undisclosed crimes can be proved." [58]

* * * * *

A few relevant statements about Nixon should be made here. Nixon was convinced that he was cheated out of the 1960 election by Mayor Daley, who allegedly tampered with the ballot boxes in Chicago, thus throwing Illinois' electoral votes, and the election, to Kennedy. In 1968 he started Operation Integrity, the main purpose of which was to keep an eye on Illinois' voting practices. [59] Nixon put H. Louis Nichols in charge of this operation. Nichols had worked for Schenley Distilleries, whose president, Louis Rosenstiel, had been linked to Meyer Lansky. [60] Nixon was also quite displeased with Robert Kennedy, who had called Nixon's aide-de-camp Murray Chotiner to testify before the McClellan Committee investigating organized crime. Kennedy wanted to know about alleged influence peddling; he also wanted to know why so many of Chotiner's clients were organized crime figures. Yet in 1973 Nixon was quoted as saying that if Kennedy had instituted ten more wiretaps he would have been able to discover "the Oswald plan." When questioned by the press about this statement Nixon modified it: "I said if ten more wiretaps could have found the conspiracy, if it was a conspiracy, or the individual, then it would have been worth it. As far as I'm concerned, I'm no more of an expert on that assassination than anybody else..." [61]

Hitler's rise to power was preceded by a long series of assassinations and discreditations of his opponents. There is no denying that the Robert Kennedy killing, Chappaquidick and the Wallace shooting benefited Richard Nixon. Nixon had close ties to hardline conservatives—Richard Moore, the frail, graying old man who testified on Nixon's behalf at the Watergate hearings, was executive director of the American First Committee which Gobbells termed "...truly American and truly patriotic." [62] John J. Wilson, Haldeman and Ehrlichman's lawyer, represented Interhandel Corp., owned by GAF, itself controlled by I.G. Farbin, which supplied chemicals for the gas chambers during World War II.[63] With Nixon in power, Nazi sympathizers held high positions in the Republican party.[64] Nixon's men funneled money to the Nazis and Nixon himself voiced admiration for Albert Speer.[65] And Jack Anderson has reported that Gordon Liddy once arranged for a showing of Nazi propaganda films for high members of the Nixon Administration at the National Archives.[66] In his writing Liddy professes admiration for the Nazis: "Compare if you will the mind-set of the WW II Marine Corps or SS Division Leibstandarte, as either went into battle, with the ill-disciplined, often drugged dropouts that make up a significant portion of the nation's Armed Forces today." Liddy also writes that "there is nothing more natural than for a man to refer to his country as 'fatherland.' "[67] Henry Peterson and Nixon may have been making an oblique reference to these "tendencies" of Liddy's in the following exchange that was recorded on the White House tapes:

Peterson: Liddy's a nut you see.
Nixon: I have never met the man. I don't know.
Peterson: He's a—he's kind of a super patriot—
Nixon: I understand.
Peterson: In a sense.[68]

Frank Sturgis and the Tall Tramp

The close resemblance between the Oldman-tramp and Howard Hunt parallels the resemblance between the tallest tramp and Hunt's number one operative, Frank Sturgis (real name, Frank Fiorini), another man caught tampering with democracy in Watergate. When we measured the wall the tallest tramp was standing against, we discovered that his height was six foot one inch, Sturgis' height exactly. On page 221, taken in 1959, Sturgis is wearing a July 26 armband while standing on the mass grave of seventy-one Batistaites he had just executed in order to maintain his credibility with Castro. Notice the similarity in the ears; although the tramp's earlobe looks like it is flat against the side of his head in P3, this is merely an effect of the lighting, as P2 on page 208 shows.Notice how the lips, nose and deep-set eyes match in the next set of comparison shots. (see 218) The only feature different is the hair which has been de-greased and dyed, giving the tramp a more Nordic appearance than the Cuban-looking Sturgis. Compare the shapes of the head and ear, the flare of the nostrils, and the clefts of the chin. Notice the tramp's military step in P3. Sturgis was with the Armed Forces for nine years. Notice how the tramp keeps his thumbs in, another military habit.

Frank Sturgis was born in Philadelphia of Italian stock—thus, his real name Frank Fiorini. He joined the Marines right after he graduated from high school. After an action-packed five years in the military he quit in 1945 to become a drifter and soldier of fortune traveling "up and down the eastern seaboard—Norfolk, Virginia Beach, Washington, and Miami—trying one job after another—motorcycle cop, bartender, nightclub manager,"[69] until 1949 when he enlisted in the Army.

In 1949 Howard Hunt wrote *Bimini Run*, a spy-thriller starring an ex-Marine, gambler and soldier of fortune named Hank Sturgis. It is obvious that somewhere along the line, Hunt's and Fiorini's paths had crossed. Hunt denies it. After Dick Gregory, through the media, showed the tramp-comparison shots to the American people Hunt told the Associated Press that he "...did not meet Frank Sturgis until 1972, nine years after we were allegedly together in Dallas."[70] In a way Hunt is telling the truth; he did not know *Sturgis* then, instead he knew *Fiorini*. He does the same thing in his autobiography: "...Frank Sturgis...was known during CIA days as Frank Fiorini. I had previously not met Sturgis..." until 1972.[71] Sturgis, on the other hand, says he met Hunt in 1961.[72]

Sturgis used his real name up to about 1963. In numerous interviews with Jack Anderson in 1961 he is known as Fiorini. The first mention of "Sturgis" occurs in an FBI report dated November 27, 1963.

Hunt would like us to believe that it was mere coincidence that made Sturgis choose a Hunt character's name for a pseudonym in 1963. Is it also just coincidence that his operatives in Watergate were using the names of other Hunt characters for pseudonyms in 1972?

In a recent article in the New York *Daily News*, a spy recruited by Sturgis said that when cash was needed it came from a CIA man she later recognized as Howard Hunt. The man would meet with Sturgis and her in a Miami safehouse. This was in the early 1960's.

During his second stint in the Armed Forces in the early 1950's, Sturgis took part in the Berlin airlift and also worked in Latin America and Mexico. Howard Hunt arrived at the American Embassy in Mexico City on December 13, 1950 and worked there until 1953 when he was assigned to the overthrow of Arbenez. Both men's activities during this period remain a mystery.

In 1953 Sturgis became a civilian again, moved back to Miami, married a Cuban nightclub entertainer, and by 1955 he was running clandestine night flights into Cuba for Prio, who had made a deal with Castro. In return for arms and money, Castro promised to give the deposed President his office back after Batista had been overthrown. Prio gave Castro an enormous amount of cash, some of which he used to purchase the yacht, Granma, which was converted into a troop transport. Prio had also formed an anti-Batista army in Miami which "invaded" Cuba in 1957.[73]

By 1957 Sturgis had become one of Castro's favorite "Yanquis," and a close confidante of the nationalist leader. Sturgis stated: "The July 26th Movement, since 1957 I was in it. That's why, last year, Fidel said I was one of the most dangerous agents the CIA ever had."[74] In 1958 Sturgis was arrested by Batista's Secret Police and accused of being a courier for Castro. The U.S. Embassy intervened on his behalf knowing his real mission was to penetrate the July 26th Movement.[75] Around this time he began associating with Pedro Diaz Lanz, a pro-Castro pilot, and was known to make frequent trips in and out of Cuba. There is also some evidence that Sturgis was doing contract work for Howard Hunt, who was a CIA agent in Uruguay around this time. Sturgis told Michael Canfield: "Howard Hunt was an attaché down in Uruguay. He did this and that, got information, etc. Me, I participated in the action. Skullduggery, et cetera. Back in the fifties."

When Castro deposed Batista in 1959 Sturgis was made Chief of Security and Intelligence for the Cuban Air Force and Minister of Games of Chance in Havana. During this period he "recruited a number of people in Havana for intelligence" (actually he constructed and controlled an espionage network in Cuba), and offered his services to the American Embassy in regard to a plot to kill Castro. Sturgis did not have much to say about this period except that Havana was definitely a "hub of intrigue," and that "I also broke into foreign consulates and business offices in Cuba, for the purpose of obtaining information, and into a...import-export office in Caracas, Venezuela, that was a front for the KGB (Soviet Secret Service)."

In early 1960 Sturgis left Cuba. The fact that he had to steal a plane in order to leave indicates that he may have been wanted for anti-Castro activities by the Revolutionary Government. He immediately began to fly leaflet flights over Cuba using a B-25 that was probably supplied by the CIA. Because he had fought as a soldier in a foreign army, Sturgis' citizenship was revoked by the State Department and the registration of his B-25 was cancelled by the F.A.A. He went to Washington to protest this and found an ally in Senator Smathers of Florida. Smathers, a good friend of Batista[76] who had won his Senate seat using red-baiting tactics similar to those of Richard Nixon, *hated* Fidel Castro. In 1970, when some of the files of the John F. Kennedy Library were made public, a tape recording revealed that Smathers constantly pestered Kennedy to assassinate the Cuban leader. Kennedy categorically refused.[77] Kennedy also told Smathers that the CIA frequently did things he didn't know about, and he was unhappy about it. He complained that the CIA was almost autonomous.[78] Recent revelations into CIA domestic surveillance operations have brought to light the fact that Claude Pepper, Smather's number one opponent, was being carefully watched.[79]

By late 1960 Sturgis and Victor Panque had formed the International Anti-communist Brigade (IAB) and were flying supply missions to guerillas in the Escambray mountains in the Las Villas province of Cuba from a secret base in the Bahamas. Panque helped him locate the eighty or so members of Batista's army who had holed up there hoping to avoid the firing squad. It was around this time that Jack Anderson conducted numerous interviews with Sturgis, making him famous as a soldier of fortune. In one of these interviews Sturgis complained that Castro executed a friend of his named Angus McNair. Extensive research turned up an Angus McNair who was executed on April 20, 1961 as a suspected CIA agent. Sturgis admitted that McNair was part of the espionage network he ran in Cuba, and was apprehended by Castro while trying to create a diversionary action during the Bay of Pigs invasion. [80]

Frank Sturgis played a prominent part in the Bay of Pigs operation.

> I went to Guatemala with Diaz Lanz for a meeting with President Idigoras Fuentes to arrange for bases there...There were big headlines in the newspapers. All over Latin America in the television and the radio that I was there trying to get bases...In order for the United States government to protect itself, when I got back a (unintelligible) grabbed me and held me and lifted my citizenship—which was a ploy on their part to appease Fidel...[81]

Pedro Diaz Lanz was a former Castro supporter who smuggled arms to him from Florida while he was still in the mountains. Lanz had a falling out with him in July 1959, when the Cuban leader began appointing communists to prominent positions in the Air Force. Frank Sturgis arranged for Lanz's escape to the United States in a stolen B-26. Lanz immediately testified about Castro's communist orientation before the Senate Internal Security Subcommittee, soon after which Hunt gave him a job with the CRF, despite objections from the State Department, who considered Lanz an "unstable reactionary." Lanz, who was head of the Cuban Air Force under Castro, was Sturgis' co-pilot during his leaflet runs over Havana. Hunt admits knowing Lanz and also says Lanz knew Sturgis during this period,[82] yet denies knowing Sturgis himself.*

In 1960, Trujillo offered CIA agents Frank Sturgis and Pedro Diaz Lanz $1 million to lead an invasion of Cuba from the Dominican Republic. But this wasn't the kind of invasion the Administration would give a green light to.

In between anti-Castro missions, Sturgis trained pilots at the base in Guatemala in preparation for the Bay of Pigs and was probably working on a plan to assassinate Castro. When asked about this by Canfield he said, "Well, there were several (assassination attempts) through word of mouth from associates, there were several attempts and several assassinations that were going on inside Cuba." He was also part of Operation Forty's Assassination Section (see page 80). His friend Max Gonzales reported, "Two attempts against Castro's life were made in the early part of 1959. Both failed. The assassins then waited for a green light from Frank Fiorini Sturgis. A third attempt was made in 1960."

Like everyone else involved in Bay of Pigs, Frank was disappointed at its outcome:

Sturgis: Oh, I was mad. I was mad. We had people inside of Cuba...We were doing Green Light Operations. And after a while they cut the assistance to the underground...because of the policy. The President says stop all these things and we stop them.

Canfield: Who's failure was it? Kennedy's?

Sturgis: Both President Kennedy's and the CIA's. Can't lay the blame on one man. But he takes responsibility for the whole thing...Now I met President Kennedy. I took President Carlos Prio of Cuba to speak with President Kennedy. [To plead the cause of the anti-Castro Cubans, no doubt.] President Prio...is a good friend of mine. I go to his home.

---

* In the interview with Canfield, Sturgis also admitted to working with Artime's group: "We had a place on Brickel Avenue that we used to use which is not there today. That was somewhat of a meeting place for the MRR organization." Sturgis knew both Lanz and Artime, two of Hunt's close friends—yet Hunt denies knowing him.

After the invasion Sturgis' International Anti-communist Brigade merged with a group known as the Intercontinental Penetration Force (Interpen), composed of Cuban and American anti-Castroite soldiers. Jerry Patrick Hemming was the leader of Interpen and his men trained in the Everglades and on No Name Key,[83] which had been used as a secret training center during the Bay of Pigs. The FBI reported that, like Sturgis, Hemming had fought in the mountains with Castro in 1958.[84] Another member of Interpen-IAB was Howard Kenneth Davis, who the FBI described as having been associated with "American mercenaries involved in Cuban revolutionary activities for the past six years." Davis had been Castro's personal pilot[85] and, like Sturgis, a high officer in Castro's Air Force. On July 5, 1961 a Department of Justice spokesman warned Hemming that an investigation into the IAB was under way.[86]

Interpen-IAB was indeed a curious organization. Hans Tanner, an Englishman who worked with the Christian Democratic Movement, one of the groups Sturgis was connected with, described it in his book *Counterevolutionary Agent*. Tanner said that Interpen was part of the IAB commanded by Frank Fiorini, "an American adventurer who first fought for Castro then crossed over. Hemming's men formed the parachute battalion of Fiorini's brigade and included Americans, Cubans and men from several Central and South American countries. U.S. citizens are forbidden to be combatants in foreign military operations which could prove awkward. The brigade was probably financed by dispossessed hotel and gambling room owners who operated under Batista."[87]

In late July 1962 six men from Interpen were picked up for vagrancy in Miami by the Sheriff's office. Tanner wrote, "The general clampdown on anti-Castro activities was well under way. More arrests were expected."

Despite this minor harrassment Interpen-IAB was more or less left alone by the Justice Department until about a month after the Cuban Missile Crisis in December 1962. Kennedy had made a deal with Khrushchev to stop anti-Castro activities in return for removing the missiles, and Sturgis' group was the first to suffer because of it. Hemming and Wilson were arrested by Federal agents at No Name Key along with Lawrence Howard and William Seymour, who become important later on. [88] Sturgis, who was also working for the CIA at the time must have known about this raid before it happened and managed to avoid arrest.

Sturgis was not one to be intimidated by the Justice Department; he only took orders from the CIA. The head of an organization called Los Pinos Nuevos, told the FBI that Sturgis participated in an anti-Castro operation in March 1963: "At a point off Key West, Florida, Jerry Buchanan was put aboard the Violin Three from a small launch which was also occupied by Frank Fiorini and Alexander Rorke." [89] Jerry Buchanan was the ex-convict brother of James Buchanan, a close friend of Sturgis and a possible CIA agent, who, as we shall see later, may have worked with the omnipresent Howard Hunt.

Hunt probably also knew Rorke, an ex-Army Intelligence agent who owned the Violin Three, because both men did anti-Castro propaganda work in America.

After the thirty-five foot twin engine launch, Violin Three, was seized by British authorities as it headed for Cuba fully armed, Rorke said that the U.S. Government knew about the raids in advance, or at least the CIA did because it was the Agency that furnished the money for "leaflet raids" carried out by the Violin Three in October and December of 1961. Rorke also told the media that the boat, which had already made eleven trips to Cuba, would continue to be used in future operations, because the trips were made simply to land agents and resupply forces within Cuba. [90] Just as the Justice Department could not control Sturgis, they could not stop former prisoner-of-Castro Rorke; later that April he participated in a bombing raid of Esso and Shell refineries in Havana. The New York *Times* called this action "the first bombing raid since Bay of Pigs" and stated it was made "despite U.S. Government orders." A few days after the attack Rorke addressed a group of Christian Democratic Party members and told them to keep on fighting despite Kennedy's policies. [91]

Jack Anderson reported that during the Bay of Pigs invasion, a group of "freedom fighters" flying over Havana "radioed (that they were) over the Esso refinery in Havana and asked permission to bomb it, along with the nearby Texaco and Shell refineries" only to be told to steer clear by their CIA command post.[92] When Frank Sturgis was arrested in Watergate, one of the people who came to his bail hearing was Jack Anderson, who told the judge that Sturgis had been a "source" of his for many years. Was Sturgis the source of this story? Anderson also reported that Mike McLaney, "an American gambler who ran a casino in Havana and stayed on for eighteen months after Castro's takeover" sent the CIA a detailed plan for destroying the refineries. Mike McLaney had purchased the National Casino in Havana from Syndicate frontman Moe Dalitz in 1958, just three weeks prior to Castro's takeover.[93] He continued to operate under Castro, hoping to become the Gambling Czar of Cuba; but in late 1960, Castro nationalized the casino and deported him. McLaney lost a fortune on the deal and blamed it on Castro.

Victor Panque, another friend of Sturgis', was arrested on July 31, 1963 as a result of the agreement Kennedy had reached with the Russians. He was picked up by Federal agents on an anti-Castro training camp outside of New Orleans rented by Mike McLaney's brother. Most of the men in this camp were connected with the Christian Democratic Movement which Sturgis was an indirect member of.[94]

After the Kennedy assassination an employee of Parrott Jungle in Miami told the FBI that on November 1, 1963, an unidentified male made some remarks which led her to believe he was acquainted with Lee Harvey Oswald. The man told her he had a friend named Lee who was an American Marxist, spoke Russian, and was a crack marksman to boot. He made references to Kennedy and "shooting between the eyes" and added that his friend was now in either Texas or Mexico. On March 6, 1964 the man returned to Parrott Jungle and the employees there were able to find out his name and took down his license plate number.

He turned out to be Jorge Soto Martinez, who had been a customs inspector in Cuba for most of his life until Castro fired him. Martinez was brought to the United States by Mike McLaney, who also hired him to work at his casino. Martinez's father also had a grievance against Castro—he had been a successful lawyer until the revolutionary regime seized his property. Martinez denied making any statements about Oswald to the FBI, and like Pena and Novel, demanded a lie-detector test to prove he was telling the truth. He also expressed displeasure at the United States Government for not ridding Cuba of Castro.[95]

Despite the arrests at McLaney's farm, anti-Castro activities continued throughout that summer. The remnants of the Cuban Revolutionary Council (which had been cut off from their $200,000-a-month CIA subsidy after Council President Cardona had publicly accused Kennedy of reneging on a promise to invade Cuba) claimed they landed fifty counter-revolutionists in Cuba.[96] Five Interpen-IAB members were arrested near their training camp, on Federal Arms violations, by Treasury agents; Artime's group, the MRR, made another attempt to destroy Havana's oil refineries.[97]

On September 15, 1963 Rorke was summoned to the U.S. Customs Department headquarters where he was cautioned against violating the munitions control laws and told that his activities went against the foreign policies of the United States. Frank Sturgis was given a similar warning,[98] even though he was an employee of the CIA at the time.

Kennedy had rebuffed, double-crossed, arrested friends of, and threatened, Sturgis. Sturgis *must have* seen him as an obstacle to the assassination of Castro and the liberation of Cuba. His associates from the days he was Gambling Czar of Cuba like McLaney, did not like Kennedy any better, nor did his friend Everette Howard Hunt, the CIA's expert on engendering coups, nor did the Cubans, many of whom had participated in the Batista totalitarian government, in which political assassination was an accepted practice. There is no doubt that Frank Sturgis had a motive to kill John Kennedy. But did he do it?

After the tramp shots were widely disseminated, he told Michael Canfield:

> I've been asked whether I was in Dallas on November 22, 1963 and I gave the press no comment. They asked me if I was in Dallas at all and I gave 'em no comment. They asked me if I wasn't denying it. I told 'em

I'm not denying it or I'm not acknowledging it, one of those things, I gave all my testimony to the Senate Watergate Committee.

He had also said:

I can show you clippings where they say I was involved in the assassination of President Kennedy...I even got investigated by the Watergate thing. They asked me where I was and I told them I knew nothing about it. I was home watching television.

In another interview he was asked, "Where were you when Kennedy was killed?" and he said:

Sturgis: I have no comment on that.
Canfield: Because last time we talked you said you were watching television.
Sturgis: I love to watch television. I don't care if it's Washington or any place else, I'll watch television.

Hunt's lawyer said Hunt was in Washington that day, at home with his family.[99]

It is not a fact that Frank Sturgis was in Dallas on November 22, 1963; but it is a fact that one of the three tramps picked up resembles him beyond coincidental factors. It is also a fact that on November 23, 1963 the FBI paid Sturgis a visit and questioned him in regard to the assassination. Mae Brussell uncovered a document in the National Archives about this before the Watergate affair was exposed. Last summer we looked through *every* document but could not find it. For a while we believed a CTIA member, who said that the document was a figment of Brussell's imagination. But when Canfield spoke with Sturgis he found out that the FBI had indeed paid the visit. Sturgis said:

I had FBI agents over at my house...right after it happened...They told me I was one person they felt had the capabilities to do it. Heh, heh, heh. They said 'Frank, if there's anyone capable of killing the President of the United States you're one guy that can do it.' Heh, heh, that's funny.

The document was probably stolen from the Archives right after the exposure of Watergate.

I did find the FBI reports about how, a few days later, James Buchanan had written an article for the Pompano Beach *Sun Sentinel* which quoted Sturgis as saying that "...Oswald had telephone conversations with the Cuban Government G-2 Intelligence Service during (a) November 1962" visit to Miami. He also contacted "Miami-based supporters of Fidel Castro...," gave out his famous leaflets and tried to infiltrate a Cuban anti-Castro group which turned out to be the International Anti-communist Brigade. He failed because he could not outsmart their leader, Frank Sturgis. When questioned about this by the FBI, Sturgis said it was just speculation.[100]

A few weeks later Buchanan phoned the Miami office of the FBI to ask them about Oswald's connections with the DRE while in Miami. He said that the DRE had material which proves Oswald killed Kennedy on orders from Castro, but the FBI confiscated the DRE bulletins and took three members to Washington for extensive questioning.[101]

FBI agent O'Conner, who did not seem to like the Cuban community—he occasionally describes the anti-Castro Cubans as "Cuban agitators"—conducted a thorough investigation of Buchanan's story, which had been printed in the *Sun Sentinel*. After speaking with two DRE officials, O'Conner concluded that Eduardo Diaz Lanz might know something about it. Eduardo, the brother of Sturgis' friend Pedro Diaz Lanz, had arrived as an exile in June 1963 after working with the DRE's underground in Cuba. He told O'Conner that his friend Sturgis had mentioned something about bringing a newspaperman to the DRE's office but doubts that he did so. Lanz denied all of James Buchanan's allegations and referred O'Conner to an exile who told him that the only thing he knew was that Lanz introduced Sturgis to the DRE's Miami office where Sturgis made about four appearances and had given a lecture.

O'Conner then interviewed the director of the DRE who told him he believed Lanz had given the information to Sturgis. Tired of getting the runaround O'Conner questioned FBI informant MM T-1 who said that Buchanan was trying to get the government to act against Cuba.

On January 15, 1964 Sturgis was questioned by the FBI for a third time about matters relating to the killing of John F. Kennedy. Sturgis denied knowing anything about Buchanan's article. O'Conner then interviewed an informer who knew Sturgis and was told that "Fiorini (Sturgis) represents himself as the 'inside man' with all Cuban organizations in Miami." [102]

Four months later the FBI was back for a fourth visit. Sturgis told them that the Vice-President of IAB was imprisoned by Castro and that Jim Buchanan was Director of Propaganda. Sturgis claimed to have quit the IAB because of Buchanan's excessive attacks on the FBI "...even going so far as to describe the former President John F. Kennedy as a communist." [103]

This visit was triggered by an interview with Buchanan's brother, Jerry, whom Nathaniel Weyl had fingered as the man who fought with Oswald. Jerry said that in October 1962 certain members of the IAB were involved in a fight with members of the FPCC in Miami and that Oswald "was there." [104] The FBI traced Jerry's activities from the time he was released from prison and found he could not have been in Miami in October 1962. Sturgis told the agent he knew nothing about the alleged fracas. [105]

Of course the FBI wanted to contact Buchanan about this but he could not be found—they tried everywhere. Finally the FBI contacted Sturgis at a used car lot he was working in and Buchanan happened to be there. Buchanan and the Federal agents arranged to have a meeting.

Buchanan told the FBI that his source for the Oswald-G-2 fight story was Sturgis and that he knew the name of the printer who did Oswald's leaflets, but could not divulge it. He was advised by the FBI that John Martino and Nathaniel Weyl had reported the alleged fight to them. [106]

Martino and Weyl may have been working for the domestic propaganda section of the CIA at the time because they were involved in the production of a book called *I Was Castro's Prisoner*. Howard Hunt headed this section and the CIA may very well have subsidized it. A look at both men's backgrounds is revealing.

Martino told the Secret Service that he was a manufacturer of electronics products in Miami. [107] Was this firm named Double-Chek? Or was it Zenith Technological Services, an alleged obscure electronics firm doing weapons research for the Department of Defense, which the Miami *Herald* says was "at the time (1962) the CIA's largest installation anywhere in the world outside its headquarters in Langley, Virginia."[108]

Martino was the nation's most famous former Castro prisoner. He had been arrested in Havana in 1959. Witnesses at his trial said he had landed a light aircraft on a highway in the course of clandestinely entering Cuba. It is likely he was engaged in anti-Castro activities because he says he identified Castro as a communist in 1953. Martino was a friend of Capt. William Morgan, who had fought alongside Castro from 1957-59. After Castro took power, Morgan and Major Menoyo thwarted an attempt to oust him by acting as a double agent and luring supporters of Batista and Trujillo into a death trap. In September 1960 Morgan had been sent to the Escambray Mountains to dispatch the anti-Castro guerilla forces active there, but was accused of aiding them by Cuban Military Intelligence. After a brief trial, the former war hero was executed by a firing squad in Havana, and instantly became an anti-Castro martyr. [109]

* * * * *

When questioned about the alleged fight by the FBI, Martino told them that his source was a Cuban exile in Miami. [110] After four more inquiries by the FBI he said his source was on his way to Miami with some new recruits for MRR (Artime's group).[111] In the next interview he told the FBI that his source was Oscar Ortiz whom he described as "forty to forty-two years of age; about six feet tall, 180-190 pounds, dark curly hair parted in the middle, accustomed to wearing long sideburns, in good physical condition, a good dresser, fluent in Spanish and English." He also said that Ortiz was a member of an anti-Castro organization too sensitive to name (Operation Forty?), was "known in Washington D.C. and could even be a double-agent." [112] The description fits Sturgis perfectly and he *was* working for the government at that time. Sturgis had boasted to Canfield: "I had another Cuban leader say I was worth fifty men to them. These are people who knew me but didn't know I was a government agent...Jack Anderson made me famous as a soldier of fortune and he told me 'I never knew you were working as an agent for the United States Government.' "

Martino also spread the rumor that Castro had threatened Kennedy while making a speech in the Cuban Embassy in Brazil, and Oswald was paid by Castro to kill Kennedy, and so on. [113] As we shall see many CIA front groups parroted the same line.

Martino's friend, Nathaniel Weyl, may have been an early deep-cover agent in the Communist Party. A former OSS operative, Weyl claimed to be in the same cell as Alger Hiss whom he had helped expose. [114] Nixon made his reputation as a "red-hunter" by successfully prosecuting Hiss; many people think Hiss was framed. Frank Meyers, who is cited as reference for the Weyls in CD662 often wrote for the *National Review,* the editor of which was Hunt's confidante William Buckley. The Weyls were also friendly with Victor Lasky, who became an important figure in the Rockefeller confirmation hearings when it was revealed that Lawrence Rockefeller had financed a book he had written "exposing" one of Nelson's political opponents.

*   *   *   *   *

When questioned about the alleged fisticuffs, Buchanan said he never discussed the matter with his brother Jerry. Instead he got the information over the telephone from a man who lived near MRR headquarters, and was a member of an exile group called Los Pinos. [115] The FBI interviewed the leader of Los Pinos Nuevos and was told that James Buchanan was unknown to them, but they did know Rorke, Jerry Buchanan and Frank Sturgis in connection with the Violin Three, which, the spokesman said, was going to sink a ship off the Cuban coast before it was seized by British authorities. [116]

Eventually O'Conner questioned everyone around Bayfront but no one could recall a pro-Castro demonstration in a park that was known as a hangout for anti-Castro soldiers of fortune. The only demonstration that was remotely like it was put on by the Committee for Nonviolent Action in front of the offices of the Cuban Revolutionary Council. [117]

Because Buchanan was heavily involved in anti-Castro propaganda, he may also have worked under Howard Hunt. The FBI's informant reported that he used to own part of the Pompano Beach *Sun Sentinel*; after he pulled out, he began his own news service known as Caribbean Press Associates. He was also the editor of the IAB bulletin which had a lead article by Frank Sturgis and a filler from a Miami press service called Agency for Newspaper Information that was linked to the DRE. After the assassination Buchanan stamped each IAB bulletin with the words "Communism Killed Kennedy." [118]

Many rumors similar to the ones spread by Buchanan and Sturgis began to surface after the assassination. A rightwing Miami radio personality said that when some of Interpen's members were on the air in December 1962, he received a telephone call from a New Orleans man, a former Marine who wanted to join Interpen. According to the broadcaster, the man identified himself with some variation of Lee Harvey Oswald's name. When the FBI checked out this rumor with Howard Kenneth Davis, the man who the call was referred to, he denied the tale. [119] The former news director of a radio station in Dallas, who was briefly imprisoned by Castro in 1959, also claimed to have been contacted by Oswald. This time it was in the course of a drive to recruit pilots for anti-Castro activities. Oswald allegedly telephoned and asked him for a list of the recruits. [120]

* * * * *

Sturgis and his friends were extensively questioned by the FBI about matters linked to the Kennedy assassination. Sturgis was questioned about the actual killing. A classified document exists in the National Archives about Sturgis and the assassination. [121] There is reason for it.

> Sturgis: You have to look at my past. I've done a lot of things. I've been on assassination attempts...I was involved in so many things. Skullduggery, intrigue, espionage...

Canfield: When you say assassination attempts...

Sturgis: Well, in other countries... I've taken presidents of foreign countries to speak with our president. That was John F. Kennedy. And there's records of it. I've been closely associated with about thirteen presidents of foreign countries and the United States. Presidents and prime ministers...You see, where I live at, a lot of people in that area before the Watergate thing, they never knew who I was...and here I am involved in every goddamned thing imaginable. And I've never used Sturgis in any of my activities. I've always used Fiorini, Fedrini...so if any publicity ever came out, it came out under a code name...I was asked by my friend, who was a CIA agent, he asked me if I was interested in participating, or doing an assassination with the company. I told him yes, providing I would sit down with this case officer and go over the details, that I would do it.

Canfield: Domestic or foreign?

Sturgis: It would be domestic. The reason for that, he asked me how I would go about it. And I told him, well, if it was going to be domestic, well, I could do it in several ways...I did not want nobody to be a part of this, I would do it by myself, but I definitely wanted to meet the case officer who wanted this done, and I wanted to see him, and get it right from him, so I would be sure it would be someone with authority, and not just a lower-level agent such as he...

Sturgis' activities throughout the latter 1960's remain a mystery. He claims to have run a big "sweep" on Edward Kennedy in 1971 and by May 1972 he was hired by Bernard Barker to disrupt a rally at which Daniel Ellsberg was present.

A month later Sturgis' cover was blown when he turned up in Watergate. Sturgis told one-time intelligence agent and former Castro prisoner, Andrew St. George, that his assignment was to photograph two thousand documents that night, and other targets he would hit included Ted Kennedy. In this interview Sturgis suddenly claims to hate Barker, blaming the Cuban former Secret policeman for the famous tape-on-the-door and the failure of communications. This is very curious. Most of the evidence points to McCord, yet Sturgis disassociates himself from Barker in much the same way Hunt does from Cabell. This interview ended with Sturgis saying, "The liberals have twisted everything—if I had my way I would kill them all."

Right after Sturgis was caught in Watergate he was charged with an old Dyer Act violation (stolen cars) in a Federal court in Miami. He claimed he was being punished further for not naming his superiors and did not say a word throughout the trial. [122] Jerry Buchanan and Max Gonzales were Sturgis' co-defendants. Eventually he was sentenced to nine months but appealed this decision. [123]

Sturgis was called before a closed-door session of the Watergate Senate Select Committee to testify about the John F. Kennedy assassination. He told Canfield about it.

> They felt the CIA might be behind it. So they wanted an investigation of E. Howard Hunt and myself on the assassination of President Kennedy...And they asked me about other attempted assassinations. I said yeah, Cuba. Some people say 'if you attempt to assassinate people outside the United States, wouldn't you be capable of assassinating the President of the United States?' I said, well, the thought never entered my mind. But I'm capable of doing many things. I'm that type of man...

After Watergate broke, a French soldier of fortune named Jose Luis Romero said that he was approached by two men who looked just like Sturgis and Barker around May 1961. He was offered a large sum of money if he would kill Kennedy and make it look like an attempt on the life of Charles de Gaulle. [124] Victor Marchetti has stated that Hunt, Sturgis, Barker and others on the Watergate bugging team worked with Clay Shaw and David Ferrie on the Bay of Pigs. Marchetti says he believes they worked together afterwards.

Sturgis served fourteen months in a minimum security prison facility at Elgin Air Force Base and was released on appeal bond in January 1974. As soon as he was released his friends in the Cuban community gave him a testimonial dinner.

How did Sturgis react to the tramp shots?

> I think Dick Gregory is on the radical Left and I think Dick Gregory and his group are being financed by foreign outsiders in order to put pressure on the CIA, using both Howard Hunt and myself as a tool for that. I don't think they can stand the idea that Oswald was of the Left,

one of their own people, took the rap, at least one of the persons who took the rap for killing the President of the United States...I believe there was a conspiracy...I expect I'll be drug up to Washington before one of these Congressional Committees. I think there's five more different committees being formed for CIA investigations...They're getting the biggies first and unfortunately they got Helms and they're calling Helms a liar...they said Helms told a lot of lies...and they're gonna drag him back. I don't care what I would tell the press—they wouldn't believe me anyway. Do you think anybody would believe Hunt? The best thing to do is keep quiet...And here, this bum here, is bringing up all this stuff. He's going out and trying to help bury CIA, too. You know they can't function with all this publicity. On and on and on. And the enemy loves it. Because the enemy figures, hey, we're doin' somethin' that's screwin' them up—let's give these bums money—and not just anybody—I mean a guy like Dick Gregory—he's on the radical Left. The Left is not too bad but when you get up to being radical like he is—then it can be very harmful for the country...Hunt is mad as a firecracker. Howard and I are both concerned about this in more ways than one—'cause you can get some damn kooky guy come down here and want to kill him and kill me. This is a terrible accusation he's making. He said we had something to do with killing the most powerful man in the world...I hope he can prove his accusations. Because if he can't he's gonna have problems. He'll have legal problems if he can't prove it...I'm hoping it will just die away, personally.

Sturgis went on to say that he would wait and see what other evidence Gregory and his group had before making any statements. When asked where he thought Gregory got the information from he responded, "Well, I imagine with the money he's been getting from different groups of people, I imagine he's dug up some choice things and because of Watergate he dug up Howard and myself. I don't know, I imagine through investigations."

But Sturgis' last remarks were ominous. After telling us that Gregory was an agent of a communist power and that the assassination of Kennedy was a leftist plot he suddenly does a turnabout:

Sturgis: We're talking off the record—he may be digging up things that other people may not want dug up—know what I mean? Well, let's say if there was a conspiracy, right, and, ah, people like him going around the country—not the fact that he's accusing Howard and me and CIA but let's say that other people—other than them—suppose he's wrong, that's one thing—but he may stumble upon something or somebody who probably might have been involved in it and then they'll decide to go ahead and do something about him. He's big enough stuff that maybe people will get a little itchy about—you know what I mean—give him problems.

Canfield: Physical?

Sturgis: Well, I don't know—it would depend on whoever the people were—I don't know...so I think he's wrong in doing what he's doing...I think he should let things lie—leave it alone...

CHAPTER SIX

The Oswald-Double

The third tramp closely resembles Lee Harvey Oswald. If he were seen at the sixth-floor window of a building, he could very easily be mistaken for Oswald.

The "Oswald-double" is first mentioned in a Warren Commission document dated June 3, 1960: "Since there is a possibility that an imposter is using Oswald's birth certificate—any current information the Department of State may have concerning the subject will be appreciated." This FBI memorandum from J. Edgar Hoover went out when Oswald first began living in the USSR. After he decided to return to America, a State Department memorandum contained a similar passage—"...passport should be delivered to him only on a personal basis" because his file contained information that there was "an imposter using (his) identification data." (See page 281.)

These reports dovetail with Commission Document 75 page 677 in which the FBI reports that in January 1960 two representatives of Friends of Democratic Cuba—Guy Bannister was one of the founders of this organization—tried to buy several pick-up trucks at Bolton Ford in New Orleans. They insisted that the head of this company sell them the trucks at cost because they were intended for use against Castro. One of these men identified himself as Lee Harvey Oswald. [1]

William Huffman, who ran a marine gasoline station in the Florida Keys, told the FBI that he had seen Oswald "sometime after Fidel Castro came to power in Cuba." Oswald had pulled in for gas for his forty-three-foot Chris-Craft diesel and was accompanied by four or five Cubans. Huffman went on to say that someone named "Ruben" soon showed up and paid for the fuel. Could this man have been Jack Ruby? The FBI never pressed the issue even though Ruby was reported to be in the Miami-Key West area around this time. [2] Was this boat being used in anti-Castro missions like Rorke's Violin Three?

The Oswald-double sightings subsided until a few weeks before the assassination. Suddenly many responsible people spotted "Oswald" at several rifle ranges, ostensibly practicing for the "big day." Malcolm Price, the owner of the Sportsdrome rifle range, saw him drive up in an old Buick. "Oswald" had him sight-in his rifle after which he scored three bulls-eyes. [3] Even the Warren Report had to concede that Oswald was in Mexico around the time this incident occurred. Garland Slack also said he saw "Oswald" at a rifle range, but the Warren Commission reported he was mistaken because the evidence indicated that Oswald was at the Paines' house at the time. [4] A doctor and his son claimed they had a conversation with Oswald at another range, while E.P. Bass saw someone who was "possibly identical to Oswald" and an excellent marksman. "Oswald" was also seen in a gun store by Dewey Bradford. [5] After the President was murdered, the Dallas *Times Herald* received an anonymous tip that Oswald had a rifle sight mounted at the Irving Sports Shop. When the gunsmith, who was operating the store at the time of the alleged transaction, was questioned by the FBI, he said that he had found a repair tag with Oswald's name on it, but had no recollection of seeing Oswald or of doing the job. [6] Finally, a Ms. Penn told the FBI that Oswald had been practice shooting on her land, and had left in a white Chevrolet. [7]

Ruth Paine testified that a few weeks prior to the assassination she had driven Oswald to the Department of Motor Vehicles so he could get a learner's permit because he did not know how to drive; another of Oswald's friends in Dallas confirmed this. [8] So, for someone who did not know how to drive, Oswald definitely got around. Dallas car salesman Albert Bogard reported that "Oswald" went for a test drive with him on November 9, 1963. "Oswald" told him he would have plenty of money within two or three weeks but declined to reveal the source of his funds, merely telling Bogard that he "had it coming." He also said he was from Oak Cliff (the area where the real Oswald lived), but declined to give Bogard an address. After the assassination Bogard came forward with his story. Unfortunately he had thrown away the piece of paper he had written "Oswald's" name on, but his boss, Mr. Pizzo, confirmed his tale and he successfully passed a lie-detector test. [9]

Either Oswald was a *very* busy man around this time or someone was trying to frame him by having his double practice at several rifle ranges, and brag about coming into a large sum of money. It is also possible that the tag found in the Irving Sports Shop had been planted there as part of the frame-up.

Was the third tramp the man at the rifle range, car lot, and so on? When Pizzo described the man he saw speaking with Bogard he said that his "face resembles him more than the hairline" because the man he saw looked older and his hairline was further back. [10] Mr. Brennen, the Warren Commission's star witness, described the man he saw in the Texas School Book Depository window in a similar manner : "...he looked much younger on television than he did from my picture of him in the window—say five years younger." [11] Most of the people we have questioned believe that the Oswald-tramp looks older than Oswald, primarily because of his hairline. Check comparison shots P1 and page 222.

Many people have pointed out the fact that the Oswald look-alike tramp is an extremely mean-looking person. Garland Slack told the FBI that "Oswald" had fired at Slack's target and almost got into a fight with him. He also said that the man he saw looked more cocky than he did in the photos shown to him by the Dallas Police. [12] E.P. Bass said the "Oswald" he saw was rough in appearance and very rude, [13] while Dewey Bradford said that "Oswald" came into a gun store and grabbed the rifle he was examining right out of his hands. Bradford said the man moved with a "military bearing" (notice how the tramp lifts his knees when he walks in P6) and had a "repugnant and obnoxious attitude." [14] Albert Bogard confessed that "Oswald" scared him by driving "really wild" at 75-85 miles an hour. [15]

Another man who allegedly saw Oswald at a rifle range said that "only the profile of Oswald resembled the shooter," and Ms. Penn said only "the full-face view resembled him." [16] The Oswald-look-alike tramp never lets himself be photographed full-face or in profile in any of the tramp shots. The closest we get to a full-face shot is P1, which we believe looks very much like Oswald.

Dr. Peter Dale Scott has probably uncovered an important clue to the identity of the Oswald-look-alike tramp simply by putting together several documents found in the National Archives. In order to do this, one has to know all the documents by heart to begin with, which Dr. Scott does.

Take a look at the Sheriff's Department report reprinted on page 282. The late Buddy Walthers may not have known how to spell, but he was an honest Dallas policeman. This document did not mean very much until CD1085, the FBI reports on anti-Castro activities in America from 1960-63, was released. This document revealed that Alpha 66, an anti-Castro organization, had headquarters in Dallas, located at 3126 Hollandale. What was Oswald doing around there if he was a supporter of Fidel Castro? According to the document Alpha 66 was part of a coalition of groups that included the 30th of November Movement, the Second National Front of Escambray (SNFE), and the People's Revolutionary Movement (MRP).

* * * * *

The 30th of November Movement was founded by David Salvador, who had been the first Secretary-General of the Cuban Confederation of Workers, an anti-communist CIA-financed labor group. When Castro came to power Salvador resigned from this position and was subsequently imprisoned. The movement had at one time been affiliated with the Cuban Revolutionary Council but had broken off from that group to protest its lack of military action. By the middle of 1963, the 30th of November Movement was staging hit-and-run attacks on Cuba, and was running into opposition from the Administration. Several of their members were arrested by the Coast Guard and Customs Service. The movement threatened to stage a march in Washington if Kennedy did not stop interfering with their activities. By August 1963 they were carrying banners which read, "President Kennedy—Please Don't Arrest Any More Cuban Fighters."

SNFE /Alpha 66 was led by Major Eloy Gutierrez Menoyo, who had commanded the Castro forces in the Escambray Mountains in the Las Villas Province of Cuba. His deputy was William Morgan.

After Castro came to power, Menoyo remained in his government for about a year, then had a disagreement with him and fled to Miami by boat, along with a dozen of Castro's top military men.

When they reached Miami, the Cubans called them communists and abused them. The immigration authorities sent them to a detention center for six months. Upon release, they started Alpha 66 and by September 1962 they machine-gunned three vessels in Cuban waters and claimed to have a three-hundred-man force scattered in small units throughout the Caribbean. An Alpha 66 spokesman told the press that the group had a hundred-thousand-dollar war chest, so it is quite likely that the CIA was funding them. On October 11, 1962 Alpha 66 raiders attacked Cuba itself, but a few weeks later they were forced to curtail their activities as a result of the Cuban Missile Crisis. [17]

By March 1963 they were active again, and the group was suspected of launching a raid against Soviet ships moored in a Cuban port. A few weeks later Major Menoyo was apprehended by the Coast Guard while attempting to carry out an anti-Castro mission. [18]

In early April the Justice Department, then headed by Robert Kennedy, quarantined eighteen Cubans to the Miami area to prevent them from conducting raids against Castro and Soviet shipping; many were members of SNFE/Alpha 66. On April 9, 1963 Menoyo himself was restricted to Miami, but on April 10,

1963 he announced that the raids would continue. SNFE/Alpha 66 held a press conference in Los Angeles on April 18, 1963 at which they criticized the Kennedy Administration for frustrating their efforts to rid Cuba of Castro. By September 1963 they were back in action. According to a letter intercepted by the FBI, SNFE/Alpha 66/MRP was "training...men for a specialized reserve brigade in various types of guerilla warfare." The FBI also reported that in October, Menoyo came to Los Angeles where he announced "the organization would be in Cuba in less than six months." In November 1963 SNFE/Alpha 66/MRP were working together on the "Omega Plan." [19]

A Member of Alpha 66 Looked Just Like Oswald

Take a look at Commission Document 23, two pages of which we have reprinted on pages 282-283. Compare this information with the following data extracted from the recently declassified Commission Document 1085, an extensive FBI report on a man named Manuel Rodriguez Orcarberro who is doubtless the same man named in CD 23. Rodriguez was president of the Dallas unit of SNFE/Alpha 66/MRP and was known to be "violently anti-President Kennedy" according to FBI informant Dallas T-1. The report also said that he had worked with Coca-Cola in Cuba until 1958, when he joined Castro's army. He defected after Castro took power, went back to work for Coca-Cola and probably worked clandestinely against Castro. Soon he took refuge in the Brazilian Embassy in Havana and came to America in November 1960. He took a job as a dishwasher in a Miami Beach hotel and stayed there until September 6, 1963, when he registered as an alien in Dallas. The document says, "A photograph of Rodriguez appears in this file." Again it was missing from the National Archives. Rodriguez's fingerprint classification was also included in the report yet the Bureau stated that they had no file on him. When interviewed by the FBI, Rodriguez said that SNFE was just a fundraising organization that had been relatively inactive in the Dallas area until recently. He said that meetings were held at "3126 Hollandale" and that he had made no contacts "with any American persons or other persons concerning the purchase of arms or ammunition by SNFE (Dr. Scott reports he was involved in the purchase of arms for use in the Bay of Pigs). Rodriguez stated that he had been an admirer of President Kennedy, both as a person and as a politician. He said he believed President Kennedy had been a fighter against communism and a friend of the Cuban people—never had he made any derogatory statements against President Kennedy. He pointed out that SNFE had bought and placed flowers at the site of the Kennedy assassination.

There are four secret files on Rodriguez that are still classified.

Report	Agent	Subject	Date	City	
853.	SS	Memorandum from Chief Rowley, SS, re: Manuel Rodriguez w/attachments......	4/24/64	Wash., D.C.	S
	Warner	(a) Manuel Rodriguez—Reaction by Cuban Exile Community to Pres. Kennedy's Death—5310 Columbia, Dallas, Texas.....................	1/17/64	Dallas	S
		(b) Protective Research Referral Memorandum re: Manuel Rodriguez, 5310 Columbia, Dallas, Texas..........	3/18/64		S
		w/attached FBI Identification Record........................	3/9/64		
	Aragon	(c) Manuel Rodriguez, 5310 Columbia, Dallas, Texas (Reaction by Cuban Exile Community to Pres. Kennedy's Death)........................	1/31/64	Miami	S

The Secret Service compiles Protective Research Referral Memoranda on people they believe are potential assassins of the President. It seems likely that after the assassination, Rodriguez said or did something that made the Secret Service issue a belated PRS.

In April 1975 we filed a request for Rodriguez's address with the Immigration and Naturalization Service under the provisions of the Freedom of Information Act. Within ten days we were given his address in Puerto Rico. A week later Canfield was in San Juan interviewing the former leader of Alpha 66.

At first we thought that Rodriguez might be the Oswald-double. After all, Doctor Socarraz told the FBI he looked like

Oswald. Many researchers would have jumped on this and the other reports as an excuse to unjustifiably accuse the Cuban exile. But we try to rely more on field work than speculation. Rodriguez looked nothing like Oswald.

Canfield set up an interview which he tape recorded. Rodriguez told him that he moved to Puerto Rico because he had been persecuted in the United States for being a strong anti-communist. He had vowed to dedicate his life to fighting communism after having been bitterly betrayed by Castro—Rodriguez played an important part in the struggle against Batista and had been jailed and tortured for doing so. When he was released from prison he joined Castro and after the revolution he was made a Province leader. When he fled to America he worked closely with the Cuban Revolutionary Council and helped start SNFE/Alpha 66. Soon he moved to Dallas where he became an FBI informer "talking with them* about Castro infiltrators and the like for the last ten years."

When Canfield questioned him about the incident at the service station in Oklahoma, Rodriguez said that "someone thought one of (his) friends was Oswald" and that "it was just one big mistake that was soon cleared up." At first Rodriguez said he was never questioned by the FBI, but when Canfield produced an FBI report he suddenly remembered, then said he did not want to talk about the assassination. When he was shown a photo of the Oswald-like tramp, he said the man was never in Alpha 66. When we displayed the photographs of the Oswald look-alike tramp to the owner of the Oklahoma gas-station, he said—"The best that I can remember—it resembled him."

* * * * *

Shortly after John Kennedy was killed in Dealy Plaza, two people, Dora Causa and Marguerite Klinner, came forward with stories that linked SNFE/Alpha 66/MRP with the murder. An

---

* The agent in Dallas with whom he conferred was probably James Hosty, the same man who was assigned to keep an eye on Oswald. Hosty was in charge of establishing informants within the Cuban exile community.

FBI report filed in Miami stated that, "Another government agency which conducts intelligence and personnel investigations, advised that one of their sources stated that he heard one Dora Causa relate that Eloy Gutierrez Menoyo had stated on November 21, 1963, that 'something very big would happen soon that would advance the Cuban cause.' " When questioned about this by the FBI, Causa denied everything. [20] The other person who linked SNFE/Alpha 66/MRP with the killing was the wife of John Klinner, an ex-convict who had been imprisoned by Castro after a shipwreck off the Cuban coast. She said her husband, who had been released by Castro on April 10, 1963, was in a large Miami department store on November 22, 1963. When he heard that Kennedy was dead he immediately wanted to go home and make a phone call to "The Major." Marguerite told the FBI that her husband asked the Major—"Was it us?" or "Was he one of our boys?" or "Was it one of our group that did it?"—then immediately began to speculate on the possibility of arrests in Florida. When the FBI reached Klinner he denied everything but said he did know a Major who was connected with Alpha 66, a group that had unsuccessfully tried to recruit him into their ranks.

Klinner was probably lying to the FBI about his affiliation with Alpha 66 because his wife reported that he had been in touch with Cuban freedom fighters and had told her in November 1963 that he had just returned from Cuba. And that is not all. One of the men he was shipwrecked and imprisoned with, was suspected by Castro of working for the CIA because he had been jailed in Cuba in 1961 for anti-Castro activities. [21] Was the "Major" Klinner telephoned Major Gutierrez Menoyo?

About a month after the assassination of Dr. Martin Luther King, former FBI agent Bill Turner realized that the first police sketch of King's killer looked just like the Oswald-look-alike-tramp. This sketch had been provided by a Mexican artist who drew it from a description furnished by the FBI when it was rumored that a sharp-nosed man who was connected with the King murder was headed for the border. [22] Turner held a press conference about it on the West Coast.

The next day a group called the Kennedy Assassination Inquiry Committee showed the comparison to the media in New York City. An article appeared in the New York *Times* about this press conference, which extensively quoted Richard Sprague. Sprague said the tramps were taken in within 45-60 minutes after the killing and that the Oldman-tramp may have been the drunk who was picked up near the railroad tracks (see page 61). Fortunately, the *Times* printed the sketch and the comparison photo. A few weeks later the FBI disclaimed the sketch: "The FBI said today it had not distributed any sketch of the King assassin. The sketch circulated in Mexico was apparently made from radio broadcasts giving the FBI's description. No sketch was authorized by the FBI." [23]

James Earl Ray was eventually convicted for the murder of King and sentenced to life imprisonment. In the early 1970's, Ray decided to allow Bernard Fensterwald of CTIA to represent him. By May 1974 Fensterwald's associate, Robert Livingston, had obtained a hearing for Ray before Judge McRae that was scheduled for October. He suddenly announced that someone was going to come forward and confess that he had been hired by "four wealthy, prominent American citizens" to kill King, if he was granted immunity from prosecution. Livingston was also quoted as saying that "There are three men who propose to testify to give a complete exposé of the King murder case..." [24]

But when Ray's hearing rolled around these men never materialized and the judge was presented with very little tangible evidence that Ray deserved a new trial. About six months after, McRae ruled against Ray, denying him a new trial. However, some interesting things did come out in the hearing. The New York *Times* reported that

> In questioning by his attorney this morning, Mr. Ray said he had been shown 'ten or twelve pictures' of 'Latin appearing' individuals while he was awaiting trial in 1968. One of these photographs, he said, was of a man who had been arrested in Dallas for questioning on the day that President Kennedy was assassinated there in 1963. 'I was asked if I would identify the man if he was brought to Memphis,' Mr. Ray said. 'I

said no, although he did look similar to the party I was involved with.'
The man arrested in Dallas was not charged, and his name was not
mentioned in the courtroom today. He was identified as an
anti-communist Cuban. [25]

It should be pointed out that Ray claims he was set up to take
the blame for the killing by a blonde Latin named Raoul who
convinced him he was working for anti-Castro Cubans in a gun
smuggling operation.

Was Raoul, Manuel Rodriguez's friend? Was he also present
at the King assassination? These are questions which only a
full-scale Congressional investigation can answer. In the
meantime we can only speculate on the many similarities between
the two murders—a rifle with a telescopic sight which was easily
traced back to its owner was found at both crime scenes; a map
with the Texas School Book Depository prominently marked was
found in Oswald's possession—a map with King's house and
church marked on it was found in Ray's car; there was also a
lack of witnesses to both shootings.

Ray dismissed his first lawyer who was an ex-CIA agent [26] and
chose to allow Bernard Fensterwald to represent him despite the
fact that Gerald Alch testified that James McCord funded CTIA
while he was working for the CIA.

CHAPTER SEVEN

Odio and the Mysterious Mr. Martin

On November 29, 1963, Ms. C.L. Connell of the Catholic Cuban Relief Committee informed the FBI that Sylvia Odio called her and said she knew Lee Harvey Oswald. [1]

The FBI did not interview Odio until December 19, 1963 and when they did, they sent two CIA-linked agents to do it—Bardwell D. Odum and James P. Hosty.

Odum was the agent assigned to question Oswald's mother immediately after the killing and was given a photo, allegedly of Oswald leaving the Cuban Embassy in Mexico City (see page 297) by the CIA. [2] Hosty was the Dallas FBI agent in charge of monitoring the activities of anti-Castro Cubans, and was also the agent assigned to Oswald's case (he had interrogated Ruth Paine about Oswald a few weeks before the killing). Oswald had Hosty's phone number in his address book, but the FBI omitted this fact when they typed up his address book for the Warren Commission. [3]

The Hosty report is reprinted on page 284. Note how the pair describe Oswald as a cynical ex-Marine who wanted to use JURE's* hatred for America to achieve his own ends. When the

* **Junta Revolucionaria** (Revolutionary Junta), a socialist exile group led by Manolo Ray. The acronym comes from the first two letters of each word.

"member of JURE" replied to Oswald's remark that Kennedy should have been killed for his actions during the Bay of Pigs, he did not sound sincere. "According to Mrs. Odio," the report states, "Leopoldo told them that the Cuban people bore no malice toward President Kennedy because of the Bay of Pigs episode."

Odum and Hosty also omit the fact that Odio never believed the men were really from JURE [4] despite the fact they knew her father's cryptonym. She mentions this in almost all of her other interviews with the FBI, the Secret Service and the Warren Commission, and probably related it also to Odum and Hosty because she was anxious to absolve the Cuban exile community.

We believe that this report was deliberately slanted against JURE. It differs immensely from later FBI reports and from Odio's testimony before the Warren Commission.

As far as we can determine from our research in the National Archives nothing was done about the Hosty-Odum report until Odio was called to testify before the Warren Commission in July 1964. She told Welsey Liebler that around September 27, 1963 she was visited by three men. Two of them were Cubans and called themselves Angelo and Leopoldo. The other was an ex-Marine named Leon Oswald. They knew all about her father's imprisonment by Castro on the Isle of Pines and told her they were members of JURE and the "revolutionary council."* The "Cubans" repeated the name Leon Oswald twice and wanted her to translate letters to various corporations appealing for funds for JURE. Before they left they let it be known they were going on a trip.

A day or so later one of them called her on the telephone and said that Leon was crazy. He thought the Cubans should have killed Kennedy after what he did to them in the Bay of Pigs and that exiles had "no guts" since it was *so easy* to do. The Cuban went on to describe Leon as "the kind of man that could do anything—like getting underground in Cuba, like killing Castro." He also said that Leon was an expert marksman, who thought Kennedy was "holding the freedom of Cuba..."

---

* The Cuban Revolutionary Council.

After the Kennedy assassination Odio had fainted when she saw Oswald's photo on television and heard his name. During her testimony about this she asked Liebler, "Can I say something off the record?" Afterward Liebler said, "At this point let's go back on the record. You indicated that you thought perhaps the three men who had come to your apartment had something to do with the assassination?" Odio said "Yes." [5]

She was a highly credible witness. The daughter of a Cuban millionaire, she attended a Catholic school in Philadelphia and studied law at the University of Illinois. She spoke four languages and was working as a secretary at the time of the visit. With her mother and father in Cuban prisons, and her brothers in an orphanage, she was having trouble adjusting to life in Dallas and consulted with a psychiatrist about these problems. Hosty spoke with this psychiatrist as part of his follow-up to the Connell report and was told that "she does not have any problems concerning hallucinations...she is telling the truth and not exaggerating..." [6]

Unsatisfied with this report, the FBI questioned all of her friends about her mental health. With the exception of Ms. Connell, who said Odio and her sister both suffered from grand hysteria, all of the Cubans queried said she was "nuts" while the Americans said she was "sane." [7]

But Sylvia Odio could not be written off so easily: First, her sister had also seen the men and corroborated her story. Both had identified Oswald from FBI photos as the man who visited them. Second, before Ms. Connell had spoken with the FBI, Odio had told her priest about the incident. Miami Secret Service agent Ernest Aragon reported he was unable to locate the priest who was allegedly living in Florida. [8]

The Warren Commission was quite upset by all this. J. Lee Rankin called it a case of mistaken identity because Oswald was supposedly on his way to Mexico City at the time of the visit. The Commission then set about trying to prove Oswald could have stopped off in Dallas on his way, by checking bus schedules and hotel registers, all to no avail. But they still had to admit that "Odio may well turn out to be right. The Commission will look bad if it turns out that she is. There is no need to look foolish by grasping at straws to avoid admitting there is a problem." [9]

A paragraph in the first draft of the Warren Report stated that Odio "came forward" with her story. A memorandum about this by J. Lee Rankin pointed out that "she didn't come forward at all and was quite reluctant to get involved..." As a matter of fact, Odio had good reason to keep her story to herself—it turned out she lost her job because the FBI visited her place of employment. [10]

In all likelihood Odio was visited by two rightwing Cuban exiles and the Oswald-double in an attempt to discredit JURE, the most left-oriented of the exile groups. After the assassination they knew she would recall the visit by "Oswald and his buddies in JURE"; perhaps to make certain, they mentioned the name "Oswald" at least twice and associated him with the idea of the assassination.

The man who put them up to it also knew Oswald was heading for Mexico since the visitors gave Odio the impression that they were taking "a trip"; [11] had inside information about the state of imprisoned exiles in Cuba; had one of his "characters" mention Kennedy, the Bay of Pigs and the assassination of Fidel Castro. Could this man have been Howard Hunt? It is a well established fact that Hunt hated Manolo Ray and his organization JURE and in his book about the Bay of Pigs invasion he has more derogatory references to Ray than anyone else.

Ray had been chief of Castro's underground in Havana and had organized a general strike against Batista. After the revolution he became Minister of Public Works and did not defect until about a year after the Batistaites left. [12] According to Hunt, just before he fled, Pedro Diaz Lanz told Ray that Castro was a communist. Ray allegedly told him he did not care. Lanz was a good friend of Sturgis and Hunt (see page 95).

Hunt also claims that an article accusing his friend Artime of being a communist could be traced back to Ray and that after Ray arrived in the U.S. in late 1960, all his associates were of the "extreme socialist Left." [13]

A few months after Ray arrived he formed the MRP (See page 117) which Hunt claims soon became known among exiles as

"Fidelismo sin Fidel."* Ray refused to bring MRP into the Cuban Revolutionary Front while Varona was the leader and the Administration wanted every exile group included, except for the Batistaites. So Hunt was put under pressure by his superiors to admit Ray and replace Varona. Rather than do so, Hunt resigned,[14] but agreed to remain as "a propagandist" for the new Cuban Revolutionary Council (CRC) and the Bay of Pigs invasion, which was soon to take place.

Hunt could never work with, or trust, Ray, He described him as a "Marxist opportunist who had not rebelled even when Castro forced Ray's brother, Rene, to kill himself following his arrest for alleged misappropriation of $400,000." Hunt also said he "...blamed the United States for Cuba's troubles, hated the landowning classes and saw a socialist revolution for Cuba's post-Castro future." Despite all of Hunt's objections and his resignation, when the Council was formed on March 18, 1961 Ray was made Chief of Sabotage and Internal Affairs,[15] yet he was not informed about the upcoming invasion. Shortly after Bay of Pigs, Ray complained about this to the press, adding that "The CRC, seemingly acting with the CIA's blessings, is recruiting former officials of the Batista dictatorship while turning its back on the MRP."[16] By 1962 Ray had become a persona non grata with the CIA and was forced to resign from the MRP which had been co-opted by SNFE/Alpha 66/30th of November and the CIA (see page 116).Ray started JURE about this time.

The Odio family was closely linked with Ray and his allies. Although they initially supported Castro, they turned against him and began to work with Aureliano Sanchez Arango. Castro discovered a cache of arms on their farm and they were jailed. Before this, they hid Manolo Ray prior to his escape.[17] It is interesting to note that Sanchez, one of the more liberal members of the CRF, quit after Varona was elected chairman. Hunt believed that his resignation ultimately led to a broadening of the Front's political base and the inclusion of Ray.[18] Arango charged that the CIA chose the leaders of the Front "so they could be easily subdued to the hidden policy and orders of the CIA" and

---

* Castroism without Castro

started his own group—JUNTA—which eventually merged with JURE.[19] Odio was criticized by the rightwing exiles in Dallas for being a part of this organization.

The Odio incident can also be connected to Howard Hunt through Maurice Ferre, whose family had extensive industrial holdings in Puerto Rico and South Florida. Just before Odio was to appear at the FBI's Miami office for questioning on October 1, 1964, Ferre called the Bureau and told them that she had attempted suicide several times and was under a psychiatrist's care. Maurice Ferre's bodyguard, Ramon Orozoco Crespo, is the partner of Angel Ferrer, the Watergater who was registered at the time of the break-in but was not picked up by the police.[20]

The Mysterious Mr. Martin

In Ms. Connell's historic call to the FBI, she also told them she was suspicious of someone everyone called "Mr. Martin," a contact man from "Uruguay" who tried to obtain guns for anti-Castroites in the Dallas area. She distrusted this man because he claimed to be an airplane engineer, while Sylvia Odio had told her that he operated a laundry in Dallas.[21] About two weeks later FBI agent Hosty interviewed Juan B. Martin. We've reprinted his report on page 284. Notice how short the report is and how there is no mention of Martin's gun-running activities in violation of Federal law (see CD 205). Hosty is minimizing Mr. Martin's importance.

Because of incomplete reports like this one, James Rowley, Chief of the Secret Service, ordered Thomas J. Kelly, the Secret Serviceman who had questioned Oswald after the assassination without transcribing or recording the conversation,[22] to conduct an investigation of the Odio incident. Kelly assigned the task to Miami Secret Serviceman Ernest Aragon; he told him to run a background check on Odio and Father McChann (the priest Odio had confided in) as well as one Juan Martin, "believed to be in the state of Florida." His report on Odio was slanted against her. He said he studied the background of her parents and they were strong anti-communists, implying that there was some question about her. He also reported that the police in

Puerto Rico were making inquiries about her "but the reasons for the inquiries are unknown" and that she was "believed to have a mental disorder." After questioning the head of the Miami archdiocese, Aragon reported he could not locate Father McChann and that he was still working on Juan Martin. [23] About a week later he filed another report, this one even more curious than the first. Aragon still could not find McChann or Martin and "in accordance with a long distance telephone call from Inspector Kelly" he interviewed Rogelio Cisneros (alias Eugenio), an officer of JURE at Miami, Florida.

Cisneros told him that he flew to Dallas in June 1963 "specifically for the purpose of contacting Sylvia Odio who was to introduce him to a person in Dallas who was interested in selling them (JURE) small arms." Cisneros related that the man to whom Sylvia Odio introduced him was believed to be an Uruguayan who was well known to Sylvia Odio from previous contact in Cuba. Cisneros said he did not approve of the Uruguayan's tactics and had discounted further negotiations with him. Cisneros added he did not recall the Uruguayan's name." The next day Aragon called Kelly and told him about the interview after which he "recontacted Cisneros by telephone and the name of Juan Martin was mentioned to him. Cisneros spontaneously exclaimed that Juan Martin was the name of the Uruguayan who had been introduced to him by Sylvia Odio. Cisneros then related that Juan Martin operates a well-established laundry believed to be known as 'Dixie'...he stated he only made one contact with Juan Martin at the laundry..." [24]

Cisneros' story conflicts with Juan Martin's (who said there was never any meeting with Odio) and with that of Odio herself, who told the Commission that she was trying to contact John Martin of Uruguay to buy arms from Brazil. In spite of this contradiction, Aragon closed down this part of the investigation.

Aragon is an expert at closing cases. When a long distance operator in Mexico City monitored an international phone call on November 24, 1963 she heard someone say that "the Castro plan is being carried out. Bobby is next. Soon the atomic bombs will begin to rain and they won't know from where." When the phone numbers were traced one of them belonged to Emilio

Nunez Portuondo, a former "Cuban Ambassador to the United Nations during the Batista regime" and a rightwing political figure in the exile community who had recently "become bitter at the United States" to the point where a file was kept on him by the Protective Research Division of the Secret Service. The other phone number belonged to Jose Antonio Cabarga of Mexico City. According to Portuondo, "Carbaga was in close contact with the U.S. Embassy in Mexico City and was a good investigator who could develop information in the event the plans to assassinate the President were formulated in Mexico City." Despite telegrams to Washington by an honest Secret Service agent who worked under Aragon, the Washington office of the Secret Service failed to send an agent to interview Carbaga and here again the case was closed. [25]

Dissatisfied with Aragon's investigation of the McChann and Odio affair in general, the Chief of the Secret Service, James Rowley, ordered Inspector Kelly to question Father McChann himself. Kelly located McChann in a rest home in New Orleans. McChann said he had headed the Cuban Catholic Committee's re-settlement office in Dallas and tried to stay aloof from Cuban politics. He "stated that he was introduced to John Martin (Juan Martin) whom he described as a Latin but not a Cuban. He stated Mr. Martin came to Sylvia Odio's apartment one evening while he was there. Martin did not stay very long and after he had left Odio stated that Martin represented a Cuban group or was doing a job for a Cuban group in Dallas. Father McChann was under the impression that Martin had an apartment or house in Dallas and had a family in some other city." In a telephone conversation later that afternoon Odio told the priest, "John Martin is an Uruguayan who is supplying arms purchased in some South American countries to some Cuban groups." [26]

McChann went on to say that he had been contacted by the FBI prior to the assassination about other matters—why couldn't they find him after the assassination?—and generally verified Sylvia Odio's story. The priest told Kelly that Odio's downward plunge in economic status was responsible for her illness, and that her mental condition had been aggravated by "her concern that the Cuban community might be involved in some way with the assassination in view of their association with Oswald shortly before the event."

Kelly had McChann call Odio and question her about the incident once again. The priest came back with the usual story except for one thing: Odio now claimed Cisneros was one of the men who visited her. The men writing the Warren Report jumped on this inconsistency but were rebuffed in a memo from one of the Commission counsels: "The story of Father McChann is over-emphasized. We should state that Odio never told anyone else that Eugenio had been one of the men with Oswald. How can we conclude McChann would not have become confused when he was apparently in a rest home of some sort and we have never seen or spoken with him?"[27]

About three weeks before the Warren Report was scheduled to go to press the FBI re-interviewed Odio, hoping to tie up the loose ends her story had engendered. By this time she had moved in with her brother in Miami. Although she had changed her residence, her story remained intact. All the FBI got was a bit more information on the mysterious Mr. Martin: "Mrs. Odio stated that a gun seller called Johnny Martin had spoken before small groups of Cuban refugees in Dallas."[28] Apparently unwilling to track down the elusive Mr. Martin, the FBI also decided to question Manolo Ray and his deputy, Rogelio Cisneros, in their never-ending quest to make the Warren Report credible. Ray told them he knew the Odios and they were good people but that Sylvia had to be imagining the story about Oswald. Cisneros told them "...Mrs. Odio arranged a meeting with a South American named Juan Martin, who lived in Dallas, and who claimed to be able to supply weapons. Mr. Cisneros stated he made the decision against any negotiations with Martin for weapons."[29]

Watergate provides an interesting hypothesis for explaining the mysterious Mr. Martin. In an article in *Harper's*, Eugenio Martinez revealed that the Watergaters used the same false names they had used during the Bay of Pigs. When James McCord was caught bugging the Democratic National Committee Office in the Watergate he was using the name Edward J. Martin. Hunt was using the code name Mr. White. Was the mysterious Mr. Martin who was going to sell arms to JURE James McCord?

It is interesting to note that an ex-political informant for the Los Angeles Police Department, Louis Tackwood, said at a press conference, held several months before Watergate, that he had been indirectly approached by a Mr. Martin and a Mr. White and been asked to incite a riot at the 1972 Republican Convention. How did Tackwood know the code names of McCord and Hunt before the Watergate story broke?[30]

There is some evidence that McCord was involved in Cuban affairs in the 1960's—after Watergate the CIA issued the following: "In a separate memorandum of 21 June we advised you that a review of the duties and assignments of Mr. James McCord provided no indication he was involved in Cuban matters and that he was not assigned to the Bay of Pigs operation. We stated, however, that he might have developed personal acquaintances which are not recorded in official personnel and security records. We have no information regarding Mr. McCord's activities with Cuban exiles since his retirement."[31]

It is also interesting to note that in the book *The Invisible Government*, Wise and Ross state that Ernesto Aragon was Cardona's right-hand man on the Cuban Revolutionary Council. Cardona was well acquainted with Howard Hunt.*

---

* Charles Colson has stated that the CIA has infiltrated the Secret Service.[32]

CHAPTER EIGHT

Loran Hall and the Free Cuba Committees

A week before the Warren Report went to press, a man named Loran Hall was located by the FBI and he told them he was the one who had visited Sylvia Odio in Dallas in late September 1963. Hall said he was there to raise money for anti-Castro forces training in the Florida Keys and he had contacted three professors—one of them was named Odio. He was introduced to Sylvia by Kiki Ferror and visited her accompanied by William Seymour (who allegedly looked like Oswald) and Lawrence Howard, a few days later.[1]

Hall fought in the mountains alongside Castro in 1958 but was arrested by the Castro Government in April 1959 on a charge of training recruits for an expedition whose purpose was to overthrow the government of Nicaragua.*[2] This plan was alleged to have been prepared by the CIA to demonstrate to the world that Castro was exporting his revolution and had to be wiped out.

After his release, Hall left Cuba and took up the fight against Castro in the States. In the early fall of 1963 Hall, towing a trailer-load of arms to the Interpen-IAB training camp at No Name, was arrested by Federal agents.[3]

---

* A few weeks after Castro's takeover, Major William Morgan (see page 106), Frank Sturgis and Alex Rorke (see page 107) participated in a similar plot. At least two of these men were working for the CIA.

Hall could not get either of his friends to back up his story. The FBI questioned Seymour who told them that he had met Hall at a training camp in the Keys and had been arrested with him in Dallas. He denied visiting Sylvia Odio or ever hearing the name and told the FBI where he was working during the period he was supposed to have been in Dallas. The story checked out. [4] William Seymour was one of the Interpen-IAB fighters arrested for training on No Name Key (see page 100) and he does not look very much like Lee Harvey Oswald (see picture on page 297).

Lawrence Howard, who had also been arrested at No Name, said that around September 1963 he left Miami for Los Angeles, accompanied by Celio Castro, Loran Hall and "a Cuban named Frank." In Los Angeles, Hall picked up a trailer-load of arms and they all headed back for Miami—except for Frank. On the way back they stopped in Dallas, but Howard denied visiting Odio, and told the FBI that the only Kiki he knew was Kiki Masferrer, the brother of Rolando Masferrer, a former Cuban senator under Batista and an active anti-Castroite. [5] Masferrer was one of the exiles singled out by John Kennedy. Just before the Bay of Pigs, Federal agents in Miami arrested this notorious Batista henchman, whose private army had roamed Cuba, killing, stealing and committing rape. Masferrer was charged with violating the Neutrality Act and Kennedy said that his arrest should serve as a warning to other Cubans that the United States was not about to resurrect the Batista regime.

Rolando was a member of the Christian Democratic Movement, which shared personnel with Sturgis' IAB.*

On September 20, 1964 Hall was again interviewed by the FBI. He told them he was mistaken about Seymour (he had traveled with Seymour and Howard on separate occasions) and in reality, he was accompanied by a man named Wahito, who turned out to be a Castro plant. Hall stuck to the Kiki story, but now he said he met her in a nearby phone booth rather than in her apartment building, and admitted he was "confused," because he had been to Dallas five times that year. (He was there as late as October 1963.) Finally he denied ever meeting Odio but says the

---

* See paragraphs on Panque on pp. 96 .
* See paragraphs on Panque on pp. 96 .

name and the fact that her father was a prisoner of Castro were familiar to him.

Hall's timing was perfect. His first statement to the FBI was included on page 324 of the Warren Report.

> On September 16, 1964, the FBI located LORAN EUGENE HALL...He told the FBI that in September of 1963 he was in Dallas, soliciting aid in connection with anti-Castro activities. He said he had visited MRS. ODIO. He was accompanied by LAWRENCE HOWARD, a Mexican-American from Los Angeles and one WILLIAM SEYMOUR from Arizona. He stated that Seymour is similar in appearance to LEE HARVEY OSWALD; he speaks only a few words of Spanish, as MRS. ODIO testified one of the men who visited her did. While the FBI has not yet completed its investigation into this matter at the time the report went to press, the Commission has concluded Lee Harvey Oswald was not at Mrs. Odio's apartment in September of 1963.

No mention was made of the fact that Hall retracted his statement or that when the Odio sisters were shown pictures of Hall, Seymour, Howard and a certain Mr. Alba they said these were definitely *not* the men who had visited them. [6]

Loran Hall was the subject of another FBI report which appears on pages 285 through 286—and is, to our knowledge, one of the strangest FBI reports in the National Archives. First, there is no Justice Department letterhead or insignia and the report is unsigned. It is credited to S.A. Gamberling in an index of documents in the National Archives yet Gamberling could not have written it because he worked with the Dallas Bureau. [7] It seems to be about Dick Watley from its heading, but it actually concerns a "private detective" named Richard Hathcock, Loran Hall and our old friend from the Interpen-IAB training camp on No Name Key—Gerald Patrick Hemming. What the document boils down to is this: On September 18, 1963, Loran Hall took a rifle out of pawn that was described as being identical to the one "shown on television on November 23, 1963 as being used in the assassination of President Kennedy," by a man who had accidentally witnessed the transaction. The man contacted the FBI and they immediately interviewed the people involved—except, of course, for Hemming and Hall. Richard Hathcock told them that the transaction did take place, but the rifle was different from Oswald's. Hathcock, private detective, one-time owner of a hangout for soldiers of fortune, was associated with members of the *"Brigada Internationale"*—also known as the International Anti-communist Brigade, which was led by Frank Sturgis of Watergate fame. Hathcock volunteered the information that Hall paid for the rifle with a check drawn on "The Committee To Free Cuba." Since Hathcock would not lie about the rifle being different the anonymous agents curiously concluded, "No further investigation was conducted as it is obvious that the rifle mentioned above was not used in connection with the assassination of John F. Kennedy." The FBI could have followed up numerous leads made evident by this report. They also could have checked out the possibility that the "Cuban named Frank" who traveled to Los Angeles with Hall in September 1963 (when the transaction took place) was Frank Sturgis, since both men were in Interpen-IAB and both had fought with Castro when he was in the Sierra Maestres.

If they would have checked out the Committee To Free Cuba they would have found their way to a CIA-financed can of worms. The Committee To Free Cuba, like the Free Cuba Committee, Citizens for a Free Cuba, Crusade to Free Cuba, Crusade to Free Cuba Committee, Cuban Freedom Committee, and the Committee for Free Cuba, was merely a CIA front group established in order to account for funds the CIA was pumping into various exile groups. Either directly or indirectly, they could all be traced back to Watergate mastermind, Everette Howard Hunt.

The Free Cuba Committee was headed by E. Del Valle—the same man who paid David Ferrie and died the same day he did. David Ferrie had been linked to Frank Sturgis and Howard Hunt by ex-CIA agent Victor Marchetti.

Citizens For a Free Cuba was founded by Guy Bannister, who probably worked with Hunt on the overthrow of Arbenez and the Bay of Pigs invasion. He was closely associated with Arcacha Smith who was a member of the Cuban Revolutionary Front and Council which were both closely linked to Hunt.⁸

Committee members of The Crusade to Free Cuba openly admitted it was a Cuban Revolutionary Council fundraising front. Arnesto Rodriguez told the FBI the Crusade was founded "primarily to raise funds with which to buy arms and supplies for use by the CRC." [9]

The Citizens Committee for a Free Cuba, the Cuban Freedom Committee and The Free Cuba Committee, all located in Washington, D.C., were really one organization. Mr. Bethel worked for the Citizens Committee For a Free Cuba and the Free Cuba Committee [10] at the same time. In *Undercover* Hunt says a Washington-based public relations firm named Mullen & Co. "established and managed a Free Cuba Committee for the CIA." [11] In Watergate Exhibit 142 it is apparent that Mullen & Co. was also involved in setting up the Cuban Freedom Committee, which is the same thing. At this point note that when Dallas District Attorney Henry Wade stated that Oswald was a member of the Free Cuba Committee at a late night press conference on November 22, 1963, none other than Jack Ruby "interrupted Wade when he made that statement and pointed out that Oswald was a member of the Fair Play For Cuba Committee and there was a great difference" between the two. Was this the committee Howard Hunt had in mind when he wrote—"But for Castro and the Bay of Pigs disaster there would have been no such 'committee' and no such assassin named Lee Harvey Oswald"?* [12]

Loran Hall was an officer of the Committee To Free Cuba—also known as the Free Cuba Committee. [13] So what we have here is a CIA front group taking a rifle "out of pawn" that looked like Oswald's a month before the assassination. This man also happened to be associated with Frank Sturgis, who may very well have appeared in Dealy Plaza disguised as a tramp. In fact, Frank may have driven to Los Angeles with Hall and may be the mysterious "Cuban named Frank." And J. Edgar Hoover was willing to take Hall's word about the Odio incident, going as far as saying that Odio may have mistaken the name Loran Eugene

---

* Although the preceding was taken out of context, it is worth reflecting upon nevertheless.

Hall for Lee Harvey Oswald because there is a phonetic resemblance.[14] This is one of the strongest pieces of evidence indicating that there was a conspiracy on the part of some members of the FBI to suppress the truth and protect the assassins. Then Representative Gerald Ford once asked J. Edgar Hoover if he was going to keep the case open. Hoover replied, "It will be an open case till the end of time."[15] About a week after Dick Gregory showed the tramp comparison shots obtained from us to America, Nixon appointee Clarence Kelly, head of the Federal Bureau of Investigation, told the Dallas Press Corps, "From time to time, of course, someone will come up and say the trajectory was wrong and the place from which the bullet was fired was wrong. We have done so (reopened the case) from time to time (but) we have no information to indicate that (Hunt was at the scene)...To our knowledge and from our investigation of the photograph, he is not that man."[16]

In February 1975 I called the Los Angeles Bureau of the FBI and tried to find out which agents filed this report. Normally this would be a complete waste of time because all FBI documents are kept strictly confidential, but this happened to be one of the few in the public domain.

Special Agent Kananskie was unable to find a document with the same Los Angeles file number, so he looked under the names of the people involved. When I called him back he told me, "I have the information here but it is not in the same form you have it. I think the agent in Dallas must've reworded it...I have the first two paragraphs on one page and the next paragraph I have on another page so apparently the agent in Dallas put them all together."

Perhaps that is why the report was credited to Gamberling; it had been forwarded to him for watering down.*

I asked Kananskie who the agents were who had originally written the report. "I only have his initials and he's no longer here. They're different than the ones on your document...I can't give them to you...(what) I have is on a standard FBI form."[17]

---

* Ninety per cent of the other FBI reports went straight to the Warren Commission and the FBI in Washington, D.C. from the field offices where they were filed.

During the Watergate cover-up attempt, Nixon was also funneling illicit funds through a "Cuban Committee." In discussing the payment of hush money to Watergate defendants with his counsel, John Dean, he said, "They put that under the cover of a Cuban Committee or (unintelligible)." Dean replied, "Yeah, they, they had a Cuban Committee and they had—some of it was given to Hunt's lawyer, who in turn passed it out. This, you know, when Hunt's wife was flying to Chicago with ten thousand, she was actually, I understand after the fact now, was going to pass that money to, uh, one of the Cubans." The money had "Good Luck F.S." written on it. [18]

* * * * *

Now that we know who was really behind the Committee, it puts the rumors they helped spread in a different perspective: the CIA, most likely, was trying to make up for the fact that Oswald did not have the Cuban visa on his person when he was arrested, by spreading stories that made it seem like Castro was behind the Kennedy killing.

Paul Bethel, of the Free Cuba Committee, helped disseminate the rumor that an "admitted Castro agent" had been arrested a week before the assassination for plotting to kill John Kennedy. Actually, "the agent" was a schizophrenic methedrine addict. [19] Other "Free Cuba" officials put out the stories that Oswald visited Cuba prior to assassinating Kennedy, [20] and that Castro had threatened to "knock off" any political leaders that gave him trouble. [21] The Free Cuba Committee also stressed the "Ruby as Communistic Jew" angle by spreading the story that he met with a Solomon Pratkins in Havana, after Castro came to power. [22] They also repeated a Cuban plan to assassinate U.S. ambassadors in all parts of the world revealed by Sturgis' confidante, and one-time intelligence agent, Andrew St. George. St. George told them this on November 22, 1963 when he happened to be passing through Washington and stopped by their office—which was run by Mullen & Co. [23] The DRE, another CIA-controlled exile organization, [24] was often the source for these rumors and may have been behind a letter signed by Pedro

Charles postmarked "Havana, November 28, 1963," which arrived at Oswald's old Post Office box. It said Charles saw Oswald in Miami (where Frank Sturgis and his friends also saw him) and that he had told the Chief about Oswald's marksmanship. Charles recommends he "close business as soon as possible" and says he's awaiting Oswald's arrival in Havana. Other letters were sent to Robert Kennedy and Lyndon B. Johnson. These were allegedly from someone in the anti-Castro underground in Cuba who wanted to inform on Charles. They said he was an agent of the Cuban Security Department and that Oswald killed the President on his orders, hoping the blame would fall "on the Republican Party" of Texas. [25] Both these letters were typed on the same machine and the FBI dismissed the whole thing. [26] Ex-military intelligence agent Fletcher Prouty, of CTIA, claims Hunt may have been behind the Pedro Charles episode, because when he called Lucian Conien, he had Colson use the pseudonym Fred Charles. It could have been a scheme of Carlos Bringuier's because, in a letter published by the Warren Commission, he links Ruby, Clay Betrand and a Castro official through the common bond of homosexuality, and parenthetically states that Oswald's leafletting friend in New Orleans was named Charles. [27] The amateurism in using the same typewriter for these letters would almost certainly rule out Hunt as their originator.

Salvadore Diaz Verson, who was a friend of Bringuier's, took a similar line. The former Chief of the dreaded Cuban Military Intelligence Service and the current President of the Anti-communist League of Cuba, said that Castro had put Oswald up to it. Diaz states that a close friend of his was a director of the anti-Castro radio program called Voice of Cuba. The Voice of Cuba was sponsored by Mullen/CIA's Cuban Freedom Committee. It was extremely likely Diaz knew Bernard Barker. It is strange that Diaz first heard the story about Oswald while attending an International Federation of Journalists Convention in Mexico City. According to ex-CIA agent Philip Agee, this organization works closely with the CIA. [28]

Bringuier also tried to prove that Oswald was a Castro agent by linking him to a letter that a disgruntled member of the

Christian Democratic Movement had sent to the Cuban Ambassador in Mexico City, hoping to be allowed back into Cuba in return for information on the activities of the anti-Castro exiles. The CDM got this man to confess by putting a rope around his neck and a gun to his head. The letter they originally intercepted had a reference to "remain alert until the 8th of August." Bringuier claimed Oswald had tried to infiltrate the DRE prior to the eighth of August and that he had found out about McLaney Training Camp Farm from the confessed spy. Frank Sturgis' friend, Victor Panque, was mixed up in this affair.

Hunt seems to have also been behind a similar rumor. In his friend William F. Buckley's column of March 26, 1964 he ponders the possibility that Oswald was a Soviet agent by citing the hypothesis of a "recently retired member of the CIA." This "friend," who was "extensively schooled in espionage," told him that before Oswald left Russia he was recruited as an agent. Hunt had "recently retired" from the CIA to become a "contract agent" around this time, and was very close to Buckley. Jack Anderson reported that William F. Buckley was "behind a defense fund to pay Hunt's lawyers what the secret Watergate hush funds didn't cover." [29]

Back at the Texas School Book Depository

Patrolman Baker, who was riding a motorcycle at the end of the motorcade, saw pigeons fly off the roof of the Texas School Book Depository. He got off his bike and ran into that building in the blink of an eyelash while people were still "grabbing their children" thinking that the firing was continuing. Baker hurried up to the second floor where he encountered a cool, calm Oswald. [30] How could Oswald have killed the President, wiped off the rifle, wiped off the empty cartridges, hidden the rifle and run down the stairs in so short a time? The Commission had to prove something like this could be done so they staged a grand re-enactment, complete with Baker on his motorcycle and an agent up on the sixth-floor window. Without wiping off the rifle or cartridges the FBI found that the times were within three seconds of each other, if Oswald bought the Coke he was drinking *after* he encountered Baker. There is some question about this. David Belin discussed this in his book *You Are The Jury*. Oswald told Fritz and others that when he met Baker he had a Coke in his hand and a TSBD secretary saw him holding a bottle when he left the building. The two men who ran into Oswald (Baker and Truely) were never questioned about this until after the re-enactment. By this time they had gotten the idea that the whole Warren Commission Report was dependent on this little bit of testimony. Baker said Oswald's hands were empty, while Truely told them he was not sure. There is no obvious reason why Oswald should lie about when he bought the Coke because he could not have known the role it would play in the investigation.

The validity of the re-enactment is highly questionable because it is difficult to duplicate the conditions that existed. Nevertheless, David Belin, who is now investigating the CIA for the Rockefeller Commission, bases a good deal of his case for Oswald-as-lone-assassin on flimsy evidence such as this.[31]

Oswald slipped out of the depository before Harkness sealed it up, and judging from the rest of his actions that day, he must have realized almost immediately that he had been set up as a patsy for John F. Kennedy's killing. The first thing he did was go back to his room and presumably get his pistol,[32] after which he headed for parts unknown.

On the way he encountered Officer J.D. Tippit, who could have been assigned to kill him. After all, what better way for Oswald to die than in the course of "resisting" a legitimate arrest? Tippit would be just doing his duty. There are several curious things about Tippit—first of all, ex-Syndicate hooker, Nancy Perrin, testified that when she first came to Dallas she was referred to Tippit by the mob.[33] Tippit also happened to work for a functionary of the John Birch Society on weekends[34] and was a "double" for Bernard Weisman, the man whose name appeared at the bottom of the black-bordered "WELCOME TO DALLAS MR. KENNEDY" advertisement which ran in the Dallas *Morning News* on November 22, 1963. Mark Lane told the Warren Commission he had evidence of a Tippit-Ruby meeting and an associate of Ruby's told them the same thing.[35]

Tippit was out of his patrol district when he stopped Oswald according to early reports from the Dallas Police Department.* [36] Tippit questioned Oswald on a description that seemed rather broad. [37]

Many other assassination researchers have stated that Oswald did not kill Tippit. They cite the fact that both witnesses to the actual murder gave the police descriptions of Tippit's assailant that did not fit Oswald. One of these witnesses ended up getting shot while the other's son was arrested. They also point out that the jacket Oswald allegedly discarded after killing Tippit could not be traced back to him, despite an extensive FBI investigation during which hundreds of laundry owners were questioned. [38]

But, assuming Oswald did not kill Tippit, what motive could the assassins have for killing the officer? Did they want to associate Oswald with another killing? Was there not enough heat on him already for being a Marxist and ex-defector who worked in the building the President was allegedly shot from? Let us suppose this was not enough for them, would they not have the Oswald-look-alike commit the murder? But the Oswald-look-alike was probably being questioned by the FBI around this time.

There is strong evidence that Oswald killed Tippit. First of all, we believe that Oswald realized he was a patsy and was going to die—so he had nothing to lose; seven eyewitnesses saw Oswald with a gun in his hand. (No one saw him holding the rifle in the TSBD.) Ballistics tests showed the shells that were found on the scene came from his gun. Mark Lane cites the fact that Tippit was hit with two different kinds of bullets in the course of proving his thesis that Oswald did not do it. He neglects to mention that Oswald had two different kinds of bullets in his pocket after he was apprehended. The paraffin tests administered by the Dallas Police proved positive for his hands and negative for his cheek—indicating he had recently fired a pistol. [39] Finally, the murder weapon was found in Oswald's possession and had his fingerprints on it. David Belin states that if you believe Oswald killed Tippit it follows that he killed Kennedy.

---

* Later they said he was there on special instructions.

This kind of reasoning is specious at best, but has nevertheless fooled many people for a long time.*

Aware that the police were out to murder him, Oswald ran into a movie theater where he would be surrounded by witnesses. Knowing it was him or them, he put up a struggle when apprehended and reportedly tried to shoot it out with the police. What difference did it make? He was a dead man anyway. [41]

By this time the police searching the TSBD had found the assassin's lair, the spent shells and the rifle. None of the shells had any fingerprints on them and one of them looked like it was planted because it was far away from the others and had an uncharacteristic dent on it. Ballistics experts were unable to link this shell to "Oswald's" rifle. [42] The *Mannlicher Carcano* rifle also had no prints on it [43] but was easily traced back to Oswald because it had been sent to his Post Office box under the name A.J. Hidell. When Oswald was taken into custody the police found extensive false identification for an A.J. Hidell in his wallet. Oswald also used the name Hidell on his literature, vaccination certificate, employment references and revolver order. How could he have expected that the rifle would not be traced back to him? At this point one might wonder why Oswald had to order the murder weapon from a commercial mail-order house if he was part of a CIA plot to kill Castro and John Kennedy? Why did the CIA not supply him with a gun?

Watergater Eugenio Martinez supplied us with a possible answer in his article in *Harper's*. "If you were caught in one of these operations with commercial weapons that you could buy anywhere," he wrote, "you could be said to be on your own. They teach you that they are going to disavow you."

The lack of fingerprints is also characteristic of a CIA/Hunt type of covert operation. When the Watergaters were caught they were all wearing surgical gloves. Eugenio Martinez claims that the gloves are not one hundred per cent effective. "According to the police we were using gloves and didn't leave any fingerprints. But I'm afraid that I did because I didn't wear my gloves when I

---

* We also find it very bizarre that none other than Priscilla Johnson (see page 25) reviewed Belin's book for the New York **Times**. [40]

put the tape on the window—you know—sometimes it's hard to use gloves. . ."[44] There were some unidentified fingerprints found on the sixth floor of the TSBD that day. The FBI made a half-hearted attempt to identify them by comparing them with the prints of the depository employees they had on file. None matched.[45] They did not bother to compare them against all the other prints they had on file.*

Oswald was taken to the Dallas jail where he was thoroughly searched. Let us suppose for one moment that he had been granted the visa by the Cuban Embassy and that this visa had been on his person. The implications of a Cuban collusion would have generated incredible pressure for U.S. military action in that country. Hunt's mission of ". . . ridding Cuba of Castro and his henchmen, regardless of personal cost and effort" would have been accomplished.

In Hunt's book about the Bay of Pigs, *Give Us This Day*, he presents us with an incident very much like the above hypothetical situation. Hunt recalls that just before the overthrow of Arbenez the CIA "was treating [sic] with three exiled leaders: Col. Castillo Armas, Dr. Juan Cordova Cerna and Col. Miguel Idigoras Fuentes." Hunt favored Cordova. Armas was chosen—only to be "assassinated by a member of the Presidential bodyguard in whose pocket was found a card from Radio Moscow."

Although the police did not list it, they found on Oswald a small slip of paper with the number of a pay phone located in the lobby of a Fort Worth apartment building. We came across this fact in an obscure document dealing with the activities of the Warren Commission.[46] Throughout the Watergate hearing there were references made to "sensitive" phone calls that had to be made from pay phone to pay phone, in order to avoid any possible wiretaps. Was Oswald calling a confederate from pay phone to pay phone?

---

* Howard Hunt's prints were not on file until he was arrested in connection with the Watergate affair in 1972. Now we can compare them, although there is a slight problem—the FBI refused to give us a copy of the unidentified fingerprints and the D.C. Police Department refused to give us a copy of Howard Hunt's. A Congressional investigation, conducted independently of the FBI, should be able to answer questions like these.

While all of this was going on, John F. Kennedy's body was being rushed to Washington D.C. for an autopsy by the military, and a bullet, practically in mint condition, fell out of Governor John Connally and onto his stretcher right after an unidentified CIA agent appeared on the scene.[47]

Oswald's interrogation was equally bizarre. He was questioned by Will Fritz (see page 191), James Hosty (see page 67), Secret Service man Kelly (see page 130), Postal Inspector Holmes (see page 86), and three other local Federal officials—U.S. Marshall Robert Nash, FBI agent Jim Bookhout and Dallas Secret Service head, Forest Sorrells. None of these men called in a stenographer or recorded this historical interrogation and we have to take their word for what transpired.

While Oswald was in jail he held a brief press conference during which he said he was "just a patsy in this deal."[48] He was visited by H. Louis Nichols, the president of the Dallas Bar Association.[49] Oswald also made several phone calls which the Dallas Police said they kept no record of[50] and the pages containing the Dallas Police Department telephone records for November 1963 have been withheld from CD 1472.

Independent researcher Sherman Skolnick was able to come up with the document reprinted on page 287. In the summer of 1974 Mike Canfield called John David Hurt and tried to find out why Oswald called him. The following is an edited transcription of the conversation.

Hurt:	I never heard of Lee Harvey Oswald 'til the tragedy occurred...
Canfield:	But there's this document...
Hurt:	Never heard of him 'til the tragedy occurred...Had some telephone conversations with Kennedy's assistants though. I'd never talked to President or Mrs. Kennedy but I was greatly interested in them and a real Kennedyphile. Every time I'd be interested in their comings and goings and every time I'd talk to their administrative assistant. I never got to talk to either of the Kennedys... I was in the counterintelligence corps in the Army during World War II for about three years...
Canfield:	I wonder why they had this record down at the Dallas jail?
Hurt:	I can't tell you to save my life...he never called...I never

> spoke to him in my life—the only connection I ever had was just seeing him on TV...

(Mrs. Hurt picked up the extension and Canfield questioned her about the call.)

Canfield: Why do you think this record exists?

Mrs. Hurt: It puzzles me to death, I'd like to know too.

Hurt: My interest was from the standpoint of the Kennedys—in fact, I'd be inclined to take the same action Ruby took—I would have loved to have put a bullet in him. I wish I could give you some leads but I can't 'cause I don't have the slightest idea of how this thing came about.

Canfield called Hurt back in February 1975 and found out that he made the calls inquiring about the Kennedys before their Dallas trip. He also commented on Bay of Pigs: "I think we should have gone on in there and taken things over and I think (JFK) felt the same way...I don't think we should have an enemy of the United States sitting ninety miles off our shore."

Judging from its signature and form, the document appears to be authentic. But it does not come from the National Archives.

In a recent development the New York correspondent of the Rome newspaper *Il Messaggero* reported that Lawrence Trackman, an "American Adventurer" who was arrested in Manila in 1972 because of his alleged involvement in an assassination plot against President Marcos told his inquisitors that JFK was "the victim of a plot by fifteen Cuban and American mercenaries enlisted two years earlier by the CIA for the abortive Bay of Pigs Invasion." Truckman was allegedly under the influence of sodium pentathol at the time of his confession. Was this group Interpen-IAB? When Bill Turner recently spoke with Patrick Hemming about the photograph of "Oswald" entering the Cuban Embassy in Mexico City (see page 297) he was reportedly told the man was "William Deveraux"–another member of Interpen-IAB. Finally the author of *Walking Tall*, William Morris, said that while visiting the alleged assassin's grave on the third anniversary of his death he encountered an agent who'd worked with Oswald in the CIA. This was the man who Daniel Schorr put on the CBS-TV national news recently in silhouette, since he didn't want anyone to know his identity. According to Morris, the man fought in the mountains of Cuba with Sturgis and Hall and may have been a member of Interpen-IAB.

According to Morris, Agent X told him that Hall was in Dallas on November 22, 1963 and was part of the assassination squad which was directed by Eugene HaleBrading. He also claims to have tapes of Hall making threats on Kennedy's life and says that Hall was in Mexico City about a month before the assassination for a strategy meeting.

When questioned by Canfield, Sturgis denied knowing Hall but admitted "So many names . . . there are so many names." Hall moved to Mexico in July 1975.

CHAPTER NINE

Ruby, Lansky, and the Death of Oswald

Oswald was a doomed man from the moment he was taken into custody by the Dallas Police. He denied the Tippit and Kennedy shootings at his press conference, but never got a chance to elaborate because Jack Ruby, a well-known figure among the Dallas Police, shot him in the stomach on Sunday, November 24, 1963 before millions of television viewers.

The old adage "dead men don't talk" seemed to apply very well to the situation and President Johnson had to create the Warren Commission perhaps more in order to calm the resulting strong fears and anxieties than to determine the truth about the assassination and give an irate and troubled people the full story.

Only the Warren Commission could conclude that Ruby was a patriotic nightclub owner who slew Oswald because of his love for the Kennedys and their children. Only the Warren Commission could overlook the overwhelming evidence that Ruby started out as a Hoffa*-oriented labor hoodlum and soon became a full-fledged gangster who worked under Meyer Lansky and had a special interest in Cuban affairs.

In 1939 Jack Rubenstein, as he was known back then, formed the Waste-Handlers Union in Chicago, and shortly thereafter

---

* The Teamster Union leader.

became its Secretary/Treasurer. After the lawyer who helped him in this effort was found shot to death, Ruby relinquished his union role and was replaced by Paul Dorfman, ex-boxer and chief Hoffa henchman. The McClellan Committee, whose chief investigator was Robert Kennedy, associated Dorfman with many organized crime figures [1] and described the Waste-Handlers Union as a link between the underworld and James Hoffa. [2] When Robert Kennedy finally brought Hoffa to justice Paul Dorfman's father, Allen, was one of the defendants in the Hoffa jury-tampering case. [3] Dorfman worked closely with Carlos Marchello (see page 44) in his futile attempt to get Hoffa cleared. [4]

"Needlenose" Labriola, a labor gangster who was eventually found strangled to death with a steel wire in the back of a car, was also a Ruby associate in Chicago, [5] as was Barney Baker, [6] a close friend of Jimmy Hoffa's [7] who was questioned by Robert Kennedy during the McClellan Crime Committee Hearings.

After the McClellan investigation, Edward V. Long, a Senator from Missouri, was persuaded to hold hearings into the abuses of civil rights that occur during Congressional investigations. *Life* claimed that Jimmy Hoffa was the guiding hand behind this investigation. [8] Long hired none other than Bernard Fensterwald and ex-McCarthy chief counsel, Roy M. Cohn, to expose how Robert Kennedy had trampled on these poor gangsters in the course of investigating them. [9]

When Robert Kennedy became Attorney General he set up a special Justice Department organized crime squad to "get" people like Jimmy Hoffa, which was headed by William Hundley, Robert Peloquin and William O. Bittman. Kennedy's "get Hoffa" squad managed to get Edward Partin, a Teamster leader from Louisiana, to testify against Hoffa. Partin also said he knew of a plot to kill Robert Kennedy and was allegedly involved in smuggling arms to Castro. [10] Eventually Hoffa was sent to prison, primarily on the strength of Partin's testimony.

Just before shooting Oswald, Ruby called Barney Baker. Baker, who had just gotten out of prison, was in touch with Earl Scheib (according to Baker's telephone records [11]), whose son,

Philip, was friendly with Eugene Hale Brading. Philip Scheib was also a close friend of Dennis Mower, who would soon join Eugene Hall and others in an attempt to sabotage the Garrison investigation. [12]

Ruby also called the head of the Teamsters Southern Conference and a Teamster bondsman [13] before he killed Oswald for having "a communistic look" on his face.

Many of the people involved in the Hoffa case became important figures in the Watergate scandal. Bernard Fensterwald, who had suddenly stopped attacking Robert Kennedy and started CTIA (to "investigate" things like the Kennedy murders) became James McCord's lawyer. William O. Bittman became Howard Hunt's attorney and went so far as to collect hush money for him and involve himself in a possible case of obstruction of justice. [14] William Hundley, who had represented John Mitchell, was closely associated with the new Watergate prosecutor, James Neal, who was also part of Robert Kennedy's "get Hoffa" squad. Neal was also associated with Charles N. Schaffer, John Dean's lawyer and Warren Commission staff member. [15]

Hoffa had also been associated with Meyer Lansky. A man who tried to infiltrate Kennedy's "get Hoffa" squad was tied up with Lansky, and Hoffa was questioned about his association with the ultra-conservative kingpin of syndicated crime. [16] Peloquin and Hundley were eventually hired by INTERTEL, which certain observers regard as a Syndicate front, [17] while others, among them Charles Colson, believe INTERTEL is a CIA cover because "you can't tell where the Hughes Corporation begins and the CIA leaves off."* The Hughes-CIA Russian submarine adventure completely bears Colson out. But, as we shall soon see, it is also hard to tell where the Syndicate leaves off and the CIA begins.

The FBI investigated the connections between Ruby and Hoffa and officially found that there were none, [18] although there are FBI documents in the National Archives that contradict this. For example, FBI File #DL 44-1639 reports that a Ramos Ducos told

---

* INTERTEL is ostensibly owned by Hughes.

the FBI that he had heard that Miguel Cruz had said the Teamsters were involved in Kennedy's death. An "M. Cruz" was picked up during the Bringuier-Oswald fight in New Orleans. Ramos Ducos, a former Teamster official, also said that Frank Chavez had told him he was going to attend a meeting at which Ruby would be present. Frank Chavez, a former Teamster official himself, wrote threatening letters to Robert Kennedy after the assassination and was killed by his own bodyguard after he openly threatened to kill the Attorney General. [19]

On December 28, 1973, accused Martin Luther King assassin, James Earl Ray, issued a fifteen-page statement about his suit against the state of Tennessee which implicated "a New Orleans man close to a Louisiana Teamster official."

Jimmy Hoffa is free now, thanks to a pardon from Richard Nixon that was arranged by Charles Colson. Nixon also showed up at a Teamsters Executive Board meeting in June 1971 and dropped charges against Hoffa's successor's son.

When the Syndicate needed another man in Dallas, they sent Ruby there, where he joined Benny Binnion and Paul Jones. [20] Binnion was running a gambling house just outside of the Dallas city limits called The Top Of The Hill. [21] Jones, who worked with the Chicago mob, had managed to bribe the Sheriff of Dallas for quite a number of years, probably on behalf of Binnion and Company. When a new Sheriff took over and he tried to bribe him, Jones wound up getting indicted for bribery. All this took place before Ruby came to Texas. Jones claims that he met Ruby through his sister Eva Grant, who had come to Dallas to open a nightclub. Grant testified that Jones had contacted her regarding some "metal pipe." Shortly thereafter, Jones was arrested for forty pounds of opium. Jack Ruby was questioned about this arrest. During the Kefauver hearings Lt. Butler of the Dallas Police Department was also questioned about a meeting he had with Jones.

Robinson: Well, do you recall having a conversation with him around October 9, 1946, in which Mr. Jones stated to you that he was connected with a Syndicate that operated from coast to coast, and Canada and Spain?

Butler: That is right, sir.

Robinson: What was the purpose of having this conversation with him?
Butler: To establish whether these rumors concerning him and his connections were true.
Halley: You just visited him and identified yourself?
Butler: Well, I had already arrested him and he knew me...I was questioning him about some men who had been brought down to Dallas from Chicago...[22]

Jones advised the FBI that he had seen Ruby in early November 1963 and that if they wanted further information they should contact the head of the Dallas Syndicate.[23]

There is considerable evidence that sometime in the mid-1950's Ruby became involved with Carlos Prio (see page 95) and helped him smuggle arms to anti-Batista forces inside Cuba. He also sold them to exiles in the United States. Ruby was doing this with the approval of Meyer Lansky, who was living in Cuba and was very close to the Batista regime, but was hedging his bets by supporting both men.

Jimmy Hoffa was also linked to weapons-dealing with Castro: The Senate Rackets Committee discovered that an aide of Hoffa's had shared a Miami hotel room with someone who had sought to sell planes to Castro.[24]

Notice how the documents reprinted on pages 287 and 288 both associate a Jack Rubenstein with arms purchases shortly before Castro came to power. When the CIA checked their files, they only looked under "Ruby," and so they reported back that they had found nothing.

After the murder of Oswald, several people came forward and linked Ruby with Prio and arms smuggling. Mary Thompson of Kalamazoo, Michigan told the FBI that on or about May 30, 1958, she visited her brother and sister-in-law, James and Mary Lou Woodard, who had a cottage in Islamadora, Florida. They introduced her to a man named Jack who was originally from Chicago but had moved to Dallas where he ran a bar. Jack had met James in Dallas, during the time he was a police officer there. Thompson added that Jack's real name was supposed to be Leon and that he drove a car with Texas plates. Her sister-in-law, Mary Lou, had related that "Jack had a trunkfull of guns and inferred that Jack was going to supply them to the Cubans...This was at the time of the revolution in Cuba."

When Mary Thompson observed Jack Ruby's picture on television on November 24, 1963 she found that he was identical with "Jack." The FBI questioned Thompson's daughter and she verified the story and added that she had gotten the impression that Jack was in the "Syndicate." In another FBI report a woman named Simmons reports seeing Ruby around this time in nearby Isla Camorada. [25]

Although the FBI could not locate Woodard, they did come up with an interview they had conducted in September 1963. We have reprinted the document which contains this excerpt on pages 288-289. Woodard says he participated in an invasion of Cuba prior to the Castro regime and had furnished arms to Castro forces. We know of only one such invasion (see page 95), so it is very likely that Woodard was working for Prio.

Woodard definitely knew Jack and may very well have known Sturgis, who worked for Prio from 1955-57 in a similar capacity. Woodard may have also been a member of Interpen/IAB—he says he took part in the Bay of Pigs invasion and was now supplying anti-Castro exiles with arms. On October 8, 1963 the FBI questioned him about some dynamite found in his home, which was located south of Miami near the area in the Everglades which Interpen/IAB used for training purposes. Woodard also fit the profile of the typical Interpen/IAB member—he had helped Castro to power only to be "double-crossed" by him.

An informant, assigned the code number AT T-2, also linked Ruby with Prio and gun smuggling to Castro. We have reproduced this document on page 290. Notice the part about Ruby arranging illegal flights of weapons for Castro and being the owner of two planes used for these purposes. Compare it with the following excerpt from an article on Sturgis by Andrew St. George printed in *True*:

> In 1955 Frank began to run clandestine night flights into Cuba for former President Carlos Prio Socarras, sometimes delivering passengers (agents, contactmen, underground organizers) sometimes cargo (tommy guns, hand grenades, plastic explosives) to be employed, in one manner or another, against Batista. [26]

In a reinterview, AT T-2 said it was all right to use his real name—Blaney Mack Johnson—and added that he had seen Ruby around a private airport and had also known Ruby to run guns by boat. Johnson picked out a photo of Ruby as someone he had seen before. Blaney Johnson went on to say that the Colonial Inn was the sole property of the National Mob headed by Frank Costello, Frank Erickson and Joe Adonis.[27]

According to Hank Messick, a recognized authority on organized crime, Costello, a New York Mafia chieftain, owned a share of the Colonial Inn as did Frank Erickson, a bookie at the Rooney Plaza Hotel in Miami Beach and Joe Adonis. As a matter of fact, there were at least eight partners in the Colonial Inn and Jack Ruby may very well have been one. Meyer Lansky was the man in charge, because he owned the biggest share, and had moved to Miami in 1945 in order to run it. The Kefauver investigation closely examined the Colonial Inn and the men who owned it, and they were hurt by all the publicity. Adonis was deported and Erickson jailed. The Colonial Inn had to close down.[28]

The FBI questioned all of the people Johnson had named in the document—Browder, who was locked up in a Federal penitentiary, denied everything, but admitted knowing Marrs. Marrs denied everything and described Johnson as a shady ex-Canadian Air Force pilot. Johnson admitted making numerous flights to Cuba but insisted that he was not involved in smuggling.[29] The former police chief also denied knowing Ruby,* as did a former airline pilot, who said the Colonial Inn was closed in the early 1940's and Johnson was a liar. Robert Vollmer, who worked in the Records Bureau of the Miami Police Department, also said Johnson was "off the beam."

In early 1959 "Rubin" was spotted in Key West with a man who looked like Oswald (see page 114) and later that year Ruby admitted he was involved in a "jeep deal" with Castro. During his historic testimony to the Warren Commission he said there was a "government article that they would need jeeps...the United States Government was wanting person [*sic.*] to help them

---

* Ruby had been known to cultivate the friendship of policemen.

at that particular time when they threw out the dictator, Batista. And [*sic.*] one particular time there was a gentleman who smuggled guns to Castro...His name was Longley out of Bay something—Texas—on Bayshore...He was given a jail term for smuggling guns to Castro...He had a boat and lived somewhere in the center of Texas."[30]

The FBI said that Ruby was referring to Robert Ray McKeown, who was arrested by agents of the Alcohol and Tobacco Tax Unit in 1958 and charged with trying to smuggle goods to Cuba. He was fined five hundred dollars and given a two-year suspended sentence. The FBI located McKeown in Bay Cliff, Texas and he told them he knew Castro personally and when the Cuban leader visited Houston he had met him at the airport and had his picture taken with him. He said that "Castro stated he would give (me) a government position in Cuba or perhaps might give (me) some franchises or concessions there." McKeown was also very close to Prio. The FBI reported that the daughter of McKeown's wife by a previous marriage was closely associated with Prio "on an intimate basis."[31] McKeown had obtained funds to open the drive-in he managed from Prio, and was involved in smuggling arms for the former Cuban President. (see page 289)

McKeown said that Ruby had obtained his phone number through the local Sheriff's Department (rather than from Prio) and had offered him five thousand dollars for each person he could get out of Cuba. He told him that someone in Las Vegas was footing the bill but refused to pay him the money in advance so, like so many of the deals Ruby was involved in, it never went through. Ruby visited McKeown a couple of weeks later and said he held an option on some jeeps in Louisiana and wanted McKeown to write him a letter of introduction to Castro. Once again nothing came of the proposed transaction.

Despite all this evidence of a Ruby-Prio link, the Warren Commission concluded that with the exception of the jeep deal, "no substantiation has been found for rumors linking Ruby with pro- or anti-Castro Cuban activities." They also decided there was no "significant link between Ruby and organized crime." Some members of the Commission dissented. Said Boggs, "The most difficult aspect of this is the Ruby aspect." Rankin commented, "...you have some clear proof of some kind of Cuban connection there and there is a difference of testimony of what it is."[32]

After Ruby's name became a household word many people came forward with stories linking him to smuggling. A former Oklahoma policeman said that when he worked for the Oklahoma Crime Bureau a local hoodlum drove a car loaded with guns and ammunition through his town. The officer gave chase and the man was finally arrested in Texas. Subsequent investigation by the Texas Department of Public Safety allegedly revealed that a man named "Rubenstein" was involved.[33] Then there was Eileen Curry, a former prostitute whose pimp-boy-friend, James Breen, had introduced her to Ruby in 1955. Breen told Curry that Ruby had taken him to a place where he was shown movies of various border guards, narcotics agents and contacts and that he thought his operation was extremely efficient. Soon Breen went to Mexico and came back $2400 richer.[34]

The most detailed story of Ruby's involvement in Cuban affairs came from Nancy Perrin, who, like Curry, had a long record of prostitution and mental instability. Perrin, whose real name was Zaidman, worked for Ruby in the summer of 1961, quitting after Ruby slapped her during an argument.

When Perrin saw Ruby's picture on television she called the FBI in Oakland, California and gave them all the information she had on him. Shortly thereafter she was re-interviewed at her home and agreed to sign a statement about her charges. The FBI even went as far as giving her a lie-detector test—the results of which proved inconclusive because she had ingested a powerful stimulant before submitting to the test.

Perrin told the Bureau that before moving to Dallas she had worked for the Syndicate in Denver. By "Syndicate" she stated she meant the Italian "Mafia."* She said it was headed by Vito Genovese and she had worked under a man named Dragna who was close to Mickey Cohn and Virginia Hill.[35]

---

* We have put Mafia in quotes because that is the way it was in the FBI Report—J. Edgar Hoover never acknowledged its actual existence.

Vito Genovese worked under Luciano [36] who worked with Lansky. Dragna and Cohn had both tried to take over the leadership of the West Coast mob after Lansky had his partner, Bugsy Siegel, murdered. [37] Frank Costello, an agent of Lansky, worked out a deal between the gangsters in order to avoid unprofitable bloodshed. Virginia Hill was Siegel's mistress. [38] After he died she lived with Joe Adonis (see page 157).

Most of these gangsters were pretty notorious at the time and Perrin could have gotten her information from the newspapers. In Denver, Perrin met Piggy Marchese from New York, and was involved in fixing card games with him. Julius "Piggy" Marchese was a small-time hoodlum who had been arrested by "New York's Finest" back in April 1945 and charged with running a heroin manufacturing plant. [39] The fact that she knew this man lent weight to the veracity of her story.

From Denver, Perrin moved to New England where she worked as a "lobbyist" for the liquor interests in the New Hampshire State Legislature. Everything was going well until she had a fight with her husband, Robert Perrin, who left her and moved to Texas. In an effort to locate him she called the Dallas Police Department, probably on the advice of one of her friends in the Syndicate, and spoke with none other than Officer Tippit—the same officer Oswald was later alleged to have killed. When she came to Dallas, Officer Rayburn found her an apartment and she was soon reunited with her husband. It was around this time that she got a job as a barmaid at Ruby's Carousel Club, which she said was frequented by Dallas policemen, such as her boyfriend, Rayburn, along with Syndicate men from Chicago and St. Louis who went there to make payments to Ruby. Five weeks after Ruby hired her he hit her and she quit. She tried to file charges against Ruby, but the District Attorney refused to act, and advised her not to try to bring charges against the nightclub owner. A couple of weeks after speaking to the authorities she was arrested for prostitution.

That summer her husband was approached by Ed Brunner of Grand Prairie, Texas and was asked if he was interested in attending meetings of a group concerned with getting refugees out of Cuba. He knew Brunner (the Commission also calls him

"Brawner") from Miami, where both men had worked with automobiles; and Perrin had experience in smuggling that dated back to the Spanish Civil War, when he had smuggled guns for Franco. Nancy Perrin said her husband also knew a man named "Youngblood."*

Nancy Perrin said that the first meeting between her husband and the group took place sometime between August and November 1961. A bartender and alleged pimp introduced him to "The Colonel," who was dressed in an Army uniform. The Colonel offered her husband twenty thousand dollars to take an old Coast Guard cutter, possibly loaded with *Enfields*, into Cuba.⁴⁰ About two weeks later another meeting was held which was attended by twelve people including the Colonel and someone she described as "Vito Genovese's son." The topics discussed ranged from how to get refugees into Miami to what beaches would be best to land on in Cuba. During this meeting none other than Jack Ruby walked in and seemed to transfer some funds to the unidentified Army Colonel. Perrin said she thought the arms were going to Castro but was probably lying in an effort to discredit Ruby, whom she hated. When Mark Lane questioned her about this meeting she told him that after it ended she was taken to a yard in back of the building where she thought she had "run into an Army supply depot." Burt Griffen, who later became head of the legal services program of the Office of Economic Opportunity under the Nixon Administration, allegedly had this part of her testimony stricken from the records.⁴¹

A third meeting took place two days later at which the Perrins told the Colonel that they had to turn down his offer. A short time later she and her husband were arrested by the Dallas Police. In August 1962 Robert Perrin died of arsenic poisoning in New Orleans.

---

* She is probably referring to Jack Youngblood, a soldier of fortune who helped overthrow Arbenez then began to work for Castro and Prio. Youngblood had arranged a meeting between his two employers and flew Prio to Cuba after the Revolution. He was present during the slaughter of seventy Batistaite military-men at San Juan Hill (see page 93) and was arrested for plotting to kidnap Rolando Masferrer (see page 136) while acting as an agent of Castro. There is no doubt that Youngblood was an important figure in the exile community and the fact that she mentions him indicates she is probably telling the truth about the meetings.

The FBI questioned all the people she had mentioned—they all agreed she was a liar and a whore. The Bureau seized upon the fact that she was a prostitute to destroy her credibility, just as they did in the case of Eileen Curry. They failed to realize that Perrin's credibility might have been enhanced by this fact because people like Ruby associated almost exclusively with the criminal element. Only someone like Perrin would be in a position to know. They also discounted a letter of reference from the Oakland Police Department which stated that Perrin had worked as an undercover agent in an abortion case and had supplied them with valuable information. According to the FBI and Secret Service, Perrin was not to be believed. [42]

Many researchers have wondered who "The Colonel" really was. Some have suggested it was Colonel Castorr who was described by Father McChann as "...a retired Army Colonel...generally interested in the plight of the Cuban refugees (who was) 'playing the role of an intelligence officer' in his contacts with the Cubans...he seemed more interested in their political beliefs than in their economic plight..." [43] Maybe Frank Sturgis can throw some light on this—he told Canfield that in Cuba in 1959 his contact was "...an Army Colonel...I told him more than one time, within a six-month period [that he could kill Fidel.]" Note that the Interpen/IAB forces were "training in the Everglades [with] thirty surplus *Enfield* rifles." [44]

Jack Ruby Visits Cuba

To date, the general impression has been that the only thing Jack Ruby had to do with Cuba was the fact that he once ate in a Cuban restaurant. It may therefore come as a shock to the reader to find out that Ruby visited Cuba shortly after Fidel Castro came to power in 1959.

When he first came to Dallas in 1947 Ruby was introduced to the pitman of The Top Of The Hill casino, Lewis J. McWillie, by his friend from Chicago, Benny Binnion. McWillie and Ruby immediately hit it off and when McWillie's mother was questioned by the FBI she told them that they saw each other on a daily basis around this time. [45]

In 1958 McWillie moved to Cuba and immediately went to work at the Tropicana Casino in Havana. Shortly after Castro came to power in 1959, McWillie wrote a letter to Ruby and asked him if he wanted to visit Havana for a week "extend(ing) this invitation as one would to a brother." According to Ruby, he needed a vacation and McWillie had mailed him the tickets, so he figured he might as well go there "for rest and relaxation." As he was about to enter Cuba he was detained by Castro's Customs officials. He tells about it in his testimony to the Warren Commission reproduced on page 291. Ruby says that he was stopped because the officials recognized a picture of him with "Mr. Fox." Extensive investigation by Weberman and Professor Scott has yielded no information on the identity of this "Mr. Fox." We believe that he does not in fact exist. Perhaps "Fox" was a pseudonym—notice how Ruby says on page 291 that "evidently they had me pretty well lined up as to where I come in the picture of Mr. Rivera Fox. I can't think of his name."

If the Customs inspectors recognized Mr. Fox so quickly he must have been a very important person in Cuba. It was this clue that led us to first believe that the Fox brothers were really the Lansky brothers—Meyer and Jake—two gangsters who had played an important role in Cuban affairs for decades.

During World War II, Meyer Lansky, head of the National Crime Syndicate (an alliance of primarily Jewish, Italian and Irish gangsters) was asked to visit Lucky Luciano in jail in order to enlist the Mafia's support in preventing sabotage in America's ports, which they controlled through the Longshoremen's union. Because the Mafia was at war with Mussolini in Italy (they never liked competition), Luciano agreed.

Lansky worked closely with Naval Intelligence in this unique operation during which organized crime and the intelligence community worked together for the first time. By 1944 Franklin D. Roosevelt was using Lansky as sort of an unofficial diplomat: he sent Lansky to Cuba with a message to Batista to hold elections or else! A few months later Batista held a free election, lost, and was forced to flee Cuba. In 1948 Prio was elected

President and proved to be one of the most corrupt leaders in Cuban history. During his term of office there were scores of unsolved political assassinations, often involving the wrong people. Things were so bad even the Syndicate could not function properly; in 1950 Lansky allegedly transferred a Swiss bank account containing a quarter of a million dollars over to Prio, in return for his letting Batista back into the country. [46]

Batista had won the Army over to his side and had gotten Prio's bodyguard to act as a spy for him. One day he showed up at the Presidential Palace and told Prio he knew every move he was going to make that day, including what movie he had planned to see and how he was getting there. He also announced that the Armed Forces were behind him. Prio went to the countryside and tried to rouse the peasantry, but they had nothing to fight for and turned a deaf ear to him. So he fled to Miami where he formed an anti-Batista private army.

In 1951 Lansky's Florida casinos, including the Colonial Inn, had to close down on account of Kefauver's investigations. As Lansky biographer Hank Messick put it, "...it can be safely said that the shutdown of Lansky's Florida casinos in 1951, and the return to power of Sergeant Batista in 1952, was no mere coincidence."

By 1953 Lansky started to invest heavily in Havana casinos and in 1954 he moved there. [47] He became close friends with Batista, yet he still remained on good terms with Prio, because he wanted to be on top of the situation no matter who was in power. Lansky was so close to Batista that when Castro took over he had to flee alongside the deposed dictator—leaving many of his henchmen behind.

Notice that Ruby says in the transcript on page 290 that the Fox brothers were in exile at the time...so were the Lansky brothers. Take a look at page 86 line 6 (page 291): "At the time they knew the Fox brothers weren't going to *jell*, or something was going to happen." Is this a typographical error? The word "jail" would seem to make more sense in that context. It would also support our hypothesis that the Fox brothers were really the Lansky brothers because throughout their infamous career the Lanskys constantly had charges dropped against them or received favorable verdicts. Meyer Lansky has not been in prison for several decades.

Take a look at page 63 lines 24-25 (page 293): "Any thought of ever being close to Havana, Cuba" is a fragment rather than a sentence. When we tried to get the original stenographic notes and tapes of Ruby's testimony in order to find out if anything preceded this we found they were withheld from research.

In another part of his testimony Ruby points out that the Volk's Apartments, where he stayed, were only three blocks from the Hotel Nacional, where Lansky's brother Jake had been pit-boss. He says that one of the Fox brothers' first names was "Rivera"—Lansky owned the Rivera Hotel and Casino in Havana.[48] Ruby also says that the Fox brothers owned the Tropicana where McWillie was pitboss. When questioned by the FBI, McWillie said the Tropicana was Cuban-owned.[49] On the other hand, Prof. Scott reports that Norman Rothman owned it. Rothman was part of the Lansky-dominated National Crime Syndicate; he tried to stop the Castro steamroller in 1958 by smuggling a planeload of arms to anti-Castro forces in Cuba.

According to police and Federal sources, Rothman was high up in the Cuban crime syndicate and shared his rackets profits with Batista's brother-in-law. When the CIA and the Syndicate joined forces against Castro, the liaison picked for the project was reportedly Norman Rothman.[50] In the mid-1960's Rothman worked with Donald Browder, an associate of Mack Blaney Johnson (see page 157).

If Ruby had met with Lansky before going to Cuba, then Castro's police had good reason to suspect him of anti-Castro activities.

In yet another part of his testimony, reproduced on page 290, Ruby tells us some more about the Fox brothers. First, he calls them "the greatest that have been expelled from Cuba," then goes on to say that they are now living in Miami. The Lanskys took up residence in Miami after leaving Cuba. Then he says they know everything about McWillie (who is linked to Lansky by the FBI in the document reprinted on page 294) "and know the officials." He does not say which officials. Could he have been referring to Frank Sturgis who was the official of the Castro Government in charge of Games of Chance?*

The next part of Jack Ruby's testimony makes very little sense. According to Ruby, one of the Fox brothers came to Dallas to collect a gambling debt owed to the "Cotton Gin Company." Could one of the Lansky brothers have come to Dallas to collect a debt owed to the Syndicate?

After this matter was disposed of, "Mr. Fox's" lawyer, Dave McCord,† invited Ruby to join himself, Mr. Fox, Juanita McWillie and a lawyer named "Leon" for supper at a restaurant at Love Field. Independent researcher Craig Karpel, writing in the *Village Voice*, carefully studied Ruby's testimony and found out that of the ten or more officials present at Ruby's "hearing" before the Warren Commission, the only person Ruby refused to speak with was a Dallas attorney named Leon Jaworski. This led Karpel to believe that the lawyer named "Leon" might be Leon Jaworski. Ruby then asks if Leon was connected with the Fox brothers' lawyer, after which there is a blank followed by the fragment "and there was McClain." Justice Warren immediately knows who Ruby is referring to and tells him "Alfred was killed in a taxicab in New York." Has something been deleted from Ruby's testimony? It is also very strange that in an earlier part of Ruby's testimony we find out that Ruby and Warren both knew an attorney named Dave Lane, who was also killed in a taxicab accident.

We tried to find an obituary for an Alfred McClain who died in an auto accident in New York City, but were unsuccessful, although we did find an attorney named Chester McLain who died of a heart attack in 1953. McLain was a Special Advisor to Warren Commission member John J. McCloy.[51] Dr. Scott, on the other hand, was able to locate a New York attorney named Alfred McClain who disappeared mysteriously in 1960. He is currently investigating possible links between this man and Ruby.

---

* as Castro officially referred to gambling.

† Efforts to reach McCord and find out if he ever represented Lansky have been unsuccessful.

Until the tapes of Ruby's testimony are declassified and certain ambiguities cleared up, all we are left with is conjecture.

Did Ruby visit Cuba in 1959 on a mission for Lansky? Warren Commission counsel Leon Hubert wrote that there was credible evidence that Ruby had been there several times prior to 1959 when Lansky was an extremely powerful figure. Also, if Ruby's visit was purely for recreational purposes, why did he return to Cuba a week after his Labor Day visit for only a day? [52]

The information given by Elaine Mynier, McWillie's ex-girl-friend, is relevant here. Mynier said she had served as a courier between Ruby and McWillie during a May 1959 trip to Cuba, and that she memorized Ruby's message, then wrote it down after she went through Customs. [53]

Keep in mind that at the time Ruby visited Havana, Frank Sturgis was Minister of Games of Chance and was in charge of the casino where McWillie worked.

Canfield: Did you ever know a guy named McWillie?

Sturgis: Yeah, that name is very, very familiar. I forgot what he is or who he is but McWillie—yeah...I knew...Santo Trafficante...the Lansky brothers...Mike McLaney. I was in charge of all the gambling casinos for the Cuban Government. For a very short period of time.

Sturgis told the New York *Daily News* that when Castro took over the Syndicate was "very, very mad. Those casinos were worth $100 million a year to the American crime syndicate. Every important mob boss in the United States had points (percentages) in the Cuban casinos." Sturgis said that the Syndicate offered him $100,000 to kill Castro.

According to an early Commission memo McWillie was scheduled to testify in April 1964 but nothing ever came of this. Prio, whose name is mentioned in several Commission documents, was not even scheduled to testify before the Commission nor was he questioned by the FBI. In 1972 the former Cuban president led the anti-Castro demonstrations staged to coincide with the Democratic Convention in Miami Beach and was a strong supporter of Richard Nixon. [54]

In order to understand the significance of Ruby's trip to Cuba, one must have some insight into the character of the man he visited, Lewis J. McWillie, who Elaine Mynier described as a "big-time gambler who had always been in the big money and who was operating top gambling establishments here in the United States and Cuba...he always had a 'torpedo' living with him for protection." After all, when Ruby shot Oswald he said "...this McWillie flashed across me, because I have a great fondness for him."[55]

Lewis J. McWillie

McWillie was born May 4, 1908 in Kansas City, Missouri. At seventeen he was arrested for stealing a car in Memphis, Tennessee and was sentenced to two years in a reformatory. It did not do too much good as you can see by looking at the bottom of the document reprinted on page 293. In 1940, McWillie was employed in a gambling house in Mississippi and in 1942 he turned up in Dallas and began working at The Top Of The Hill. Elaine Mynier said that around this time McWillie was "...a well-known Dallas and Fort Worth gambler who paid off local police." In 1945 McWillie was arrested for violating the Gas Ration Act and in 1946 he killed a man who tried to hold him up. Up to this point McWillie's life is very similar to that of Eugene Hale Brading—both men had served time before they were 20, both were accused of black-marketeering during World War II and both were linked to gambling.

McWillie met Ruby around 1947 and aside from an occasional gambling arrest everything was going fine for him until Estes Kefauver began his famous investigations. The heat was on the Lansky mob and The Top Of The Hill had to close down. McWillie's Social Security records show "no earnings reported" for most of 1952-1958 but this does not necessarily mean hard times. Elaine Mynier told the FBI she "frequently saw Ruby and McWillie at the airport, going on their frequent trips" and said that McWillie was running the Four Deuces Gambling House in Fort Worth around this time. In 1958 McWillie moved to Cuba and began his career as pitboss of the Tropicana. Eva Grant stated that McWillie was involved in the famous "jeep deal." "Jack was in a jeep deal with McWillie—up to eight hundred jeeps." [56] After Castro came to power, McWillie became the manager of the Tropicana hotel—a fact which he denied—and Ruby describes him as ". . . a key man over the Tropicana down there. That was during our good times. Was in harmony with our enemy of our present time." [57]

In May 1960 McWillie quit his job at the Tropicana and started working at the Capri hotel casino. The Capri was a long-time Lansky property. The FBI admits McWillie's links to the kingpin of organized crime (see page 294). The trouble with this FBI report is that it fails to point out that almost all these people worked for Lansky. Santo Trafficante worked for Lansky in Cuba and Tampa hoping to become gambling czar of Havana. Dino Cellini worked for Lansky in Havana. As Frank Sturgis put it, "The gambling interests in Cuba did support Batista. The two main people who controlled the gambling interests in Cuba were Meyer Lansky and Santo Trafficante. They controlled (it). . . for the National Crime Syndicate." [58]

McWillie fled Cuba in January 1961. Ruby said he was "the last person to leave" and called him frequently around this time. Although McWillie was never imprisoned by Castro, his friend Harvey Harr, manager of the Lansky-owned National Casino, did a year in jail. He was arrested a day after McWillie left. [59] In the Kefauver hearings there is a reference to the Harr brothers being in partnership with Lansky associate Abner "Longie" Zwill-man. [60] McWillie was also a friend of Captain Morgan (see page 106).

As fate would have it, Jack Ruby's best friend, Lewis J. McWillie, got into a fight with a member of the Fair Play for Cuba Committee on the plane going to Miami. McWillie was leaving Cuba with very little—most of his assets had been confiscated by Castro and his temper was short. [61] In October 1961 the FBI made an inquiry to the Miami Crime Commission about McWillie's activities. They said they knew nothing (see page 294). By this time McWillie had gone to work at the

Cal-Neva Lounge, whose owner's income tax returns were a source of concern for the Kefauver investigation.* From the Cal-Neva McWillie went to the Riverside Casino in Las Vegas and ended up at the Thunderbird Casino which Lansky had purchased in 1948. †

In early 1963 McWillie and Ruby may have worked together on a Syndicate-CIA plot to kill Castro. Ruby hints at this during his testimony before the Warren Commission. According to Ruby, McWillie contacted him and asked him to purchase four Cobra pistols and mail them to his address in Las Vegas. Ruby contacted a gun dealer named Ray Brantley, who had previously had dealings with McWillie and asked him to sell him the fire-arms. But Ruby says Brantley would not sell him the pistols because "evidently he feels, maybe he feels it would be illegal to send guns out of the country." Why does Ruby say "country" when he previously testified that the guns were going to Las Vegas? Ruby also says, "That was the only relationship I had of any mention, outside of phone calls, to Mr. McWillie, or any person from Havana, Cuba." This sentence suggests Ruby was in touch by telephone with someone in Havana, Cuba, outside of McWillie.

McWillie told the FBI that the pistols arrived at the Post Office but he never picked them up.

This was going on around the time the CIA was encouraging gangsters to assassinate Castro. According to Jack Anderson, a CIA agent named Robert Maheu, who later managed Howard Hughes' Las Vegas gambling interests and who probably worked out of Mullen & Company in Washington, D.C., was assigned the task. Maheu hired Las Vegas gambler Johnny Rosselli, an ex-Capone lieutenant who had moved to the West Coast. Rosselli, with the help of two CIA agents and Syndicate money, paid for everything, including the expensive boats. Cover for the operation was provided by Cuban refugee groups.

---

* They were filled out by an Internal Revenue agent yet he owed six or seven hundred thousand dollars. [62]

† There was a big scandal in Nevada when Lansky's ownership of the Thunderbird was exposed in 1958. [63]

The initial plan had been to poison Castro with a substance that would make it look like he had died a natural death. The toxin was smuggled to a relative of Castro's chef. It almost worked! Castro got sick just before Bay of Pigs but recovered just in time. In early 1963 they used a more conventional approach—four assassination teams, equipped with walkie-talkies and high-powered rifles (sound familiar?) which were of Belgian manufacture so they could not be traced back to the CIA, were dispatched to Cuba. But even the men who make careers out of murder were no match for Castro and the protective, totalitarian society he had set up to prevent the CIA from fomenting and financing a counter-revolution. All four death squads met their fate at the hands of Cuba's militia.

Was Ruby supplying the pistols to the Las Vegas gambler McWillie so they could be passed on to Rosselli, another Las Vegas "gambler" who worked for Lansky, then used in a plot against Castro? If the Rosselli assassination squad was apprehended it would be very difficult to trace the pistols back to the CIA since Ruby had purchased them in an out of the way gunstore in Texas.

The Warren Commission exhibit reprinted on page 294 is an Army Intelligence report that was attached to a letter from the Secretary of Defense which certified that Oswald "was never an informant or agent of any Intelligence Agency under the jurisdiction of the Department of Defense." Notice how the sentence about Ruby and Oswald being "connected in some way" was followed by the line "there is a one million dollar reward for the assassination of Castro." The evidence we have compiled in this book tends to indicate that although it is unlikely Ruby and Oswald knew each other personally, the thread that connected them was the CIA/Syndicate plot against Castro.

Hank Messick reports that eventually the Justice Department under Robert Kennedy cracked down on the anti-Castro groups who were providing cover for the Syndicate's operations. According to Messick, "Several weapons caches were confiscated in the Everglades and the Florida Keys...the full story of organized crime's private war with Castro remains a mystery." [64] To the best of our knowledge, the only group whose cache of weapons was seized and who trained in the Everglades was Interpen/ IAB, led by Frank Sturgis—who knew all the Syndicate figures personally from his stint as Castro's aide in charge of gambling in Cuba.

Just before he died, Lyndon Jonhson told a reporter for *Atlantic Monthly* that he felt the Kennedy assassination was part of a conspiracy. Pointing to the fact that the United States "had been operating a damned Murder Incorporated in the Caribbean," Johnson speculated that Kennedy's death had been in retaliation for a thwarted attempt against Castro's life. [65]

Dr. Peter Scott has speculated that Hunt was probably the man who convinced the CIA to use the Syndicate against Castro. As the major proponent of killing Castro, Hunt had been linked to other attempts on the Cuban leader's life. Andrew St. George, an ex-Intelligence agent who had spent 1957-1959 with Castro, reported that Alexander Rorke (who probably knew Hunt and was a close friend of Sturgis) was plotting with Col. Johnny Abbes, Trujillo's Intelligence Chief, to kill Castro. Rorke piloted a speedboat to Cuba where his agents machine-gunned Castro's aides but missed Castro himself. A few months before Kennedy was gunned down, Rorke went down in a mysterious "plane crash" a few miles from Cuba. [66]

Sturgis had this to say about Rorke:

> He was a freelance photographer and reporter involved in many different Latin American, uh as a reporter, many Latin American intrigues. Alex participated in a number of operations that went into Cuba, also into Mexico. And if you remember there was a big search by the United States Coast Guard, both air and sea, a number of years ago, where he left Opalocka airfield, and he went, or at least was going to Nicaragua, and supposedly it is rumored that he was shot down near Cuba...I, with a number of other people I will get to at a later date, sat with Rorke where his plane was parked at Opalocka airfield which is close by here,the day he made his ill-fated trip. And I will get the names of everybody that knew about the trip and so forth, that the FBI investigated, I believe even the CIA investigated that... [67]

Robert Maheu, who was alleged to be in charge of the CIA's part of the effort to assassinate Castro, had worked under

Guy Bannister in the FBI's Chicago Field Office during World War II. [68] In the 1950's Maheu operated an investigative and "problem-solving agency" in Washington called Robert A. Maheu Associates and by 1955 he was an employee of Howard Hughes. Mr. Maheu handled political and governmental matters for the reclusive billionaire. One of his first major missions was attempting to squelch a story about a $205,000 loan from Hughes to President Nixon's brother, Donald.

In 1966, when Mr. Hughes moved secretly into the Desert Inn in Las Vegas, he took Maheu with him and swiftly made him his "chief Nevada executive" at $520,000 a year. Hughes had him collaborate with alleged Lansky-frontman Moe Dalitz in managing the casinos Hughes' tool company had purchased in Las Vegas. Nixon's friend Richard Danner was also hired by Hughes and kept on after Maheu was fired in December 1970. [69]

While trying to kill Castro Maheu probably used the same cover Hunt used when he was directing the White House Secret Police—Mullen & Company, a firm with a very unique background. At the time Maheu was allegedly there, the Washington-based "public relations" firm with offices across the street from the White House was headed by Robert Mullen, a one-time press aide to President Eisenhower who ran the Marshall Plan's propaganda arm. Mullen had known Howard Hunt, who worked for Gen. Marshall's ECA, and liked him. [70] One of Mullen's biggest accounts was General Foods, whose Washington representative, Douglas Caddy, operated out of the Mullen office. Caddy who would later become Hunt's lawyer, was a Goldwaterite who helped form Young Americans for Freedom, along with William F. Buckley, Jr. and Robert E. Bennett. Caddy was also active in Youth for Nixon and was a member of Lawyers Committee to Re-elect the President.

Hunt states that Mullen & Company always had close ties with the CIA and that its office in Europe was paid for by the Agency.* For all practical purposes, Mullen worked like an arm of the CIA. Thanks to Watergate, we know that after he "retired" from the CIA on April 30, 1970, Hunt went to work for

---

* Philip Agee reports that Mullen & Company had offices in Mexico City in 1963.

Mullen the next day. This would be the second time Hunt retired from what was essentially the same organization: He was listed as a retired government official when he planned Castro's assassination in Spain.[71]

By the time Hunt arrived at Mullen & Company, it had been purchased by former Nixon Administrator, Robert E. Bennett, whose father was an ultra-conservative Republican Senator from Utah. Bennett brought the Howard Hughes account with him and helped Nixon set up dummy groups to raise campaign funds. Colson believes Hunt was working for the CIA at the same time he was working for Mullen and the White House. Judging from Mullen's close ties with the Agency in the past, Colson is probably right.

There is strong evidence that plans for Castro's assassination had been made in the offices of Mullen & Company. Loran Hall's Committee to Free Cuba may have been a Mullen & Company front. Mullen may have paid for a rifle, reportedly identical to the one used by Lee Harvey Oswald.

None of this came out during Jack Ruby's "trial." When the District Attorney asked Brantley "if the defendant Jack Ruby had you ship a Centennial Model S&W .38 Special to a man in Las Vegas?" and Brantley said he had, Ruby's attorney objected. "Well, that is immaterial to the case," he said, "we ask that it be stricken." The judge agreed.

But it did come out in one of Johnny Rosselli's trials. In 1969 government lawyers argued against deporting Rosselli on the grounds that he aided national security. Rosselli and Maheu were quizzed by the Senate Watergate Committee about their activities. Both refused to disclose their roles in the anti-Castro plot and the Committee did not press the issue.*

---

* On March 9, 1975 two former key aides to the late Robert F. Kennedy, Adam Walinsky and Peter B. Edelman, said that the late Attorney General told them in 1967 that agents of the CIA had "made a contract with the Mafia to hit Castro" and that he played an active role in stopping the assassination attempt. Kennedy had learned of the CIA-Mafia link while working for the McClellan Committee in the late 1950's. "He was out in Las Vegas and a mobster told him, 'You can't touch me, I've got immunity,' " Walinsky recalled. When Kennedy asked who granted him this "immunity" the mobster said "CIA." Kennedy checked it out and found that "They had made a deal with this guy."

According to Eva Grant, Ruby "made many calls to
McWillie...at least ten calls in these three months" (Sept.-Nov.
1963) and McWillie was questioned a number of times by the
FBI. He told them that although Ruby "might be acquainted
with some figures in gambling and other illegal activities, Ruby
had no underworld connections" and his association with him
was "strictly social, without any intertwined business or gambling
interests." [72] McWillie said he never picked up the pistols and
that "Ruby had no contact with anyone interested in the sale of
weapons or jeeps under any circumstances." He also said there
was "no understanding between the gambling interests and
Castro's supporters" and there was only a lot of "speculation as
to the fate of the gambling interests should a change in government come about..." He "knew of no arrangements or liaison
between the gambling interests and Castro."*

McWillie also characterized Ruby "...as being completely
apolitical"; the only connection with politics Ruby had was with
Rep. Bruce Alger (see page 86), whose "wife was a patron of
Ruby's club." McWillie admitted that "Ruby probably knew
most of the members of the Dallas Police Force" because he
"had a genuine liking for law enforcement officers" [73] and said
he never called Ruby from a pay phone, but had called him on
his home phone in November, in regard to a "labor matter."

There is little doubt that McWillie and Ruby were big-time
gangsters working for Meyer Lansky. McWillie is currently employed by Mike McLaney at his casino in Haiti. Ruby may have
been put in charge of paying off the police in Dallas after Jones
was arrested. Thanks to Ruby, The Top Of The Hill and other

The New York **Times** reported on March 16, 1975 that after the Rockefeller
Commission to Investigate CIA Domestic Operations obtained testimony about CIA
involvement in the John F. Kennedy killing from Dick Gregory and others it was ready to
go on to the "more credible" questions of CIA plots to kill foreign leaders. Will the
Commission question Lewis J. McWillie? Was he also given immunity by the CIA? Will
the Commission look into the charges made in this book that Jack Ruby was involved in
a plot to kill Castro? There are many questions to be asked, and many that the
Commission could provide answers for if it really tried.

* Frank Sturgis was the liaison between the gambling interests and Castro but never
mentions this job throughout his numerous interviews with the FBI—at least not in the
ones available to researchers.

Syndicate establishments operating in and around Dallas stayed open.

Did the CIA assign the Syndicate the task of "rubbing out" Oswald? Lansky had worked with the OSS on Operation Underworld and also had contact with the CIA in regard to joint ventures to assassinate Castro (Rosselli worked for Lansky). Both groups had a tremendous interest in overthrowing Castro—an operation which, to some, had become synonymous with killing Kennedy—and both the CIA and the Syndicate were prone to violence.

One "legitimate" way for Oswald to die would be in the course of resisting arrest; and the Syndicate made it a practice to keep tabs on all the corrupt cops in Dallas. Ruby worked closely with corrupt, rightwing cops like James Woodard (see page 296) and was generally a corrupting influence with his sleazy nightclubs which catered to policemen. So, could he have hired Tippit to shoot an unarmed Oswald after making it seem like he was resisting arrest—then no questions would be asked? Could Oswald have caught on that he was a patsy very early in the game? When Baker stuck that gun in his ribs and he found out that the Texas School Book Depository was under suspicion, the thought could have hit Oswald that with his background, he would be a prime suspect. So he immediately went home and got his gun; when Tippit stopped him he shot Tippit before Tippit could shoot him. If this is true, then Ruby's man had botched the job so the burden of disposing of Oswald fell on him. Ruby told his psychiatrist, Dr. Werner Teuter, that he "had been part of a plot to kill Kennedy" and he was "framed to kill Oswald." Ruby insisted he went to the Dallas Police Headquarters because of "a phone call from Fort Worth" and told Teuter to read Buchanan's book which states that Ruby was assigned to kill Oswald.

Buchanan may have been privy to something. A CIA document declassified in July 1973 reveals that he was the subject of intensive investigation by the CIA and that Raymond Rocca, who resigned during the CIA Domestic Operations scandal, was in charge of his case. This document is reprinted in full on page 295. Notice how they stress the point that his articles allege that

Tippit was part of a rightwing plot and how they are worried about his upcoming book being published in the United States. Were any steps taken to discourage these publishers from printing the book? According to the document, Houghton-Mifflin was interested in Buchanan's book, but were in the process of publishing "two 'official' books on President Kennedy with United States Government backing." When we called the company in 1975, we were told that they had never published anything about the Kennedy assassination. Were other pro-Warren Report books given "United States backing"? We also called Buchanan's alleged literary agent—they said they had never handled him. Is this document indicative of the accuracy of CIA documents? Notice how item six is still classified—it obviously contains Buchanan's biography and if our hunch is correct, it makes derogatory accusations. There was probably a concerted effort on the part of the CIA to discredit Buchanan and his work. Hunt's friend, William F. Buckley Jr., wrote two columns attacking Buchanan's book—in one of them he calls the author a "profiteer."

Since a higher-up in the Syndicate ended up with the job of killing Oswald it should have been easy for the FBI to connect the assassination with organized crime. But they just looked the other way. For example Nancy Perrin had told the FBI that a man named Ed Brunner had invited her husband to attend the anti-Castro arms smuggling meetings. On November 24, 1963 Ruby named Fred Brunner as his attorney. The FBI made no effort to locate Mr. Brunner or make any feasible connections.

McWillie's telephone toll records revealed he called a man named Warren Barlow.[74] When Weberman ran a check on the number, he found it was not Barlow's; instead, it belonged to the Hidden Valley Country Club, where Barlow worked as a cook until late 1963. The FBI never bothered to inquire who constituted the membership of this club; nor did they investigate the nature of the telegram Earl Ruby (Jack's brother) sent to Havana in April 1962, despite the fact that when the IRS questioned him about it "he became noticeably agitated and unable to give an explanation of the nature of the telegram."[75] The FBI also failed to look into the coincidence that in early November Earl placed a call (apparently on his brother's behalf) from Detroit to the Triangle Manufacturing Company in Oshkosh, Wisconsin and Lee Harvey Oswald received a call from Oshkosh, Wisconsin in mid-November 1963. [76]

When the FBI found that Ruby had the telephone number of a Mexican Government official in his address book they spent most of their investigation trying to locate a man with the official's code name. They questioned the official but never investigated him. [77] Nor did they investigate a certain member of the Permanent Delegation of South Africa who Ruby had called. They also failed to put the fact that Ruby had the telephone number of a member of the Dallas John Birch Society named Thomas Hill in his notebook together with the fact that Tippit worked for a "Bircher on weekends." [78] Ruby only worked about five hours a day in his club yet he owed forty-four thousand dollars in back taxes. [79] His gangsterism stuck out like a sore thumb. Nevertheless the FBI and the Warren Commission failed to check out the leads.

Ruby, who was strongly anti-Nazi, began to worry about the assassination being blamed on the Jews and spent the weekend after the assassination trying to track down the origin of the black-bordered "Welcome Mr. Kennedy" advertisement in the Dallas *Morning News* that was signed by Bernard Weissman. By the spring of 1964 Ruby must have realized that very few Americans believed Oswald had acted alone and that he was considered Oswald's most likely co-conspirator. Once again, a disturbed Ruby believed, the Jews might be blamed. He began to rant and rave to everyone he could about how "they" were "putting the Jews in kill machines" and slaughtering them on the streets. He also tried to explain to them how he was responsible for this "terrible tragedy" and how there "is only one kind of people that would do such a thing, that would be the Nazis." [80]

Ruby attempted suicide several times and told Dr. Teuter— "They're trying to make another Dreyfus out of me." When the Warren Report came out in September 1964, Ruby believed it was of little value in dispelling the rumors that he was part of a plot to kill John Kennedy. Just before he died of lung cancer in

1966, Ruby had engaged William Kunstler as his attorney and may have been planning to talk. [81]

Ruby lost everything he owned and suffered immeasurably for his part in the plot. Marina Oswald, on the other hand, became rich. Immediately after the assassination the Dallas *Morning News* gave her sixty-eight thousand dollars for her story [82] and a friend of Richard Sprague who worked for *Life* paid her five thousand dollars for the Oswald-with-rifle-photos. By October 1, 1964 Marina was worth about a fifth of a million dollars. She had received twenty-five thousand dollars for the rights to the photographs she had in her possession and a hundred thousand for the rights to tell her story in a book. Marina had been approached by Issac Don Levine (see page 33) about doing a book. [83] Levine offered her twenty-five thousand dollars for her story and eventually testified before the Warren Commission about his meeting with her. [84] Some of Levine's books were published by David McKay Co., Inc., a subsidiary* of which, Hunt admits, worked closely with the CIA. [85] This book, however, was supposed to be published by Meredith Press. † Levine also contacted Ruth Paine. Marina was approached by none other than Priscilla Johnson in regard to doing a book. [86] Somehow, in spite of all these efforts, no book by or about Marina Oswald was ever published.

Aside from this money, the "assassin's widow" received seventy-thousand dollars in contributions from unnamed sources. Was this laundered hush money? The channels for this kind of thing had already been established—the Cuban Revolutionary Front had been funded "through a series of foreign banks"; there is no telling how much Marina actually received. Warren Commission counsel, Norman Redlich, wrote a memo that stated, "the amounts that she has actually received are considerably more than the figures which have been made public." [87] There are several documents about Marina's wealth and relations with her attorneys that are still classified. [88]

A prominent member of the Dallas White Russian community whose FBI file was heavily censored, became Marina's advisor,

---

* Fodor Travel Guides, Inc. McKay, however, only recently acquired this company.
† Levine did not say whether or not Marina Oswald was ever paid the $25,000.

and the man who allegedly "discovered" Oswald, became her official interpreter.[89] Marina eventually married a Dallas electronics worker and now lives on a fifteen-acre estate.

CHAPTER TEN

The Warren Commission

"The resources that have been put *against* the whole investigation to date are really incredible...it's truly a larger investigation than was conducted *against*, uh, the after inquiry of the JFK assassination."

John Dean to Richard Nixon
House Version of White House Tapes
(Italics ours.)

The Warren Commission report is a lie. The documents in the National Archives that it is based on, do not back up its conclusions. The report is the single greatest cover-up in American history.

First of all, the vast majority of Warren Commission members and special counsels had ties to the people and organizations who could be implicated in the coup. Secondly, approximately sixty-five per cent of the counsels ended up being closely associated with Richard Milhous Nixon.

Earl Warren, the titular head of the Warren Commission was a "liberal" Republican, and former Governor of California who had been chosen as the Republican Party's Vice-Presidential standard bearer in 1948. Warren shared the ticket with the former District Attorney Thomas Dewey, who would refuse to appear before the Kefauver Committee to discuss the pardon he had granted Lansky's partner, Lucky Luciano. Eventually Dewey would become a stockholder in the Mary Carter Paint Company, which many regard as a Lansky front.[1] President Eisenhower appointed Warren to the Supreme Court in 1953 and he began handing down decisions the Conservatives did not like. In fact, the only actions Warren ever did that drew some praise from the Conservatives were to issue the Warren Report[2] and announce his retirement. He seems to be easily manipulated by Nixon and his friends. In the White House tapes we find that they first considered setting up another "Warren Commission," complete with Earl, to "investigate" Watergate: Haldeman says, "But if you would want Earl Warren, he'll do it..."[3] Another Nixon-Warren link surfaced after Warren died and his papers were turned over to the California State Archives. All of the correspondence between Warren and then U.S. Senator Richard Nixon had been stolen.

Chief Justice Warren told the staff of his Commission that when the position had first been offered to him he declined it, on the principle that Supreme Court justices should not take on this kind of role. His associate justices concurred with this decision. At this point, however, President Johnson called him. The President stated that rumors of the most exaggerated kind were circulating in the country and overseas. Some rumors went as far as attributing Kennedy's assassination to a faction within the government wishing to see the Presidency assumed by Lyndon Johnson. Others, if not quenched, could conceivably lead the country into a war which could cost forty million lives. No one could refuse to do something which might help to prevent such a possibility. The President convinced Warren that this was an occasion on which actual conditions had to override general principles.[4] Warren's mixed feelings may have resulted in a moral compromise: The Commission would quell the destructive rumors, but would ferret out the truth and classify it for many years, letting it out a little at a time. Could this be why Warren told the American people that the entire truth about the Kennedy assassination would not be known for a hundred years?

* * * * *

President Gerald Ford was on the Warren Commission although it seems like he tries to hide the fact. He failed to include it in his biography for the *Congressional Directory*; it is also not mentioned in *The Biographical Directory of the American Congress, The International Who's Who,* and *Who's Who In America.* When Nixon appointed Ford as Vice-President, very few news sources mentioned it.

Nixon asked Johnson to appoint Ford, and it was no accident that Ford's chief aide, John R. Stiles, had been field director of Nixon's first Presidential campaign. Ford had been mentioned as a possible Vice-Presidential running mate for Nixon in 1960, was chairman of the House Republican Caucus, and was a leading member of the CIA oversight committee. [5]

Congressman Ford heard more witnesses and asked more questions than anyone else on the Commission. He also made more money; Ford received a ten-thousand dollar advance for a book on the assassination called *Portrait of THE Assassin.* The reason "the" is in capitals is because it has never been legally established that Oswald was the assassin. The Warren Commission was not a court of law and under the Constitution had no right to rule on anyone's guilt or innocence. Ford also used the transcript from an Executive Session of the Warren Commission that had not as yet been declassified and was the FBI's prime suspect in the leaking of Oswald's diary to the press. [6] Ford stood behind the findings of the Commission with one qualification: "This is not to say that some significant piece of evidence might not turn up tomorrow or next year..." *

America's first unelected Vice-President, Nelson Rockefeller, was not on the Warren Commission himself. But two people very

---

* A day after the Warren Report was released, the Senate passed the Twenty-fifth Amendment which allows the President to appoint another Vice-President if anything happens to the duly elected one. It is ironic that this law led to a Commission member becoming President.

close to him were. Commissioner John J. McCloy was almost an honorary member of the Rockefeller family. The law firm he was associated with had represented Standard Oil, a Rockefeller property, in the 1920's and 1930's. Ironically, Standard Oil "bought out fifty-one per cent of the Nobel family's giant oil fields," which were partially owned by DeMohrenschildt's father.[7] The former owners of these fields sued Standard Oil. Part of the giant conglomerate believed indemnities should be paid. Did McCloy arrange for the payment of reparations to the DeMohrenschildts? In a brief telephone conversation, McCloy denied having any dealings with Nobel.

McCloy engineered the merger of the Chase and Manhattan banks into the Chase Manhattan, which now provides David Rockefeller with a strong financial base. McCloy later became Chairman of the Board of the Chase Manhattan, a director of the Rockefeller Foundation, and a board member of United Fruit (see page 49). He had a strong background in intelligence as assistant to the Secretary of War during World War II, High Commissioner to Germany, and was appointed by Dulles as a disarmament negotiator under Eisenhower. Hunt says he was an important part of the power base of the Office of Policy Coordination, the predecessor to the CIA.[8]

Commission counsel William T. Coleman was Rockefeller's number two man who worked for J. Richardson Dilworth, the law firm that handled Rockefeller's assets (see page 49). After Rockefeller was appointed Vice-President, Coleman became Secretary of Transportation.

* * * * *

Even though Kennedy had virtually fired Allen Dulles as Director of the CIA, Johnson nevertheless appointed him to the Warren Commission. Allen Dulles was *the CIA*. He had shaped it into an invisible government during his eight years as head of the Agency, working closely with Howard Hunt. Before he retired in 1961 he appointed Howard Hunt to his staff.[9] Dulles had also worked with Nixon on the National Security Council and was president of the Rockefeller-dominated Council on Foreign

Relations. Dulles was more interested in stopping "wild stories circulating abroad" than in finding out the truth about the Kennedy assassination. In a recently declassified transcript of an executive session of the Warren Commission, Dulles admits that he would lie to his associates regarding Lee Harvey Oswald and the CIA. "I would tell the President of the United States anything...I wouldn't necessarily tell anyone else..." He also admitted that his agents *would* lie about whether or not Oswald worked for the CIA. This is perhaps why CIA Director McCone's final statement about Oswald and the CIA was not as strong as it could have been: "I have determined to my satisfaction he had no such connections."

* * * * *

John Sherman Cooper, a Republican from Kentucky, was educated at Harvard and Yale and served in the diplomatic corps. He joined forces with Richard Russell and threatened to write a minority report if the Commission did not stress the "informational gap" regarding Oswald's activities in Mexico City.[10] After the Warren Report was issued Cooper never said another word about this and was appointed Ambassador to India by Nixon.

Russell, the Democratic Congressman from Georgia, had experience mediating disputes between the Executive and the Military. He had investigated the MacArthur-Truman tussle, but was reluctant to serve on the Warren Commission. As the Chairman of the House Armed Services Committee, Russell did not go too far in his dissent, but did say that he disagreed with the single-bullet theory and the parts of the report that dealt with outside influences and Lee Harvey Oswald. Russell may have also believed that there was a connection between Ruby and Oswald. In January 1970 he publicly expressed his doubts about the validity of the Commission's findings on a WAB-TV taped interview in Atlanta. A short time later he died of "natural causes."[11]

Hale Boggs also had second thoughts about the findings of the Warren Commission. In 1971 he gave a speech in Congress about how the FBI used Gestapo tactics. During the Warren Commission investigation, Boggs was shown files on the private lives of Commission critics like Mark Lane (the FBI had a photo of Lane in bed with two women) and suspected that they were spying on *him*. Boggs was convinced that his phone was tapped—he was probably right. About a year later Boggs was killed in a mysterious plane crash in Alaska.[12] Soon, the airline he had flown with—the Alaska Inter-Air—was the recipient of extensive government contracts in Europe and Africa. Laura Bergt, the wife of the airline's president, was appointed to the National Commission on Indian Affairs and some time later she went seal hunting with William F. Buckley, a close friend of Howard Hunt's.

* * * * *

J. Lee Rankin, the Solicitor-General of the Eisenhower Administration, was the General Counsel for the Commission. When Nixon needed a Special Prosecutor for the Watergate case he chose Archibald Cox, former Solicitor-General of the Kennedy Administration, and when Rockefeller put together his "Blue Ribbon" CIA panel he appointed Erwin Griswald, former Solicitor-General of the Nixon Administration.

The assistant counsels were allegedly chosen on the basis of their law school grades. However, other intervening factors may have affected the choices. Assistant Counsel W. David Slawson's father was a good friend of Gerald Ford. Before studying law Slawson worked as "...a mathematical physicist for the Chemical Corps at Dugway proving grounds, in Utah, a poison gas testing center."[13] Slawson did his job well and in the 1970's was appointed General Counsel to the Price Commission by Richard Nixon.[14]

Arlen Spector was more than just an average enlisted man. During a stint with the Air Force, he had been a special agent for the Office of Special Investigations. He came back to his hometown, Philadelphia, and was appointed Assistant District Attorney. Spector was able to obtain the convictions of six Teamster officials after a ten-week trial and may have been put on the Warren Commission to relieve the pressure on the Teamsters. In the 1970's Spector became chairman of Pennsylvania Committee to Re-elect the President and was asked by Nixon to help out in the Watergate defense.[15]

David Belin, who supported Spector's single-bullet theory, was a Republican attorney from Iowa in charge of investigating the death of Officer Tippit. In 1968 Belin was the head of Lawyers for Nixon-Agnew, and in 1975 he was appointed Chief Investigator of Rockefeller's Blue Ribbon CIA panel. Dick Gregory gave Belin copies of the tramp photographs. He was the first man connected with the Warren Commission to publicly acknowledge the existence of the photos. Lt. Wayne Posey of the Dallas Police Department's Intelligence Division makes the claim: "These pictures were made available to the Warren Commission and they attached no significance to them." This is *an outright lie*; we read every document in the National Archives and found absolutely NO mention of the photographs.[16]

A.C. Albert Jenner was hired directly by Warren to investigate the conspiracy angle. He traced Oswald's movements and was in charge of interviewing the Dallas White Russian community. During the Watergate affair Albert became Nixon's Minority Counsel on the Judiciary Committee. We have already dealt with William Coleman and there is not much to be said about Assistant Counsel Francis W.H. Adams, a Democrat politician and former New York Police Commissioner, except that he hardly did anything. Assistant Counsel Joe Ball, a prominent West Coast attorney, represented Ehrlichman on the Ellsberg case and A.C Melvin Aron Eisenberg was appointed to the Price Commission by Nixon.[17]

Carlos Bringuier went berserk when Norman Redlich, a member of the Emergency Civil Liberties Union (which had ties with the American Communist Party), was chosen as an assistant counsel. But Bringuier had nothing to fear because Redlich did not object to the cover-up. He later became New York City's Corporation Counsel and was a member of the City's Board of Education.

One of the more honest men on the Commission was Leon D. Hubert Jr., a former New Orleans District Attorney who was once Jim Garrison's chief. Hubert had been a U.S. Assistant Attorney and had served on the Judge Advocate's staff in the Air Force. Yet he and Burt Griffen wrote a memorandum to the Commission which virtually stated that Jack Ruby was heavily involved in "Cuban affairs." There is no record of Hubert's being hired by the Nixon Administration.

Wesley Leibler, who investigated Oswald's activity in New Orleans and overlooked the leaflets with 544 Camp Street stamped on them was appointed to the Federal Trade Commission by Nixon[18] and Burt W. Griffen has been linked to the National Office of Economic Opportunity.[19] Sam Stern's activities after he left the Commission are a mystery, as are those of Howard P. Willens, liaison for the Department of Justice and the Commission. Willens' chief in the Justice Department, Herbert Miller, became Nixon's attorney.

Miller had another subordinate on the Commission. He was staff member Stuart R. Pollak who was his staff assistant.[20] He also sent two secretaries to work for the Commission's General Counsel, J. Lee Rankin.[21] On November 27, 1963 Miller sent a "Tentative Outline of Report Summarizing Investigation of the Assassination of the President" to the newly formed investigative body.[22] J. Edgar Hoover referred many questions about the FBI's part in the investigation to him.[23] As John Ehrlichman says in the White House version of the tapes: "There's a lawyer here in town by the name of Herbert Miller. You may know him. He was head of the Criminal Division at the Justice Department...He was there through '61 to '67, Kennedy and Johnson, but he's a Republican."

The Warren Commission staff was composed of people on loan from other branches of the Federal Government. Many of them came from the Department of Justice and the two men who had literary, as well as military, experience, were the logical candidates to write the actual report: Alfred Goldberg and Arthur K. Marmor were both historians with the United States Air Force. Goldberg wrote a large part of the Report. He was a member of the Center for Strategic Studies at Georgetown University. The Director of this CIA think-tank was Arleigh Burke, a member of the Free Cuba Committee.[24] Other notables at the Georgetown center included William Baroody, who later became an assistant to President Nixon; George Smathers (see page 96) and Gerald Ford. [25]

Leon Jaworski was also in close contact with the Warren Commission, and is mentioned numerous times in its literature. He first comes into the picture on November 23, 1963, when he called H. Louis Nichols, the head of the Dallas Bar Association after Nichols paid a visit to the imprisoned Oswald. Jaworski told Nichols that he represented the American Trial Lawyers Association. He neglected to mention that he was also Special Assistant to the Attorney General, [26] a member of the Board of Directors of the M.D. Anderson Foundation, a notorious CIA front. [27] After their conversation Nichols wrote a long letter describing the visit. Was someone worried about Oswald revealing his Agency connections?

When Texas Attorney General Waggoner Carr needed personnel for his "Texas Court of Inquiry" into the Kennedy assassination, he chose Jaworski as a Special Counsel, along with Robert Gerald Storey, another attorney with CIA connections. Storey had worked for the State Department as "Representative in the Far East and Middle East" and was on the Board of Directors of the International Educational Exchange, a part of the CIA's Institute of International Education. [28]

If they ever made a movie about Oswald's "attorney" on the Warren Commission, Walter E. Craig, they would have to call it *The Invisible Man*. He was hardly seen nor heard. Craig was appointed after he conferred with J. Lee Rankin and Lewis F. Powell (former Chairman of the American Bar Association), even though his background was almost exclusively in corporate law. [29] Lewis F. Powell was eventually appointed to the Supreme Court by Nixon.

* * * * *

Senator Richard Russell called the Report a "sorrily incompetent document." The Cuban News Service was quoted as saying, "The murder of the century has created the lie of the century." President Johnson ordered Douglas Dillon, Nicholas

Katzenbach, John McCone and George McBundy to study the Report for him. Dillon turned up as a member of the Rockefeller Blue Ribbon CIA Panel in 1975 and John McCone now works for ITT. George McBundy was Kennedy's personal representative to the Special Intelligence Coordinating group 5412.[30] As you may have already guessed these distinguished gentlemen found nothing irregular about the Report and recommended ways for Johnson to implement its findings. Everything looked fine for the assassins and conspirators until Jim Garrison, the District Attorney in New Orleans, resurrected the case. Garrison had been inspired by the work of Harold Weisberg, who carefully studied the Commission documents relating to Oswald's activities in New Orleans. Most of the people he initially went after were connected with the Cuban Revolutionary Front and/or Council (Arcacha, Smith, Novel, etc.) On February 21, 1967 Garrison announced to the media that arrests were imminent and a source in his office told a New York *Times* reporter that the "assassination grew out of a plot by anti-communist forces to kill Premier Fidel Castro of Cuba."[31] Four days later, Garrison's top suspect, William Ferrie (see page 43) was dead.

Several witnesses who may have contributed valuable information to the Watergate hearings also died before they got a chance to testify—Lou Russell, a former House Un-American Activities Committee investigator who had worked on the Hiss case[32] was allegedly the middleman between McCord and CTIA. (see page 2) Russell died during the hearings.[33] CIA agent Lee Pennington helped James McCord burn or remove his files shortly after the covert entry team was apprehended. Pennington died a few months before his name was revealed in the course of the Baker investigation.[34]

Garrison's critics included Carlos Bringuier, who said he used old documents that the FBI had already rejected as being unsound, and Gerald Ford, who thought Garrison should turn over whatever evidence he had to President Johnson. When Garrison refused, Ford said he was "...amazed that public officials would refuse to cooperate with Federal authorities."[35]

By mid-1967 the Invisible Government began a concerted effort to sabotage the Garrison investigation. Ex-CIA agent Victor Marchetti has stated that Richard Helms wanted to make sure Clay Shaw, (see page 39) was getting all the Agency support he needed; for all we know this may have included feeding Garrison false leads so he would indict an innocent party...which is exactly what Garrison did.

On December 21, 1967 Garrison filed an "Information" (tantamount to a warrant of arrest) in New Orleans accusing Eugene Edgar Bradley of conspiring to murder Kennedy. Bradley had been fingered by Loran Hall, along with Minuteman Dennis Mower and American Nazi Party member Carol Aydelotte.

Garrison was nobody's fool, but he overlooked the facts that Hall had furnished misinformation to the Warren Commission in the past and that Aydelotte and Mower were feuding with Bradley. [36]

Former Dallas policeman Roger Craig then told Garrison that Bradley was the fake Secret Service agent he encountered on November 22, 1963. Craig was either working for the Government or was just plain crazy: He was the only policeman who heard Lee Harvey Oswald confess to Fritz by saying "Now everyone will know who I am!" He cast doubt on Rowland's story of two assassins (see page 64) by reporting Rowland had said the older man was white; [37] and he also turned back people as they headed for the railroad tracks.[†][38] Finally Richard Sprague was able to egg Garrison on by convincing him that Bradley was the tallest tramp. [39] Philadelphia attorney Vincent Salandria, who was very close to the Garrison investigation told us—"Sprague, he's a clever one and he's one of them. Big Jim Garrison made a terrible error based on Sprague regarding Bradley...he's poison...he was the first to bring out the Bradley thing..." [40]

When Bradley heard he had been indicted he said, "I know I had nothing to do with it and I know nothing about it. Either someone is feeding (Garrison) wrong information and he's doing it sincerely and honestly or else he's trying to harm someone I'm associated with."[*] He also told the media that he had been approached by police officers looking for a man with a similar

---

* Bradley was the West Coast representative of Carl McIntyre's nonviolent Christian anti-communist group.

† Craig committed suicide in May 1975.

name. Was this man Eugene Hale Brading? (see page 61) California Attorney General Evelle Younger ordered Bradley's arrest; he was released on his own recognizance so he could prepare his defense.[41]

After the Bradley indictment, the controversy about the Garrison investigation began to grow. Garrison stuck to his guns and set up a meeting with his star witness against Bradley, Loran Hall, who told him that the Christian anti-communist was at a meeting where the assassination was discussed and was definitely with the CIA.[42] After the meeting Garrison gave Hall a clean bill of health: "It is apparent that Hall was in no way personally connected with the events culminating in the assassination...other individuals and agencies caused Mr. Hall's name to be in the exhibits of the Warren Commission." Garrison fell for Hall's story completely. In a few months many of the same people who convinced him the tall tramp was Bradley had him believing that the Oldman-tramp was a man named Fred Lee Chrisman, a rightwinger from Tacoma, Washington. (see page 297 for pictures of Chrisman and Bradley.)

Governor Ronald Reagan eventually refused to extradite Bradley but Chrisman came to New Orleans voluntarily in order to make a fool out of Garrison.[43] In 1970 Garrison dropped his complaint against Bradley; Sprague decided it could not be Bradley because he was shorter than the six-foot, four-inch tramp.

Garrison had initially indicted a whole nest of Howard Hunt's friends in New Orleans. Some of the District Attorney's statements were truly prophetic; he once said that "Fascism will come to America in the name of national security." Nixon used "national security" as an excuse for his crimes throughout the Watergate affair.

In July 1971 Garrison was indicted by the Justice Department for allegedly taking bribes from pinball machine operators. The government's star witness eventually confessed that he had been promised a job by the Justice Department in return for his testimony. F. Lee Bailey successfully defended Garrison but the smear had done its job and he was defeated in his bid for reelection. In 1972 Garrison was charged with income tax evasion.[44]

Rockefeller's Panel

Nelson Rockefeller's "Blue Ribbon" CIA panel was supposed to look into the Agency's domestic activities but almost everyone on the panel was closely connected with the intelligence community and previous cover-ups of CIA domestic operations. David Belin was on the Warren Commission; Douglas Dillon reviewed CIA activities as Undersecretary of State, was Chairman of the Rockefeller Foundation and was also on Johnson's special committee to study the Warren Report (see page 190). He was head of the Treasury Department at the time of the assassination and was called on to testify by the Warren Commission. Some of Dillon's men helped search for the tramps.

Warren Commission member Lyman Lemnitzer was Chairman of the Joint Chiefs of Staff from 1960 until 1963 when Kennedy made him Supreme Commander in Europe. A few days before Kennedy was sworn into office, Lemnitzer expressed admiration for the dictator of Paraguay.[45] He was the man who first introduced the Bay of Pigs plan to the Kennedy Administration. Under Eisenhower, the plans for the attack had been developed by "...CIA and the Pentagon through the Joint Chiefs of Staff."[46]

The Chiefs of Staff had sent a representative to the training base in Guatemala and a company of Green Berets to help out. The first landing was originally targeted for Trinidad, a small port city in Cuba, but Kennedy did not want the civilian population to get caught in the middle of the fighting, so the landing was changed to the Bay of Pigs. The Joint Chiefs were angry and gave the invasion less than a fifty-fifty chance of succeeding. Lemnitzer, who would later advise Kennedy to resume nuclear testing and use nuclear weapons in Southeast Asia[47] must have been especially incensed about the failure of the invasion, and may be the member of Rockefeller's panel appointed because he had a vested interest in making sure nothing was revealed about the CIA's domestic assassination program.

Not very much is known about Edgar F. Shannon Jr. but everyone knows the kind of pro-Nixon politics Ronald Reagan has come to epitomize. John T. Conner is Chairman of Allied Chemical, a multi-national corporation, and a director of David Rockefeller's Chase Manhattan Bank.[48] When Blue Ribbon Commissioner Erwin Griswald was Solicitor-General, he "argued in the Supreme Court that the Army's domestic surveillance of civilians from 1967 to 1970 violated neither the Constitution nor Federal law."[49] Rounding out the Rockefeller CIA Whitewash Commission is Joseph Lane Kirkland, the number two man in the AFL-CIO Labor Union, and a top man in AFLID (American Institute for Free Labor Development), a CIA front group led by DeMohrenschildt's friend's son, J. Peter Grace (see page 30). Most of the funding for AFLID comes from DeMohrenschildt's old employer, the Agency for International Development (AID). In 1963 AFLID helped overthrow the government of Cheddi Jagan of British Guiana by means of a Chile-style general strike. Jagan wrote a letter to the New York *Times* blaming AFLID for the coup.[50] AFLID is doubtlessly engaged in counter-insurgency to this very day.

The New York *Times* reported that the Rockefeller Commission is looking into allegations put forward by Dick Gregory

> that E. Howard Hunt Jr. was seized by the Dallas Police near the Kennedy assassination site...The Gregory group's charge is founded on photographs published last year in underground newspapers and elsewhere purporting to show Mr. Hunt and Frank A. Sturgis, one of the convicted Watergate burglars, being led away by the police...Mr. Hunt reportedly told the Commission staff that he was at home in the Washington D.C. area on the day of the Kennedy assassination, had dined that evening with his family and supplied the names of witnesses who could attest to his whereabouts...

Hunt's current attorney, William Snyder, told us that he had received a letter from the Commission assuring him that the tramps were not Hunt, Sturgis or McCord. As for Belin, after Gregory gave him the tramp pictures, he was quoted as saying, "Thus far I have found no hard evidence whatsoever to indicate that there was any person involved in the assassination of John F. Kennedy other than Lee Harvey Oswald."[51]

It is more likely that the Rockefeller panel was really a forum for a public purge of hardline, anti-Soviet agents than any sort of investigation. Some of the agents who were implicated were Richard Helms, the retired Oswald-in-Mexico-City expert who is now Ambassador to Iran; James Angleton, head of the CIA Counterintelligence Department and liaison to Israeli Intelligence. In an interview with the *Times* reprinted on page 296 Angleton was asked about alleged wrongdoing. He answered, "I've got problems... A mansion has many rooms, and there were many thing [*sic.*] going on during the period of the [antiwar] bombings." And seemingly out of nowhere, Angleton adds: "I'm not privy to who struck John." [52]

Raymond Rocca, another Oswald-in-Mexico City expert, had to resign as a result of the allegations. Rocca spied on Warren Commission critics and was one of Angleton's top deputies.

*   *   *   *   *

The last hope this country has to bring the assassins of John Kennedy to justice is the United States Congress.

Just after the Watergate affair was exposed, Congressman Gonzalez (D-Tex), who was in the motorcade with Kennedy, began to wonder where the Watergaters were on November 22, 1963: "I didn't put any credence in the theory that some of the CIA was involved in the Kennedy assassination until the revelations last year about CIA-connected persons involved in the Watergate crimes... My suspicions were greatly aroused as a result of some of the Watergate testimony regarding CIA-related activities and the Bay of Pigs... One of the most disturbing aspects of Watergate is the involvement of the CIA in certain domestic affairs... There is a total void of knowledge surrounding the exact activities of the Waterbuggers—their careers and their doings at the time of 1963 are shrouded in complete silence and mystery. There seems to be a gap of a two-three year period in their activities around this time..."

On February 18, 1974 Congressman Gonzalez introduced House Resolution 204 "calling for the Speaker of the House to name seven members of the House to a select committee, on of whom he shall name Chairman, to conduct an investigation and study of the circumstances surrounding the deaths of John F. Kennedy, Robert Kennedy and Martin Luther King, and the attempted assassination of George Wallace...We must find out if the President's death was in retaliation to the Bay of Pigs invasion against Cuba, and what connection did Oswald's murderer, Jack Ruby, also dead, have to do with all of this...I believe there is reason to subpoena E. Howard Hunt and Charles W. Colson..."

In mid-May 1975 Congressman Gonzalez introduced a resolution "to study circumstances of deaths and assassination attempts." Among the members of the House of Representatives who supported him were: Bella Abzug, Yvonne Brathwaite Burke, Shirley Chisholm, Ron Dellums, Herman Badillo, and Thomas Murphy.

America needs the Gonzalez Committee. The Rockefeller Panel is limited by its charter to investigate allegations of domestic spying. The Senate Select Committee on Intelligence headed by Senator Church (D-Idaho) will have its hands full investigating the allegations leaked through CBS and *Time* that the CIA had been "involved in assassination plots" against Castro, Trujillo, Duvalier and others. [53] These reports caused *Times* columnist Tom Wicker to wonder if "covert techniques and personnel can be imported into domestic politics," and if those techniques include assassination—"why might not that too someday be seen as a necessary tool for 'national security' right here at home?" [54]

CHAPTER ELEVEN

Pictures from Dallas
A Photo Analysis

Because photo technology has advanced to a point where authorities can now use television and still cameras to record crimes and later use these photos to positively identify suspects, photo identification has become a highly developed forensic science. Most foreign countries use photo interpretation; for example, the German government has been using the process to capture ex-Nazis for many years. U.S. authorities apprehend bank robbers photographed by camera surveillance systems now used in just about every bank in the U.S.

Many techniques are used to determine if two different photographs are of the same person. We have used the acetate layover method, one of the major techniques in photo interpretation, on the photos of the tramps arrested in Dallas. We took the tramp photos, and blew them up to a specific size; we then took a photo of a suspect we feel could be the unknown tramp, blew it up to the same size, and compared the two. The photo we used in the first comparison is a wire service picture of Frank Sturgis (page 223) which was taken at the Watergate break-in trial. In order for the comparison to be viable, the comparison photograph should have been shot from the same angle.

If there is a great difference in size and angle between the two, the features will not match and it will not be a valid comparison. For the comparisons of Hunt and Sturgis to the tramps, we tried to find photographs of them taken at the exact angles as the tramp photos to insure a valid comparison. But because Hunt and Sturgis were professional spies, there are very few photographs of them available to choose from. We've used the ones with the most similar angles, but they are still not exactly the same. Also, lighting conditions are different for each shot, creating different shadows as well. The final test, however, comes when the photo that is printed on plastic is laid over the tramp photo. If it is the same person in the two photos, the features will match; if the features do not line up together, then obviously they are two different people.

In the Frank Sturgis comparison we see that the facial features line up perfectly. When you match the ears, you will see that the shape and size of the ears are exactly the same and that the cartilege inside the ear also matches up perfectly. To a photo expert, an ear match is as conclusive as a fingerprint.[*] In fact, every facial feature of Frank Sturgis' matches with the tramp's. Note the way the shape of the noses and the oblong nostril holes correspond. The face creases match; the way the light falls off the curve of the cheek just below the eye is the same. Although the expression of the face is a bit tight-lipped in the tramp photo, the lip line is the same distance from the other features in both pictures.

There are two discrepancies in the Sturgis comparison: the hair line and the neck line. The tramp seems to have a hair line that recedes further than Sturgis'. Hair lines, of course, can be temporarily altered by simply cutting off hair at the desired area. In the wire service photo, Sturgis' body is facing the camera while his head is twisted around in a profile with his chin jutting out. In the tramp photo, the tramp has his body turned almost

---

[*] Also, if you compare the tall "tramp's" **left** ear on page 220 to the **left** ear of Sturgis on page 221 you will find that they match.

90° from the camera with his chin tucked in, thus possibly changing the relationship between the facial features and the neck line.

Again, in the E. Howard Hunt comparison, although we could not find a photograph with the exact same angle, (see page 223), we see that we have a near perfect match—every feature of the tramp aligns with Hunt's features. The only exception is the ear, which is on a different angle. Although the general shape appears to be the same, most of the detail of the ear has been washed out by the intense light coming from the tramp's right. The photo is overexposed and blown up eight times to this final size; shadows obscure the top of the ear. This is the worst of the tramp shots for an ear study. A better shot is on page 208. The profile of the short tramp on the far left shows the outline of the ear clearly. Notice the shadow that falls off the top of the ear (see Figure 2 page 201). This would indicate that the ear is of the convex type, which matches with the ear shown in the frontal shot of Hunt on page 207. If you look closely at the photo of the small tramp that we have used in the photo layover on page 223, you will find that there is something obscuring the neck line of the small tramp. Look at the photo this was blown up from on page 215 and you will see that the shoulder of the tall tramp is blocking a portion of the neck line of the small tramp, obscuring the entire neck line of the small tramp in the comparison photo on page 223.

In an April 24, 1975 article in *Rolling Stone* magazine, Robert Blair Kaiser printed, without Michael Canfield's permission, two photos of the tramps which Canfield had lent the *Rolling Stone*. Kaiser claims to have had a photo report done by the Institute of Forensic Science in Oakland, California. In the report, which was not published, Kaiser claims that the tramps could not be Hunt or Sturgis for two reasons. Using the tramp shot on page 217, he said the tramp has a concave ear and Hunt has a convex. But as you see here, the tramp has a *convex* ear. Kaiser used the worst ear shot of the small tramp as an example. He had the better profile shot on page 208 but did not print it, probably because it disproves his thesis. Kaiser's so-called photo experts also used the misinformation that the tall tramp is six foot five inches or taller. It is not known how they reached this conclusion. We will show you how we reached ours.

The Height Controversy

Many people in the media have argued that the tall tramp could not be Sturgis, who is six foot tall, because the tall tramp appears to be at least six foot five inches tall. This has proven to be misinformation. It was first propagated by Richard Sprague in his article in the Los Angeles *Star*. Sprague said he measured the wall which is in the background when the tramps are pictured walking along (see page 208), and he found a height discrepancy of six inches between the tallest tramp and Frank Sturgis. We decided to conduct our own investigation, and Michael Canfield went down to Dallas, Texas.

What we did was run a scale and two graduated yardsticks up the wall at the exact point on the Texas School Book Depository that the tramps were at when the photo on page 208 was taken. The way we determined the exact position on the wall was to find the same imperfections in the brick work that are evident in the photographs. These coordination points are labeled A, B, C, D and E in the tramp photo matched up in the height study on the following page.

In trying to determine the height of the tramps, one must take into consideration the angle of the photograph and the position of the tramps in relation to the wall. There are two factors that make the tallest tramp seem taller than he really is.

The position of the camera when the shot was taken is about chest high of the tallest tramp on the right. This was determined by the fact that the bottom of the ornamental brick work on the first row is visible at the right of the tall tramp's head (see Figure 1, page 201). This indicates that the camera was held a few inches below that point.

The tallest tramp is two feet closer to the camera than the wall in which the scale is attached. So with the laws of perspective in operation the tramp appears higher on the scale than he really is. Taking into account the diminishing point and camera angle, we find that the tramp is approximately six foot tall give or take a half inch, *not* six foot five inches tall. Sturgis has been listed as six foot or six foot one inch. Now, comparing the smallest tramp, on the far left of the photo on page 208, to the scale on page 209, we see that his hat barely comes to the inner square of the second brick, which is approximately five foot eleven inches on the scale. Subtracting about two inches that the hat adds to the height and an inch because of the camera angle and the diminishing perspective optics law, the height of the small tramp is five foot eight inches. Hunt has listed his height as five foot eight inches on his personal employment resume.

Thus, the tallest tramp and the small tramp are approximately six foot and five foot eight inches, respectively.

Figure 1

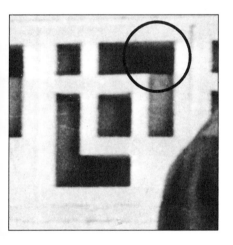

The underside of the brick just behind the Tall Tramp is visible indicating that the camera was held below this point. Blow-up **P2,** page 208.

Figure 2

Shadow indicating curved ear.

Shadow from the curved top of ear.

Photo Section

Nov. 8, 1963

Dear Mr. Hunt,

I would like information concerning my position.

I am asking only for information. I am suggesting that we discuss the matter fully before any steps are taken by me or anyone else.

Thank You,
Lee Harvey Oswald

This letter to E. Howard Hunt was written just before the assassination by Lee Harvey Oswald. Reports connect Hunt to the Mexico City CIA Office during that time period. Handwriting analysis experts for the HSCA were unable to prove that this document is a forgery.

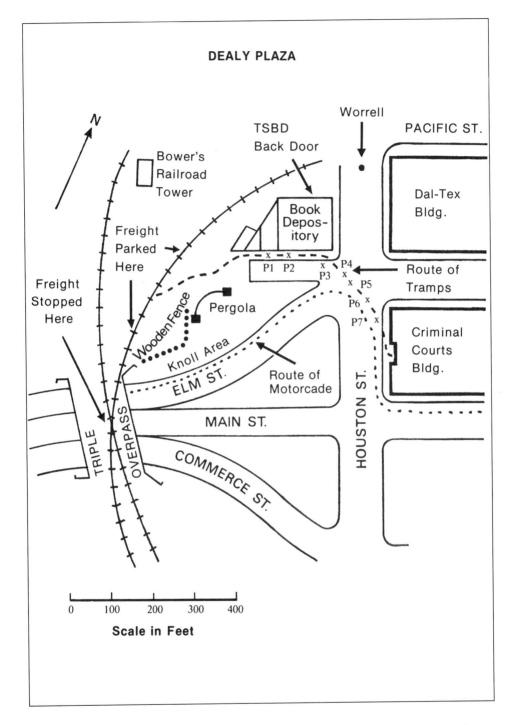

DEALY PLAZA

Map of Dealy Plaza shows an overview of the assassination scene and indicates the path of the tramps under police guard from the train yard behind the grassy knoll to the Criminal Courts building. The points marked **P1** through **P7** indicate their position as each photo was taken.

P1- In this first photo taken of the tramps the head of the short tramp is hidden. However, a third man's feet are clearly visible. *Photo by George Smith, Fort Worth Star Telegram.*

Blow-up of **P1** shows the tip of the short tramp's large left ear. The rest of his face is hidden.

Howard Hunt prior to 1963. The left ear is large and tips away from the head in the same formation as the tramp's. The report from the HSCA revealed that Hunt had cosmetic surgery on his ears shortly after the Kennedy assassination.

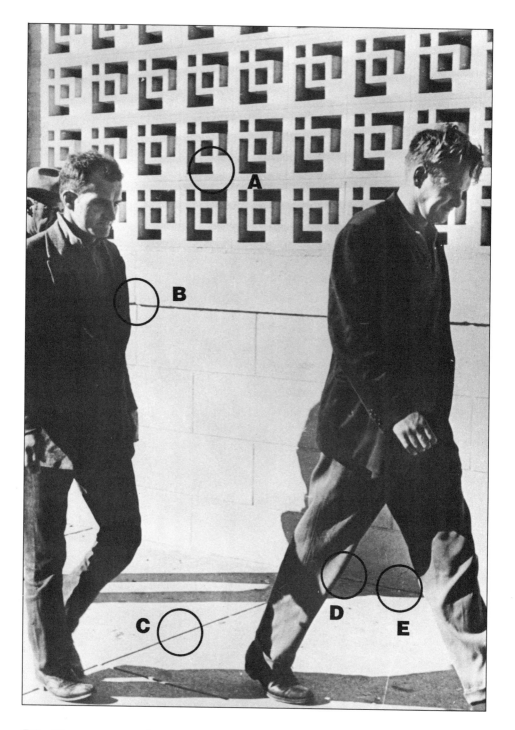

P2 - The tramps as they passed the Texas School Book Depository. The camera was held low, below the heads of the men, because the bottom of the ornamental brick is visible. *Photo by George Smith, Fort Worth Star Telegram.*

The angle of the camera and the position of the tramps to the wall gave the illusion that the tramps were taller. Therefore, a head-on shot of the tall Tramp would show that at most he is only 6' 1" tall. Imperfections of the wall and sidewalk (marked A-E) were used to determine exact positions for the height comparison.

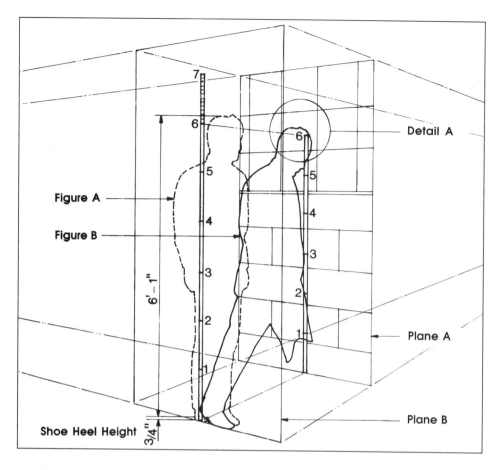

Figure A

Figure B

6'–1"

Shoe Heel Height

3/4"

Detail A

Plane A

Plane B

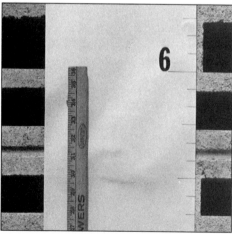

Engineered perspective drawing uses vanishing points to establish the true height of objects. After accounting for the tilted head, uplifted heel, and thick shoe sole our drawing indicates that the Tramp's height is 6'1" when standing upright.

P3 - The tramps crossing the street from the Texas School Book Depository. The low camera perspective makes them appear taller than their actual height. *Photo by Jack Beers, Dallas Morning News.*

P4 - The tramps crossing Houston St. to the Criminal Courts building.
Photo by Jack Beers, Dallas Morning News.

P5 - Tramps in police custody being marched to the temporary homicide headquarters set up by the Dallas police in the Criminal Courts building. Note that while the short tramp appears to be hiding behind the tall tramp to avoid being photographed, his leg and shadow can be seen behind the tall tramp's left leg. *Photo by William Allen, Dallas Times Herald.*

P6 - Tramps in custody. The short tramp's face can be seen clearly. *Photo by William Allen, Dallas Times Herald.*

P7 - Tramps about to enter the Criminal Court building. The short tramp is hiding to avoid being photographed. However, his leg and shadow are visible. *Photo by William Allen, Dallas Times Herald.*

Blow-up from **P7**, page 215.
A brush stroke covers the small
part of the short tramp's face
that would have been visible
and extends into the cheek of
the man in front.

Blow-up from **P3**, page 211.
Since Hunt's ear is very
distinctive, the ear of the short
tramp has been changed in this
photo. The remaining shadow is
too deep for the new ear and a
minute notch from an art-knife
can been seen. It is unknown
who did the retouching, since the
photographer, Jack Beers, died
of a heart attack in 1975.

Blow-up from **P5**, page 213.
Two white spots were placed in
front of the short tramp's face.

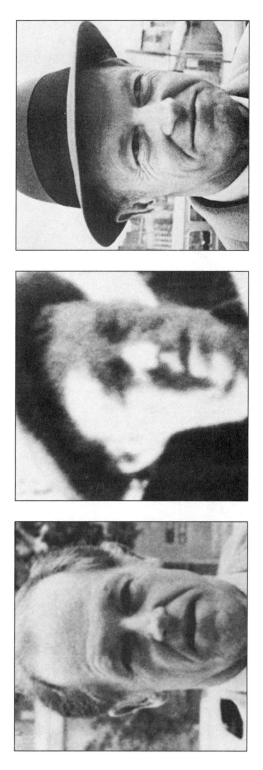

The photos on the left and right are E. Howard Hunt taken during the Watergate Trial. The center photo is a blow-up of the short tramp from **P6**, page 214. Similarities are the overall shape of the head, a slightly open-mouthed expression, and the shape of the nose typified by flatness on the tip of the nose, the slope, and the lines running to the mouth.

A blow up of the tall tramp as seen in **P5**, page 213. The shape of the head, nose and mouth match the photo of Sturgis on page 219. Both men have a muscular build and short neck. The shoulder line and the proportion of the torso to the legs are the same.

Frank Sturgis being arraigned for auto theft, Miami, Jan. 7, 1972.

A blow-up of the tall tramp as seen in **P3**, page 211. The mud on his shoes is consistent with witnesses' testimony to the mud behind the fence on the grassy knoll. The left ear of this tramp has the same shape and cartilage pattern as the ear on Frank Sturgis on page 221.

Sturgis, 1959, standing on a mass grave of 61 Batista supporters he had just killed. When Castro's brother, Raúl, voiced doubts concerning Sturgis' loyalty and possible CIA connections, Fidel handed Sturgis a gun and commanded him to execute the Batistites as proof of his sincerity.

221

Blow-up of the "unknown" tramp sometimes referred to as "Raoul," "Frenchy" or "Dan Carswell" shows a resemblance to Oswald. Blow-up from **P1**, page 206.

Oswald taken during his very short press conference at which he stated, "I am a patsy."

This is the only photograph of "Carswell" that the CIA submitted to the HSCA. It is of little value since this is a frontal shot and the tramp's face is always shown at an angle.

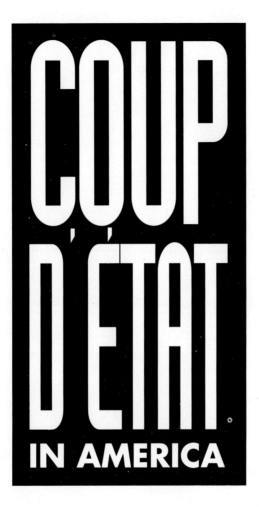

COUP D'ÉTAT
IN AMERICA

THE FORENSIC EVIDENCE

THE THREE TRAMPS
Dallas, Texas
November 22, 1963

OSWALD-LIKE TRAMP

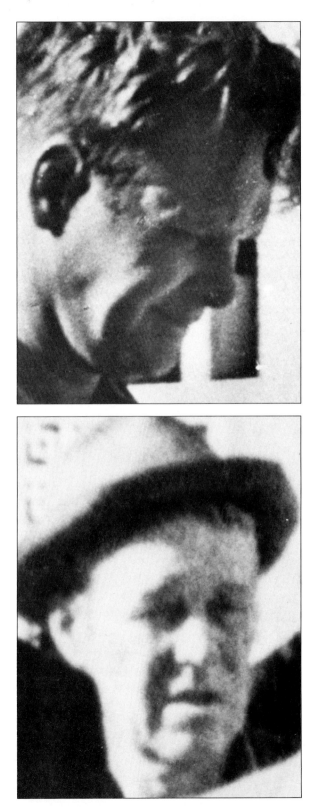

TALL TRAMP

SHORT/OLD MAN TRAMP

CHAPTER TWELVE

Unanswered Questions

In spite of the efforts we have put into the preceding, many questions still remain unanswered. It is quite possible that new facts may come up to refute some of the arguments we have made. As our interest is solely to raise the important questions regarding the assassination and to attempt to answer as many as we can, we wholeheartedly welcome any further illumination of the subject—even if it contradicts us.

Among some of the questions which need answers are the following:

The FBI found fingerprints in the Texas School Book Depository which to date, they have not identified. The most obvious thing to do is to crosscheck them with those of the Watergate burglars.

Seymour Weitzman and John Marshall Smith encountered a "Secret Service agent" behind the grassy knoll. Weitzman identified the man as Bernard Barker but so far there is no known evidence to confirm this claim. One of those who could shed light on this might be Patrolman John Marshall Smith.

Was there an Oswald double? If so, who was he? Could this double be identical to the man in the tramp photos who looks like Oswald?

Who, in fact, is the third tramp? As of the time of going to press we have been unable to identify him.

A floorplan drawn in the same ink Oswald used while making notations in the Cuban Embassy in Mexico City was found in his notebook. Was this in fact a floorplan of the Embassy?

Were Hunt and Sturgis in Dallas on November 22, 1963? According to Howard Hunt, he was in Washington, D.C. on November 22, 1963, attending a CIA meeting. Bernard Fensterwald has stated that Hunt has affidavits from twelve CIA officials who will swear he was there. Richard Sprague says that Richard Helms, Enrique Williams (the leader of the Cuban Committee of Liberation—see page 78) and Lyman Kirkpatrick (the Inspector General of the CIA at the time of the Bay of Pigs) were also at the meeting. Before the tramp story broke, Hunt's lawyer told us he was at home with his family that day and not at any meeting.

When Canfield first interviewed him, Sturgis said he was in Miami with his family, watching television. But when Canfield questioned him again after the tramp shots had been disseminated, he implied that he might have been in Washington, watching television. Sturgis went back to his first story when he testified before the Rockefeller Commission, citing his wife, nephew and mother-in-law as witnesses.

One area of obvious importance in any investigation would be to clarify the apparent links between Oswald, Jack Ruby, Carlos Prio, the Watergate burglars and Meyer Lansky and the Syndicate. There are many questions to be answered in this area.

At the time of going to press, preliminary plans for Senate hearings on CIA activities are still in the process of being formulated. Congressman Gonzalez has also introduced a bill, HR 204, aimed at reopening the investigation of the Kennedy assassination. Obviously, only Congress has the resources and authority to carry out the kind of extensive inquiry necessary to answer most of the outstanding questions on this subject. It is possible however that some crucial witnesses might hesitate to testify unless they are granted immunity. Their concern for their safety might not be a purely legal one. The list of potential witnesses and others in any way connected with the Kennedy assassination who have died under clearly mysterious circumstances is sufficient to scare many people. Under these circumstances, Congress may have to offer protection to some potential witnesses. Although there may be no connection between these efforts to reopen the investigation of the assassination and recent events affecting him, it is worth noting that while in San Antonio, Congressman Gonzalez's parked car was fired at with a high-powered rifle.

Perhaps the most important question to be answered is whether or not the CIA, officially or otherwise, knowingly or by default, may have been involved in all or part of the planning, execution and cover-up of the Kennedy assassination. There is no doubt that there has been a tremendous cover-up by both the FBI and CIA of the true assassination story. The official (now declassified) FBI and Secret Service documents that we have discussed and exhibited here decisively prove that the Warren Report was a fraud. It was the greatest cover-up in American history.

It is possible that for genuine but debatable reasons of national security and the emotional well-being of a nation in shock, the Warren Report may have been deliberately designed to protect the nation from potentially painful repercussions of the harsh reality of the facts of the assassination.

It is more than twelve years now since John F. Kennedy was killed. After Watergate the American people must certainly have the resilience to come to terms with the truth.

Editor's Note: This chapter and the appendices that follow complete the book as published 1975. The authors' current research begins on page 303.

Canfield: I was just thinking, all the publicity you've gotten out of this would cost millions of dollars. You know, if you wanted to go to a public relations firm and do advertising. You know you've gotten a lot of free publicity, and that would help with a book. You just put your name on it and it's going to sell.

Sturgis: Yeah, Jack Anderson, too. In his column.

Canfield: How long have you known him?

Sturgis: About twenty years. You see, Jack Anderson came to my home a day before my trial, and he says, 'Frank, let me tell you something, you might not be aware of it, but the people over you, whether you know them or not...they're going to double-cross you and they're not going to stand up behind you. You're being sold down the river. You're being betrayed.' Now he says, 'If you want me to help you, I can help you.' I says, 'Jack, I'm sorry, nobody can help me. I've got nothing to say. He says, 'Well you think about it, 'cause they're not going to stand behind you.' I said, 'You know how I am in Washington. I do have my contacts with the FBI, the CIA, I do have my contacts with the government.' And he says, 'You and your friends are going to be betrayed. I know you, for many years. You're a loyal guy. But your loyalty ends on betrayal.' I said 'Jack, I have no other choice but to do what I have to do.'

Canfield: Did you feel you were betrayed?

Sturgis: Not really. Because I didn't know the people upstairs involved. So I didn't know what was going on. Only the people in close contact would know what was going on.

Canfield: Yeah, but did you expect them to back you up? And get you off the hook?

Sturgis: Sure, I was an agent for the United States government. For what reason should I feel otherwise?

Canfield: Right. I'd be pretty angry myself. If I was working for someone in that position, and they told you to do a job and you went out and did it. And then you got into some trouble because of what you did for them. And then they wouldn't back you up, I would...I don't know.

Sturgis: You have to look at my past. I've done a lot of things. I've been on assassination attempts. I was involved in so many things. Skullduggery, intrigue, espionage.

Canfield: When you say assassination attempts...

Sturgis: Well, in foreign countries.

Canfield: I see.

Sturgis: You have to remember one thing. I've jumped from airplanes, I've made bombing raids, I've made leaflet raids, I've bought agents, you know, threw them out of airplanes with parachutes. I took weapons behind foreign countries for the underground. I've risked my life quite a bit. I've been shot at, I've been wounded, I've been beaten, been tortured. You know, I been through the whole realm. And there are records, this just isn't something I fabricate. There are records! For instance, in the Congressional Record, one Cuban leader said I was one of the greatest soldiers Cuba ever had. And that's a Cuban leader. I've had Cuban leaders say to newspaper people, which I have the clippings of, that I was a big hero...a hero to the Cubans. I had another Cuban leader say I was worth fifty men to them. These are people who knew me but didn't know I was a Government agent. These are people who talk to me as a person.

Canfield: Right.

Sturgis: Jack Anderson made me famous as a soldier of fortune and he told me, 'I never knew you were working as an agent for the United States government. Here I am, I made you famous saying you were a soldier of fortune and now, Frank, you're one of the most famous soldiers of fortune in the world.'

Canfield: It's true, it's true. When did you get involved in the Cuban thing?

Sturgis: I've been involved in Cuba many years ago.

Canfield: Before Castro?

Sturgis: Yeah.

Canfield: Before Batista?

Sturgis: During Batista's time. So, this is what people think of me. I've taken Presidents of foreign countries to speak to our President—that was John F. Kennedy—and there's records of it. I've been closely associated with about thirteen Presidents of foreign countries and the United States. Presidents and Prime Ministers. You see me where I live at? A lot of people in that area before the Watergate thing, they never knew who I was. They figured I was a workingman just out working. I'm a salesman. I go off two or three weeks at a time. Then I come back home. I go five, six weeks at a time. A normal guy, I work, mind my own business. And here I am, involved in every goddam thing imaginable. And I've never used Sturgis in any of my activities. I've always used Fiorini, Fenelli, Fedrini—code names that I've used. So if any publicity came out it came out in a code name. I left Sturgis alone. And I had Fidel in his official newspaper, government paper, *The Granma,* said that I was the most dangerous agent the CIA ever had. Heh, heh, heh. Now that's the Prime Minister of a country. And he was my enemy.

Canfield: Right.

Sturgis: And I knew him. I infiltrated his organization and spent two years in the mountains with him—the things I did to get close to that man. I got very friendly with him.

Canfield: Were you an agent then?

Sturgis: Yeah, sure, I infiltrated the 26th of July Movement. Nobody knew that; nobody still knows that; except the Senate Watergate Committee. That's why last year Fidel said I was the most dangerous agent the CIA ever had. Because he found out.

Canfield: But he found out after you got out of Cuba?

Sturgis: At the Watergate hearings, he found out.

Canfield: It came out in that?

Sturgis: He knew I was involved in the Bay of Pigs invasion. Somewhat involved in it, you know.

Canfield: You actually infiltrated the Castro movement?

Sturgis: Right. The 26th of July Movement. Since 1957 I was in it.

Canfield: When did you break out of it?

Sturgis: I left Cuba when I arranged for the escape of the Chief of the Air Force.

Canfield: How high up in the Cuban thing did you get?

Sturgis: I was a commander, I was Chief of Security and Intelligence for the Cuban Air Force. I got a star just like Fidel's. That's how high I went up. And while he was

Prime Minister, I knew President Dorticos; I knew President Urruatia, President Prio, who is a good friend of mine. President Rivero. I know all these people. I associated with them. I go to President Prio's home.

Canfield: Did you know Castro very well?

Sturgis: Oh yeah. I went to his home in Mexico City. He has a beautiful home. I knew Che Guevara. And I had pictures of...I can't find the pictures I had with Che Guevara. Goddam that makes me mad. I lent them to a friend to hold for me, and she can't find them.

Canfield: Do you have pictures with you and Castro?

Sturgis: Up in the mountains of Cuba.

Canfield: I'd like to see them. You know that whole Cuban thing is a series of books in itself.

Sturgis: The Cuban involvement is a story itself.

Canfield: Do the Cuban nationalists, that is the people who fled Cuba, still have hopes of returning?

Sturgis: Oh yeah. It would take months of research. I've done so many things to try and remember all I've done, it's impossible. I would have to take my tape recorder to all the places I've been. I could go to all the exile leaders, the ex-President of Costa Rica, Trujillo of the Dominican Republic, Idigoras of Guatemala, President of Argentina, etc. Howard Hunt was an attache down in Uruguay. He did this, did that, got information etc. Me, I participated in the action. Skullduggery, etc., back in the fifties.

Canfield: Were you involved in projects in all parts of those countries?

Sturgis: I was involved in operations in all those countries and Mexico many times. I had to be careful of KGB agents down there.

Canfield: You must have been very disappointed when the Bay of Pigs failed.

Sturgis: Oh I was mad. I was mad! We had people inside of Cuba. That's when I started to do...ahh, you know we were doing green light operations.

Canfield: Green light? What's that?

Sturgis: Permission. No problem. And after a while they cut the assistance of the underground.

Canfield: Why did they do that?

Sturgis: Well, because of the policy. The President says stop all things and they stop them.

Canfield: Eisenhower?

Sturgis: No, Kennedy. Kennedy was the President during the Bay of Pigs.

Canfield: Didn't it originate in '58 or '59?

Sturgis: It was started in 1957 with Eisenhower, but I'm talking about after the failure of the Bay of Pigs invasion, they let the underground down.

Canfield: Whose fault was it? Kennedy's?

Sturgis: Both President Kennedy's, CIA. Can't lay blame on one man. But he takes responsibility for the whole thing.

Canfield: I know in Hunt's books he's very adamant towards Kennedy.

Sturgis: See, he plays politics a little bit. I don't. Because I was on a low level and being Republican or Democrat don't make no difference to me. But understand this. There's times when I've received orders from the Company (CIA) and I made my own decision. If I didn't like the order, I'd voice my opinion and I wouldn't do it. This is the worst part of being an employee, you have to do it. If you're not an employee, I'd tell them to go to hell. If it came to a point where the orders were leaning towards a pro-communist thing, I'd tell them to go to hell.

Canfield: Did you ever feel that way towards the Bay of Pigs invasion itself, when Kennedy started cutting back?

Sturgis: Yeah. I figured he made a deal. In that we had to cut back. I felt that was wrong. He deserted the people. I felt that was wrong. That's why all the news people had me in the newspapers. Hey, I can show you clippings where they say I was involved in the assassination of President Kennedy.

Canfield: Who said this?

Sturgis: Newspapers, I even got investigated to that by the Watergate thing. They asked me where I was. I told them I knew nothing about it. I was home watching television. They felt the CIA might be behind it. So they wanted an investigation of E. Howard Hunt and myself on the assassination of President Kennedy. What the hell do I got to do with the assassination of President Kennedy? I may have disagreed with his policies, and so forth, but that doesn't warrant killing the President of the United States. And they asked me about other attempted assassinations. I said yeah, Cuba. Some people say if you attempt to assassinate people outside of the United States, wouldn't you be capable of assassination of the President in the U.S.? I said well, the thought never entered my mind. But I'm capable of doing many things. I'm that type of a man. But I see no grounds for me doing something like that. You know, he was my Commander-in-Chief.

Canfield: What about other people in the CIA?

Sturgis: The CIA had a lot of different factions, some of which I didn't trust.

Canfield: Are you convinced that the Warren Commission Report was correct?

Sturgis: On what?

Canfield: On the Kennedy assassination.

Sturgis: Let me tell you something about the Report. Nobody knows what's in that Report. Only what they wanted to give out. And I don't believe the Report is complete. I think there is a conspiracy involved in the assassination of President Kennedy, and they covered it up.

Canfield: Who do you think did it?

Sturgis: I don't have the slightest idea. But I think it's one big cover-up.

Canfield: That's strange that they would investigate you for that.

Sturgis: Well, they sure did. I had FBI agents over at my house.

Canfield: For the assassination?

Sturgis: Yeah.

Canfield: When? Right after it happened?

Sturgis: Right after it happened.

Canfield: Why did they come to you?

Sturgis: I asked them that. They told me I was one person they felt had the capabilities to do it. Heh, heh, heh. They said, 'Frank, if there's anybody capable of killing the President of the United States, you're the guy that can do it.' Heh, heh, that's funny. I told them, 'I'm not mad at you or nothing, I had nothing to do with it, but that amuses me.'

Canfield: Do you think the Cuban people did it because Kennedy messed up the Bay of Pigs thing?

Sturgis: (Looking at the backside of a girl walking by) This is what the Cuban people brought over here. All those...(at this point I turned off the tape.)

Canfield: What about other political groups?

Sturgis: Well, I don't know anything about political groups. Really. I've never got that involved with political groups.

Canfield: You wound up working for a pretty big political group, actually.

Sturgis: No, how do you figure?

Canfield: Well, Nixon and . . .

Sturgis: I worked in the Special Intelligence Unit that was formed by the President of the United States. There were complaints about national security, leakage of important documents, military documents, for instance, the Pentagon papers. And these were things I received top clearance on, in order to become part of this intelligence group. Now, if that was being handled wrongly by the people upstairs, well, that's not my responsibility. My responsibility was to take orders. I spent many years involved in these things. With, naturally, top people; military commanders, I know all the top military commanders in Cuba. I had dealings with them before, during and after, 'til I left. And Cuba at that time during the revolution and after, was a hubbub of intrigue.

Canfield: What did you do after the revolution?

Sturgis: Like I say, I was a commander. I was in the rebel army and I transferred over from Oriente Province, came down from the mountains and went to Havana and talked to my friend who got to be the Chief of the Air Force. He's Commander Pepe Vialonze, and I had him appoint me Chief of Security, Director of Security for the Cuban Air Force and Director of Intelligence. I also recruited a number of people in Havana for intelligence. There was a friend of mine, a woman who lives here in Hollandale, Florida. Her name is Geralding Shama, and she was an agent in the government.

I don't know if you remember, but when James Donovan, the lawyer who represented the U.S. Government, went to Cuba to negotiate for the release of the Bay of Pigs invasion, she was one of the last persons to leave Cuba. He arranged for her release. She spent three years in a Cuban prison outside Havana. She lost a twenty million dollar business that her husband had in Cuba. Her husband's name is Suarez. They had a tobacco business. Do you believe that she applied to the government here for aid for the business she lost there and they claim that she was a revolutionary and because she was a revolutionary, convicted by the Cuban tribunal for revolutionary activities, they couldn't do anything about it. Here she was an agent for the American government whom I recruited and her contact was Major Van Horn who was out of the American Embassy and which I thought was very ridiculous. She came back almost physically destroyed and her mental being was not what it was. She was, if you remember, the go-between the underground in Havana and the people here. That was Artime's group which was the MRR. We had a place on Brikel Avenue that we used, which is not there today. That was somewhat a meeting place for the MRR organization. And Geraldine was there constantly. And because of her activities going back and forth between Miami and Cuba with the underground and the U.S. government, she was eventually captured, and put in prison. And yet the American government denies her, says she was a revolutionary acting on her own. I know different because I recruited this woman for the American government.

Canfield: Did you tell the American government that?

Sturgis: What do they know? They don't know. And I arranged for her escape, of course, and the Chief of the Air Force to come over here. I arranged for him to be in touch with various agencies of the military government, rather, agencies of the American government. I went to Guatemala with Diaz Lanz for a meeting with President Idigoras, to arrange for bases there.

Canfield: Before the invasion there?

Sturgis: Before the invasion.

Canfield: For training?

Sturgis: Well, for bases, which was training bases for the invasion forces. And naturally, there were Cuban and Russian agents there, so there were big headlines in the newspapers. All over Latin America in the television and in the radio, that I was there trying to get bases from President Idigoras in Guatemala, to invade Cuba, which really came about a year later. So naturally the President was embarassed with them and we spent almost a week there trying to leave. In order for the United States government to protect itself when I got back a (unintelligible) grabbed me, and held me and lifted my citizenship—which was a ploy on their part to appease Fidel, you know.

Canfield: I see.

Sturgis: Well, you know he did this on his own, not for us, and I don't know if I'll be...

Canfield: It seems that you're always doing...that they don't support you, you know. You do things for them, but then when it gets down to the...

Sturgis: That's part of the game.

Canfield: nitty gritty, they cut you loose. I guess that's...that's understood, eh?

Sturgis: Yeah. You know that old saying, if you're caught, you're on your own. Heh, heh, heh.

Canfield: They deny all contacts with you, right?

Sturgis: Sure. You can get killed.

Canfield: Did you . . .

Sturgis: I was captured by foreign countries four or five times, in the last fifteen or twenty years. The government always came to my rescue. The only time they didn't come to my rescue, is when I'm captured by my own government. Heh, heh, heh. They fed me to the dogs.

Canfield: Watergate.

Sturgis: It's funny.

Canfield: It's ironic, isn't it?

Sturgis: Yeah, well it sure is. The way things worked out.

Canfield: Later on I'd like to get into a specific incident. Like this general thing is good, but I'd want to get into a specific incident. You can pick it. I don't care what it is. So the publisher can get an idea of some of the things that actually happened.

Sturgis: Well, actually, it depends on what it is.

Canfield: Well, you can generalize about it, you don't have to get specific. But something major like as—you know something major—as exciting as you want to make it. Like you said you participated in assassination attempts.

Sturgis: In Cuba, against Fidel. Against some of his top (unintelligible).

Canfield: Were you always in the Cuban military? Did you ever get out of it, into the private sector?

Sturgis: Not really. In a communist country, the military controls, at least in Cuba the military controls, everything.

Canfield: But he wasn't communist right away, was he? I thought he had a lot of people fooled?

Sturgis: They have evidence of his activities in Bogota, Columbia. Evidently, he must have had some people here, in this country here who thought he wasn't much of a threat. Remember, he wasn't that big of a revolutionary until he went into the mountains. Herbert Matthews, of the New York *Times*, made him such a big deal.

Canfield: Yeah, but with your contacts you must have known that he had the potential to be successful?

Sturgis: Look, anybody had the potential to be successful in Cuba at that time, because Cuba was ripe for revolution. The American government supported Batista. The American government knew of the corruption, tortures, prison, what Batista was doing to the people. So it was only a matter of time before the people got up in arms and supported somebody who would revolt against them. And here came Fidel Castro. The American government was interested in Fidel Castro because they had a number of people who tried to infiltrate. I believe that I was the only American who infiltrated the 26th of July Movement.

Canfield: Do you mean that America was interested in him to replace Batista?

Sturgis: No, no, no, I didn't say that. The American government knew of the crime and corruption in the Batista regime. And they did nothing to stop all this corruption. You had various revolutionary groups who were up in arms against Batista and the American government supported nobody at that time. It so happened that the American government, certain people, officials, had sympathy for him. The reasons for these sympathies I don't know.

Canfield: Were you sent in by the CIA?

Sturgis: No. I went in on my own. I had contact with the people. What happened was the Consul General of Santiago, the American Consul General there, his name was Park F. Wooler, wanted me to work with him. That's how I got started, with Park F. Wooler in 1957...(he) was a consulate official and normally most consulate officials are Agency people.

Canfield: Right, was he?

Sturgis: No, I couldn't say. What guy is going to say, 'Hey, I'm a CIA official.'?

Canfield: Right. Nobody does that.

Sturgis: Nobody's going to...

Canfield: Blow their cover. Right.

Sturgis: There are lots of consul officials using their positions to cover up their activities. My job was to give him the names of the top military commanders, the units, the strength of the units, the weapons, so forth.

Canfield: Then you were reporting to him while you were working for Castro?

Sturgis: He told me I was playing a very dangerous game, and to be very, very careful, because I could have both sides after me.

Canfield: Did you actually fight for Castro, you know, see action?

Sturgis: I participated in a number of activities up there with him. Not directly kill anybody, but if it was necessary to defend myself, you know. I was almost trapped by their patrols. And one time the people I was with were trapped. Most of the time we were dodging them. We would see them, we would hide, stay low.

Canfield: You said you were in the Air Force. Did you fly?

Sturgis: We'd fly all the time. Matter of fact, I was a flight instructor in the Civil Air Patrol plus Operations Officer for a squadron.

Canfield: And that's what you did for Castro?

Sturgis: I flew while I was up there; in order to get close to him, I flew a bunch of guns and equipment.

Canfield: From where?

Sturgis: The United States. Using secret landing fields. I'd go buy guns and equipment, I'd package them up, bring them to the air field, load them on the plane, run over and back to Cuba. I had to do all these things myself, personally in order to get close to him. I had to show him that I had the intelligence to get him equipment that he needed very badly. I spoke to him while I was in Mexico over one of the clandestine radio transmitters we had in Ecuador that would go directly to Cuba.

Canfield: Did he ever suspect you of being an American agent?

Sturgis: We got very friendly.

Canfield: Is there any truth in the report that Batista was supported by Americans like Meyer Lansky?

Sturgis: The gambling interests in Cuba did support Batista. The two main people who controlled the gambling interests in Cuba were Meyer Lansky and Santo Trafficante. They were the men who controlled all the gambling in Cuba for the National Syndicate.

Canfield: Did Castro keep the gambling casinos open and just run them?

Sturgis: They closed them all down.

Canfield: Right after the revolution?

Sturgis: Several months after he took over. I forget when, but they closed up in '60, before the invasion. I don't know the date, that will have to be researched.

Canfield: Did you ever know a guy by the name of McWillie?

Sturgis: Who?

Canfield: McWillie.

Sturgis: Yeah. That name is very, very familiar. I forget what he is or who he is but McWillie, yeah.

Canfield: I think he was a gambler of some sort.

Sturgis: Well, there you had so many of them.

Canfield: I thought he was a big man in the Syndicate or something?

Sturgis: I knew....I met there, Santo Trafficante, I met the Lansky brothers, I met there Charlie Terrini; they call him Charlie the Blade, I met him there. I met Errol Flynn. Heh, heh. I met a lot of movie actors there.

Canfield: Where?

Sturgis: At the casino. I met Mike McLaney there. He was in charge of the national gambling casino.

Canfield: How? Were you just hanging out there?

Sturgis: No, that was another part of the job there. I was in charge of all the gambling casinos for the Cuban government—for a very short period of time.

Canfield: For Castro?

Sturgis: For Castro. The woman who was in charge of that was Casterta Nunnas. She was up in the mountains with me, and she got to be in charge of that. It came under her ministry. Fidel, one day at the Prime Minister's office, asked me if I would help Casterta with the gambling casinos. I told him, yes, which, of course, was a short time, because I had all these other jobs and I was involved with all this intelligence work.

Canfield: Do you know when that was?

Sturgis: 1959.

Canfield: I bet when he closed all the casinos, when he took over the casinos, the Syndicate was pretty angry.

Sturgis: It didn't bother them. At the very beginning.

Canfield: Didn't he kick them all out?

Sturgis: Later, yeah.

Canfield: And then they got angry!

Sturgis: There wasn't much they could do about it.

Canfield: Did the Syndicate ever help go back and take Cuba?

Sturgis: Naw, naw.

Canfield: They just let it go?

Sturgis: They had to let it go. The American government was involved. They didn't want to get involved in anything that the American government was involved in.

Canfield: Did Nixon ever go down there? During that period?

Sturgis: Not to my knowledge. I don't think he did.

Canfield: Of course he was Vice-President prior to '60.

Sturgis: With all the trouble that was going on in Cuba at the time, I don't think he made it one of his tours; at least not to my knowledge.

Canfield: He was down in South America.

Sturgis: But he never went to Cuba.

Canfield: Did you ever know him or ever meet him?

Sturgis: Who's that?

Canfield: Nixon.

Sturgis: No, I never met President Nixon. Now, I met President Kennedy. I took President Carlos Prio of Cuba to speak with President Kennedy. I met Secretary of State Christian Herter; a few other State Department officials.

Yeah, Mexico was a place that was very intriguing— a lot of conspiracies down there. I did several things while I was back in Havana, you know, there was so much intrigue going on. I was smuggling out different military personnel that were against the Castro government...(end of this tape)

Canfield: Let's talk about the domestic activities that are just being revealed.

Sturgis: Let me go ahead and say this here. I realize like in today's paper, I saw where it said CIA did domestic intelligence on Eartha Kitt—

Canfield: Right.

Sturgis: —and a number of other people and so forth. Okay, well, I think I told you earlier that I don't know if I'm a CIA agent or was a CIA agent or not because the top brass in CIA first denies me then they acknowledge me, then they deny me, so I don't know what the hell I am, but all I know is I've been involved in a lot of activities for the United States government, from the very beginning—from the time that I joined the United States Marine Corps when I first turned seventeen years old up until the present day, and I have three honorable discharges from the service. I served in Europe, United States, Latin America, and I served in Asia. Now as far as domestic intelligence, I can say this, that I believe that before, during and after the Bay of Pigs invasion there was a lot of domestic intelligence going on, and I believe it's still going on to the present day, because Miami is the hub of international intrigue here. You've got a lot of Asians here—

Canfield: As far as Latin America is concerned—

Sturgis: I'm saying as far as Latin America, which extends all the way to China and Russia. Latin America, you've got the Chinese colonies, and Cuba, and different parts of Latin America. So that means you do have Chinese communist intelligence agents that are here in Latin America. You've got Russian agents—always. Before Fidel took over Cuba, the Russian government had the largets spy network in this hemisphere working out of their Russian embassy in Mexico City. They had over two hundred agents working out of that embassy there. Since Cuba came about with Fidel, they transferred the bulk of their agents, naturally, in Havana, Cuba. This hemisphere is loaded with Russian communist agents. Still in Mexico, my Mexican operation, I had to be careful of Mexican KGB agents there—which I have names of them in 1968; I have the names of all these people here.

Canfield: How far back does your Mexican involvement go?

Sturgis: I would say my Mexican involvement goes back as far as 1957, '58 to the present day. To the present day, would you believe?

Canfield: Now you worked with Hunt down in—well, you didn't work *with* him. Did he ever work in Mexico?

Sturgis: Oh yes. Howard Hunt? Yeah. Yeah, he worked in Mexico, sure.

Canfield: When was that?

Sturgis: I forget what year, I'd have to research that. But he operated out of Mexico, certainly. Now let's get back to domestic intelligence. I do have the names of over a dozen Americans, that they're activities have been reported to CIA. Observed and reported, surveillance—all their activities, yes. And I can also give you names of other CIA agents that were involved...

Canfield: You actually participated in the surveillance operation?

Sturgis: Oh, yeah, of Americans, sure—

Canfield: Are they prominent people that—

Sturgis: Well, they're ordinary people that, uh, who did not believe in communism, and believed in anti-communism, and naturally these same people helped in many ways—

Canfield: Well why would you put anti-communist people under surveillance?

Sturgis: Government orders.

Canfield: Why? I don't understand.

Sturgis: It's orders that came down from upstairs.

Canfield: Wouldn't they say *pro*-communist people?

Sturgis: My activities in this area here was against pro-communist elements, who were Americans and foreigners, plus anti-communist elements who were American and foreigners.

Canfield: Any prominent people, that the American public would know?

Sturgis: I would think that CIA had the dossier of many, many prominent people, and people who were not prominent; but regardless of their prominence, from what I understand just recently, the 1947 Act on Domestic Intelligence that the CIA had, they're not supposed to do that, it's against the charter. And regardless of their prominence, they're still Americans citizens.

Canfield: Right, well, I'm just saying it would be a very interesting thing if it was known.

Sturgis: Well, I would think so. You know who Sherman Billinglsy* is? He was the owner of the—what's that famous nightclub in New York?—um, oh my goodness,—(The Stork Club)

Canfield: Well...

Sturgis: Famous nightclub, it's been for many years—

Canfield: We can look that up later......

Sturgis: Anyway, I can't remember his name, uh, the name of the nightclub, but Billingsly is his name, he's a very very famous man, and his son-in-law, the man who

---

* Sherman Billingsly owned the Stork Club, a plush New York City restaurant. In the early '60's six employees of the Stork Club were arrested for not registering with the police as "cabaret employees." Roy M. Cohn represented Billingsly. The Stork Club also refused to recognize the Hotel and Restaurant Workers Union even though they picketed his establishment for four years.

married his daughter, name was Alex Rorke. He was a freelance photographer and reporter, involved in many different Latin American, uh, as a reporter, many Latin American intrigues. Alex participated in a number of operations that went into Cuba, also in Mexico. And if you remember there was a big search by the United States Coast Guard, both air and sea, a number of years ago, when he left Opalocka airfield, and he was going to Nicaragua, and supposedly it is rumored that he was shot down near Cuba, into the water, there were reports he was captured but evidently my information—there was nobody inside of Cuba that was captured by the name of Alex Rorke. I assume he either got shot down over water and his body and the plane have disappeared. I, with a number of other people which I will get to at a later date, sat with Alex Rorke where his airplane was parked at Opalocka airfield which is close by here, the day before he made his ill-fated trip. And I will get the names of everybody that knew about the trip and so forth, that the FBI investigated, I believe even CIA investigated that, I'm not sure, but they may have been in on the investigation, plus other agencies of the United States government, (unintelligible)...of his disappearance.

Canfield: What about surveillance of other people; any specific people that you remember?

Sturgis: Well, I can't, I have to really search my memory, I've got a meeting tonight with a friend of mine that participated in operations with me; one of the people that I personally had under surveillance, and I know that other agents had him under surveillance.

Canfield: Electronically, and by other means?

Sturgis: I would say by other means, really—

Canfield: Not so much electronically.

Strugis: Not so much electronically; other means. As a matter of fact, there's one party (unintelligible)—that he bought. Now if you remember that particular time, there was a lot of discussion about the Russian missiles that were inside of Cuba. And this party had the airplane in the hangar being worked on; he told me that this airplane was going to go to Cuba to seek out these missile bases and take pictures. Also at the same time there was rumors that he was going to go over there and do some bombing and strafing. So naturally, people I was associated with got wind of it, and told me to investigate it, which I did; and I ran across another CIA friend of mine who wanted to see and meet this party who I was in touch with. So I made arrangements and I told my friend who was under surveillance, that I had someone I knew by the name of a Mr. B., who was a company man, he worked for the outfit—these are the words you use to describe agents for the CIA—and he said, OK, I'll see him, provided it's with you. I said OK and I set up the arrangements, and we went over to Mr. B's home. I went into his office where he had files, like he had maybe a good half a dozen or more file cabinets full of documents of people, that he or the Agency that came over to him, and gave him information on foreigners, or Americans—

Canfield: And he kept tabs on a lot of different people.

Sturgis: Oh, quite a bit, yeah. And plus the man that I worked for, my case officer, also did the same thing.

Canfield: Explain, as you did before, on our way over here, some of the other things that the company asked you to do, and approached you, like on the 40 committee, etc.

Sturgis: Well, I was an associate, while I participated in Operation Forty. Operation Forty was formed before the Bay of Pigs invasion, it was a top secret government operation; it consisted of many Cuban intelligence officers, who worked for the Central Intelligence

Agency, and this organization. Their job primarily was to train people to infiltrate a foreign country, to make contact with members of the underground, make contact with people in the political sector of the government, foreign government, make contact with people in the military sector of the foreign government, plus there was also a group formed in which was the assassination section, which I was part of, that if necessary, this assassination group would upon orders, naturally, assassinate either members of the military in the foreign country, members of the political parties of the foreign country that you were going to infiltrate, and if necessary some of your own members, who were suspected of being foreign agents. Now at the same time, I was asked by my friend, who was a CIA agent, he asked me if I was interested in participating, or doing an assassination with the Company. I told him yes, providing that I would sit down with this case officer and go over the details, and that I would do it.

Canfield: Domestic or foreign?

Sturgis: It would be domestic.

Canfield: Here in the United States?

Sturgis: Oh, yeah. The reason for that, he asked me how I would go about it. And I told him, well, if it was going to be domestic, well, I could do it several ways. I could do it either in the Everglades, I could do it by boat, or I could do it by air. But, that if it was going to be done, I did not want nobody to be part of this, I would do it by myself, but I definitely wanted to meet the officer who wanted this done, and I wanted to see him, and get it right from him, so I would be sure that it would be someone with authority, and not just a lower-level agent, such as he.

Canfield: Did this come out of the Forty Committee, or the Agency itself?

Sturgis: This is what the Operation of Forty was trained for, by the Agency—to do all this type of work.

Canfield: Do you know if they ever did carry out any operations like that?

Sturgis: Yeah, oh yeah. Sure. Operations were being done, infiltrations were going on inside of Cuba, and contacts were made with political elements in Cuba, also in military and—

Canfield: I mean the assassination teams.

Sturgis: Well there were several from word of mouth through associates, there were several attempts and several assassinations that were going on inside of Cuba. Nothing large—

Canfield: Any other countries?

Sturgis: Not that I know of. No, we were concentrating strictly in Cuba at that particular time. Actually, they were operating out of Mexico, too; CIA activities were in Mexico through Nicaragua, Costa Rica, in Panama, in Guantanamo Bay, Puerto Rico, South Florida, all the way to Andrews Air Force Base. This is how the activities stretched all over.

Canfield: What about domestic activities, did they ever attempt a domestic assassination?

Sturgis: Not to my knowledge, no. But the only thing I can say on that is, when I was asked to do domestically, myself—

Canfield: Right.

Sturgis: Of anyone else, no, not to my knowledge; which brings the why all this stuff I've been reading in the papers where they want me to be part of the investigation of the assassination of President Kennedy, I have no knowledge of anything like—

Canfield: Did anyone ever approach you about—

Sturgis: The assassination? Yeah, oh yeah.

Canfield: No, I mean, to *do* the assassination.

Sturgis: No, no, oh no. The Cubans were very angry with the
            Kennedys, they were furious with Kennedy because of
            the failure of the Bay of Pigs invasion. But the only
            thing that I had as far as the assassination was con-
            cerned, naturally, is the investigation by the FBI. And
            they said, 'Well, Frank, this is strictly a voluntary
            thing, if you want to talk with us, if you don't want to
            talk with us'—And they told me that they felt that I
            was one of the persons capable, if I wanted to assassi-
            nate somebody as high as the President of the United
            States, that I was capable of. . .

Canfield: Do you think that maybe some of those other people in
            the Forty Committee were capable of doing that?

Sturgis: Well, I'll be very honest with you, I told you that the
            Cubans were furious with what happened and so forth.
            It seems that the proof is Oswald, who was involved
            with the assassination, who supposedly killed President
            Kennedy, anybody was capable of it. Whether they get
            away with it or not, is another thing. I think there was
            a tremendous conspiracy going on in that assassina-
            tion, that the Warren Commission has not told all,
            that they covered up a lot of things that they didn't
            want the American people to know. And I think there
            are people in various Federal agencies that may have
            covered up.

Canfield: Why would they do that?

Sturgis: I really don't know. Because we were on the brink of a
            war, and it could have very easily touched off a war, a
            nuclear war.

Canfield: Because of Cuba, because of the Missile Crisis? Had
            you ever had any suspicions about any other people on
            the Forty Committee that were in the assassination—

Sturgis: Oh yeah, I had suspicions that some of the members of Operation Forty were communist agents. Certainly.

Canfield: Getting back to some of those domestic activities that you participated in. We were discussing your suspicions of other Forty Committee members. Did you ever have any proof or any leads that would indicate that they were involved in assassinations—like Kennedy's?

Sturgis: No, no I didn't. The only thing I can say, there were rumors in the intelligence circles. You see a lot of these people, the American intelligence, had contact with a number of students inside of Cuba during this time. They left Cuba when Fidel took over; they came to the United States, and they still maintain contact, mainly, naturally, CIA. And you gotta understand the situation in Cuba. When Fidel came in, a lot of these people went over to Fidel's side. They turned in a lot of Cubans, and at the same time when they found out that their situation was difficult, and didn't like what was going on themselves, some of these people had contact with the American agencies; and you gotta understand that some of these people that came over were already indoctrinated and trained to be special agents, so they came over here, and some of them more or less, worked as double agents. Not only working for (tape break). We still have that problem today, except there's been a change...They have infiltrated many fields here. Cubans are agents, intelligence agents, they have infiltrated the unions here, they have infiltrated all kinds of business in this area. I imagine all the different agencies here are aware of this, they should be, because I am. And being that this country is a democracy, they know what is going on, so naturally they don't touch it, unless it's something serious that's going on.

Canfield: You were approached though to do assassination jobs—

Sturgis: Oh, yeah. Also an associate. And it can be proven that he is or rather was, at that time, a CIA agent.

Canfield: Was he involved in any of the things that went on later?

Sturgis: . . . intelligence?

Canfield: No, involved in, yeah, involved in domestic intelligence—involved in Watergate?

Sturgis: Well, I don't want to go ahead and say at this point. But if I'm ever called in front of a Congressional committee, which I assume I would be, I'll tell them . . .

Canfield: Would you tell, uh, say we were going to do a book, a publisher, you know. And he would be very much interested in breaking something like that in a book before it got to the Congressional investigation where everyone would hear it. Would you reveal that name before?

Sturgis: Well, it would be more than one name . . .

Canfield: Would you do that then?

Sturgis: Sure.

Canfield: Would you do it now?

Sturgis: I wouldn't do it for the press, but I would do it more or less if an offer was made in book form.

Canfield: OK, great. Is it someone that we would know?

Sturgis: I would expect that it would be people who—at least some of them would be known, yeah.

Canfield: Did they ever tell you who was to be assassinated?

Sturgis: No.

Canfield: Did you have any ideas?

Sturgis: No, no. I don't even know if it was another agent, or a double agent, or a fool or what. The only one who would know are the people involved in CIA.

Canfield: Do you know if they had ever done this, with another agent?

Sturgis: No, not to my knowledge, no.

Canfield: They never did assassinate anybody in the United States?

Sturgis: Not to my knowledge, no.

Canfield: Interesting. If they did, my God, that would be a great piece of material right there.

Sturgis: This is what would happen to the committee, the committee would get all that out. The committee would have to go ahead and subpoena people, and the subpoena would have to go ahead and say who, when, where, what and where...with what went on with Watergate...(unintelligible)...orders were given to that effect. On this assassination thing, I would figure well, it's gonna have to come up from someone a little higher than this agent right here. It's gonna have to come from someone with a little authority.

Canfield: Did you tell him that?

Sturgis: Oh, yeah.

Canfield: And what was his response?

Sturgis: He told me that he would make contact with someone higher up, and pass on that information, and so forth.

Canfield: Did you ever get any feedback from him—or anyone else?

Sturgis: No.

(Tape Break)

Sturgis: Remember I told you that I made the arrangements for
           President Prio many years ago, with phone calls from
           Washington, D.C. to see and meet and speak with the
           President of the United States who at that time was
           President John F. Kennedy, right? OK, just recently in
           the last few months, I was contacted by certain leaders
           in the exile community to try and form some kind of a
           unity Party among the Cubans. I arranged for the
           three ex-presidents of Cuba, that's President Urruatia,
           who I knew personally, President Carlos Prio, who I
           know personally, and President —, oh I got a blank
           mind, well I got these three ex-Presidents to come
           to an agreement for a political base, of unity,
           and help liberate Cuba, providing that they would not
           break any American or international laws. Throughout
           this whole period they did a tremendous job. I was
           contacted by leaders in the organization and many
           times sat down with them and told them that I think
           that they should get contact with the OAS which is the
           Organization of American States, with the UN,
           which is the United Nations, that I also made contact
           for them with various government agencies. They
           asked me about them forming a committee, a dele-
           gation, what I thought about it, and, uh, going with
           them to Quito, Ecuador in order to protest the lifting
           of sanctions; and I advised them before that I think
           that they should work on this. They took my advice,
           sent a delegation to Quito, Ecuador, with the help of
           the Ambassador of Chile, and they were under house
           arrest in Ecuador, and because of them being under
           house arrest they got tremendous international publi-
           city, which really blew up Cuba's chance, Fidel's
           chance of the OAS lifting the sanctions. So the world
           does know that with the publicity that this delegation
           got, that was headed by the ex-President Carlos Prio,
           that the vote went against lifting the sanctions. They

came back, I was notified that they were going to arrive at the international airport, I went there to make sure that they had no problems of re-entry, and they came in, they had a big ovation. I'm still in touch with these people today. This is the historical event for them, and a disaster for Fidel.

Canfield: Did you know anything about the bombing in Washington that was connected with that?

Sturgis: No, no. These are groups. One reason why I've been advising these groups to rally around the three ex-Presidents is to help the American government in keeping down the terrorist bombing. I felt that they wouldn't do the Cuban exiles any good, but all this activity, and I felt that if they had some form of unity, which—everything that they did do would have to be legal—this would give incentive to the Cuban exiles; not to really do anything.

Canfield: Anything else?

Sturgis: No, no I don't think so. He gets people who are close to the individual, you know, who could do the thing, 'cause usually agents are not close to the individual.

Canfield: I see, like say you're gonna do in a President of some country, you would, uh—

Sturgis: For instance, Fidel; when I was in Cuba there, I told my CIA contact, I said, look pass the word upstairs, you want me to kill Fidel, I'll kill him, if he comes to the Air Force base. I'm here in control of the military police, of the security of all the Air Force bases in Cuba. I said, if he comes here with Che, if he comes there with all the top military people, with many of the ministers, I can kill him in two minutes. If you people want it done, I will do it with my people...and I'll just wipe the whole three jeeps right out, just taking two minutes to do it. Or if you want me to do it inside the base. But I am in a position to do it, see. Because I was close with Fidel.

Canfield: Right, and he would trust you.

Sturgis: You know what I mean? I sat down in the Prime Minister's office with Fidel talking with Fidel right in the Prime Minister's office, you know, these are things, you've got to go ahead and get people who are close to someone, instead of someone who's not close, for the simple reason, how are you going to get in the Prime Minster's office? No way you can, because of all the security. But I pass through like nobody's business...the commander!

Canfield: So what did they say when you put this to them?

Sturgis: They'd let me know. At that time, if you remember, the American embassy was very pro-Fidel.

Canfield: Oh, I see, this was before?

Sturgis: In 1959, yep. A few weeks after '59. The Embassy, I didn't trust a lot of people in the Embassy because they were pro-Fidel; Americans were. But I trusted the man that was my contact. He was an Army colonel—not an Army colonel, he was a colonel...a military man. I told him more than one time, within a six-month period. And I was involved with other people trying to kill Fidel. But they wanted it a different way, and I told them no, it's not gonna work, and it didn't work. The only way to get him was right at that Air Force base.

Canfield: They didn't go your way, they went some other way and they failed?

Sturgis: Right, well these were not the CIA people, these were Cuban leaders, top ranking Cubans who were against Fidel, and they wanted to do it their way, and keep me out of it. Well, OK, 'cause I heard there was going to be an attempt to kill him and so forth; and I told them hey, I hear this, this, this, this, and if you're gonna do it, I suggest you don't do it. The only way to do it is here at the Air Force base. I'll tell you how to do it. 'You're not to be involved. We'll do it our way. We got our own plan.' (Laugh). The plan never worked, he's still there. Now on research, where it comes to the Cuban problem, Christ, there's so much people working here, Cubans who were working on the CIA payroll, and the things that they were doing, the things I was involved in, there's a lot to it. I'll be honest with you. To research a lot of things I did, it'll take a good six months. Really. Working hard, making contact with people. And these are people who were associated with CIA, with the Cuban government.

Canfield: Like in the Forty Committee? They just took people that had already been trained in this?

Sturgis: Operation 40 were a bunch of Cubans that were sent to the Army to receive intelligence training. They received it; their job was...infiltration into Cuba, to make contact with the underground, and to assist the underground with money for guns, equipment; also make contact with the local politicians and military people, and if they would not cooperate...

Canfield: And they were all trained in assasssination? Or just a group of them?

Sturgis: Just a group, a team of them.

Canfield: Five, ten, fifteen—

Sturgis: No, more than that.

Canfield: Twenty?

Sturgis: More than that. When we get into the research of it, there's a lot—you see a lot of these people who belong to it didn't know me. Only the top chief of the operation, only the top man. Like agents, they don't expose themselves to everybody. You don't do that. What good is an agent if everybody knows? You wind up getting killed. Agent is an agent that nobody knows, only the men he works with. Now this intelligence group, they all knew only the people working close with them.

Canfield: Any other domestic activities that you participated in, or know of that other agents participated in, that would be interesting to a publisher; the American public, you know, the readers.

Sturgis: Well, I'm going to have a meeting tonight with one of the persons who were under surveillance by me and CIA, and I'm gonna talk with him...names, places, and refresh my memory with him...

Canfield: These are some of the operations that you and he went on together?

Sturgis: Yeah. He participated with me. I used him—

Canfield: Will you be able to reveal his name, or can you reveal his name right now?

Sturgis: Well, I'll reveal it tonight after I sit down with him and get all that information, I will get it down on paper.

Canfield: Would you make that information available to a publisher then?

Sturgis: Yeah.

Canfield: Under contract—

Sturgis: I may have to hold it with the names. To be very honest with you, at least the names of the agents involved, for reasons...but as far as the names of the people who were under surveillance, I would give them to you.

Canfield: You will reveal the agents for the committee?

Sturgis: Oh, yeah, for the committee—

Canfield: Why for the committee and not your publisher?

Sturgis: Because that is a legal body and there might be legal technicalities involved, and I want to make sure that I am protected legally.

Canfield: Well, the only protection the publisher can—

Sturgis: There's no protection a publisher can give me.

Canfield: Well, except money. Money can protect you, in a sense—

Sturgis: No, no, it can put you in jail, unless you got immunity, my friend—

Canfield:. If you were offered immunity, what kind of revelations would you make?

Sturgis: Well, I would give the names of all the agents that were involved, that I know were involved in domestic surveillance. And this would be my card for protection from prosecution. So why should I go for even a hundred thousand dollars or even a million dollars, put myself in jail for that.

Canfield: You can always leave, avoid prosecution with that kind of money; stay on appeal until doomsday—

Sturgis: No way, no way. Listen, I got involved in one of the greatest scandals that this country ever had in its history—

Canfield: What?

Sturgis: And I had no protection whatsoever.

Canfield: Why would the government offer you any more protection on something else?

Sturgis: Because they would want to know about this domestic surveillance, and I would be willing to give all that information for my own protection. Once I go in front of a committee and I get my immunity and I give them information, then there's no problem.

Canfield: Do you think there are any more scandals?

Sturgis: This is a scandal.

Canfield: Do you think it's bigger than Watergate?

Sturgis: No.

Canfield: Do you think there's anything bigger than Watergate?

Sturgis: Not in a long time. There's a number of scandals that wouldn't come close to Watergate. The operation I had in Mexico was a scandal. Nobody knows anything about that. And I told the Senate Watergate committee about it, but naturally they...

Canfield: Can you tell us a little bit about that?

Sturgis: Yeah, it was a Mexican operation that I was in. In association with one or more CIA people that I knew for many, many years and worked with for many, many years.

Canfield: What was your purpose? What were you doing?

Sturgis: Well, I told this group of Americans that we were going to make a commando raid in Cuba. That was the purpose at the beginning. But when I went to see my contact in Mexico City at one of the big name hotels there called the—I have a mental block for the names of hotels—I was told secretly by him that I was to participate with another boat to capture a Russian vessel that was going to be off the coast of Cuba, and I was to pretend that my ship that I was on was disabled that they would stop to pick me up, at the same time I was to arrange the capture of this Russian vessel and proceed to take this Russian vessel off the coast of Venezuela where I would receive assistance, and to use the ship and the crew members as hostages to negotiate for the release of the SS Pueblo and the crew members who were captured in...

Canfield: What happened to this?

Sturgis: A storm came up, I got caught on a reef, the captain wasn't familiar with that particular area, the rudder and the propeller was bent, we sprung a leak, had to throw a lot of stuff overboard in order not to sink, come into Belieze which is British Honduras, stayed there for two hours, tried to get repairs, after two hours later the government officials came there and made us all...(unintelligible because of train noise) but I assume the operation was aborted. I was contacted while I was at the British Honduras prison, by an official of the American governement who was very firm and stern with me. Finally after x amount of days while we were in prison there, we then went to court there and people were, you know we were treated like celebrities there, we walked past people, crowds in the street...'cause it is a black nation, so we were somewhat of celebrities. I gave a beautiful speech to judge there...(he) then deported us back to Miami in three separate flights; the reason for that is they were afraid of hijacking. And at the same time in that prison we made very good friends with their black prisoners; as a matter of fact, there were a coupla times where they wanted to break me out; I was put in solitary confinement, and they wanted to have a big breakout there to get me out of prison,...and I told them no, I didn't want that, I wanted to see how the trial went...In this breakout they wanted to go to the hills and help us organize...(train noise) One day less five years later I got caught with Watergate; Archibald Cox, Federal Watergate Prosecutor, told Judge Sirica that I would not cooperate with him, and at the same time, a few days later I was handed down an indictment on three counts. Indictment came pertaining to my Mexican operation. I went to court at the first trial

...I got found innocent on car theft...hung jury on the other two counts, went back for a second trial, got found guilty on interstate transportation of stolen vehicle, plus conspiracy. I could have got up to ten years, my lawyer threatened to call the CIA director station chief in Miami and the station chief in Mexico City and the Consul General of British Honduras, and I refused, I refused to get on the stand to defend myself, because I felt that these were trumped-up charges being put on by Archibald Cox and my lawyer told or asked him why did the government wait one day less five years because if I was guilty of any wrongdoing, they had all these years to do it in. Why do it at the last minute.

Canfield: But they were doing it because you were—

Sturgis: I was not cooperating.

Canfield: Why wouldn't you cooperate?

Sturgis: Well, Archibald Cox wanted me to go ahead and admit the things that I felt were lies, which would have helped him in his investigation of the Watergate break-in. I felt it was not right—

Canfield: Like what things?

Sturgis: He wanted me to admit that I received executive clemency from the President of the United States; he wanted me to admit that I was pressured to plead guilty; he wanted me to admit that I was to receive 'hush money.' And I told him no, I would not admit to these things, because I felt that these were lies, that him wanting me to admit these would help his committee. He said, for instance, 'I have a jigsaw puzzle here, and there is a spot open on this jigsaw puzzle which you don't fit into. I need you to fit into that. Can you answer these questions truthfully, then you will be part of this jigsaw puzzle.' He says, 'There's the door, and you can go free, right now.' I told him,

'Nope, I'll stay in jail.' And I stayed in jail for over fourteen months.

Canfield: Have you ever regretted that since then?

Sturgis: No, I was asked if I had this opportunity to do the things again, knowing what I knew, would I do it, and I told them yes. They said why, they thought I was a fool. I says well, I maintain now, like I maintained then, that I was an agent of the United States government; the truth was there, that all these officials in the government. . .

Canfield: Paid you to do these things—

Sturgis: Hired me to do what I had to do, what I thought was a legal thing, for national security. Who am I to go and dispute an order, from someone higher than me, knowing that they are officials of the United States government?

Canfield: Did you feel you were protecting these people?

Sturgis: Nope, I felt I was doing my job. As I had done in the past, for my country, for national security, and in the same way you operate when you're working with intelligence organizations.

Canfield: I see. Hmmm. Any other domestic revelations that you could—?

Sturgis: Well right now I can't think of any more, maybe after tonight after I deal with this friend of mine, it's possible that in talking with him, you know, we could more or less think of certain things, certain operations and so forth that will come out, you know.

Canfield: OK, let's talk for a minute on the break-in. Did you help break into Ellsberg's office? Did you do any other break-ins besides Watergate?

Sturgis: Yeah, in Cuba I did several break-ins, while I was there in Havana. As I told you before, I was involved in a lot of intrigue there. With Cuban officials and so forth, but, you know, this information was for the national government...Mexico. I was involved in a number of things in Mexico, but not—I have to think about Mexico.

Canfield: Did you ever go to Viet Nam?

Sturgis: No.

Canfield: Just Latin America primarily.

Sturgis: Europe, Latin America. Well, I was in the Pacific in the Second World War.

Canfield: And there weren't any other break-ins that you participated in, in the United States?

Sturgis: In Cuba, yes. In the United States, no.

Canfield: Just Watergate.

Sturgis: Just Watergate, yes. That's the one I got caught at.

Canfield: What about the Chilean embassy?

Sturgis: No, I denied that.

Canfield: You denied that, but did you do it?

Sturgis: I denied it.

Canfield: (laugh). OK, um. You said that was the only one you ever got *caught* at.

Sturgis: Right.

Canfield: I see, OK. How are we gonna interest our publisher, if, you know, we don't have any material?

Sturgis: I don't know, really. This is usually what happens with, you know, with publishers and people that go ahead and say, well, well, we got this, we got that, we gotta have something new, and so forth. What else is new?

Canfield: Yeah, but Congress is going to get out—

Sturgis: Oh, there's going to be a number of things. There's gonna be a lot of TV coverage, a lot of things going on.

Canfield: Think anybody will be prosecuted?

Sturgis: I hope not. How can they be prosecuted? You know, doing something that they had orders to do.

Canfield: Well, how were they prosecuted for Watergate?

Sturgis: Good question. Good question.

Canfield: So, if it's gonna come out in that, don't you think, you know, you should benefit by it? You know, this way, if you get it out, before it comes out in Congress, you can make something from it, you know, instead of just taking a rap, or whatever is going to happen—

Sturgis: Well, I don't think there's going to be any rap taken, because there's too many high officials involved at the time, and if an order did come down, which, remember, Colby said that there was domestic intelligence...CIA orders—

Canfield: CIA, or did somebody order the CIA?

Sturgis: They'll have to dig even more into that. They'll have to dig into that and see, who ordered it, whether it was the CIA director, or whether it was somebody in the State Department, or whether it was somebody in the government itself.

(end of tape)

CD 533

NY 100-10310

In addition to passport and identification papers, the following other items were noted in VON MOHRENSCHILDT's effects:

Letter dated April 5, 1941, to VON MOHRENSCHILDT, 109 East 73rd Street, New York, from K. MAYDELL, Facts and Films, 33 West 60th Street, New York City, mentioning getting necessary letters from NELSON ROCKEFELLER.

Letter from ROGELIO SANCHEZ CORRAL, Federal Congressman, dated Mexico City, March 31, 1941, expressing pleasure that VON MOHRENSCHILDT was coming to Mexico to make a picture.

Letter from OLIVER G. LUCUS, President, National Bank of Commerce, New Orleans, Louisiana, to R. A. THORNTON, President, Mercantile National Bank, Dallas, Texas, dated May 4, 1939, stating that VON MOHRENSCHILDT was looking for a position and was interested in the oil industry.

Letter dated July 29, 1939, from GEORGE REYER, Chief of Police, New Orleans, Louisiana, "to whom it may concern" advising that VON MOHRENSCHILDT had been residing in New Orleans, since March 5, 1939, and was enroute to Colombia and Venezuela.

Eight one hundred dollar American Express Company checks, numbered R 3, 201,100 to 107, inclusive.

Letter of credit from Chase National Bank, New York City number C16745, dated May 3, 1941, for $1250.00.

Letter of credit from First National Bank, Houston, Texas, number 1487, dated May 13, 1941, for $4500.00.

Memo reflecting transfer on May 12, 1941, of $1100.00 from National Bank of Commerce, New Orleans, Louisiana, to Chase National Bank.

- l:g -

Commission No. *1080*

In Reply, Please Refer to File No.

UNITED STATES DEPARTMENT OF JUSTICE

FEDERAL BUREAU OF INVESTIGATION

Boston, Massachusetts

May 22, 1964

MARILYN DOROTHEA MURRET

Reference is made to memorandum dated May 7, 1964, at Washington, D. C.

The 1964 Staff Directory for Massachusetts Institute of Technology (MIT), Cambridge, Massachusetts, lists Harold R. Isaacs as Research Associate at the Center for International Studies at MIT.

The current Greater Boston Directory lists Harold R. Isaacs as residing at 75 Varick Road, Newton, Massachusetts.

On May 21, 1964, Mrs. Claire Edwardson, Secretary, President's Office, MIT, advised the records reflect the following regarding Harold R. Isaacs: Born September 13, 1910, New York City. Before coming to MIT, he specialized in Far Eastern affairs, was a "Newsweek" correspondent in the Far East, and a special writer for the "Christian Science Monitor" on Far Eastern affairs. He commenced employment at MIT August 20, 1953, as a Research Associate in the Center for International Studies and is so employed at the present time. During this period of time, he has also been employed as a lecturer in the Economics Department at MIT. Mrs. Edwardson stated that the Center for International Studies is endowed to a great extent by the United States Government. She said that much of Isaac's work takes him away from MIT and consists of international travel and concentration on study in India.

On April 4, 1950, Harold R. Isaacs, who resided in China from 1931 to 1936, furnished the following information concerning his activities in China:

At the age of twenty-one he obtained a job in the Merchant Marine on a ship going to China, and left this ship at a Chinese port in 1931. He remained in China for the next five years, the first two or three years being in Shanghai, where he edited a weekly newspaper in English called, "The China Forum."

Commission No. 436

UNITED STATES DEPARTMENT OF JUSTICE
FEDERAL BUREAU OF INVESTIGATION

WASHINGTON 25, D.C.

February 25, 1964

In Reply, Please Refer to
File No.

LEE HARVEY OSWALD

Marina Oswald was interviewed on February 24, 1964.
She stated that approximately two weeks after the General Walker
incident and while they resided on Neely Street in Dallas,
Oswald, some time between 11 a.m. and 1 p.m., dressed himself
in a suit and tie and put a pistol underneath his jacket. (The
General Walker incident occurred on April 10, 1963.) She said
Oswald was unemployed at this time. She said she inquired where
he was going, to which Oswald replied approximately, "Nixon is
coming and I'm going to take a look."

Mrs. Oswald said that at the time she realized she had
to act fast, whereupon she walked into the bathroom and told
Oswald to come into the bathroom with her, which he did. She
said she then quickly jumped outside the door, closing it as she
left the bathroom. She said she forcibly held the bathroom door
shut holding on to the knob and bracing her feet against the wall.
She said Oswald attempted to get out of the bathroom and was
yelling, "Open the door." She said she forcibly held the door
shut for about three minutes. In this respect she said that she
cannot at this time accurately recall the length of time she
forcibly held the bathroom door closed. She said she told Oswald
it was difficult for her to hold the door and commented to him
that something might happen to the baby. She said that she was
pregnant at this time.

She said she told Oswald he was not going to shoot at
anyone else and that if he wanted to come out of the bathroom, he
would have to walk across her body. She said she reminded Oswald
of his promise to her after the Walker incident that he would not
try to do anything else like that. She recalled she said something like, "Hold it. How can you deceive me after you gave me your word?"
She said, "I told Oswald she would open the door if he would give
his word to remain in Oswald the bathroom and not go anywhere and if he
would undress and give her his clothing and pistol. Mrs. Oswald
said that her husband agreed to this and she opened the bathroom
door after holding it, as stated, for approximately three minutes.

CD 535

WFO 100-1689

REVIEW OF THE INTERNATIONAL COOPERATION
ADMINISTRATION FILES RE GEORGE DE MOHRENSCHILDT

On February 25, 1964, examination of records
maintained by the Security Division of the Agency for
International Development (AID) of the International
Cooperation Administration (ICA), made available by Miss
BETTY K. PIZZARELLE, indicated that GEORGE DE MOHRENSCHILDT,
11631 Hillcrest Road, Dallas, Texas, was a contract employee
of the agency during 1957. The file contained a memo of
request for clearance which was date-stamped June 6, 1956,
and also contained a handwritten notation that the request
was not referred until August 9, 1957. The request
indicated that DE MOHRENSCHILDT was being considered on a
contract basis to act as a consultant in oil resources for
the Government of Yugoslavia. He expected to depart for
Yugoslavia as soon as cleared or in about eight months.
It was stated that he would not have access to classified
information. The file indicated he entered on duty
February 3, 1957.

A copy of a memo from ICA to the Yugoslav Consulate
referred to an agreement of January 15, 1957, regarding GEORGE
DE MOHRENSCHILDT stating the financial provision agreement
had been approved in the amount of $13,000 subject to the
terms specified in the agreement.

The file contained no information indicating the
date on which DE MOHRENSCHILDT's contract terminated except
a notation dated November 21, 1957, stating the results of
the investigation conducted by the Civil Service Commission
were not reviewed since DE MOHRENSCHILDT had completed
the contract and returned to the United States.

Miss MARINA APEL, Contract Division, AID, advised
that the only information she had reflected that DE
MOHRENSCHILDT entered on duty February 3, 1957.

The file contained copies of results of a Civil
Service Commission investigation conducted of DE MOHRENSCHILDT
at the request of the International Cooperation Administration.

4

The rest of this document is classified.

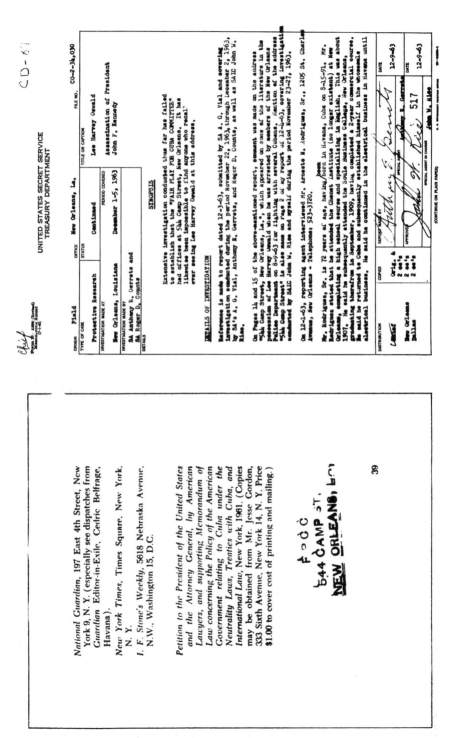

CD-87

UNITED STATES SECRET SERVICE
TREASURY DEPARTMENT

ORIGIN Field	OFFICE New Orleans, La.		FILE NO. CO-2-34,030
TYPE OF CASE	STATUS	TITLE OR CAPTION	
Protective Research	Continued	Lee Harvey Oswald	
INVESTIGATION MADE AT	PERIOD COVERED	Assassination of President	
New Orleans, Louisiana	December 1-5, 1963	John F. Kennedy	

INVESTIGATION MADE BY
SA Anthony E. Gerrets and
SA Roger D. Counts

DETAILS

SYNOPSIS

Extensive investigation conducted thus far has failed to establish that the "FAIR PLAY FOR CUBA COMMITTEE" had offices at 544 Camp Street, New Orleans. It has likewise been impossible to find anyone who recall ever seeing Lee Harvey Oswald at this address.

DETAILS OF INVESTIGATION

Reference is made to report dated 12-3-63, submitted by SA A. G. Vial and covering investigation conducted during the period November 22, 1963, through December 2, 1963, by SA's A. G. Vial, Anthony E. Gerrets, and Roger D. Counts, as well as SAIC John W. Rice.

On Pages 14 and 15 of the above-mentioned report, comment was made on the address "544 Camp Street, New Orleans, La.", which appeared on some of the literature in the possession of Lee Harvey Oswald when he was arrested by members of the New Orleans Police Department on 8-9-63 for fighting with several Cubans. Mention of the address "544 Camp Street" is also made on Page 2 of my report of 12-1-63, covering investigation conducted by SAIC John W. Rice and myself during the period November 23-27, 1963.

On 12-3-63, reporting agent interviewed Mr. Arnesto M. Rodrigues, Sr., 1205 St. Charles Avenue, New Orleans - Telephone: 523-3720.

Mr. Rodrigues, Sr. is 72 years of age, having been born in Havana, Cuba on 8-15-91. Mr. Rodrigues stated that he attended the Cnenet institute (no longer existant) at New Orleans, completing a high school course and specializing in English. This was about 1907. He said he subsequently attended the Soule Business College, New Orleans, graduating therefrom in September, 1909, having completed a 2-year commercial course. He said he returned to Cuba and subsequently established himself in the wholesale electrical business. He said he continued in the electrical business in Havana until

DISTRIBUTION	COPIES	REPORT MADE BY		DATE
USSS	Orig. & 2 cc's	Anthony E. Gerrets SPECIAL AGENT		12-9-63
New Orleans	2 cc's	APPROVED		DATE
Dallas	2 cc's	John W. Rice SPECIAL AGENT IN CHARGE 517		12-9-63

CONTINUE ON PLAIN PAPER

National Guardian, 197 East 4th Street, New York 9, N. Y. (especially see dispatches from Guardian Editor-in-Exile, Cedric Belfrage, Havana).

New York Times, Times Square, New York, N. Y.

I. F. Stone's Weekly, 5618 Nebraska Avenue, N.W., Washington 15, D.C.

Petition to the President of the United States and the Attorney General, by American Lawyers, and supporting Memorandum of Law concerning the Policy of the American Government relating to Cuba under the Neutrality Laws, Treaties with Cuba, and International Law, New York, 1961. (Copies may be obtained from Mr. Jesse Cordon, 333 Sixth Avenue, New York 14, N. Y. Price $1.00 to cover cost of printing and mailing.)

F ᵒ O G
544 CAMP ST,
NEW ORLEANS, Lᵒ⁻

39

Commission No. 1085e2

UNITED STATES DEPARTMENT OF JUSTICE

FEDERAL BUREAU OF INVESTIGATION

New York, New York
May 28, 1964

In Reply, Please Refer to
File No.

Re: Lee Harvey Oswald
    Internal Security - R - Cuba

Directorio Revolucionario Estudiantil
(Cuban Student Directorate)
(DRE)

Detective John Caulfield, Bureau of Special Services, New York City Police Department, on April 16, 1963, advised that five members of the Cuban Student Directorate were arrested in New York City on April 14, 1963. Detective Caulfield advised that the five members of the DRE were charged with disorderly conduct and creating a nuisance. The five DRE members were given a hearing on April 14, 1963, and received suspended sentences.

Detective Caulfield further advised that the five DRE members were arrested in the vicinity of the Radio City Music Hall, as they demonstrated and shouted anti-Fidel Castro slogans, and also demonstrated against recent United States Government orders imposed upon Cuban exiles carrying out armed attacks against Cuba.

A confidential source, who has furnished reliable information in the past, during 1963 furnished copies of the bi-weekly newsletter put out by DRE in Miami, Florida. This biweekly newsletter is captioned "The Cuban Report" and has the return address of Post Office Box 805, Miami, Florida.

Detective John Caulfield, New York City Police Department, during December, 1963, advised that the DRE sponsored no public meetings or participated in any picketing with the exception of the incident which took place in New York at Radio City April 14, 1963. Detective Caulfield advised that the activity of the DRE in the New York area during 1963 was confined to propaganda activities.

Page 3
CO-2-34,030
December 9, 1963

the "FAIR PLAY FOR CUBA COMMITTEE" was using the address of 544 Camp Street, New Orleans, former address of the "CUBAN REVOLUTIONARY COUNCIL," an anti-Castro organization, whereas the "F P C C" was pro-Castro. Mr. Rodriguez said he did not know of anyone who had belonged to the "F P C C."

Mr. Rodriguez stated that recent newspaper articles had indicated that Oswald's former landlady at New Orleans had stated that Oswald's wife often attended meetings at New Orleans, yet she could only speak Russian, giving rise to the suspicion, in Mr. Rodriguez's mind, that there must have been other Russian speaking persons attending such meetings. (Subsequent to this interview with Mr. Rodriguez, Sr., reporting agent contacted Mrs. Jesse J. Garner, 4911 Magazine St., New Orleans, Oswald's former landlady. She denied having made any statements to the effect that Oswald's wife had frequently attended meetings at New Orleans, explaining that, as far as she knew, Oswald's wife very seldom left their apartment and when she did leave the apartment it was mostly to go to a neighborhood grocery to buy bread, milk, and items of that nature. She said she did not know of anyone who would have looked after Mrs. Oswald's 14 year old child while she would have been attending such meetings. It was her definite belief that Mrs. Oswald did not attend any such meetings and certainly not on a frequent basis.)

On 12-1-63 interviewed Mr. Manuel Gil, 912 Esplin St., New Orleans - Telephone: 944-1171, mentioned on Page 15 of SA Viala's report of 12-3-63. Mr. Gil stated that he did not know Oswald personally and had never seen him. He said he had seen photos of Oswald on television and in newspapers since President Kennedy's assassination.

Mr. Gil stated that he has been a member of the "CUBAN REVOLUTIONARY COUNCIL," for about the past two years. He said that this organization formerly had offices at 544 Camp St., 2nd floor, for about six months during 1961-62; that Sergio Arcacha Smith had been the New Orleans delegate to the "C R C." He said that Luis Rabel, Arnesto N. Rodriguez, Sr., Armesto N. Rodriguez, Jr., Sergio Arcacha Smith, and himself were authorized to sign checks in behalf of the "C R C", as was Carlos J. Grimalder, CPA.

Mr. Gil stated that Corliss Lamont, publisher of the booklet entitled "The Crime Against Cuba" is a notorious Communist or so he has heard. He also stated that the "FAIR PLAY FOR CUBA COMMITTEE" is a well-known Communist front and is directed from Havana.

Manuel Gil stated that he is presently employed as Production Manager by THE INFORMATION COUNCIL OF THE AMERICAS, explaining that he makes tape recordings of information received from refugees from Communist countries, which recordings are broadcast in Latin American countries, as indicated that some of these recordings are also used in some Louisiana schools. "THE INFORMATION COUNCIL OF THE AMERICAS, INC." has offices at 620 Gravier Street, New Orleans - Telephone: 523-3641.

On 12-2-63 interviewed Mr. Luis Rabel, 4651 Marigny St., New Orleans - Telephone: 282-7981 (next door). This is actually the telephone number of Charles I. Camp, Mr. Rabel's son-in-law.

Oswald's lack of money. And, apparently, the very first thing that Oswald did when he arrived in Dallas was to go to the Texas Employment Commission to apply for an unemployment compensation check.

Examination of the address book in the original shows that Oswald used pens and inks of many different kinds in making various entries. For example, on the page which contains the names and addresses of the embassies in Mexico City all these names and addresses are obviously from the same pen and the same ink, but the name, "Silvia Duran," is in a different ink and was probably written with a ball-point pen. This strongly indicates that Oswald got the names and addresses of the embassies at some earlier time, perhaps before he left New Orleans, and that he wrote down Silvia Duran's name after he had met her at the Cuban Embassy. It would be interesting to know if the same ball-point pen that was used to write her name was also used to make other entries in the notebook. This would be especially significant because what appears to be an alternate telephone number for the Russian Embassy in Mexico City seems to be from a pen which is different from both that used to write "Silvia Duran" and from that used to write the names and addresses of the several embassies. This points to the fact that Oswald did not have a pen with him but was borrowing pens to make these entries and therefore probably borrowed one pen at the Cuban Embassy to write "Silvia Duran" and another at the Russian Embassy to write the alternate telephone number. It follows from this that if any other entry in the notebook is from the same pen and ink as the "Silvia Duran" entry or the alternate telephone number, that it was probably made at the same time and place as these other entries were made. To carry this conjecture out even further, there is what appears to be a floor diagram on page 4 of this notebook and it is written in an ink which could be the same as that used for "Silvia Duran." If this proves to be the case, it could mean that the floor plan was drawn while Oswald was at the Cuban Embassy. Obviously my analysis so far is much too highly conjectural, but it indicates the kind of inferences that could legitimately be taken from a closer analysis of the address book. I recommend therefore that we ask that a CIA expert on this sort of thing be assigned the task of analyzing the entire notebook to give us a report on what entries were probably made by Oswald with the same pen and ink. If this kind of analysis is feasible, the information gained could prove to be extremely helpful.

Ruth Paine has stated that she and Marina spent the first night of their journey to Irving, Texas, in a motel in Texas just across the Louisiana border. (Commission No. 5, page 303.)

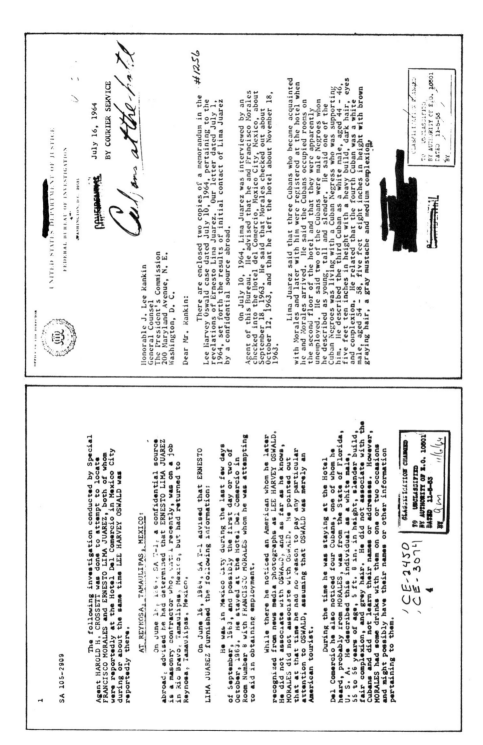

UNITED STATES DEPARTMENT OF JUSTICE

FEDERAL BUREAU OF INVESTIGATION

WASHINGTON, D. C. 20535

July 16, 1964

BY COURIER SERVICE

#1256

Honorable J. Lee Rankin
General Counsel
The President's Commission
200 Maryland Avenue, N. E.
Washington, D. C.

Dear Mr. Rankin:

There are enclosed two copies of a memorandum in the Lee Harvey Oswald case dated July 10, 1964, pertaining to the revelations of Ernesto Lima Juarez. Our letter dated July 1, 1964, set forth the results of initial contact of Lima Juarez by a confidential source abroad.

On July 10, 1964, Lima Juarez was interviewed by an Agent of this Bureau. He advised that he and Francisco Morales checked into the Hotel del Comercio, Mexico City, Mexico, about September 18, 1963. He said that Morales checked out about October 12, 1963, and that he left the hotel about November 18, 1963.

Lima Juarez said that three Cubans who became acquainted with Morales and later with him were registered at the hotel when he and Morales arrived. He said the Cubans occupied rooms on the second floor of the hotel and that they were apparently unemployed. He said two of the Cubans were male Negroes whom he described as young, tall and slender. He said one of the Cuban Negroes was living with a Cuban Negress who was supporting him. He described the third Cuban as a white male, aged 44 – 46, five feet ten inches in height with a heavy build, dark hair, eyes and complexion. He related that the fourth Cuban was a white male, aged 54 – 58, five feet eight inches in height with brown graying hair, a gray mustache and medium complexion.

SA 105-2909

1

The following investigation conducted by Special Agent HAROLD H. CROSSETT was done to attempt to locate FRANCISCO MORALES and ERNESTO LIMA JUAREZ, both of whom were reportedly at the Hotel Del Comercio in Mexico City during or about the same time LEE HARVEY OSWALD was reportedly there.

AT REYNOSA, TAMAULIPAS, MEXICO:

On June 16, 1964, SA T-1, a confidential source abroad, advised he had determined that ERNESTO LIMA JUAREZ is a masonry contractor who recently was on a job in Rio Bravo, Tamaulipas, Mexico, but had returned to Reynosa, Tamaulipas, Mexico.

LIMA JUAREZ furnished the following information:

On June 16, 1964, SA T-1 advised that ERNESTO LIMA JUAREZ furnished the following information:

He was in Mexico City during the last few days of September, 1963, and possibly the first day or two of October, 1963. He stayed at the Hotel Del Comercio in Room Number 8 with FRANCISCO MORALES whom he was attempting to aid in obtaining employment.

While there he noticed an American whom he later recognized from news media photographs as LEE HARVEY OSWALD. He did not associate with OSWALD and as far as he knows, MORALES did not associate with OSWALD. He pointed out that at that time he had no reason to pay any particular attention to OSWALD, assuming that OSWALD was merely an American tourist.

During the time he was staying at the Hotel Del Comercio he also noticed four Cubans, one of whom he heard, probably from MORALES, was from the State of Florida, U. S. A. He described this individual as a white male, 55 to 56 years of age, 5 ft. 8 in. in height, slender build, fair complexion, and grey hair. He did not associate with the Cubans and did not learn their names or addresses. However, MORALES had some drinks with them on one or two occasions and might possibly have their names or other information pertaining to them.

CE-2450
CE-3074

WTC:mfd

MEMORANDUM   March 26, 1964

SUBJECT: Mexico - CIA Dissemination of Information on
         Lee Harvey Oswald on March 24, 1964

The CIA directed a memorandum to J. Lee Rankin (Commission Document No. 531) in which it set forth the dissemination of the information on Lee Harvey Oswald. I realize that this memorandum is only a partial answer to our inquiry to the CIA dated March 16, 1964 and I hope that the complete answers will give us the/additional information we requested.

We would like to know just when got the information with respect to Lee Harvey Oswald and what was the information and how was it obtained. How did the information get from Mexico to the CIA in Washington, and in what fom did it come?

At what point was the information that the Lee Harvey Oswald was probably the Lee Harvey Oswald who had defected and was married to a Russian developed so that when the telegram went from the CIA in Washington to the various agencies it contained such information. In other words, I would like to know whether this was information available in Mexico or did this additional information get in the message only after it reached Washington and the information was being disseminated to the various agencies.

As you know, we are still trying to get an explanation of the photograph which the FBI showed Marguerite Oswald soon after the assassination. I hope that paragraph 4 of the memorandum of March 24, 1964 sent Mr. Rankin by the CIA is not the answer which the CIA intends to give us as to this inquiry.

We should also determine why the Navy never furnished the CIA with copies of the most recent photographs of Oswald.

Mr. J. Edgar Hoover
Director, Federal Bureau
of Investigation
Department of Justice
Washington, D. C.

Dear Mr. Hoover:

Your letter of November 12 responded to our suggestion that it might be desirable to investigate further the sources of the original description of the President's alleged assassin that was broadcast by the Dallas police at 12:45 p.m., November 22, 1963. We had also raised whether the police engaged in searching the Texas School Book Depository were notified of this description of the alleged assassin, and if so, when.

You state that in a letter of January 14, 1964 you notified the Commission that the Dallas Police Department advised that the broadcast was initiated on the basis of a description furnished by an unidentified citizen who had observed an individual approximating Oswald's description running from the Texas School Book Depository Building immediately after the assassination. Since there is other testimony that the description was also based on information given by Howard Brennan who stated that he saw the assassin in the southeast corner window of the building, it would seem desirable to ascertain as precisely as may be possible the sources—of which there seem to have been several—on which the description was based and how and by whom the information was transmitted to the Police Department to be put out by the radio dispatcher.

In its Report, the Commission has determined that considerable time—15 minutes or more—elapsed between the broadcast of the description and the discovery of the cartons and other material evidence in the southeast corner window of the sixth floor, 37 minutes elapsed since the discovery of the rifle. An even longer time had elapsed since Brennan first told a policeman of seeing the shots come from the southeast window. Yet the men searching in the building seem never to have been notified of Brennan's statement.

Attachment A

Out Message No. 74673, dated 10 October 1963 and filed at 0800 hours, to Department of State, Federal Bureau of Investigation, Department of the Navy.

Subject: Lee Henry OSWALD

1. On 1 October 1963 a reliable and sensitive source in Mexico reported that an American male, who identified himself as Lee OSWALD, contacted the Soviet Embassy in Mexico City inquiring whether the Embassy had received any news concerning a telegram which had been sent to Washington. The American was described as approximately 35 years old, with an athletic build, about six feet tall, with a receding hairline.

2. It is believed that OSWALD may be identical to Lee Henry OSWALD, born on 18 October 1939 in New Orleans, Louisiana. A former U.S. Marine who defected to the Soviet Union in October 1959 and later made arrangement through the United States Embassy in Moscow to return to the United States with his Russian-born wife, Marina Nikolaevna Pusakova, and their child.

3. The information in paragraph one is being disseminated to your representatives in Mexico City. Any further information received on this subject will be furnished you.

1 more than one direction. One group converged from the

2 corner of Elm and Houston, and came down the exten-

3 sion of Elm and came into the high ground, and another

4 line -- another large group went across the triangular

5 area between Houston and Elm and then across Elm and

6 then up the incline. Som of them all the way up.

7 Many of them did, as well as, of course, between

8 50 and a hundred policemen within a maximum of five

9 minutes.

10 MR. BALL: In this area around your tower?

11 MR. BOWERS: That's right. Sealed off the

12 area, and I held off the trains until they could be

13 examined, and there was some transients taken on at

14 least one train.

15 MR. BALL: I believe you have talked this over

16 with me before you deposition was taken, haven't we?

17 MR. BOWERS: Yes.

18 MR. BALL: Is there anything that you told me

19 that I haven't asked you about that you think of?

20 MR. BOWERS: Nothing that I can recall.

21 MR. BALL: You have told me all that you know

22 about this, haven't you?

23 MR. BOWERS: Yes, I believe that I have related

24 everything which I have told the City Police, and

Re: ASSASSINATION OF PRESIDENT
JOHN FITZGERALD KENNEDY,
NOVEMBER 22, 1963, DALLAS, TEXAS

Caller	Conversation
61 (Patrolmen G. W. TEMPLE and R. E. VAUGHN)	We have information from the agent out here at T&P. Said that the train is stopped on the overpass, the triple over- pass; that there was a person jumping at the ninth boxcar from the front engine. Said he is hiding in a car.
Dispatcher (HULSE and MC DANIEL)	Is the train stopped there now?
61 (TEMPLE and VAUGHN)	I'm in behind the Texas School Depository. He has the train stopped. He said it is the ninth car from the engine. Gondola-type car; said he is hunkered down inside.
Dispatcher (HULSE and MC DANIEL)	Any squad Elm and Houston...
392 (Criminal Investigation Division)	392 (Criminal Investigation Division)
Dispatcher (HULSE and MC DANIEL)	392 (Criminal Investigation Division), did you receive that information?
392 (Criminal Investigation Division)	10-4. En route.
Dispatcher (HULSE and MC DANIEL)	10-4.
241 (Patrolman J. P. HOLLINGS-WORTH)	241 (HOLLINGSWORTH) en route.
361 (Criminal Investigation Division)	361 (Criminal Investigation Division) en route.

- 94 -

IRIS LEONARD
COURT REPORTER
IRVING, TEXAS

TOP SECRET

52

1   you got there?

2   MR. HARKNESS: There were some Secret Service

3   Agents there. I didn't get them identified. They

4   told me they were Secret Service.

5   MR. BELIN: Then did you stay around the back

6   of the building?

7   MR. HARKNESS: Yes, I stayed at the back until

8   the squad got there.

9   MR. BELIN: Then what did you do?

10   MR. HARKNESS: I went back to the front, and

11   Inspector Sawyer -- helped to get the crowd back first

12   and then Inspector Sawyer assigned me to some freight

13   cars that were leaving out of the yard, to go down

14   and search all freight cars that were leaving the yard

15   MR. BELIN: Then what did you do?

16   MR. HARKNESS: Well, we got a long freight that

17   was in there, and we pulled some people off of there

18   and took them to the station.

19   MR. BELIN: You mean some transients?

20   MR. HARKNESS: Tramps and hoboes.

21   MR. BELIN: That were on the freight car?

22   MR. HARKNESS: Yes, sir.

23   MR. BELIN: Then what did you do?

24   MR. HARKNESS: That was all my assignment, be-

25   cause they shook two long freights down that were

TOP SECRET

TOP SECRET

53

1   leaving, to my knowledge, in all the area there.

2   We had several officers working in that area.

3   MR. BELIN: Do you know whether or not anyone

4   found any suspicious people of any kind or nature

5   down there in the railroad yard?

6   MR. HARKNESS: Yes, sir. We made some arrests.

7   I put some people in.

8   MR. BELIN: Were these what you call hoboes or

9   tramps?

10   MR. HARKNESS: Yes, sir.

11   MR. BELIN: Were all those questioned?

12   MR. HARKNESS: Yes, sir, they were taken to

13   the station and questioned.

14   MR. BELIN: Any guns of any kind found?

15   MR. HARKNESS: Not to my knowledge.

16   MR. BELIN: I want to go back to this Amos

17   Euins. Do you remember what he said to you and what

18   you said to him when you first saw him?

19   MR. HARKNESS: I went in that crowd up there

20   near the area there, and asked did anyone see any

21   place where the shots come from, and there was an

22   unidentified person pointed to him, said this boy

23   here saw it, saw the shots, where the shots came from,

24   and he told me it was.

25   MR. BELIN: Then what did he say?

TOP SECRET

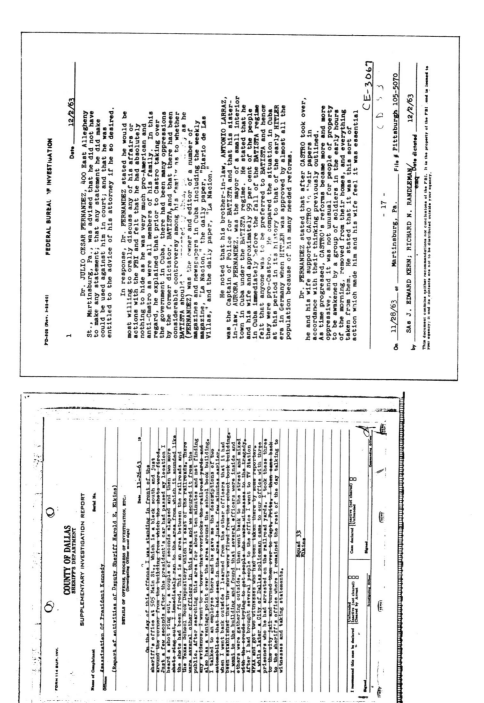

PD-302 (Rev. 1-31-60)

FEDERAL BUREAU OF INVESTIGATION

Date ___12/2/63___

1

Dr. JULIO CESAR FERNANDEZ, 400 East Allegheny St., Martinsburg, Pa., was advised that he did not have to make any statement; that any statement he did not have could be used against him in court; and that he was entitled to the advice of his attorney if he so desired.

In response, Dr. FERNANDEZ stated he would be most willing to orally discuss any of his affairs or actions with the FBI and felt that he had absolutely nothing to hide as he was very much pro-American and anti-Castro as were all members of his family. In this regard he explained that prior to Castro taking over the government in Cuba, there had been many oppressions by the former dictator, BATISTA, and that there had been considerable controversy among his family as to whether BATISTA should be supported. Dr. FERNANDEZ' brother (FERNANDEZ) was the owner and editor of a number of magazines and newspapers in Cuba including the weekly magazine, "La Nacion," the daily paper, "Diario de Las Villas," and the daily paper, "La Nacion."

He noted that his brother-in-law, ANTONIO LARRAZ, was the Captain of Police for BATISTA and that his sister-in-law, AURORA FERNANDEZ, was the mayor of a small interior town in Cuba under the BATISTA regime. He stated that he and his wife and approximately 99 per cent of the people in Cuba immediately before the fall of the BATISTA regime felt that anyone was to be preferred to BATISTA and hence they were pro-Castro. He compared the situation in Cuba at this period in its history to that of the early HITLER era in Germany when HITLER was approved by almost all the population because of his many needed reforms.

Dr. FERNANDEZ stated that after CASTRO took over, he and his wife supported CASTRO in their papers in accordance with their thinking previously outlined. As time progressed, CASTRO's reforms became more and more oppressive, and it was not unusual for people of property to be awakened by a group of soldiers in the early hours of the morning, removed from their homes, and everything taken from them. He stated that it was this sort of action which made him and his wife feel it was essential

- 17 -

On ___11/28/63___ at ___Martinsburg, Pa.___ File # ___Pittsburgh 105-5070___

by ___SAs J. EDWARD KERN; RICHARD N. RANDLEMAN___/enc Date dictated ___12/2/63___

This document contains neither recommendations nor conclusions of the FBI. It is the property of the FBI and is loaned to your agency; it and its contents are not to be distributed outside your agency.

CE 3067

CD 53

FORM 114 SUPP. INV.

COUNTY OF DALLAS
SHERIFF'S DEPARTMENT

SUPPLEMENTARY INVESTIGATION REPORT

Serial No. _____

Name of Complainant _____

Offense ___Assassination of President Kennedy___

(Report of activities of Deputy Sheriff Harold E. Elkins)

Date ___11-26-63___ 19___

DETAILS OF OFFENSE, PROGRESS OF INVESTIGATION, ETC.
(Investigating Officer must sign)

On the day of this offense I was standing in front of the sheriff's office at 505 Main St., which is a block south and just around the corner from the building from which the shots were fired. Just a few seconds after the President had passed my position I heard a shot ring out, a couple of seconds elapsed and then two more shots rang out. I immediately ran to the area from which it sounded like the shots had been fired. This is an area between the railroads and the Texas School Book Depository which is east of the railroads. There were many officers and a lot of spectators in this area. I secured it from the public. After searching this area for about ten minutes and not finding any evidence, I went to a tower that overlooks the railroad yards and also has a vantage point over the area around the school book building. I talked to an employee there and got from him the descriptions of two automobiles that he had seen in the area just a few minutes earlier. When I went back outside I learned from the other officers that it had been established that the shots were fired from the school book building. I went in the building and found that several officers were inside and others were gathering outside. I then went back to the street and asked with the crowds trying to get people who were witnesses to the tragedy. After I had brought several people to the office I went to TV Station WFAA and got pertinent data that had been taken there by news reporters. A while later a City of Dallas policeman came to our office with three prisoners who he had arrested on the railroad yards. I took these three to the city jail and turned them over to Capt. Fritz. I then came back to the sheriff's office where I remained the rest of the day talking to witnesses and taking statements.

Squad 33
Elkins

I commend this case be declared ___ Unfounded ___Inactive (not cleared) ___
___ Inactive (not cleared) ___Cleared by Arrest ___
Case declared ___Inactive (not cleared) ___Unfounded ___

Signed _____ Signed _____

Investigating Officer _____ Commanding Officer _____

3877

EXHIBIT NO. 148

July 2, 1971

MEMORANDUM FOR: H.R. HALDEMAN

FROM: CHARLES COLSON

SUBJECT: Howard Hunt

The more I think about Howard Hunt's background, politics, disposition and experience, the more I think it would be worth your time to meet him. I had forgotten when I talked to you that he was the CIA mastermind on the Bay of Pig's. He told me a long time ago that if the truth were even know, Kennedy would be destroyed.

If you want to get a feel of his attitude, I transcribed a conversation with him yesterday on it. Needless to say, I did not even approach what we had been talking about, but merely sounded out his own ideas.

NY 105-38431

On February 28, 1964, the Honorable RICHARD M. NIXON, former Vice-President of the U. S., was contacted by Assistant Director in Charge of the New York Office, JOHN F. MALONE, and furnished the following information:

Mr. NIXON advised that the only time he was in Dallas, Texas during 1963 was two days prior to the assassination of President JOHN F. KENNEDY. He vaguely thought there

3   ▬▬ Commission Exhibit 1973

NY 105-38431

was some invitation extended during the early part of 1963, probably in April, for him to come to Dallas, but that it never materialized, nor did he give any consideration to going there. Mr. NIXON could not even recall the circumstances surrounding the invitation, but did observe that conceivably there could have been some publicity indicating that he had been invited to come to Dallas. Mr. NIXON said that if anything more concrete comes to his mind or after his secretary checks his records which would indicate the circumstances surrounding this, he would immediately notify the Federal Bureau of Investigation (FBI). He did say positively that he had no intention of visiting Dallas during April, 1963.

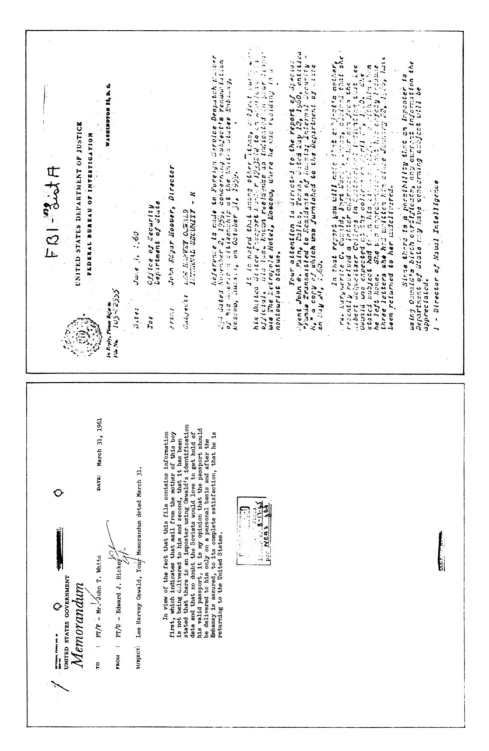

UNITED STATES GOVERNMENT

Memorandum

TO: PT/F - Mr. John T. White   DATE: March 31, 1961

FROM: PT/U - Edward J. Hickey

SUBJECT: Lee Harvey Oswald, Your Memorandum dated March 31.

In view of the fact that this file contains information first, which indicates that mail from the mother of this boy is not being delivered to him and second, that it has been stated that there is an imposter using Oswald's identification data and that no doubt the Soviets would love to get hold of his valid passport, it is my opinion that the passport should be delivered to him only on a personal basis and after the Embassy is assured, to its complete satisfaction, that he is returning to the United States.

UNITED STATES DEPARTMENT OF JUSTICE
FEDERAL BUREAU OF INVESTIGATION
WASHINGTON 25, D.C.

In Reply, Please Refer to
File No. 105-82555

Date: June 3, 1960

To: Office of Security
Department of State

From: John Edgar Hoover, Director

Subject: LEE HARVEY OSWALD
INTERNAL SECURITY - R

Reference is made to Foreign Service Despatch Number 234 dated November 2, 1959, concerning subject's renunciation of his American citizenship at the United States Embassy, Moscow, Russia, on October 31, 1959.

It is noted that among other items, subject during his United States passport under 1/23,242 to an American official, his last known residence as indicated in your report was The Metropole Hotel, Moscow, where he was residing in a nontourist status.

Your attention is directed to the report of Special Agent John W. Fain, Dallas, Texas, dated May 12, 1960, entitled "Funds transmitted to Residents of Russia; Internal Security -R," a copy of which was furnished to the Department of State on May 23, 1960.

In that report you will note that subject's mother, Mrs. Marguerite C. Oswald, Fort Worth, Texas, advised that she recently received a letter addressed to her son from the Albert Schweitzer College in Switzerland indicating that Lee Oswald was expected at the college in April 1960. She stated subject had written his last letter when he left home. She has corresponded with him only twice since the three letters she had written him since January 22, 1960, had been returned to her undelivered.

Since there is a possibility that an imposter is using Oswald's birth certificate, any current information the Department of State may have concerning subject will be appreciated.

1 - Director of Naval Intelligence

CD 23

OC 105-783

DETAILS:

At Sulphur, Oklahoma

The following investigation was conducted by SAs CARROLL L. SHIFFER and RICHARD T. LAINE on November 23, 1963:

CHARLES J. MC BEE, Chief of Police advised that WILLIS D. PRICE who operates the FINA Service Station on Broadway at 12th Street had informed him that on Sunday, November 17, 1963, a male who resembled LEE OSWALD had been in PRICE's service station in the company of people who appeared to be Cubans. PRICE stated he had seen a photograph in the Daily Oklahoman daily newspaper of LEE OSWALD who was being held in Dallas, Texas for the assassination of President KENNEDY, and the man with the Cubans resembled LEE OSWALD.

MC BEE further advised that the following are Cubans who reside in the Sulphur, Oklahoma area: Dr. M. L. SOCARRAZ, Dr. A. D. LOPAZ, and Dr. A. A. CERVERA. He believed all three of these Cubans are employed at the Oklahoma Veterans Hospital. As he remembers, he fingerprinted each of them after they arrived.

WILLIS D. PRICE, 1123 Broadway, Sulphur, advised he is the operator of the FINA Service Station at 1123 Broadway, and at about 2:00 P. M. on Sunday, November 17, 1963, a group of people who appeared to be Cubans, with a light-complexioned man who resembled LEE HARVEY OSWALD, drove up beside his service station in about a 1958 Ford station wagon, and some of them came into his station. He has seen a photograph in the Daily Oklahoman daily newspaper of LEE HARVEY OSWALD who was being held in Dallas, Texas for the assassination of President JOHN F. KENNEDY, and the light-complexioned man with the Cubans resembled OSWALD. He has since however seen television pictures of LEE OSWALD which did not very much resemble the man in the company of the Cubans. The automobile which they parked by the side of his station appeared to be of white and tan color with a white center and tan bottom. He did not know what license the vehicle carried. In the station wagon were two women who never got out of the vehicle. One of these women appeared to be about forty and the other older. The following described people got out of the station wagon and came into his service station: A woman in her late 20's or early 30's; a tall slender girl about thirteen years of age; a child two or three years old; two men, both of dark complexion, and

9.

COUNTY OF DALLAS
SHERIFF'S DEPARTMENT
SUPPLEMENTARY INVESTIGATION REPORT

Name of Complainant   Serial No.

Ref: Assassination Death of President

Offense

DETAILS OF OFFENSE, PROGRESS OF INVESTIGATION, ETC: Date 11-21-63 19

Mr. Decker,

About 8:00 am this morning, while in the presence of Allen Sweatt, I talked to Sorrels the head of the Dallas Secret Service. I advised him that for the past few months at a house at 3126 Harlendale some Cubans had been having meetings on the week ends and were possibly connected with the "Freedom For Cuba Party" of which Oswald was a member.

11-26-63

I don't know what action the secret service has taken but I learned today that sometime between seven days before the president was shot and the day after he was shot that subject Oswald had been in this house too.

Buddy Walthers

CD 23

OC 105-783

wide across the face. Both appeared to be Latins, were about 5'6.-7" tall and wore slacks. One man who resembled the photograph of OSWALD, who was of light complexion, pale, appeared to be in his late 20's or early 30's, about 6' tall, 170 pounds, thin and slender, light brown hair. The man who resembled OSWALD spoke in the language of the other people who looked like Cubans.

Before getting out of the station wagon, they asked if they could use the telephone in the station and he gave consent. When they first drove up the man who resembled OSWALD was in the back seat and by motion attracted his attention and motioned for one of the women to talk to him. She held up a small black book with a name and box number on it which he does not remember. From actions they thought the woman held up a street number or address. PRICE told her it was a mailing address and not a street address.

When the group of people came into the service station the woman who appeared to be in her 30's asked for a telephone directory on obtaining the directory, she looked up a number, and made a telephone call. The first number she attempted to call did not answer and she looked up another number. She telephoned a second time speaking in broken English. At the last of her telephone conversation, she gave some name as though referring to her own name, and said "from Cuba". She then hung up and walked to the man with light complexion resembling OSWALD in a foreign language. These people then left driving west on Highway 7, after getting into their station wagon. He does not remember which direction they came from.

The man resembling OSWALD never spoke English in the station but only used motions to PRICE. He looked American but talked in the same language as the people in his company.

MIGUEL L. de SOCARRAZ, M. D., at Oklahoma Veterans Hospital, residence, Post Office Box 200, advised he is a Cuban refugee and very anti-Communist. The following people contacted him on Sunday, November 17, 1963: MANOLITO RODRIGUEZ, with his wife and two or three year old baby; two other men both of whom were of dark complexion, one having the name of SALAZAR and the other CHITO RIVERO. With SALAZAR and RIVERO were their wives and a girl about thirteen or fourteen years

CD 23

OC 105-783

of age. SALAZAR is dark, short and husky and in his 20's. RIVERO is dark, short, thin and in his 50's. All of these people were in an older Ford station wagon of cream color. He did not know a 1958 Ford from other year models.

SOCARRAZ, after examining a photograph of LEE HARVEY OSWALD which appeared in the Daily Oklahoman newspaper, stated that MANOLITO RODRIGUEZ possibly did resemble OSWALD. However he is certain RODRIGUEZ is identical with OSWALD. RODRIGUEZ cannot speak English. He resides at 1208 Huspeth (Oak Cliff) Dallas, Texas with telephone number FR 4-5923. He is a Cuban refugee, was a lieutenant in the rebel army of FIDEL CASTRO but broke with CASTRO and obtained asylum in the Brazilian Embassy before coming to the United States. RODRIGUEZ is employed as a welder in Dallas.

SOCARRAZ advised from the descriptions of the Cubans visiting the FINA service station on November 17, 1963 and their vehicle, he feels certain they are the Cubans described above, who visited him on that date.

At Tulsa, Oklahoma

The following investigation was conducted by SA CE 2811 R. NEIL QUIGLEY:

On November 25, 1963, United States Attorney JOHN M. IMEL, Northern District of Oklahoma advised he had received a telephone call from JACK SPARKMAN, 701 North Cheyenne, Tulsa, telephone number NA 7-5389, in which SPARKMAN advised he was in possession of information proving JACK RUBENSTEIN furnished the station wagon that transported LEE HARVEY OSWALD from New Orleans, Louisiana to Fort Worth, Texas.

On November 25, 1963, JACK SPARKMAN, age 74, 701 North Cheyenne, Tulsa advised SAs THOMAS W. MC LAIN and R. NEIL QUIGLEY that he was directly responsible for Mr. IMEL's appointment as United States Attorney and had secured Capt. LARRY COLSEN, Tulsa Police Department, his job.

SPARKMAN exhibited a letter dated in 1960 from the then Senator JOHN F. KENNEDY which was in answer to one SPARKMAN wrote to Senator KENNEDY. SPARKMAN exhibited identification as an honorary deputy sheriff of Tulsa County and a special officer's badge.

SPARKMAN stated thirty per cent of all the people living in Tulsa were Communists and through his contacts with them had learned of the assassination ninety days prior to its happening (he later stated sixty days prior) but did not believe the persons telling him of the matter.

-5-

FD-302 (Rev. 3-3-59)

CO205

"EDERAL BUREAU OF INVESTIGA"

Date 12/19/63

1

JUAN B. MARTIN, 9923 Carnegie Drive, Dallas, Texas, advised he is acquainted with SYLVIA ODIO who approached him to help her with the organization known as Junta Revolucionaria, also known as JURE, however he did not help her and he had never heard of LEE HARVEY OSWALD prior to November 22, 1963, and has never met LEE HARVEY OSWALD.

on 12/19/63 at Dallas, Texas File # DL 100-10461

by Special Agent JAMES P. HOSTY:vm Date dictated 12/19/63

FD-302 (Rev. 3-3-59)

CO205

"EDERAL BUREAU OF INVESTIGA"

Date 12/19/63

1

Miss SYLVIA ODIO, 1816 W. Davis Street, Dallas, Texas, advised she is a Cuban refugee and a member of the organization known as Junta Revolucionaria or JURE.

Miss ODIO stated that in late September or early October, 1963, two Cuban men came to her house and stated they were from JURE. They were accompanied by an individual whom they introduced as LEON OSWALD. Miss ODIO stated that based upon photographs she has seen of LEE HARVEY OSWALD she is certain that LEON OSWALD is identical with LEE HARVEY OSWALD. Miss ODIO stated she is not certain if she misunderstood OSWALD as LEON or if the two Cuban men who introduced OSWALD as LEON misunderstood him. Miss ODIO stated the purpose of their visit was to ask her to write some letters to various businesses in Dallas and request funds for JURE.

Miss ODIO stated that both of her parents are presently in prison in Cuba and for this reason she declined for fear her parents would be possibly harmed. These two individuals together with OSWALD then left. A few days later one of the two Cuban individuals contacted her by telephone and stated they were leaving town presumably to return to either Miami, Florida, or Puerto Rico, the headquarters for JURE. The individual who called Miss ODIO who only gave his name as LEOPOLDO stated he was not going to have anything further to do with LEON OSWALD since he considered him to be "loco." This individual known only as LEOPOLDO stated OSWALD did not appear sincere. He told them he was an ex-marine and could help them in the underground however he appeared to be very cynical and seemed to think that all Cubans but all Americans. According to LEOPOLDO, OSWALD stated "I'll bet you Cubans could kill KENNEDY for what he did to you at the Bay of Pigs." According to Miss ODIO, LEOPOLDO told them that the Cuban people bore no malice toward President KENNEDY because of the Bay of Pigs episode.

on 12/18/63 at Irving, Texas File # DL 100-10461

by Special Agent JAMES P. HOSTY, Jr., and Date dictated 12/19/63
BARDWELL D. ODUM:vm

LA 89-75
LLB:DHA

DICK WATLEY
3350 N.W. 18th Terrace
Miami, Florida

On November 23, 1963, SID MARKS, Gardena, California, advised that about 30 days ago or a little more he was in the private detective offices of DICK HATHCOCK at 6663 Hollywood Boulevard, Los Angeles, California. At this time an associate of HATHCOCK, ROY PAYNE, was there and prior to leaving asked MARKS and HATHCOCK if anyone had been in to get a rifle for $50.00. PAYNE is white, male, 6'0" tall, 210 pounds, and shaved bald head.

After awhile an individual named "SKIP" came in and got a high powered rifle which looked identical to the one shown on television on November 23, 1963, as being used in the assassination of President KENNEDY. "SKIP" is male, Mexican, 6'0" tall, 40-45 years, slender, and a loud mouth.

On November 23, 1963, RICHARD HATHCOCK, Allied International Detectives, Suite 310, 6605 Hollywood Boulevard, Los Angeles, telephone number HO 4-5644, advised ROY PAYNE is his associate in the above enterprise. HATHCOCK advised as follows:

He, HATHCOCK, has known one DICK WATLEY for several years. WATLEY, to the best of HATHCOCK's information, currently resides at 3350 N.W. 18th Terrace in Miami, Florida. WATLEY is a male Caucasian.

Prior to HATHCOCK's present occupation, he was the proprietor of the Adventurers Corner, a shop at the corner of Sunset and La Brea, Los Angeles, which sold articles from all over the world and was an unofficial gathering place for adventurers in this area.

LA 89-75
LLB:DHA
2

Shortly after the Bay of Pigs invasion in Cuba, WATLEY, whom HATHCOCK had not seen for some time, came into the Adventurers Corner and gave HATHCOCK a shoulder patch "that had a skull and cross-bones on it plus the words, "Brigada Internationale." WATLEY told HATHCOCK that he had been in Guatemala instructing troops down there and that he had pulled out a week or two prior to the Bay of Pigs invasion and had not participated in the invasion.

HATHCOCK did not see WATLEY again until about seven or eight months ago when he came to HATHCOCK's office with two other men, all three of whom were wearing green fatigues and one of the men was wearing a "mohawk" hair cut. The men were interested in getting into the wild animal business and asked HATHCOCK where they could get some wild animals.

Approximately one year ago, JERRY PATRICK, whose true name is JERRY HEMMING, a male Caucasian, approximately 30 to 31 years, 6'4" tall, 230 pounds, well built, curly brown hair, handsome, and LORENZO PASCILLIO, also known as LORENZO HALL and "SKIP" HALL, a male Caucasian, 35 to 42 years, 5'11" tall, 175 to 180 pounds, black hair, mustache, ruddy complexion from Wichita, Kansas, came into HATHCOCK's office which was then located at 6715 Hollywood Boulevard, stating that they were broke and that they knew DICK WATLEY and WATLEY had sent them to him. They had with them a set of golf clubs and a 30-06 Johnson Semi-automatic rifle with a Bushnell Variable Powered Scope. HATHCOCK loaned them $100-$50 on each item and it was his understanding they were to pick up the articles as soon as possible. HATHCOCK only saw JERRY PATRICK once after that and that was about one week later when he again came to the office.

Several months ago, since the men did not retrieve the articles, HATHCOCK sold the golf clubs. On September 18, 1963, LORENZO HALL came in with $50 and retrieved the rifle. Shortly thereafter HATHCOCK received a telephone call from JERRY PATRICK who was then residing at 2450 N.W.

GD 1179

LA 89-75
LLB:DEA
4

LORENZO HALL, now resides at 1191 College View Drive, Apartment 7, Monterey Park, California, telephone number 261-8911 and HATHCOCK does not know where he is now employed. He last saw HALL about two weeks ago when he came by HATHCOCK's office simply to talk.

HATHCOCK reiterated that both men are anti-communist and very strongly anti-Castro.

No further investigation was conducted as it is obvious that the rifle mentioned above was not used in connection with the assassination of President KENNEDY.

298

GD 1179

LA 89-75
LLB:DEA
3

North River Drive, Miami, Florida, inquiring as to whether HATHCOCK still had the rifle. HATHCOCK told him that he had given the rifle to HALL for $50 and this seemed to irritate PATRICK to some extent. Since then HATHCOCK has sent the receipt he received from HALL for the $50 to PATRICK to convince him that he had returned the rifle.

On the day HALL retrieved the rifle, he sold him a Bolex Motion Picture Camera with telephoto lens which was then the property of HATHCOCK. HALL paid by two checks - one drawn on the Citizens Bank on the account of the Committee to Free Cuba in the amount of $350 and another in the amount of $150 on the account of a resident of La Habra. HATHCOCK gave HALL back $100.

HATHCOCK advised both PATRICK and HALL are violently anti-communist and anti-Castro and they both told him they fought in the mountains with Castro in Cuba, however, fell out with him after the revolution. LORENZO told HATHCOCK he spent seven months in prison in Cuba, however, eventually got back to the United States. PATRICK stated that he fell out with Castro and eventually got back to the United States.

(HATHCOCK has Xerox copies of newspaper articles from Florida in his office concerning the anti-Castro troops training there and PATRICK's picture appears as one of the anti-Castro troops).

PATRICK, when in Los Angeles, had an address of 1209 South Atlantic, Alhambra, (Atlantic Radio & TV), telephone number AT 1-6421, and an address of in care of HOWARD K. DAVIS, 3350 N.W. 18th Terrace, Miami, Florida, telephone number NE 4-1373.

It is HATHCOCK's information that DAVIS was Castro's personal pilot and also a close friend of DICK WATLEY.

297

DEPARTMENT OF STATE
OFFICE OF SECURITY

November 24, 1963

MEMORANDUM FOR: L - Mr. Abram Chayes

SUBJECT: JACK LEON RUBENSTEIN

Today the following departmental record checks were conducted on Jack Ruby, Jack Leon Rubenstein and similar names (e.g., Jack Rubinstein, Abe Rubinstein):

SY central files
SY crank files
SY Dallas Field Office
PPT
VO
INR
RM/R

The results were negative.

Both the FBI and Secret Service have provided us with the following information on the subject:

Jack Leon Rubenstein is originally from Chicago, where he was born March 25, 1911. He has been in Dallas several years and is well known there as a nightclub operator.

Our search did reveal a letter from a New York import firm written in 1958 by a Jack Rubenstein to the Office of Munitions Controls requesting permission to negotiate the purchase of firearms and ammunition from an Italian firm.

We also checked the file of one Abe Rubinstein in the Records Service Center, Alexandria, Virginia. This check revealed simply that the individual, a longtime resident of New York, had applied for a United Nations position some years ago.

It appears that neither of these items is significant.

Raymond W. Laugel
Acting
Deputy Assistant Secretary
for Security

cc - Duty Officer Book

O/SY:RWLaugel:mc

Collect

CITY OF DALLAS

LONG DISTANCE MESSAGE

Phone No. _____ Time _____ Minutes _____ Amount _____

Person calling Lee Harvey Oswald Dept. _____

To Raleigh N.C. 834-7430

Person called John Hurt · or 833-1253

Date 11-23-63 da (Ca) 9-1

Received Placed L. Sweeney

from A.C. 919

This document does not come from the National Archives.

CD 163

(CE 3065)

DL 44-1639
MCC:BL
1

The San Antonio Office has advised that Sheriff CONRADO HEIN, Zapata, Texas, has advised JAMES WOODARD has not been in Zapata; that he has an outstanding warrant for WOODARD's arrest.

On December 5, 1963, WALLACE SHANLEY, Assistant Customs Enforcement Supervisor, Miami, Florida, advised SA ROBERT K. LEWIS that JAMES E. WOODARD is well known to his office but his present whereabouts is not known.

On December 3, 1963, PAUL A. WOODARD, 732 Altura Court, Pomona, California, advised SA WILLIAM LEE SCRUGGS that he is a brother of JAMES WOODARD, but has not seen him since 1953 or 1954. He stated "JAMES is such a liar" that he does not believe anything he says and that "JAMES would lie when the truth would suit him better."

LOUIS ROUS, #16 Ideal Motel, Tampa, Florida, advised SAs OMNIE K. WALKER and LIONEL K. BELLANGER, he is the uncle of JAMES WOODARD, that he knows nothing of WOODARD's activities or any connection of WOODARD with Cuban matters. He stated he considers WOODARD a "drifter and irresponsible, and that WOODARD is known as a "black sheep of his mother's family" and an "inveterate liar and gross exaggerator."

#2, Coldwater, Michigan, advised SAs JAMES F. CAMPBELL and CARL C. WOODARD, 243 North Snow Prairie Road, Route CLARK F. CARTER on December 4, 1963 he has not seen his brother, JAMES E. WOODARD, in some 10 years since JAMES stole his car and machine tools. He pointed out he has a strong enmity for his brother and would attack him on sight. He said he had never known JAMES WOODARD to reside in Dallas, Texas, and he has never heard JAMES had ever worked as a policeman.

Files of the Knoxville Office reflect JAMES WOODARD, FBI # 255 317 A, has been the subject of previous FBI investigation, an official of the U. S. Customs, Miami, Florida, stated WOODARD should be considered armed and dangerous as he carries a weapon and has a violent temper with drinking.

When interviewed by Special Agents of the Knoxville Office in September, 1963, WOODARD in a somewhat rambling and

---

OPTIONAL FORM NO. 10

UNITED STATES GOVERNMENT

Memorandum

TO   : IR/D/C - Mr. ...
VIA : IR/DDC - Mr. ...
FROM : IR/DDC - Ruth ...

DATE: 11/26/63

SUBJECT: Assassination of President Kennedy and murder of OSWALD, Lee Harvey

Per your instructions today, CY index cards were re-checked for references to OSWALD and RUBY, Jack with the following results:

OSWALD, Lee Harvey file # 39-61901 charged to CY/ceross 11/22/3

FEDOROVA, Marina Nikolaevna (Oswald's wife) cross-referenced to above file

The following documents re Oswald have been received since September/63; they are incorporated therein:

FBI Report: Dallas, 9/10/63
          New Orleans, 10/31/63
FBI Memo: New Orleans, 10/2/63
CIA Teletype 3/4673 re OSWALD, Lee Henry, 10/10/3

Oswald is evidently mentioned in an FBI report prepared at New Orleans, 10/25/63 at this reference was given to me by an FBI representative when I was in Mr. Clayes' office Saturday. This document was located in IFI, and was sent to SOM/Mr. Scully in connection with this matter 11/25/63.

RUBY (RUBEN, RUBLE), Jack: (John, Sparky) -- no record

RUBY...stein, Jack: no Record other than reference to a person of this name mentioned in a 1959 Department of the Army Report concerning ... Arms dealers in Scandinavia -- A Jack Rubenstein is listed as a representative of Saunders Company in the ...

cc: IR/DDC - Mr. MacDonald

UNITED STATES DEPARTMENT OF JUSTICE

FEDERAL BUREAU OF INVESTIGATION

WASHINGTON 25, D. C.

April 17, 1964

BY COURIER SERVICE

Commission No. 797

OFFICE OF THE DIRECTOR

Honorable J. Lee Rankin
General Counsel
The President's Commission
200 Maryland Avenue, Northeast
Washington, D. C. 20002

Dear Mr. Rankin:

In response to your letter of April 3, 1964,
as it pertains to Robert Ray McKeown, I am enclosing a
letterhead memorandum entitled "Robert Ray McKeown" dated
April 17, 1964, which sets forth McKeown's connection
with a neutrality and registration act investigation
conducted by this Bureau and identifies his confederates.

The neutrality and registration act investigation
related primarily to the activities of Carlos Prio Socarras,
who, with a number of others including McKeown, was involved
in a conspiracy to ship arms, munitions, and other war
materials to Fidel Castro to assist him in his efforts to
overthrow the Batista regime in Cuba. There are no references
to Jack L. Ruby appearing in this investigation.

Other than McKeown's connection with the above
matter and material previously furnished to you in connection
with the case entitled "Jack L. Ruby, Lee Harvey Oswald -
Victim, Civil Rights" there is no other material in Bureau
files concerning McKeown.

Sincerely yours,

J. Edgar Hoover

Enclosure

CD 103

DL 44-1639
2

incoherent manner, alleged he had participated in an invasion
of Cuba prior to the CASTRO regime; that he had participated
in the Bay of Pigs invasion and has furnished ammunition and
dynamite to both CASTRO and Cuban exile forces.

On October 8, 1963, WOODARD was questioned concerning
certain dynamite found at his residence in South Dade County,
Florida, which dynamite had been stolen from a construction
company. He claimed such dynamite was stored at his residence
by Cubans to be used by Cuban exile forces against the
CASTRO regime.

(CE 3065)

8

Document continued on page 292.

CONFIDENTIAL

77

lived in his apartment. Ate directly in a place called
Wolf's, downstairs. Wouldn't know how to speak their
language. I wouldn't know how to communicate with them.

I probably had two dates from meeting some young
ladies I got to dancing with, because my dinners were
served in the Tropicana.

One thing I forgot to tell you -- you are bringing
my mind back to a few things -- the owners, the greatest
that have been expelled from Cuba, are the Fox brothers.

They own the Tropicana.

MR. RANKIN: Who are the Fox brothers?

MR. RUBY: Martin Fox, and I can't think of the
other name.

MR. RANKIN: Do you know where they are located now?

MR. RUBY: They are in Miami, Florida. They know
everything about McWillie, I heard: and know the officials.

I met McWillie because he came to the Club, and he
came to the Club to look over the show. And you get to
talk to people and meet a lot of different types of people.

The Fox brothers came to Dallas -- I don't know which
one it was -- to collect a debt that some man owed the

Cotton Gin Company here.

Do you know their name, Mr. Bowie?

MR. BOWIE: Murray, or something.

MR. RUBY: He gave some bad checks on a gambling

CONFIDENTIAL

helen laidrich

FD-302 (Rev. 1-25-60)

FEDERAL BUREAU OF INVESTIGATION

Date   December 1, 1963

1

    AT T-2 advised on November 29, 1963, that he
formerly owned interest in a club in Miami, Florida. He
stated that in the early 1950's, JACK RUBY held interest
in the Colonial Inn, a nightclub and gambling house in
Hollandale, Florida. He stated that JACK RUBY, known then
as RUBENSTEIN, was active in arranging illegal flights of
weapons from Miami to the Castro organization in Cuba.
According to T-2, RUBY was reportedly part owner of two
planes used for these purposes.

    T-2 further stated that RUBY subsequently left
Miami and purchased a substantial share in a Havana gaming
house in which one COLLIS PRIO (phonetic) was principal
owner. T-2 stated that COLLIS PRIO was within favor of
former Cuban leader BATISTA, but was instrumental in
financing and managing accumulation of arms by pro-Castro
forces.

    T-2 stated that one DONALD EDWARD BROWDER was
associated with RUBY in the arms smuggling operation.
BROWDER is reportedly incarcerated in the U. S. Penitentiary,
Atlanta, after conviction on a U. S. Customs violation.
T-2 also stated that JOE MARRS of Marrs Aircraft, 167th
Street, Miami, Florida, allegedly contracted with RUBY to
make flights to Havana. T-2 further stated that LESLIE LEWIS,
formerly Chief of Police, Hialeah, Florida, and now possibly
a pistol instructor in Dade County, Florida, Sheriff's Office,
possessed detailed knowledge of persons involved in flight
of weapons to Cuba and had specific knowledge of RUBY's
participation.

    T-2 subsequently advised on November 30, 1963,
that on the basis of viewing RUBY's photograph and knowing
that the JACK RUBENSTEIN he has described originally resided
in Chicago, Illinois, he is convinced beyond reasonable
doubt that the latter is identical with the JACK RUBY in
Dallas, Texas. T-2 also named CLIFTON T. BOWES, Jr.,
formerly captain of National Airlines, Miami, Florida, as

- 14 -

On 11/29/63 & 11/30/63 at Atlanta, Georgia   File # Atlanta 105-3193

by SA DANIEL D. DOYLE :cb   Date dictated 12/1/63

helen
laidrich

85

1 to see the same fellows at Delta Airlines.

2 MR. RANKIN: Do you recall going up the elevator

3 after the shooting of Oswald?

4 MR. RUBY: That is so small to remember, I guess it

5 is automatic, you know.

6 MR. RANKIN: Did you have this gun a long while

7 that you did the shooting with?

8 MR. RUBY: Yes.

9 MR. RANKIN: You didn't carry it all the time?

10 MR. RUBY: I did. I had it in a little bag with

11 money constantly. I carry my money.

12 CHIEF JUSTICE WARREN: Congressman, do you have

13 anything further?

14 MR. RUBY: You can get more out of me. Let's not

15 break up too soon.

16 CONGRESSMAN FORD: When you got to Havana, who met

17 you in Havana?

18 MR. RUBY: McWillie. Now here is what happened.

19 One of the Fox brothers came to visit me in Dallas with his

20 wife. They came to the Vegas Club with Mrs. McWillie, and

21 we had taken some pictures, 8 X 10's.

22 Evidently the Fox's were in exile at that time, because

23 when I went to visit McWillie, when he sent me the plane

24 tickets, they looked through my luggage and they saw a

25 photograph of Mr. Fox and his wife. They didn't interrogate

helen
laidrich

86

1 but they went through everything and held me up for hours.

2 CONGRESSMAN FORD: Castro employees?

3 MR. RUBY: Yes. Because evidently, in my ignorance,

4 I didn't realize I was bringing a picture that they knew was

5 a bitter enemy. At that time they knew that the Fox brothers

6 weren't going to jell, or something was going to happen.

7 Whether it was they were in exile at that time, I

8 don't know.

9 But they came to my Club, the Vegas Club, and we taken

10 pictures.

11 Mr. McWillie was waiting for me, and he saw me go

12 through the Customs line for a couple of hours, and he said,

13 "Jack, they never did this to anyone before." Evidently

14 they had me pretty well lined up as to where I come in the

15 picture of Mr. Rivera Fox. I can't think of his name.

16 CONGRESSMAN FORD: You spent eight days there in

17 Havana?

18 MR. RUBY: Yes, approximately.

19 CONGRESSMAN FORD: And you stayed at the apartment

20 of Mr. --

21 MR. RUBY: Volk's Apartments. I never used the

22 phone. I wouldn't know how to use the phone. Probably

23 to call back to Dallas. And the only time, Mr. McWillie

24 had to be at the Club early, so I remained a little later

25 in town -- not often -- because I saved money when I rode

78

helen
laidrich

1 debt, and they came to visit me. The lawyer, I think, is
2 Mark Lane. That is the attorney that was killed in New York?
3 CHIEF JUSTICE WARREN: That is the fellow who
4 represents, or did represent Mrs. Marguerite Oswald. I
5 think I read in the paper where he no longer represents her.
6 MR. RANKIN: He is still alive though.
7 CHIEF JUSTICE WARREN: Oh yes.
8 MR. RUBY: There was one Lane that was killed in a
9 taxicab. I thought he was an attorney in Dallas.
10 CHIEF JUSTICE WARREN: That was a Dave Lane.
11 MR. RUBY: There is a very prominent attorney in
12 Dallas, McCord. McCord represents the Fox brothers here.
13 They called me because the Fox brothers wanted to see me,
14 and I came down to the hotel.
15 And Mrs. McWillie -- Mr. McWillie was married to her
16 at that time -- and if I recall, I didn't show them off to
17 the airport at that time.
18 This is when they were still living in Havana, the
19 Fox brothers. We had dinner at -- how do you pronounce
20 that restaurant at Love Field? Luau? That serves this
21 Chinese food.
22 Dave McCord, I was in his presence, and I was invited
23 out to dinner, and there was an attorney by the name of
24 Leon. Is he associated with McCord?
25 And there was a McClain.

helen
laidrich

79

1 CHIEF JUSTICE WARREN: Alfred was killed in a taxi
2 in New York.
3 MR. RUBY: He was at this dinner meeting I had with
4 McCord. I don't know if Mrs. McWillie was along. And one
5 of the Fox brothers, because they had just been awarded the
6 case that this person owns, this Gin Company, that was
7 compelled to pay off.
8 MR. RANKIN: I think, Mr. Ruby, it would be, quite
9 helpful to the Commission if you could tell, as you recall it,
10 just what you said to Mr. Sorrells and the others after the
11 shooting of Lee Harvey Oswald. Can you recall that?
12 MR. RUBY: The only one I recall Mr. Sorrells in,
13 there were some incorrect statements made at this time.
14 MR. RANKIN: Can you tell us what you said?
15 CONGRESSMAN FORD: First, tell us when this took
16 place.
17 MR. RANKIN: How soon after the shooting occurred?
18 MR. RUBY: Well, Ray Hall was the first one that
19 interrogated me. Wanted to know my whole background.
20 MR. RANKIN: Can you tell us how soon was it?
21 Within a few minutes after the shooting?
22 MR. RUBY: No. I waited in a little room there
23 somewhere upstairs in -- I don't know what floor it was.
24 I don't recall.
25 MR. RANKIN: Where did this occur, on the third

Commission No. 686d

1

UNITED STATES DEPARTMENT OF JUSTICE
FEDERAL BUREAU OF INVESTIGATION

WASHINGTON 25, D.C.

March 26, 1964

In Reply, Please Refer to
File No.

JACK L. RUBY
LEE HARVEY OSWALD – VICTIM

The following information concerning Lewis Joseph McWillie was developed by the FBI in connection with another matter.

Records of the Nevada Gaming Commission, Carson City, Nevada, made available by Investigator Harold Anderson to SA Thomas G. Dempsey on November 21, 1963, reflect the following information:

Lewis Joseph McWillie, also known as Lewis Joseph Martin, FBI Number 4-404-064, has the following arrest record:

November 20, 1925 - larceny - Memphis Police Department, their number 8480 - disposition not shown

August 3, 1945 - USM, Dallas, Texas, number 5367 - violation of OPA Gas Ration Act - disposition not shown

December 12, 1947 - Memphis, Tennessee Police Department - investigation known gambler - fined

June 30, 1949 - Dallas, Texas Police Department - their number 28652 - investigation gambler - released

June 27, 1961 - Sheriff's Office, Reno, Nevada - applicant - number AO3382

October 4, 1961 - Reno, Nevada Police Department, number 87293 - applicant

February 15, 1963, Clark County Sheriff's Office, Las Vegas, Nevada, their number 63658 - applicant.

The Memphis Police Department has a lengthy arrest record for McWillie under their number 8480, from November, 1925, to December, 1947. All dispositions were shown as fines and released except that on November 20, 1925, he was sentenced to two years at the Boys Reformatory, Washington, D. C., for violation of Dyer Act.

---

elen aidrich

63

CONFIDENTIAL

1 MR. RUBY: No. Let me add -- you are refreshing

2 my mind about a few things.

3 Can I ask you one thing? Did you all talk to Mr.

4 McWillie? I am sure you have.

5 VOICE: Yes.

6 MR. RUBY: He always wanted me to come down to

7 Havana, Cuba, invited me down there, and I didn't want to

8 leave my business because I had to watch over it.

9 He was a key man over the Tropicana down there. That

10 was during our good times. Was in harmony with our enemy

11 of our present time.

12 CHIEF JUSTICE WARREN: Yes?

13 MR. RUBY: I refused. I couldn't make it.

14 Finally he sent me tickets to come down, airplane tickets.

15 I made the trip down there via New Orleans, and so

16 I stayed at the Volk's Apartments, and I was with him

17 constantly.

18 And I was bored with the gambling, because I don't

19 gamble, and there is nothing exciting unless you can speak

20 their language, which is Spanish, I believe.

21 And that was the only environment. That was in

22 August of '59.

23 Any thought of ever being close to Havana, Cuba,

24 I called him frequently because he was down there, and he

25 was the last person to leave, if I recall, when they had to

CONFIDENTIAL

SUMMARY OF INFORMATION
(PM-3-7)

DATE 18 Sep 1964

PREPARING OFFICE: OACSI, Directorate of Security, Counterintelligence Division, DA, Washington, DC 20310

SUBJECT: Information re the Assassination of President Kennedy

CODE FOR USE IN INDIVIDUAL PARAGRAPH EVALUATION

EVALUATION OF SOURCE:
COMPLETELY RELIABLE . . . . . A
USUALLY RELIABLE . . . . . . B
FAIRLY RELIABLE C
NOT USUALLY RELIABLE . . . . D
UNRELIABLE . . . . E
RELIABILITY UNKNOWN . . . . . F

OF INFORMATION:
CONFIRMED BY OTHER SOURCES . . 1
PROBABLY TRUE 2
POSSIBLY TRUE 3
DOUBTFULLY TRUE 4
IMPROBABLE 5
TRUTH CANNOT BE JUDGED 6

SUMMARY OF INFORMATION:

On 18 September 1964, the Deputy Chief of Staff for Intelligence, Hqs, Fifth US Army, Chicago, Illinois, furnished the following information obtained from BARTLES, Dennis, L., SSGT, RA 17 392 262, Assistant S4, Signal Battalion, Fort Carson, Colorado, during December 1963:

Sometime in December 1963, Bartles reported to the 5th MI Detachment, Fort Carson, Colorado, that Alberto de Jesus Santalo-Fuertes had told Bartles that he (Santalo) had made a telephone call to a friend in Florida shortly after the death of President Kennedy. Santalo claimed that just prior to President Kennedy's assassination, Oswald had met with Cuban Premier Fidel Castro in Mexico. Santalo also claimed that his reliable source in Florida had informed him that Oswald and the man charged with killing Oswald, Ruby, were "connected" in some way. Bartles could furnish no further information. Santalo has also remarked to Bartles that there is a one million dollar reward for the assassination of Castro.   F-6

Files of CIA and Department of State reveal no record of Fidel Castro's or Raul Castro's being in Mexico in 1962 or 1963.

The last known address of Santalo was c/o Mr. Roberto Hart, Englewood Avenue, Jacksonville, Florida.

DISTRIBUTION
1 cy - DIA; 1 cy - CRF

DA FORM 568

Files contain a letter from the Crime Commission of Greater Miami dated October 11, 1961, from Daniel P. Sullivan, Operations Director, who advised he could locate no information regarding McWillie in connection with operations of former Havana, Cuba, gambling casinos.

Investigation by Confidential Source reflected that at Dallas, Texas, McWillie was a member of the "so called gambling syndicate" operating in the Dallas area before the city and county of Dallas were closed in December, 1946. On April 11, 1946, McWillie killed one George Arthur McBride, a Dallas, Texas thief with an extensive record, at Dallas when McBride attempted to hold him up. This case was no billed by the Dallas County Grand Jury. As of May, 1960, McWillie was pit boss at the Riviera Casino, Havana, Cuba. Report reflects that it would appear McWillie solidified his syndicate connections through his association in Havana, Cuba, with Santo Trafficante, well known syndicate member, for Tampa, Florida; Meyer and Jake Lanski; Dino Cellini and others who were members of or associates of "the syndicate". McWillie has been in Nevada since June, 1961. From 1941 to about 1948, he resided in the Dallas, Texas, area and was a prominent figure in illegal gambling in that area. He left Dallas and went to Havana, Cuba, where he was known to associate with nationally known gambling characters such as Willie Bischoff, also known as Lefty Clark, Jake Lansky, Trafficante, and others.

McWillie was former Casino Manager at the Riverside Hotel, Reno and he began his employment in the casino at the Thunderbird Hotel, Las Vegas, on February 14, 1963, as an assistant to Mike Rennis, day shift casino boss.

On November 20, 1963, Robert Kellerer, Identification Officer, Washoe County Sheriff's Office, Reno, advised that Lewis Joseph McWillie, born May 4, 1908, at Kansas City, Missouri, FBI Number 4-404-064, was printed by his agency on June 27, 1961, for a work card for employment as a floor man at the Cal Neva Lodge, Crystal Bay, Nevada. This card expired on June 27, 1962, and has not been renewed. His residence at that time was Glad Lake Court, Kings Beach, California. He listed his mother as Blanche McWillie, 3631 Southwest 18th Terrace, Miami, Florida.

On December 17, 1963, Pat Tuggle, Clerk, Reno, Nevada Police Department, advised her records reflect Reno Police Department Number 87293 was assigned to Lewis Joseph

2

S-E-C-R-E-T
NO FOREIGN DISSEM/CONTROLLED DISSEM/NO DISSEM ABROAD/BACKGROUND
USE ONLY

CENTRAL INTELLIGENCE AGENCY
WASHINGTON, D.C. 20505

20 April 1964

MEMORANDUM FOR: The Director of Central Intelligence

SUBJECT: Plans of British and French Publishing Firms to
Publish the Thomas Buchanan Articles on
Assassination of President Kennedy

1. A competent American observer learned, in Paris on 10 April 1964, that Secker and Warburg Ltd., in London, will publish as a book the Thomas Gittings Buchanan articles which have appeared in Paris in l'Express. The publishing firm is also approaching various publishers in the United States and the firm is rushing its edition, hoping to have it on sale by 15 May 1964.

2. Buchanan's thesis is that the assassination of President Kennedy was the product of a rightist plot in the United States. He alleges in his articles that the slain Dallas policeman Tippett was part of the plot against President Kennedy.

3. A well-informed American, who maintains excellent contacts in French publishing circles, reported that Anne Rives (in charge of foreign rights for the Rene Julliard publishing firm) stated that the Buchanan book would be published in France by the end of April 1964. Julliard is hoping to publish the book at the same time as Les Roses Rouges de Dallas by Merin Gun, who is correspondent in the United States of the Italian magazine Epoca. Merin Gun claims to have been in the car following President Kennedy's car.

4. Anne Rives described the book Les Roses Rouges de Dallas as devastating and, for this reason, it could not be published in the United States. According to Rives, the British publisher for the book will be Frederick Muller of 110 Fleet Street, London. Rives indicated that Gun was handling all foreign publication rights to his book.

5. According to Anne Rives, the German publisher for the Buchanan book will be Rowohlt of Hamburg. She states that two American publishers have made offers for the book: Houghton-Mifflin is said to want to buy but not publish right away as the

NO FOREIGN DISSEM/CONTROLLED DISSEM/NO DISSEM ABROAD/BACKGROUND
USE ONLY

SECRET

CENTRAL INTELLIGENCE AGENCY
WASHINGTON 25, D.C.

PUB 3
GA/CIA

21 APR 1964

Mr. Samuel A. Stern
President's Commission on the
Assassination of President Kennedy
200 Maryland Avenue, N.E.
Washington, D.C. 20002

Dear Mr. Stern:

Pursuant to our telephone call yesterday, I am attaching at Mr. Karamessines' request a copy of a very recent dissemination by CIA on a matter of direct interest to you, and perhaps others in the Commission.

I would interpret the attachment to come within the sensitivity precautions that we have given in other, formal, transmissions to the Commission.

If you have any questions or comments on this piece, don't hesitate to call me.

Raymond G. Rocca

Attachment

SECRET

NO FOREIGN DISSEM/CONTROLLED DISSEM/NO DISSEM ABROAD/BACKGROUND
USE ONLY

firm is now doing two "official" books on President Kennedy with
United States Government backing. The other American firm, Knopf,
wants to publish the book right away and will probably get rights
through Curtis Brown of 575 Madison Avenue, New York City, the
literary agency involved.

6.

published his book "Unicorn" in France in 1959 and a year later
the Sloane firm published the Buchanan book in the United States.

Juliard

7. Concerning Nurin Gun, it has been reported that he was born
in Rome on 22 February 1924 of Turkish parents. He has been a free
lance journalist since 1946 and has placed articles in American
and Western European publications. In 1956 he resided in Toronto,
Canada and the Turkish Consulate in that city refused to grant him
a passport to return to Turkey because he was considered by them
to be a Communist.

Richard Helms
Deputy Director for Plans

CSDB-3/660,704

- 2 -

NO FOREIGN DISSEM/CONTROLLED DISSEM/NO DISSEM ABROAD/BACKGROUND
USE ONLY

Asked about alleged wrongdoing, Mr. Angleton said, "I've
got problems." He explained his
domestic activities this way:
"A mansion has many rooms,
and there were many thing
going on during the period of
the [antiwar] bombings. I'm not
privy to who struck John."

Mr. Angleton, who had been
in charge of rooting out foreign
espionage agents in the United
States, later permitted newsmen from three television net-
works to interview him.

Asked for reasons for his resignation he was quoted as
saying: "Police state ... Soviet

William Seymour

Unidentified man at the Cuban
Embassy, Mexico City whom the
CIA claimed was Oswald.

Fred Lee Chrisman

Eugene Edgar Bradley

The Authors' Rebuttal to
The Rockefeller Commission Report

As this book went to press, the Rockefeller Commission on CIA domestic activities released its report. As expected, it stated that there was no "credible evidence" of CIA participation in the John F. Kennedy assassination. Rather than conducting an investigation of its own (using its resources as a Presidential Commission), the panel chose only to evaluate the various allegations of CIA-complicity presented to it by essentially volunteer witnesses, some of whom were ill-equipped to handle questions raised by a panel led by an attorney as steeped in the Warren Report as David Belin. Curiously shirking its responsibilities, the Commission expected witnesses and the general public to bear the burden of proof of rumored allegations. Its obvious objective was to defend not re-examine the Warren Report. In its nineteen page section concerning the Kennedy assassination, the Commission hardly used any of the abundant pieces of evidence used in this book. The bulk of this material is available in the National Archives. Let us examine some of the Panel's findings:

1. Hunt and Sturgis did not Know Each Other prior to 1972

On page 94 we say that Sturgis took his name from a character in Hunt's 1949 spy novel, *Bimini Run*. The Panel cites the fact that in 1935 Frank's mother divorced Mr. Fiorini and married a Mr. Sturgis. We stand corrected—but only partially, because this new piece of information makes our case even stronger. It is, in fact, more likely that Hunt took the name of his character from Sturgis rather than vice versa; When a real person adopts the name of a popular fictional character (for example, Saul Bellow's Moses Herzog) he tends to use the exact name. On the other hand, a novelist who models his hero after a real person (who has no objections to being fictionalized) will tend to modify the person's name slightly. Thus Helen Bess might become Elaine Bess. Or better yet, the author might use the model's nickname or other similar names. If Hunt knew the then Frank Fiorini well, he would know that Frank's mother was called Mrs. Sturgis. "Frank Sturgis" would immediately suggest itself as an ideal name for the character, and H(Fr)ank Sturgis the perfect fictionalization of it. Three years later, in 1952, Fiorini did change his name to Frank Sturgis.

2. "Frank Sturgis was not an Employee or Agent of the CIA either in 1963 or any other Time."

The Panel cites "a search of CIA records" which failed to confirm his having been engaged as a CIA "agent, informant or operative." The CIA does not keep records on its sensitive operatives and, when they get caught, disowns them (see page 246).

3. "It cannot be Determined with Certainty where Hunt and Sturgis were on the Day of the Assassination..."

This frank admission is significant. November 22, 1963 is not exactly a day people forget. Hunt and Sturgis testified they were in Washington and Miami respectively on November 22, 1963 and no witnesses but "family members or relatives" (with the exception of Hunt's maid) backed them up. The Panel admits that "less weight can be assigned to the testimony of such interested witnesses" and goes on to disclose Hunt may have been on sick leave from the CIA on November 22, 1963. Hunt could also "not recall" if he was at CIA that morning. No one even testified to having reached Hunt at home that day by telephone.

4. "The Tramps were Found in a Boxcar about One Mile South of the Scene of the Assassination."

The Commission neglected to point out that the train had left the yards when it was stopped (see page 277). It was originally parked close to the knoll area and school book depository.

5. "The Tramps in the Photos were not Hunt or Sturgis"

We stand by our photo analysis. The reader can draw his own conclusions. Note that Lyndal L. Shaneyfelt, the FBI agent who did the photocomparison study for the Panel also did a majority of the photo-analysis for the Warren Commission. The FBI's height study claims Hunt is 5'9" (Hunt says he is 5'8" in his resume) and Sturgis is 5'11" (Canfield found he was about 6'1"). They reported the tramps were 5'7" and 6'2" with a one inch margin for error in either direction.

6. The Fact that Oswald had 544 Camp St. on his Leaflets does not Mean he had any Contact with the Cuban Revolutionary Council or Hunt.

The report states: "Oswald made up the FPCC leaflets" (we agree); "The address he stamped on the pamphlets was never an office of that committee... that he fabricated a non-existent New Orleans chapter" (we agree—see page 35); "that the building in question was a former office...(of the CRC) when he made up his pamphlets..." (The propaganda section of the CRC had been discontinued in early 1962 according to 544's landlord in CE1414 but the convert section— Smith, Bannister, Ferrie [see pages 35-52] stayed on. Ostensibly the entire CRC had "disbanded" months before Oswald arrived in New Orleans [see page 78] but in reality it was still operating [see page 102].) Finally the Panel states that "Oswald had tried to infiltrate the anti-Castro organization" presumably the CRC. Actually, he allegedly tried to infiltrate the DRE (see page 41).

• • • • • • •

But beyond all of this, two newspaper reports that have appeared since the release of the Rockefeller Report are worth noting:

1. In a copyrighted story by Bob Wiedrick, the Chicago Tribune of June 15, 1975, alleges that a CIA liaison man has informed Congressional leaders investigating the Agency that "(Kennedy) Presidential aides Kenneth O'Donnell and David Powers are reported to have told investigators soon after the Kennedy assassination that they thought they had observed what might have been shots coming from a location other than the Texas School Depository. But sometime before O'Donnell and Powers submitted their report to the Warren Commission by deposition and affidavit either J. Edgar Hoover or his top aides prevailed on the men not to disclose their suspicions to the Commission." According to the report, "the FBI warned O'Donnell and Powers that testimony to that effect could lead to possible international incident and inflame public passions fed by other secret information then known by the FBI."

2. The Rockefeller Report had jubilantly quoted Dr. Cyril Wecht, a pathologist, as having said that "the available evidence all points to the President being struck by two bullets coming from the rear, and that no support can be found for theories which postulate gunmen to the front or right front of the Presidential car." Wecht called this a "flagrant" lie. The AP story which appeared in The New York Times of June 12, 1975, states that Wecht said "he still maintained that at least two gunmen were involved in the plot and that Lee Harvey Oswald alone could not have inflicted all the wounds sustained by Mr. Kennedy and former Gov. John B. Connally of Texas." "It is utterly reprehensible and despicable," Wecht said, "but also a great compliment that they would consider my testimony that much of a threat." The Commission refused to comment.

Finally, what is most surprising is that, while refusing to issue a public statement on allegations of CIA foreign assassinations on the grounds that its rather extensive inquiry into the subject was insufficient for making conclusive judgements, the Commission would take the trouble to issue a report on the CIA and the Kennedy assassination on which it obviously and admittedly did even less research.

Current Research

CHAPTER THIRTEEN

The Third Tramp Revealed

A few years after the hard cover edition of *Coup d'Etat in America* was published I interviewed Gerry Patrick Hemming (see pages 99, 137) on behalf of the *National Enquirer* in his private detective office located in Miami's "Little Havana." He was facing Federal charges at the time, for the illegal transfer of a silencer, and was acting as his own attorney.

Hemming was trying to beat these charges by "greymailing" the government, threatening to publicly expose government secrets in the course of the criminal proceedings. Luckily for me, Hemming decided I was the perfect conduit to air information because I had access to both the media and the House Select Committee on Assassinations. However my reputation as a radical made any information I released suspect. Once the information was public, Hemming didn't have to fear reprisals from the people on whom he supplied the information. Hemming knew I wasn't an undercover police officer or an informant and let me hang out at the agency–known as "Independent Research Service"–despite the fact that all kinds of "Special Operations" were being run from there.

One day I heard Hemming tell two of his associates to pull up alongside the car of a Latin American who had arrived at the Miami International Airport and take a shot at him that would deliberately miss. About two hours later a rather disconcerted looking Latin ran in screaming in Spanish that his enemies had tried to kill him. I quickly realized that it was dangerous to hang out with Hemming. If he didn't actually murder you he might try to set you up.

In fact, Hemming once tried to set me up as a terrorist. We were discussing homemade nuclear devices. Hemming offered to drive me to a college campus which had a laboratory in which such a device could be constructed. Just going for a ride to further a criminal conspiracy of this nature is punishable by a long prison term. I told Hemming, "I feel just like Lee Harvey Oswald." Hemming admitted knowing Oswald and helping to set him up.

I liked Hemming, though he did try to frame me. I am grateful to him for the first-hand information he provided, and I believe he is a key to the Kennedy assassination. He confirmed, "Frank was firing from the Records Building." Hemming is courageous and would testify about the assassination if he were granted total immunity from prosecution.

Hemming and all the characters from my book who showed up in his office fascinated me. Hemming's crew is mentioned in the credits of Oliver Stone's movie **"JFK"**, and includes Larry Howard (pages 135-137), Howard K. Davis, etc. (page 108). When these guys eyeballed me they asked, "Hey Gerry, who's the hippie?" He'd tell them, "It's Weberman, a hot-shot investigator into the Kennedy assassination. He thinks that me and Frank did Dealy Plaza. I let him stay alive because he comes up with a good joke once in awhile."

One night, after Hemming had called me every obscenity in the book, he pulled out two photographs. "Hey A.J., I'm going to give you two photos, but keep your hands on the table. You know that "third tramp" you keep bugging me about?"

I blurted out, "It's him!"

I called Gaeton Fonzi, then an investigator for the House Select Committee on Assassinations–"Gaeton, put a siren on top of your car. It's an emergency. Hemming is talking!"

I asked, "Who is this guy getting off the plane?"

"Listen carefully, A.J." Hemming said. "I know you've been smoking pot all night before you got here and your mind is all over the goddamned real estate. He's a spook who used the name "Dan Carswell" when he got caught in Cuba in 1960. He was running an operation against the Chicoms, you know who the Communist Chinese are Weberman, you probably are one of them yourself."

"Hey, get off my case man, garbology* is illegal there. What kind of operation was he running?"

"A real simple one. Carswell and his crew set up shop in an apartment that was located right above **Hsinhua**, the Chinese news agency that was really the local spy shop. The Commies had a clandestine transmitter and codebooks there. Carswell's group was going to get the codebooks without the Chinese even knowing they had them. They might have to take out a few guys to do it, but it would look like an accident anyway. See, Weberman, they were going to pump kitchen gas into the place, blow the place up, enter and grab the books, and then set a big goddamn fire. The Chinese would think the codebooks had been destroyed in the fire and not change the codes. The agency supplied them with some outdated bugging equipment and told them to say, if they were caught, that they were bugging the place on behalf of the U.S. Embassy."

I checked the story out. On September 15, 1960, "Daniel L. Carswell", "Eustace H. Vanbrunt" and "Edmund Taransky" (at least those were the names on their passports) were arrested in an apartment above the New China News Agency when they were found in possession of electronic listening devices. "Carswell" told the G-2 agents who questioned him that he was on his way back to the United States when someone in the American Embassy asked him to do a "small favor"–fix some electronic equipment in their apartment.

As a result of this incident, two American Embassy officials were expelled from Cuba and the United States Ambassador was restricted to a ten-block radius. Cuban-American relations plummeted to a new low, and the U.S. government was unable to find out if the Castro dictatorship was planning to align itself with the Maoists or the Soviets.

Hemming said that when word of "Carswell's" arrest reached his case officer in Langley, "he hit the goddamned ceiling." He said, "'Carswell' knew about every CIA assassination operation they had going and had to be exfiltrated from Cuba at all costs."

This information also checked out. Columnist Jack Anderson reported[1] that the CIA contacted Charles Siragusa, a former OSS officer who was a high official in the Federal Bureau of Narcotics. The

* Garbology: The study of refuse (garbage) as a means of examining lifestyles and cultural habits of living subjects. It is an extension of archaeological and anthropological techniques. See: **My Life in Garbology** by A.J. Weberman, Stonehill Press, 1980

CIA asked him to contact individuals known to him in the National Crime Syndicate (the Mafia) and offer them one million dollars to break "Carswell" out of prison and bring him to the United States. Anderson stated that one reason the CIA was so desperate to bust "Carswell" out was because "...one of the men ("Carswell") knows the names of the Cubans involved in the operation."

Hemming disagreed with Anderson on the last point. He thinks the CIA wanted "Carswell" out because he was their number one stone cold killer who possessed the proverbial "license to kill."

I discovered some historical precedents for Hemming's scenario. The *New York Times* reported[2] that during the overthrow of Kwame Nkrumah, the leader of Ghana in the early 1960's, the CIA station chief of Accra requested that a group of paramilitarists storm the Chinese Communist Embassy, kill everyone there, and then steal the codebooks and records of the installation. Before leaving, the group was to blow up the building so it would look like the embassy personnel had been killed in an accidental explosion.

Further research[3] revealed that on December 18, 1960 "Carswell" was found guilty at a military trial and on January 11, 1961 he was sentenced to thirty years in the hell-hole known as "La Cabana" fortress prison. His co-defendants received identical sentences.

At La Cabana "Carswell" met Frank Sturgis's close friend, John Martino (see page 105). In his book, *I was Castro's Prisoner*, Martino recalls his first conversation with "Carswell."[4] "He told me–'We had drilled through the floor, which is the ceiling of the Chinese News Agency, and we were about to lower a microphone into the next room so we could put everything that was said there on tape...'" "Carswell" and Martino became close friends and "Carswell" shared the special food he received from the American Embassy with Martino. Both men also shared a common lawyer. When "Carswell" was released in April of 1963 he gave all his personal possessions to Martino.[5]

"Carswell's" release was secured by the intelligence community. William Donovan, the grandfather of modern American intelligence and the first head of the OSS, arranged the prisoner exchange. In return for "Carswell" and his crew, the United States released four Castro G-2 men, including the notorious Francisco "The Hook" Molina, a low life Castro bodyguard who was serving a twenty year sentence for the murder of a nine year old girl. Governor Rockefeller, who would later head a commission that attempted to ascertain the identity of the "Carswell" tramp, personally pardoned Molina.

On April 23, 1963, "Carswell" landed at Homestead Air Force Base in Florida, where he received a hero's welcome. That day in New York City, the now defunct *World Telegram and Sun* ran a banner headline which read, "CIA TRIO SLIPS PAST CASTRO IN SWAP." The article stated that "Carswell's" and his two associates' CIA employment had been confirmed with reliable government sources.

"Carswell" left no forwarding address with the American Red Cross. I spent hundreds of hours trying to track down the name "Carswell" when I realized that Hemming had been telling the truth when said it had been a pseudonym. "Carswell's" identity remains a mystery today. The House Select Committee on Assassinations investigators who handled the "tramp" aspect of the investigation were never given his real name. Instead, the CIA interviewed him, somewhere in suburban Virginia, and subsequently verified his contention that he was at work in the CIA headquarters in Langley on November 22, 1963.

The CIA investigators and "Carswell" are lying. "Carswell" was in Dallas that day, photographed along with his buddies E. Howard Hunt and Frank Sturgis, all disguised as tramps. "Carswell" had probably made contact with Hunt and Sturgis in Miami or New Orleans where he became part of the CIA conspiracy to kill John Kennedy. He had every reason to do so–Kennedy had let him rot in prison for three years where he was mistreated and tortured. Martino relates in his book that during the Bay of Pigs invasion he was told he would be shot should the invasion succeed.[6]

CHAPTER FOURTEEN

The House Select Committee on Assassinations Report

Perhaps you have a friend that looks like one of the tramps. In fact, I knew someone who looked like the Hunt tramp. It is very possible. Let us say that there is a 1 in 10 chance of this happening. Now, let's say that you knew two men who knew each other who each looked like one of the tramps. What are the chances of this happening? We must switch from an arithmetical model to a logarithmic one. The chances of knowing two people who know each other and who each resemble a different tramp are, say, 1 in 100. The chances of three people fitting the same criteria are 1 in 10,000. Hunt, Sturgis and "Carswell" all knew each other. They were all world class players connected with the CIA, the Bay of Pigs, assassination attempts against Castro, and Watergate. Hunt had participated in the overthrow of democratically elected left wing governments abroad and Sturgis was questioned about the assassination a day after it happened. If these men left even the slightest traces of their presence in Dealy Plaza that day, which is all men like Hunt, Sturgis and Carswell would leave, these minute traces alone should be enough to arouse a great deal of suspicion about their role in the Kennedy assassination.

Even if the Hunt photo only looked a little like Hunt and the Sturgis photo only looked a little like Sturgis and the "Carswell" picture only looked a little like "Carswell," when you put them all together they would still spell "CIA assassination."

When you take into account the fact that in 1972 two of these men were employed by President Nixon, a man who benefitted from the Kennedy assassination, you have political dynamite that the Establishment media will not touch.

The House Select Committee on Assassinations (HSCA) study of the tramp shots was a cover-up. The man in charge of the tramp shot photo comparison was Clyde C. Snow, B.S., Ph.D., Chief, Physical Anthropology Division, Civil Aeromedical Institute of the FEDERAL Aviation Administration. Dr. Snow was no flake. Let's say he would have written a report in which he said that Hunt, Sturgis and Carswell were on the scene of the Kennedy assassination disguised as tramps. This would imply that democracy in America was overthrown in a coup in 1963. I don't think he would advance much further in his government job.

Dr. Snow was a forensic anthropologist, not a photoanalyst. The HSCA anthropologists looked at the photographs and made some measurements trying to take into consideration certain differences in the cameras that were used, then they made up a little "scientific" chart. They did not do anything involving digital photoenhancement, a technique that did not exist in 1963, when the tramp shots were doctored (see page 72). In fact, the issue of doctored photos is not even addressed in their report. This was despite the fact that the Rockefeller Commission qualified their conclusion that Hunt and Sturgis were not the tramps with the words "as shown in the photographs submitted." The HSCA went on to say that in response to a 1975 Newsweek[7] story (*Coup* was first published in 1975) the CIA conducted "a physiological comparison of the Hunt and Sturgis photographs with the tramp photographs." The CIA study reached the same conclusion as the Rockefeller Commission. Neither group used a photoanalyst.

The HSCA concluded that Carswell, Hunt and Sturgis "were not the tramps."[8] Nonetheless, they did do more of a "hang-out" than the Rockefeller Commission or CIA when it came to Frank Sturgis.[9] "In terms of these indices, Sturgis most closely resembles Tramp B in mouth height relative to lower face height, the length of his ear lobe relative to total ear length and the total ear length relative to face height...The average deviation between the six facial indices analyzed here is 4.0 points. An average deviation of 5 or less may be considered as evidence of a strong resemblance between the subjects of analysis... This is low enough to make it impossible to rule out Sturgis on the basis of metric traits alone." Since Frank couldn't be ruled out on "metric traits" the HSCA had to note the following "morphological differences" between Sturgis and the tramp: "Hair-Sturgis is a very dark brunette with strongly waved hair; tramp B had medium dark hair with a slight wave." Didn't these anthropologists ever hear about hair dyeing and straightening? Only Frank's hairdresser knows for sure! Earlier, they admitted that the tramps' outfits "might be a disguise" due to the fact that the Hunt tramp looked like "he had been fired from a cannon through a Salvation Army Thrift Shop..." But they then stated, "...their footwear seems consistent with their classification as vagrants." However, the shoes worn by the tramps looked new (page 62). The next "morphological trait" that rules out Sturgis is his "hairline." "The hairline of tramp B shows more bilateral recession than is observed in Sturgis." I assume our anthropologists never heard of a haircut with electric clippers. Moving on to Frank's nose, "Tramp B has a concave nasal profile with a rounded, slightly bulbous, nasal tip. Sturgis' nasal profile is slightly convex and the nasal tip is less bulbous than that of the Tramp." What is really being said here is that the two noses are quite similar. Both have bulbous tips and although one is concave the other is only "slightly convex." It should also be taken into consideration that Frank is flaring his nostrils on page 211 and 213. Next, the chin–"The most striking difference between the two men is the form of the chin. Sturgis' is massive and square; Tramp B has a small and rounded chin." Turn to page 211 again. Frank is contorting his neck. Turn the page and he is doing it again. His neck is downward on page 215. By contorting his neck he is changing the shape of his chin. Check the tramp's chin vs. Frank's chin on pages 218, 219. The squareness of the tramp's chin is still visible despite Frank's contortions.

Frank's ears are very important. The HSCA thought the ears of the tramp and Frank's were quite similar. But now they point out a dissimilarity–"Tramp B's ears are considerably more projecting than those of Sturgis which are rather close set." I really don't see this when I compare the photograph. Even if this is true, ear projection can be changed by inserting a wedge of gum behind the ears to make them protrude more. Finally, physique. "Tramp B appears to be considerably more linear in body build than Sturgis, who is broad and stocky in physique." Body weight can be changed through dieting, hard living in a para-military training camp, etc.

The report does not state in what years the comparison photographs were taken. This is significant because time even takes its toll on Presidential assassins and they too grow fat. For a while it seemed that Frank was trying to eat his way out of looking like the tramp. Judging from the photos reprinted by the HSCA the comparison shots used were far apart chronologically from the tramp shots.

From the above points the HSCA concludes, "Sturgis can be excluded as being Tramp B."

The HSCA report doesn't mention who "Carswell" is historically. They describe Hunt as "a principal figure in the Watergate burglaries and an employee of the CIA at the time of the Kennedy assassination." and Sturgis "Watergate burglar" but say nothing of "Carswell."

The part of the report refuting the "Carswell" tramp connection is only one paragraph long.[10] "Of the three men who have been proposed as Tramp A, the resemblance between the latter and Carswell is least impressive...they diverge in facial index values by an average of seven points. Carswell's face is relatively long and narrow; Tramp A's is short and broad. This length difference is especially expressed in the lower face with Carswell's chin and upper lip being very long when compared to the tramp's." The problem with this "difference" is most apparent when one compares the tramp with the one photo of Carswell supplied to the HSCA by the CIA. I supplied the other of the two photos the HSCA used to make their determination. Hemming had allowed me to make copies of his photographs.

The CIA's photo looks like it was taken much later than 1963 and is a front view. Tramp A was never photographed in a head-on angle, so a direct comparison is impossible. The configurations of "Carswell's" ears are not visible in the CIA's shot nor is the profile of his nose. However, the profile of "Carswell" which we discovered lends itself to a comparison. See for yourself on page 222a.

As a matter of fact, if you compare the CIA's shot of Carswell with the one of him getting off a plane in 1963 it is hard to believe they are the same person, yet they are. If it's hard to believe that "Carswell" is really "Carswell" from the two photos of him, it's going to be even harder to believe that the CIA supplied photo and the one of the tramp are identical since he was also in disguise when photographed in Dealy Plaza.

The HSCA goes on to state "Carswell's" nose is much longer relative to its breadth." "Carswell" is wearing sun glasses in the photo of him disembarking at Homestead Air Force Base so one can't get a good idea of the length of his nose. But it certainly has the same overall configurations as the tramp's. The CIA's photographic contribution doesn't help solve the nose configuration question either, since it is not a profile shot (page 222).

Finally, we get to the ears. "Differences in ear structure are also striking. In the tramp, the lobes are attached whereas in "Carswell" the lobes are welded–that is, they attach to the side of the cheek with no discernable lobe at all. The antihelix of the ear (the elevated ridge just in front of and parallel to the outer margin of the ear) is well developed in Tramp A, but very poorly developed in Carswell."

I did not trust this idea so I had my own photoanalysis done. My attorney, Jerimiah Gutman, sent the negatives of the Carswell/Tramp shots to two forensic photoanalysts without telling them the photos had anything to do with the Kennedy assassination. In order to do this, I cropped the tramp shot so that only the outline of the third tramp is visible. This eliminated the other tramps and the Texas School Book Depository in the background. I have reprinted a copy of their report on pages 364-365 along with the qualifications of the men who authored it. The report's contentions that "the opening in the right ear has a geometrical shape consistent in all photographs and the ear lobe in all photographs in continuous and attached to the face" contradicts Dr. Snow's finding. The Robert Genna report also states, "Finally, and most significantly, there is a skin blemish on the right cheek noted in all three photographs." There was one problem with this part of the photo-report. In order to show the tramp and Carswell from the same angle the photoanalyst flipped the negative of the tramp so that both figures would be facing the same direction. By doing so he moved the mole visible in P4 and P5 from the left side of the tramp's face to the right side. The photoanalysts measured this mole and it happened to be in the same place as the mole on the right side of Carswell's face. In the CIA shot of Carswell (see page 222) a blemish is present in the exact same position as on the left cheek of the tramp. This blemish is very difficult to miss. What the other mole was doing there is a mystery to me. It is not impossible for someone to have a mole on both cheeks. Only the CIA and Fidel Castro's DGI know the answer to this question since both have photographs of "Carswell" during this period.

The second photoanalyst relied less on the blemish: "Given those physical attributes as described and including the apparent mole as seen in all three photographs, I would conclude that Subjects A and C are one and the same." He believes there is a "time sequence delay" between the two photographs ("Carswell" was released from Cuba in late April 1963 and was photographed in Dealy Plaza in November of that year, a lapse of seven months.) because of a weight difference in the two men. It should be noted that "Carswell" may have been stockier due to an inactive life in jail and the food provided by the U.S. Embassy. The photoanalyst writes: "The shape of the ears is similar in both of these photographs...The forehead shape and size are again similar between the two photographs. The nose and nostrils have similar characteristics. The subject in both photographs has a long thin jawline. Although the lips are turned up in Photo A, one can see that the lips in photographs A and C are similar that being long thin lips."

I am in the process of bringing the fact that the tramp shot negative was inadvertently flipped to the attention of the photoanalysts. However, matching "Carswell's" right profile to the left side of the tramp's face still allows a comparison of the shape of the head, ears and nose. I submitted the HSCA/CIA photograph of "Carswell" to Mr. Fahey so he can make a determination of the mole or blemish along with the other features. He told me the photograph was of little value because it was a frontal shot.

We have included an overlay of "Carswell" and the tramp so that you can see how the features line up. The ears match and the forehead is the same size. "Carswell" seems to disappear and literally become the tramp. The difference in profile angles accounts for the different sizes of the two images.We have also done electronic photo-imaging on the tramp shot P5 so that you can get an idea of what the tramp would look like with "Carswell's" pipe and sunglasses on (page 361). Finally, we have included an ear and thumb study of "Carswell" for your examination (page 360).

The HSCA report states, "In comparing Hunt with Tramp C, the average difference of the two men is 9.0,[11] a value significantly high to suggest no particularly strong resemblance in facial proportions." The photographic overlay provided with this book tells a different story. The tramp's features and Hunt's align perfectly despite the doctoring discussed on page 72. The HSCA went on, "In addition, in comparing the photographs of the Tramp to those of Hunt taken in the late 1950's and early 1960's, the following morphological differences were noted: Forehead: Tramp C has several well-developed transverse frontal sulci and a strong vertical interciliry sulcus. These are not observed in Hunt who, even in photographs taken years earlier, has only slightly developed transverse frontal and interciliry furrows." This is a fancy way of saying that the tramp has more horizontal and vertical furrows on his forehead than Hunt does. In which tramp shots is the Hunt tramp's forehead visible? The best shot occurs in P3 (page 211) and even here the depth of field of the camera blurs the grimacing face of the Hunt-like tramp. In P4 he is even farther back and in P5 and P7 his face is doctored-out (see page 212). In P6 his face is also a blur. Unless the HSCA had much better originals than I do I can not see how they arrived at their conclusion.

The report does state that both Hunt and the tramp have the same forehead furrows, but the tramp's are more pronounced. Perhaps make-up was used to accentuate already existing features? This theory is consistent with the HSCA analysis of the cheeks of Hunt and the tramp, "Tramp C has well developed nose labial folds whereas in Hunt these are only incipiently developed in his photographs taken at about the same time as the assassination." Hunt was made up to look older by cosmetic altering of pre-existing features. Sophisticated make-up. The HSCA ignores this and cites "age" as a morphological difference, "In general facial tone, age lines and other features, Tramp C appears to be a decade older than Hunt."

Hunt's nose is examined next, "The tramp has a relatively broad nose with a bulbous fleshy nasal tip. The nasal tip is not depressed. Hunt has a narrow nose with a salient nasal bridge and an angular, moderately depressed nasal tip." Once again, the best shot of Hunt's nose appears in P3, where he is grimacing. When you do this, your nose changes shape. In P4 he is out of focus and P6 is overexposed. Check the overlay (page 223), what can be seen of the tramp's nose lines up with Hunt's.

"Mouth-Tramp C has thick full membranous lips; Hunt is thin lipped. Hunt is pouting and open mouthed so his lips look thicker.

At last we get to Hunt's ears. "From his photographs, it is apparent that Hunt underwent surgery to correct his rather projecting ears. The date of this operation was not determined, but from the photographs, it would appear to have been within a few years before or after the assassination. In degree of projection, the Tramp's ears appear to more closely match Hunt's pre-surgical condition." What a bombshell! Hunt had plastic surgery so his unusual ear formation wouldn't give him away (see page 207 for the HSCA photo of Hunt before the surgery, and see P1 in which his elf-like ear is visible.)

The report continues. "Two features not influenced by the surgery are strongly different in the two men. One of these is the helix, the fold of flesh that forms the outer rim of the ear. In the Tramp, this fold is wide and prominent whereas it is narrower and more weakly developed in Hunt. The second difference is in the anti-helix, the secondary fold that roughly parallels the helix inside the ear. This structure is strongly developed in the Tramp and, in fact, its lower portion appears to extend beyond the helix. In Hunt, the anti-helix is weakly developed." I must concede this point because I have stated that the ear visible in P3 is not that of Hunt's and the photo has been doctored. Look at Hunt's ear in the HSCA photo on page 207. If the CIA hadn't changed that bizarre looking appendage Hunt would be locked up right now.

The last difference regards a scar. "In the tramp there is a pit-like ovid scar about one centimeter in diameter located immediately above the lateral end of his right eyebrow. This feature is not observed in any of the Hunt photographs provided for examination." I suggest Dr. Snow go see the original movie, Scarface, for an answer to the tramp's scar. In any event, Gaeton Fonzi told me he asked Jane Downey of the HSCA if the photo report would be valid if Hunt and Sturgis were heavily disguised. She said it would not be.

The American public got a real snow-job from Dr. Snow because be took his cues from the FBI and CIA. Mr. Fithian of the HSCA asked Dr. Snow, "It is my understanding that the CIA and FBI conducted their own analyses of the tramp photos that attempt to identify the individuals. Did you get into that?" Dr. Snow, "We didn't participate in either of those analyses. However, after being called in as consultants to this committee, we were furnished copies of the reports of the CIA and FBI analysis." In February of 1992 Dr. Snow appeared on "60 Minutes" to discuss Iraqi war crimes in Kurdistan at a time when the CIA is planning the ouster of Iraq's dictator, Saddam Hussein.

I still do not know Carswell's real name or address. If anyone does, you can call (212) 518-3292 or write me at Independent Research Associates, 6 Bleecker Street, New York City, New York 10012. Carswell should be considered armed and dangerous, so proceed with caution.

References

Carswell – State Department Bio Register and State Dept. For. Service List 1959,1960; A.P. Dispatch 22 April 63; New York Times report quoted in Zodiac News Service May 10, 1978; I Was Castro's Prisoner – John Martino-Devin-Adiar; conv with Larry McKnight, Rochester Institute of Technology; Ltr from CIA to AJ Weberman 25 Oct 77; Ltr to AJ Weberman from National Enq 30 March 78; Invisible Government – Ross and Wise-Random House-63 p259; Miami Herald 11 Jan 61, 18 Dec 60; 25 April 63; 25 Feb 63; Revolucion-Organo Del Movimiento 26 Julio, 17 Sept 60; Miami Herald 23 April 63; New York World Telegram 24 April 63; Anderson, Jack 4 Jan 78-Miami Herald; Wash Post 22 April 63, 17 Sept 61, 18 Sept 60; DL-100-10461 10 Sept 64-Alfred Neeley; Slack's testimony to WC; Glory No More-Ed Arthur; R145; 3H140; CD329p8; 10H340; CD7p252; 10H378; CD1063; CE3071; CD329Seclp77; CD205p122; Conv with Willis Price.

CHAPTER FIFTEEN

The Trial: Hunt vs. COUP D'ETAT IN AMERICA

In 1975 the hard cover edition of *Coup d'Etat in America* was published by Joseph Okpaku's Third Press. Shortly after its release, Third Press began to experience financial difficulties because they published a biography of President Gerald Ford. Jerry terHorst, the author, headed the Washington Bureau of the Detroit News from 1961 until 1974, when he became President Ford's press secretary early in the administration. E. Howard Hunt once published an article under terHorst's by-line concerning radical attorney Leonard Boudin.

Jerry Ford was not a very colorful character–Joe should have published a biography of Betty Ford instead–and the book was not exactly a best-seller. Third Press went into debt.

Coup went into a second printing, but Joe ran out of money and could not re-print despite heavy demand. He tried selling the paperback rights; some editors at one book company were interested but when they had a meeting with their publisher he told them, "We can't publish this book and I can not tell you the reason why." The Agency was on our case.

The hard cover version of *Coup* was generally ignored by the Establishment media. Despite the passage of seventeen years, I am sure this edition will meet with the same fate, unless it becomes a best seller.

In order to circumvent this media blackout, Canfield and I leased a van and drove around the country promoting the book and doing more research. We appeared on a lot of small radio and television talk shows and underground press interviews. Since we had no money for hotels we "crashed" in the back of the van and lived on McDonald's hamburgers. We were stone cold broke.

Then one day someone showed that they had some faith in Canfield and Weberman's ability to earn money. E. Howard Hunt sued us for twelve million dollars....

Initially, I was not happy about being sued. Attorneys cost money. I called my mother, Sara, in Miami Beach. She said, "Don't worry, darling, I'll find you an attorney who will work for free. Leave it to me." The lawyer she found, Mark J. Friedman, would later gain notoriety because of the number of parking tickets he ran up. Luckily, Mark employed a paralegal named Ron Lowy. Ronnie did the legal research and prepared the motions even though he was still attending high school. He is now a prominent attorney in Miami Beach. Friedman signed the motions and showed up at depositions to question witnesses. When we deposed Frank Sturgis, Friedman refused to read the questions in the order I had written them. I had structured them to trap Frank and had waited years for this opportunity. This was the last straw. I dismissed Friedman and went "pro se" that is, I defended myself.

After we took Frank's deposition I had a few off the record words with him. He told me that he knew I had worked hard on those questions and he was sorry my lawyer had screwed it up for me. I must admit Frank was a very understanding man....more so than my own attorney.

The Hunt vs. Weberman lawsuit afforded me the opportunity to depose Hunt, Sturgis, Richard Helms, James Angleton, CIA Hunt associate David Atlee Phillips and many others: I deposed witnesses for five years. My research turned the lawsuit into "The Weberman Commission." I even found a witness who categorically stated that she drove to Dallas with Frank Sturgis just before the Kennedy assassination–Marita Lorenz.

Marita came out of the cold in late 1975. She had been recruited by Sturgis as a spy in Castro's Cuba in the early 1960's and had been involved in an assassination attempt against Fidel Castro. Marita testified under oath in a deposition[12] that she drove from Miami to Dallas in November of 1963 with Sturgis and others.

Q.-"While you were (in Dallas) at that motel, did you meet anyone other than those who were in the party traveling with you from Miami to Dallas?"

A.-"E. Howard Hunt."

It was around this time that Hunt appeared on Tom Snyder's network television show that originated in New York City. As he entered the studio Yippie Aron Kay threw a pie at him. Hunt's response to being pied was to float a false news story about me. Just as he had done too many other "subversives" when he worked for the CIA's psychological warfare section. When Snyder asked him about his alleged role in the Kennedy assassination he claimed that he had won a lawsuit against two authors who had written a book about his alleged presence in Dealy Plaza on November 22, 1963 and had been awarded damages by the Court.

Hunt had opened himself up for a counter-lawsuit. But more importantly he had shown his vulnerability to unconventional psychological warfare. This weakness allowed me to trick him into changing his alibi for November 22, 1963.

In March 1974 Hunt supplied the following affidavit to the Rockefeller Commission: "I, E. Howard Hunt, affirm the following to be my recollection of my whereabouts on November 22, 1963: 1. On that date I was an employee of the CIA assigned to the Domestic Operations Division, located in a commercial building in Washington D.C. 2. I was driving with my late wife on H Street near 8th or 9th Street where we first heard of the Kennedy shooting on our car radio. We had been purchasing Chinese groceries at a store named, as well as I could recall it, "Wah Ling"....3. From the Chinese grocery store we drove out to Wisconsin Avenue to pick up our daughter Kevan from Sidewell friends school....4. From Kevan's school we drove directly to our home....At home was my newly born son David....Our elder son, St. John, a student at nearby Brookmont Elementary School, was probably already home. As I recall, our eldest child, Lisa, arrived soon afterward by bus...."

In June of 1977 I was able to question Hunt about his whereabouts on the day of the coup.

He stated "All I can give you is that when I first heard the news, which came over the car radio, I was on H Street about 9th N.W., Washington. I was driving home from a Chinese grocery store."

Q.-"Do you remember the name of the grocery store?"

A.-"Wah Ling."

I went to the stacks of old criss-cross directories in the Library of Congress and looked up the location where Hunt said Wah Ling's was located in 1963. It actually existed! That evening I called Gerry Hemming and told him, "You're not going to believe this, man, but I've dug up Wah Ling, the man who owned the grocery store Hunt claimed to be at on November 22 and he don't remember Hunt at all."

Hemming responded, "Weberman, I got to admit, you do your homework." Hemming passed this information on to Hunt either directly or through Frank Sturgis. The result of this was that when we called him in for a deposition in June of 1978, HUNT CHANGED HIS ALIBI.

Q.-"Where is Wah Ling's located in Washington D.C.?"

A.-"I don't think the grocery store existed or ever existed. In fact, in the testimony I gave to the Church Committee, if you recall, I said to the best of my recollection the name of the grocery store was Wah Ling. Having revisited the site–in fact, by chance having dinner in Chinatown fairly recently–I determined the name of the grocery store was probably Tuck Cheong, T-u-c-k C-h-e-o-n-g."

Q.-"So are you saying now that your alibi for the day of the assassination, Wah Ling's Grocery, is now changed to a different grocery store?"

A.-"Well, I am saying now that attempting to recollect a couple of years ago, the name of the Chinese grocery store, one of several on 8th Street, that my wife visited on that afternoon, certainly is subject to re-examination and refreshment which I have done."

Q.-"What did you purchase that day?"

A.-"I don't know. My wife made the purchases. She went into the grocery store. I stayed in the car with the children."

Q.-"If I told you there was a Wah Ling's grocery in Washington at the time you were talking about, would that surprise you?"

A.-"I would say simply that it was one of the probably several that my wife visited that day."

My attorney reminded Hunt that in previous sworn testimony he said the children were not with him on his shopping trip to Chinatown. He answered, "Then I would say that I stayed in the car with the dog, rather than with the children."

Q.-"This would be different from what you just testified to earlier?"

A.-"Well, we are talking about the recollection of a good many years ago, yes."

Q.-"So this refreshes your recollection?"

A.-"Yes, as to what I testified to earlier. This is not testified and it is not a sworn statement in any case."

Hunt, thinking I was about to produce Wah Ling as my witness, had to change his alibi to Tuck Cheong. Of course, there was no "Tuck Cheong" in the criss-cross directory or phone book in 1963 and I could never produce a non-existent witness. If I went ahead and produced Wah Ling, Hunt covered himself by saying he waited in the car. Needing a reason to wait in the car instead of accompanying his wife into the store he had to have someone in the car he had to watch. At first it was his children, then his dog. Had we pressed him further he may have told us he had to watch his pet hamster, "Skippy."

After five years, we were finally ready to go to trial. I intended to try Hunt for the JFK assassination by using "truth" as my defense. My prospective witnesses included a New York City Police Department intelligence officer who I had worked with in a separate case involving Frank Sturgis and Marita Lorenz, investigators from the HSCA, Congressman Henry Gonzalez and many others.

Canfield would show the jury the tramp shots and let them make up their own minds. I was represented by Bruce Stahl, an attorney I had met through NYPD. It would have been the trial of the century.

I was set to win the trial but Mr. Hunt disappointed me. As I was about to fly down to Miami for the trial my attorney called. "Hunt is dropping his lawsuit. There's nothing we can do. We can't force him to sue us, you know. We could go ahead with the countersuit but that would be on a rather limited basis. Hunt is willing to pay Canfield $200 in damages for his statement on the Snyder Show."

When news of the settlement reached the media the **New York Post**[13] ran a story that Hunt's actions seemed to be very suspicious in light of his statements that he wished to vigorously prosecute the case.

Hunt was later questioned about this in another legal proceeding. He responded, "When I attempted to find out from Mr. Rubin in what courthouse I should appear, what room of the courthouse I should appear for the trial the next morning, I was told by his office that there would not be any trial, that he had settled the matter, and furthermore, that he would not be in town. He had previously taken on as a client a Saudi Arabian sheik or princeling named Al Fasi and he was chasing all over the country with him, and as far as I know Mr. Rubin wasn't even in town the eve of the trial...

In any event, I had assumed that my requirements for the settlement of the case had been met by Mr. Rubin and that a check from Mr. Weberman for five thousand dollars would be forthcoming. I learned the following day Mr. Rubin had told the opposing attorneys who had come to Miami for the trail, that—I forgot the term—but it was going to equal out, nobody would charge anyone for anything and they would scrub the case. That was done, I must add reluctantly, without my authorization."

Hunt was then asked if the case was dismissed on his behalf without his being paid even a penny and that there was no apology or retraction from the defendants in that case. He answered, "That is ˙ correct." Researcher Gordon Winslow reports that Rubin checked in at the Miami Heart Institute the night before the case was to come to trial.

He agreed not to file a similar suit in the future as part of the settlement in Hunt vs. Weberman. By withdrawing his suit with prejudice against him, he essentially admitted that he was in Dallas on the day of the assassination.

CHAPTER SIXTEEN

The Authors vs. the CIA: The Pressure Sets In

The Feds had always been interested in the methods and results of my investigation. Before my book was published, the CIA had one of their younger agents sit near me on a Boston to New York shuttle flight and strike up a conversation. I began to expound on the Kennedy assassination non-stop. Every few minutes he would ask me, "So who's publishing your book?" I ignored his question and kept on talking. When he asked me again I pretended not to hear. The plane was about to land and the agent was getting nervous because he may have blown one of his early assignments. "You've told me everything about the Kennedy assassination except who's publishing your book. Please tell me so I can buy a copy." I felt sorry for the guy and told him just as we were leaving, "Okay, it's a firm called The Third Press." I knew that Joe Okpaku was beyond reproach and could not be compromised by the CIA.

When the Feds' study of my phone records revealed that a close friend of mine was related to the Gallo crime family they broke into this poor hippie artist's apartment and went through all of his papers. The only thing he found missing were some rings which they could have put in their pockets without compromising the operation when they left.

A few months later a Virginia Yippie drove me to CIA Headquarters in Langley. The security guard at the gate routinely made a notation of my driver's license plate number. About one week later someone broke into my friend's house by cutting the glass on one of the windows and then went through every paper in the place without stealing anything. My friend's parents were Seventh Day Adventists so they ended up searching through a lot of religious material.

I received a few subtle warnings around this time. When I did my research in D.C. I stayed at my friend John Foster Berlet's apartment. One evening I came home from the Archives and found all the lights out. I checked the fuses. They were all good. I went down to the basement and found that someone had removed the back-up fuses. When I returned to my home in New York City the next night I found the lights out there too. I checked the fuses in the apartment and in the basement. They were all good. I called Con Edison. They turned the lights back on but told me that someone had opened the manhole that supplied my building with electricity and had turned off the power. Was the CIA giving me a subtle hint that my "headlights" would be extinguished next?

During the years I prepared for the lawsuit I spent countless hours in the FBI and CIA reading rooms, the Library of Congress, the National Archives, Federal Documents Archives and District Courts.

In 1975, while studying a Federal Case brought against Frank Sturgis in Miami, I uncovered a document that should have been sealed, but wasn't, detailing Sturgis's role as an informant for the DEA. When **High Times** magazine published this document the FBI tried to arrest me for unsealing it. They came to the Federal Courthouse and questioned an assistant clerk, Gloria Walters. She told them that the document in question had not been sealed. The FBI took fingerprints from the document anyway.

When I returned to Miami a few months later they put me under intense surveillance. The night I flew back to New York City they followed me to Miami International Airport. When I put down a bag of worthless newspaper clippings and turned my back for one moment to make a call they snatched it. I never let the attache case with the important documents leave my hand. Nonetheless, their action against me got me very paranoid. When I deplaned in New York City and walked toward the baggage claim area two gentlemen who looked like Federal agents eyeballed me. I thought my time had finally come. Instead they arrested a Cuban fellow about 10 feet in back of me.

Intimidation, black bag jobs and media suppression of my book and my theories stopped when the Carter Administration took power in 1976. I began to mail the results of my investigation to the Justice Department on a monthly basis. During the time that Canfield and I worked with Congressman Gonzalez some strange incidents befell him and his staff. First of all, his aide, Gail Beagle, was attacked by a gang of thugs and beaten. Then someone may have helped spring Congressman Gonzalez's brother from a maximum security prison for the criminally insane. Before being recaptured a police officer was shot in the eye. Finally, someone took a shot at the Congressman as he was leaving a speaking engagement in San Antonio.

I also turned over all of my information to the House Select Committee on Assassinations and became friendly with some of the younger employees. One day I received a call from a courageous aide named Edward Lopez. He was really excited. "You are right about Hunt" he said. "I HEARD about a document, signed by Angleton and Helms which says 'Someday we are going to have to account for Howard Hunt's presence in Dallas on November 22, 1963.'"

It didn't make sense to me. You see, I do not think that there is a document which is in itself "a smoking gun" regarding the Kennedy assassination. The tramp shots are the closest thing to a smoking gun in the Kennedy case.

The tramps are Hunt and Sturgis and these fellows lead directly to former President Richard Nixon through Watergate. If Nixon was running Hunt and Sturgis in 1972 he could have been running them in 1963. Nixon was also running Hunt in 1960, as Nixon was the political action officer for the Bay of Pigs invasion in the White House, as Vice President.

Nixon was in on the hit because he is one of the world's biggest "sore losers." Nixon planning a hit isn't really that far out. A former CIA employee named Marion Cooper said that in January 1955 he attended a meeting in Honduras, at which the assassination of the President of Panama, J.A. Remon, was discussed. The hit team was present as was then Vice President Richard Nixon. The following day Remon was hit. Warren Commission document 279 "Assassination of Jose Remon, Panama" remains classified in the National Archives.

On pages 88-90 we showed that the phrase for the Kennedy hit was "Bay of Pigs." H.R. Haldeman tells us in *The Ends of Power*, "In all of those Nixon references to the Bay of Pigs (in the White House tapes) he (Nixon) was actually referring to the Kennedy assassination."[14] Haldeman also said, "The CIA literally erased any connection between Kennedy's assassination and the CIA..."

I began my investigation of the "smoking gun" document by calling former CIA official Victor Marchetti, who I thought was a friend of mine at the time. I asked Victor what he thought of a CIA document placing Hunt on the scene of the Kennedy assassination. He told me the Agency was going to burn Hunt by doing a "limited hangout" and he would check into it further. I couldn't help thinking to myself, "This is too good to be true." Marchetti claimed that he had called a man named William Corson and that Corson had verified that such a document existed.

On August 20, 1978 the *Sunday News Journal* of Wilmington Delaware ran an article by Joe Trento titled

> "WAS HOWARD HUNT IN DALLAS THE DAY JFK DIED?" "Washington: A secret CIA memorandum says that E. Howard Hunt was in Dallas the day JFK was murdered and that top agency officials plotted to cover up Hunt's presence there. The 1966 secret memo, now in the hands of the HSCA, places Hunt in Dallas on November 22. Richard Helms and James Angleton initialled the memo according to investigators. According to sources close to HSCA the document reveals, "Three years after Kennedy's murder, and shortly after Helms and Angleton were elevated to their highest positions in the CIA, they discussed the fact that Hunt was in Dallas on the day of the assassination and that his presence there had to be kept secret."

Helms and Angleton thought that news of Hunt's presence in Dallas would be damaging to the Agency should it leak out. Helms and Angleton felt that a cover story, giving Hunt an alibi for being elsewhere the day of the assassination "ought to be considered." Trento described his sources as being both inside and outside of the CIA. He could not reveal their names because he had promised them that he would not do so. His sources had actually shown him the memo.

When Angleton testified in the Hunt vs. Weberman lawsuit he was asked if he talked to Trento about his authorship of the CIA memorandum. Angleton testified, "After publication I had a telephone call from Trento in the office. He said he was calling from the office of one <u>William Corson</u>, who is the *Penthouse* representative ex-Colonel of the Marines and he, I think his first question was, 'Have you heard from Howard Hunt?' and I said, 'No,' and his next questions, it was a whole series of staccato questions, and I told him my lunch was getting cold and I was at the Army-Navy club and that was the end of it."

Corson was a retired Marine Corps colonel with good intelligence community connections that included James Angleton. It was Corson who had allegedly told Marchetti that Angleton had confirmed the existence of the internal CIA memo placing Hunt in Dallas on November 22, 1963, when Marchetti called him.

When deposed by Mark Lane, Corson categorically denied being Marchetti's or Trento's source since he stated he never saw the document in question.

What is the truth about "the smoking gun" document? Its source was probably James Angleton. Angleton seems to have passed the document on to Corson who allegedly confirmed its existence for Marchetti and may have shown it to Trento. Somewhere along the line Eddie Lopez heard about it and telephoned me.

Assuming that the document itself actually existed, Trento had to rely on his source's bona fides for the fact that it was not a forgery. Who could have had better bona fides than Angleton? His name was on the document.

I believe that Angleton fabricated the document as part of a very clever disinformation campaign aimed at turning the HSCA off to the Hunt/Dallas connection. By creating this document and letting it leak out that the HSCA had it, when they really didn't, Angleton put the HSCA in a position where they would feel sympathy for Hunt since he had been unjustly accused. HSCA Chief Counsel Robert Blakey was quoted as saying, "This memo does not exist. It never happened. It is a lie. The story has done great damage to Howard Hunt."

The HSCA report contains the following footnote:

"During the course of the Committee a rumor was circulating that the Committee had uncovered a memorandum in CIA files indicating

Hunt was in Dallas on November 22, 1963. The rumor was not founded on fact. In addition, Hunt gave the Committee a sworn deposition in which he denied the allegation, and the Committee found no evidence that contradicted Hunt's deposition."

More than ten years have passed since word of the document first surfaced, yet we have not seen the document. Angleton probably shredded his creation since he never planned to publicly circulate it. The document was bait, and Trento and Marchetti took it. They were unwitting participants in floating a false news story and all of them opened themselves up for a libel suit. That Hunt chose to sue Marchetti over this very story is no coincidence. He knew there was no such document and he might be able to get a judgement against the researcher who published a story about it. In this way, Hunt could suppress future works that linked him to the assassination.

CHAPTER SEVENTEEN

Hunt vs. SPOTLIGHT

Marchetti wrote an article about the memo, the tramp shots, etc. that was published by the crypto-Nazi publication, *Spotlight*. Hunt sued *Spotlight* for printing the article. *Spotlight's* attorney, Miles McGrain, agreed to the stipulation that Howard Hunt had nothing to do with the Kennedy assassination and was not in Dallas on that day. In his closing argument he said that the article, although false, was not libelous because there was no malice intended by Marchetti.

Marchetti refused to testify at the trial and *Spotlight* knew better that to call me as a witness on their behalf, since its' parent organization, Liberty Lobby, sponsors the Institute for Historical Review (IHR) in Torrance, California. The IHR is dedicated to proving that the mass extermination of Jews by the Nazis never occurred. The IHR is really a Nazi front.

Ellis Rubin, Hunt's attorney, read from the deposition of Walter Kuzmuk, taken December 7, 1981. Kuzmuk, a 27 year CIA veteran who was Hunt's friend and neighbor in 1963 testified: "I got into the office in the morning (of November 22, 1963) and then lunchtime arrived. As usual, several of us got together and went to lunch at Duke Ziebert's, right around the corner from where the office was located, and I was with several of my colleagues. I guess it was around one o'clock, one thirty in the afternoon...and I saw a car go by and I noticed Howard and Betty–not Betty–Dorothy...and I waved at them." Kuzmuk had kept this information to himself until he decided to volunteer it to Ellis Rubin in 1976 or 1977 after I had linked Hunt's name to the Kennedy killing.

Spotlight lost and Hunt was awarded one hundred thousand dollars in compensatory damages and five hundred and fifty thousand dollars in punitive damages by the jury.

Since *Spotlight* did not use truth as defense the judgement did minimal damage to my pending libel case. It looked as if Hunt might bankrupt *Spotlight* and put them out of business. I was happy for Howie...he fought for America in World War II and is anti-Nazi. He's a dedicated anti-communist who had a tendency to throw away the baby (democracy) with the bathwater in his fight against communism.

A Federal Appeals Court reversed the *Spotlight* conviction on a technicality and a new trial was ordered. This time *Spotlight* hired assassination researcher and attorney Mark Lane to represent them.

Lane is an experienced attorney and he did a good job fighting the Hunt vs. *Spotlight* lawsuit. First, Lane went after Kuzmuk. In *Plausible Denial* Lane writes that at the second Hunt vs. *Spotlight* trial Kuzmuk stated that, "Although he had previously testified that he and Hunt drove together to the CIA almost every morning, alternating automobiles, he could not testify that he had seen Hunt on any day of the week beginning Monday, November 18, and ending Friday, November 22, except for the time Hunt drove past the restaurant that Kuzmuk was leaving after lunch. Kuzmuk asserted that he had not driven to work with Hunt on November 22." Furthermore, to the best of his recollection, Hunt had not shown up for regularly scheduled meetings on November 20, 1963 and on November 22, 1963.

Kuzmuk's testimony conflicted with that of Hunt's secretary in 1963, Connie Mazerov, who testified for the first time at the second Hunt vs. *Spotlight* trial. Ms. Mazerov said she had seen Hunt at work early that morning. Lane writes, "As to the meetings he was supposed to have attended later that morning (according to one of Hunt's versions of events), she couldn't recall seeing him there. She never saw anyone else that morning who could have seen him."

Hunt had already changed his alibi to accommodate the Mazerov and Kuzmuk testimony as he had done in the case of Wah Ling when he thought I was going to produce him as a witness.

During a deposition that took place in December, 1981, in the course of the first Hunt vs. *Spotlight* case, he testified, "My wife had...driven downtown with our infant son, who was only about three months old, to pick me up. She wanted to buy ingredients for Chinese dinners, and we proceeded from my office downtown over to H Street where there are several Chinese restaurants and a number of grocery stores. She needed me to sit in the car while she went into the grocery store..."

Prior to this, Hunt was not sure if he had been in the office that day. He told the Rockefeller Commission that "on the afternoon of that day, he was in the company of his wife and family in the Washington, D.C. area, rather than at his employment duties. That was a Friday and therefore a working day for employees at the CIA. Hunt could not recall whether he was on duty with the CIA on the morning of that day...He used...eleven hours of sick leave in the two week pay period ending November 23, 1963...There is some indication that some of these eleven hours of sick leave may have been taken by Hunt on November 22, 1963."

In June of 1977 Hunt was also unsure if he had gone to the office that morning. We asked Hunt if he was certain about his whereabouts on the day of the assassination and he answered, "Totally certain."

Q.-"Were you in good health on that day?"

A.-"As far as I know I was."

Q.-"Did you take any sick leave during that pay period?"

A.-"I may have. I don't know."

Q.-"Would sick leave be taken on that particular day?"

A.-"It's entirely possible. I suffer from ulcers."

Q.-"Perhaps you visited the CIA that day?"

A.-"I have no idea. Certainly afterward I did."

Q.-"But you could have stopped by the office?"

A.-"It's possible I was there in the morning, yes."

Why did it take Hunt so many years to remember that he was at the office on November 22, 1963? Why did he equivocate about whether or not he was at the CIA on the morning of the coup when questioned by the Rockefeller and "Weberman Commissions"? He never said he was there yet he never said he wasn't...he left his options open.

The reason he did this was because he was unsure how much help he was going to receive from the Agency in his desperate effort to prevent other researchers from linking him to the Kennedy hit.

My investigation uncovered enough evidence to convince the CIA to lend Hunt a helping hand. For example, in Hunt's early depositions in my libel case he mentioned one Raymond Thomas, a neighbor, as an alibi witness. But when we questioned Thomas, he testified that he did not remember seeing Hunt that day or discussing the assassination with him.

It's possible that to protect itself the CIA evaluated my research progress and determined they had to help Hunt put the kibosh on things as soon as possible. No CIA agent would want to see the Agency linked to the Kennedy killing.

The Agency was very interested in my investigation. When Lane questioned Richard Helms about Clay Shaw, Helms's CIA counsel gave him a copy of his deposition in Hunt vs. Weberman.

It was only after my investigation was in operation for several years that Hunt started in with the "office/Mazerov" story. Before this, it was the Wah Ling/Tuck Cheong shopping trip. Was his cue to begin the office story the surfacing of Mazerov? Did Ms. Mazerov surface at the behest of the CIA?

The key to Kuzmuk's testimony is this: "Hunt" was in a car with his wife driving by quickly and Kuzmuk caught a brief glimpse of them. What he probably saw was Dorothy Hunt (see page 68) establishing an alibi for her husband by driving around with someone who dressed and looked like her husband. This way Dorothy could control the distance and speed at which "her husband" could be viewed. Hunt hoped that if his role in the Kennedy assassination ever came up one of the group of lunch goers would spontaneously come forward and say they saw him that day. He would have a witness who honestly believed he saw Hunt that day.

That is why Kuzmuk didn't remember driving him to, or seeing him at, the Agency that morning but only saw him driving by. This part of Kuzmuk's testimony conflicted with Hunt's who stated, "I probably rode in from Maryland with Mr. Kuzmuk that day and saw him later in the afternoon of that day as well...around twelve thirty, maybe one o'clock, something like that."

Lane made another interesting point about Hunt's alibi:

Q.-"Do you recall testifying back on December 16, 1981, that when the allegation was made that you were in Dallas, Texas, on November 22, 1963, your children were really upset?"

A.-"Yes"

Q.-"Do you recall testifying that you had to reassure them that you were not in Texas that day?"

A.-"Yes"

Q.-"Did you say the allegation that you were in Dallas, Texas, on November 22, 1963, was the focus of a great deal of interfamily friction...?"

A.-"I did."

Q.-"Mr. Hunt, why did you have to convince your children that you were not in Dallas, Texas on November 22, 1963, if, in fact, as you say, a fourteen year old daughter, a thirteen year old daughter, and a ten year old son were with you in the Washington, D.C. area on November 22, 1963, and were with you at least for the next forty-eight hours, as you all stayed glued to the TV set?"

A.-"So, it was less a question of my convincing them that I was in Washington, D.C. with them–rather, reminding them that I was–than it was to assure them that none of the charges and allegations that have been made, particularly those of the tramp in Dealy Plaza, had any substance to them at all."

Two of Hunt's children told the Rockefeller Commission that they were with him that day. The other two were too young to remember. Perhaps it was these two who questioned their father about the tramp shots? Yet they would have been told by their older siblings that the tramp story had to be totally false since they had first hand knowledge of their father's whereabouts that day.

Hunt also slipped when he used the word "assure." This is an indication of some doubt in his kids' minds about who was where that day.

CHAPTER EIGHTEEN

Oswald's Letter to Hunt and the New Orleans Connection

On November 8, 1963 Oswald mailed a letter to E. Howard Hunt, who was in Mexico City at the time (see page 204). The HSCA ignored it even though their own panel of handwriting experts could not say that it was a forgery. A copy of this letter was first mailed to assassination researcher Penn Jones from Mexico City. He received it on August 18, 1975 along with a note, which read, "...at the end of the last year I gave Mr. Kelley, Director of the FBI a letter from Lee Oswald. It is my understanding it could have brought out certain circumstances in the assassination of President Kennedy. Since Mr. Kelly has not responded to that letter, I've got the right to believe something bad might happen to me, and that is why I see myself obligated to keep myself away for a short time..." When copies of the letter were given to Director Kelley he announced, "Investigation to date has failed to produce evidence that the alleged letter was written by Oswald." When I filed a Freedom of Information request for the Lab Report the FBI based their findings on with respect to the letter, I found none existed.

The Hunt letter was discussed during the HSCA Hearings:

Mr. Klein – "At this time I would direct your attention to the document marked JFK-506, dated November 8, 1963...For the record could you read that document please."

Mr. McNally – "N-o-v 8, 1963: 'Dear Mr. Hunt; I would like information concerning (concerding) my position. I am asking only for information. I am suggesting that we discuss the matter fully before any steps are taken by me or anyone else. Thank you Lee Harvey Oswald."

Mr. Klein – "Using the blowup will you explain why the panel could not reach a conclusion with respect to that document?"

Mr. McNally – "...number one, this of course is a photo reproduction. It is a peculiar type of photo reproduction...it has some of the characteristics of being photo reproduced from a microfilm enlargement which was originally out of focus...This is an extremely good reproduction of that particular fuzzy original photo reproduction...this document itself, although the writing pattern or the overall letter designs are consistent with those as written on the other documents, this is much more precisely and much more carefully written. There is no great deviation from the writing of Oswald insofar as individual letter design forms are concerned..."

Mr. Fithian – "I have but one question. On balance, this Hunt letter, do you find more similarities or dissimilarities overall in the comparison to the other writings or letters, words that all seem to agree in the other documents?"

Mr. McNally – "There are no dissimilarities in the body of this particular letter, the context, until you come down to the signature...a part of the signature agrees with the signature of Oswald...and part of it does not agree...and for these reasons we were unable to come to any firm conclusion regarding this particular document...we are not able to accurately determine that it is specifically a forgery..."

Mr. Fithian – "Is it your opinion that it is a fake?"

Mr. McNally – "No. I am not certain on this particular document."

The HSCA could not get their own experts to state that the letter was a forgery.

Judging from the way the note to Penn Jones was written, English was not the writer's native tongue. The writer had faith in the FBI and sent its Director a copy of the letter but thinks that since he has received no response from them they may be planning reprisals against him. "...something bad might happen to me." His view of law enforcement seems to imply that the FBI agents are also political police capable of extra-legal acts, a situation that was more the case in the former Soviet Union than in the United States.

The major clue to Jones' source's identity lies in McNally's statement that the letter "has some of the characteristics of being photo reproduced from a microfilm..." I would guess that the letter was mailed by Oswald to a location in Mexico City where it was intercepted by a foreign intelligence agency that had enough of an interest in the location to routinely open, microfilm then reseal all the mail going there. Perhaps the letter was sent to the CIA Station in Mexico City and was intercepted by foreign intelligence (probably the KGB) who eventually mailed this letter to Penn Jones in 1975.

Hunt was in Mexico City in November of 1963. This was confirmed by David Atlee Phillips who stated in his deposition during Hunt vs. *Spotlight* that in 1963 said he had seen Hunt in Mexico City "...sometime between September of 1961 and March of 1965...I must have seen him once or twice before (the Kennedy assassination)." David Atlee Phillips was the official CIA Station Chief in 1963. During former CIA Director Richard Helms' deposition in the same matter, he said, "I do recall having submitted information that indicated Hunt was in Mexico before the assassination."

Let us shift to the text of the letter. Oswald was in Dallas on the date the letter was written, November 8, 1963. He begins the letter rather formally–"Dear Mr. Hunt" then becomes very ambiguous–"I would like information concerning my position." He spells concerning "concerding." Was the word "disconcerted" on his mind at the time? He seems a little disconcerted in the rest of the letter. What does he mean by position? His job with the CIA or his position in Dealy Plaza on the day of the hit?

Oswald goes on to say, "I am only asking for information." In other words, he is not trying to get out of the hit team; he just wants to be assured that with his background as a political extremist he would not be a suspect in the killing. Nonetheless, he wants Hunt to assuage his fears completely. "I am suggesting that we discuss the matter fully," before he takes any more steps that will lead to the assassination of John Kennedy. "...before any steps are taken by me" or by anyone else involved in the conspiracy–"...or anyone else."

The HSCA devoted a lot of time to the Hunt letter but never once was the name of E. Howard Hunt mentioned in relation to it. Mr. Fithian, who questioned McNally about the letter also questioned the forensic anthropologists about the "tramp shots" so he was well aware of E. Howard Hunt.

Another omission indicative of CIA co-option of the HSCA occurred when Professor Blakey described the "tramp shots" to the Committee. "For years the tramp shots were little more than conversation pieces, but in 1975, in a book called *Coup D'Etat in America*, Michael R. Cranfield and Alan J. Webermann (sic) proposed that two of these tramps were none other than Howard Hunt and Frank Sturgis...an identification of the third tramp...has also been suggested by critics connecting him to individuals whose names have come up in private investigations." Blakey failed to mention the forbidden word "Carswell."

So far, the HSCA had a photo of Hunt in Dallas and a letter to Hunt from Oswald, both of which they chose to ignore. It comes as no surprise that when confronted with the connection between Hunt and Oswald via 544 Camp Street and the Cuban Revolutionary Council, it too was ignored. "...the New Orleans chapter of the Cuban Revolutionary Council (CRC) had occupied an office for about 6 months during 1961 to 1962...since the CRC had vacated the building 15 months before Oswald arrived in New Orleans, the Warren Commission concluded there was no connection with Oswald. Nevertheless, the riddle of 544 Camp Street persisted over the years." The CRC was formally disbanded after Bay of Pigs in April 1961" so of course it was not longer at 544 Camp Street—it was no longer anywhere for that matter. But the crew that hung out at 544 stayed pretty much the same (see pages 34-36). The Rockefeller Report states that Hunt's "employment record with the CIA indicated that he had no duties involving contacts with Cuban exile elements or organizations inside or outside the United States after the early months of 1961." "The early months of 1961" is a euphemism for the Bay of Pigs. Hunt had official contacts before Bay of Pigs. After Bay of Pigs his contacts were unofficial since the CRC, which he helped manage, no longer existed.

Hunt ties into the characters Oliver Stone and Jim Garrison finger in the movie *JFK*: Ferrie, Bannister, etc. These men were linked to Oswald. The HSCA admits this but claims that, "...since Oswald consistently demonstrated a left wing Marxist ideology, he would not have supported the anti-Castro movement."

In 1979 the HSCA released its final report which put much of the blame for the JFK hit on the mob. The mob certainly played a very important role but it was the CIA that actually did the hit. The HSCA even went as far as suggesting that Oswald was mobbed up. Maybe he defected to the Soviet Union to set up a crime family there? The Justice Department never brought indictments against organized crime figures for the Kennedy assassination and everything went back into limbo.

Had Congressman Henry B. Gonzalez remained Chairman of the HSCA it would have been a whole different ball game. Henry Gonzalez is his own man and is totally independent of the CIA.

CHAPTER NINETEEN

Aftermath

Around the time the Oliver Stone movie was released in 1991 the tramps started to surface again in the tabloid press and on cable TV. One story that received a lot of publicity was that "Cheers" star Woody Harrelson's father was the tramp that looked like Sturgis. The Agency had reached a new low in disinformation.

The Harrelson Story

The Harrelson story came to light when lawmen cornered him near Van Horne, Texas in September, 1980. Wacked out of his skull on cocaine, Harrelson ranted and raved for six hours while pointing a pistol at his head and holding lawmen at bay until he surrendered. Still in a psychotic state, he confessed to the ambush shooting of Federal Judge John Wood in San Antonio, Texas, and the murder of John Kennedy in Dallas, Texas.

Why did Harrelson confess to the assassination? I believe that Harrelson was in a psychotic, suicidal state when he decided to make himself part of the whole Kennedy assassination myth. He talks like an assassination buff: "Well, do you believe Lee Harvey Oswald killed President Kennedy alone, without any aid from a rogue agency of the U.S. Government or at least a portion of that Agency? I believe you are very naive if you do."[15]

He may even possess some inside information on the assassination since he was an associate of Carlos Marchello's brother and was indicted along with him for the murder of Judge Woods. He also knew Jack Ruby's old gun-running R.D. Matthews (who was party to the "jeep sale" as mentioned on page 158) and was generally plugged into Texas crime circles.

The news media picked up the story of his confession, and when his photograph was circulated some assassination buffs were convinced that he was one of the tramps.

This was back in the early 1980s. It wasn't until late 1991 that the story hit it big in all the tabloids despite the fact that Harrelson had retracted his confession. "On November 22, 1963 I was with a friend at twelve-thirty in the afternoon having lunch in a restaurant in Houston, Texas. I did not kill JFK and it was not me in the picture. The facial structure isn't even close. I was twenty-five on the day the President was shot and this man looks as if he's in his mid to late thirties. I was not in my right mind when I confessed..."[16]

Why the lapse of eleven years between the time the story originated until it hit the tabloids? The story was intentionally widely disseminated in 1991 for a reason. The Agency knew the Oliver Stone movie was going to cause a big push to really get down to the bottom of the Kennedy hit and might bring the tramp shots back into the public consciousness. By having their CIA stringers at the various tabloids run this story they would overshadow any mention of the tramps being Hunt, Sturgis and Carswell.

Harrelson was profiled during a cable TV special titled "The Men Who Killed Kennedy" on Time Warner's Arts and Entertainment network. They presented an overlay of Harrelson and the same shot of the Sturgis tramp we used in this book for our overlay. The problem with the one on this show was that instead of overlaying a transparency of a photograph over the face of the Sturgis tramp they used a sketch! But we were assured by an assassination researcher from Dallas that a "forensic anthropologist" had studied the shots and reported that there is a better than 90% chance that the tramp is Harrelson. Not the "forensic anthropologists" again.

By 1992 another tramp had come forward. This time it was the Hunt tramp. It turned out to be Chauncey Marvin Holt, a career criminal who says that he was with Harrelson in Dealy Plaza that day. Holt looks like the Hunt tramp but does not have that wing-like ear that is visible on page 207. He also is not a very good liar. He claims that all three of the tramps were released by the cops after convincing them they were actually undercover agents assigned to protect the President. How would the cops believe that when they knew the tramps had been taken off a freight train that had already pulled out from behind the TSBD? Is this any way for undercover Secret Service agents to leave the scene of an assassination of the man they are assigned to protect?

The Tramp Tramps

The latest development in the story of the tramps occurred as a spinoff of the release of Oliver Stone's movie *JFK*. The film had enough influence on public opinion to cause the Dallas City Council to open the Dallas Police Department's files on the Kennedy assassination to the public. As a result of this release, records of three tramps picked up in the railroad yards shortly after the assassination were discovered.

Let us examine these documents, beginning with "Gus W. Abrams", the oldest of the three tramps (age 53).

"Mr. Abrams" was arrested on November 22, 1963 at 4:00 p.m. in the Texas and Pacific railroad yards at Elm and Houston in Dallas. He was charged with vagrancy and possible robbery: "These men were taken off a train boxcar in the railroad yards right after President Kennedy was shot. These men are passing through town. They have no jobs or any means of making a living." The arresting officer was W.E. Chambers and Officer Ernest Beck released them on November 26, 1963, four days later. Missing from the form was a home address, I.D. number, arrest number and thumbprint.

"John Forrester Gedney" was the next tramp, age 38. Aside from the different name and date of birth it was identical to that of "Gus Abrams".

The last arrest record was on "Harold Doyle", age 30, presumably the Sturgis tramp (he looked youngest). It was identical to the other two except in its description of the details of the arrest: "These men were seen getting on a boxcar on a train right after President Kennedy was shot. These men are all passing through, they have no jobs..."

Assuming these men were "the tramps", since Mr Abrams was the oldest, one would presume he was the Hunt tramp. Mr. Doyle is the youngest of the three so he must be the Sturgis tramp, since the

Sturgis tramp looks the youngest. Finally, by the process of elimination, Mr. Gedney must be the Carswell tramp.

I called the policeman who questioned these tramps, William E. Chambers, "You mean all that stuff in the news? They got that wrong. My name is on the document but it is wrong, I never questioned them. I might have seen them, I don't remember. I signed the reports but there was some mistake. You're not going to put this in your book...I don't like discussing this with strangers."

I then called retired Dallas Police Officer Ernest Beck and asked him if he had released them, "I don't know, I don't know. I don't remember anything about that time...it was so long ago. I don't remember any tramps." I said, "Mr Beck, it is really important for America to find this stuff out. You don't remember releasing any tramps who had been picked up in the railroad yards right after the assassination?" "No!"

Michael Canfield went down to Dallas and questioned Officer Beck in person. After three days of stonewalling, Officer Beck suddenly invited Canfield to his house. Two current Dallas Police Officers had visited Beck earlier, with copies of the arrest records of Doyle, Gedney and Abrams, and apparently had briefed Beck on what to say. He said he had no recollection of the arrest of the tramps, or of having released them. Earlier, when he had said on the telephone that he had seen the arrest records (after the police had shown them to him) Canfield asked if he had indeed signed the release of the tramps, and Beck said that it was his handwriting. When Canfield asked if Beck would testify to that in a court of law, Beck screamed, "I ain't testifying to nothing!" and hung up. The next day Beck changed his attitude and the meeting took place.

Canfield then called W.E. Chambers, the alleged arresting officer on the records, and asked him about the arrest records. At the mention of the alleged arrest records, Chambers got uptight, yelled, "I don't talk about that!" and hung up. Canfield then went to W.E. Chambers's house. He rang the bell. No answer. He called again. No answer. He knew Chambers was home because his car was parked in the driveway. Canfield waited three days but Chambers would not come out. He was probably hiding under his bed, afraid to get mixed-up in an event like the Kennedy assassination. If there was no problem with those arrest records, there should be no problem answering questions about them. If the situations were reversed and the police were asking the questions, this sort of behavior would seem very suspicious.

The next day Canfield went over to the Dallas City Archives and checked the arrest records there. Not only did he find the above mentioned three, but he found two more. John Francis Elrod was picked up walking along the railroad tracks and Daniel Wayne Douglas was picked up near the scene of the Tippett shooting. Both were released on November 26, 1963. Beck had released Douglas and probably also released Elrod. These arrest reports are identical to those of the "tramps" and do not have photos, prints etc.

Next stop was every courthouse in Dallas (Felony, Misdemeanor, Traffic, Divorce, Civil etc.) to check the docket books for November 22, 1963 and see if any of these four showed up. Nothing. The jailhouse was next. No record. The arrest reports were the only traces on these men.

Where these men *the* Tramps? Judging from the arrest records they were not. Instead, they were different tramps who happened to be picked up that day.

First of all, my early research on references to the tramps by the Warren Commission (see page 5) indicates that the men we are interested in were in a freight train that had been searched by Police shortly after the assassination. When the Police were unable to find anyone aboard it they let it leave the railroad yards behind the TSBD. When sharp eyed railroad man Lee Bowers saw one of the tramps going from the boxcar to the gondola car as the train was pulling out, he had the train brought back into the yards and searched again. It was at this point the tramps were unearthed by Police officers Roy Vaughn (who is now Police Chief of Midlothian, Texas) and D.V. Harkness. They were turned over to Officers Bass and Wise and were marched through Dealy Plaza.

The tramps in the arrest reports were seen "getting on a boxcar on a train right after the assassination." Just as they got on they were "taken off a train boxcar in the railroad yards right after President Kennedy was shot "

These are different tramps that were picked up before Hunt, Sturgis and Carswell were found. The fact that their arrest records contained so little information was not significant. The arrest records of Douglas and Elrod contained the same lack of information. The reason there are no court records for any of the four is simple. The Dallas Police, unconcerned about due process, threw these guys in the cooler for several days then released them.

After the Dallas papers carried the story that the tramps had been held for four days one of the policemen who had arrested them in the railroad yard, D.V. Harkness, appeared on local television to say that the men he arrested were released immediately and that these tramps were not them.

About two weeks after the story of the tramp records in the Dallas Police files broke, the couple who had written the story, Mary and Ray Fontaine, located Harold Doyle. They sold the story to the tabloid-style TV Show, "A Current Affair." The show did a piece on Doyle on February 25, 1992 which purported to prove that Doyle was the Carswell tramp.

The program began: "Conspiracy experts have claimed the hobos, all of them who appear to be unusually well dressed, might have been with the CIA and part of a high reaching assassination conspiracy. Others have claimed that the hobos were Watergate burglars E.Howard Hunt and Frank Sturgis...even Oliver Stone's movie JFK suggests the mystery hobos had something to do with the President's death...Only yesterday Dallas Police told Current Affair that the hobos were detained for a few hours and finding them now is highly unlikely."

The program went on to say that the LaFontaines traced Doyle down from his arrest record in which he listed Red Jacket, West Virginia, as his home. "From here (a small town flashes on the screen, presumably Red Jacket, West Virginia but no title appears) the LaFontaines traced his whereabouts to Amarillo, Texas and though long gone, neighbors still remember Doyle talking about his arrest on November 22, 1963."

Cut to Kay Lyon, former neighbor of Doyle–"Well, he told me he was in jail for two or three days and during that time he had been fingerprinted and questioned. He showed me a photograph of him when he was arrested after they got off the train and you know he was not proud of it but he didn't mind showing it to anybody."

From Amarillo the LaFontaines tracked Doyle to Klamath Falls, Oregon where he was found working in a pool hall and living in a small apartment. Here is Harold's story:

"The only thing I want to say about it, we had nothing to do with it, I can say it. I am telling you the God's and honest truth. We had nothing to do with it. We was (sic) booked and I went in front of the Judge and got six days for vagrancy and turned loose. That morning we went over to the railroad yards. We was (sic) going to Fort Worth and I seen (sic) a guy in the railroad...before we went to the railroad yards, sirens and everything was going on and all and we asked somebody what happened and they said the Presidents been shot. Then all at once someone said, 'Don't make a move.' We looked up the end we were sitting in and the far end down the side we were surrounded by policemen with guns drawn and they said, 'Don't make a move.' Because they got us out of the boxcar took us through the park...all the people was a hollering, was a going on and the sirens were going and people were taking pictures of us and people were hollering, 'Are they the ones that done it?'..they took us into the jail. They took us up and interrogated us. Kept us till they caught Oswald. He was right across the desk from us and the man that was with us said, 'You boys are sure lucky. You see the guy that killed the President in person.'"

What really happened was that Doyle had been arrested the day of the assassination in the railroad yards along with two other men. This was a big event in his life, his one minute of fame. But he had to embellish upon this story by adding that he was one of the mysterious tramps who was photographed while being marched through Dealy Plaza. This part of his story was not true.

First of all, Doyle claims to be the Carswell tramp. If he was the youngest of the three tramps he should be the Sturgis tramp. Secondly, he does not look like the tramp by any stretch of the imagination. Doyle has learned to make his mouth look a little like that of Carswell, but that is where the resemblance ends. We have reprinted a photograph of Doyle on page 363 so you can judge for yourself. Current Affair should have asked Doyle for a photograph of himself from around 1963 since thirty years have elapsed since the assassination.

Secondly, by his own admission, Doyle was arrested immediately after the assassination–"before we went to the railroad yards, sirens and everything was going on...then all at once someone said don't make a move." Doyle was pulled off the freight before it pulled out, not after. Then Doyle claims he was taken from a box car. Harkness and Vaughn claim they found the tramps in a gondola car. The tramp that Lee Bowers spotted must have been "jumping from the ninth boxcar from the front engine" and heading for an open gondola car.

Thirdly, all that Kay Lyon testified to was that she heard Doyle say he was arrested that day (which was true) and that he was one of the tramps whose photographs were widely circulated. (not true) Kay Lyon is not a photoanalyst nor does she possess any first hand knowledge of anything regarding the Kennedy assassination. She is reporting just hearsay based on Doyle's self serving statements. Doyle also told her he was fingerprinted. He was not.

Fourthly, Doyle says he was brought before a Judge and held for six days. He was not brought before a Judge and the arrest records indicate he was held for four days. Finally, the Dallas Police told "A Current Affair" that the tramps they were interested in had been released immediately after the assassination.

"A Current Affair" ended with Vincent T. Bugliosi, a former Deputy District Attorney from Los Angeles, County, famous for his role in the Charles Manson case, saying that "Finding the hobos can finally lay to rest irresponsible theories of conspiracy about them". Bugliosi is now at work on a book about the Kennedy assassination which supports the conclusions of the Warren Commission.

About one week after the "A Current Affair" program aired the following article appeared in the *New York Daily News:*

> "JFK TRAMPS, FBI SAYS, WERE JUST VAGRANTS Washington - Nearly 29 years after the assassination of President John Kennedy, the FBI has finally tracked down the mysterious "three tramps" arrested that day in Dallas - and concluded that they were just tramps. The FBI's Dallas office said it traced the tramps after their names were printed in Texas newspapers...One tramp, Gus Abrams, is dead, the FBI said, but agents found and interviewed John Forrest Gedney in Melbourne, Florida and Harold Doyle in Klamath Falls, Oregon. The said they were at a mission the day of the assassination "had gotten some food and had gotten cleaned up and *were wandering back toward the railroad yard*" when they

were arrested, said *Oliver Revell*, head of the Dallas FBI office. Some theorists postulated that the tramps were future Watergate burglars E. Howard Hunt and Frank Sturgis."

There was no photograph of Gedney included with the article so we can not compare him to the tramp. However I am sure the FBI must have checked the identities of Doyle and Gedney out so we know that these are there real names. Gedney's story, like Doyle's, contradicts Warren Commission testimony. The SAC of the Dallas Office who conducted this investigation had close ties to the Central Intelligence Agency when he served as the head of the FBI Counterterrorism Unit. He also has close ties to the Iran/Contra scandal.

Michael Canfield is not surprised at the intricate disinformation the CIA has come up with this time. "The CIA has a building with 300 people called the Department of Disinformation and all the folks there do is sit around and make up lies. When you call them, you ask the CIA switchboard operator for "Disinformation, please." They make up all sorts of false stories, facts and tabloid articles to float in the U.S. and foreign press to elicit various responses from governments and the unsuspecting public. They must have been burning the midnight oil preparing all sorts of fanciful fiction. They knew the release of Oliver Stone film would cause a rush of activity in certain areas.

We in the journalistic world must be aware that not every supposed scoop that comes down the line is what it seems to be. Every fact must be checked and rechecked. We have tried to check every fact and invite you the reader and you the researcher/reporter to do the same. This is the only way we are going to get the truth on these matters. In the words of the prophet: "Keep pressing on."

Have the tramps been laid to rest by the FBI along with the truth? It is up to you to decide.

As I write these words Canfield is on his way to Klamath Falls, Oregon to speak with Doyle. Then he is headed for Melbourne, Florida to interview Gedney.

We will keep you updated on the progress of our investigation right up until we go press and in subsequent printings with news flashes.

CHAPTER TWENTY

Afterward

Neither the Warren Commission, the Rockefeller Commission or the HSCA have told the truth about the CIA being behind the Kennedy assassination. The truth must be told. Either a Special Prosecutor should be appointed and indictments brought against the guilty CIA men, or a televised Congressional Investigation should take place. The CIA should be forbidden by law from co-opting or interfering in this investigation.

The former nations of the Communist Bloc are purging themselves of the secret police who violated their human rights during the Cold War era. We should purge ourselves of the anti-democratic elements that came to power during the Kennedy and Nixon Administrations.

President Nixon appointed Gerald Ford to the Vice Presidency, Ford appointed Bush, who had been Nixon's ambassador to China, to head the CIA. Now the Agency has its own man in the White House. Rule by the intelligence community must come to an end.

Footnotes
Chapters 13-20

[1] Anderson, Jack, **Miami Herald**, Jan. 4, 1978.
[2] **New York Times** quoted in 2NS News Dispatch, May 10, 1978
[3] The Invisible Government, (Russ/Wise)
[4] Martino, John, I was Castro's Prisoner, Denon-Adder
[5] ibid.
[6] ibid.
[7] Hearings, HSCA, appendix, vol. 6, page 258
[8] ibid. page 259
[9] ibid. page 260
[10] ibid. page 262
[11] ibid. page 263
[12] Lane, Mark, Plausible Denial, Thunder's Mouth Press, New York 1991
[13] **New York Post**, September 6, 1982
[14] The Ends of Power by H.R. Haldeman, Time Books, 1978 Cited in High Treason by Robert Groden, Berkeley Publishers, 1989, page 345
[15] Pan Arts Entertainment television special, "Investigative Report on the Men Who Killed Kennedy", March, 1991
[16] Ibid.

Oswald-like Tramp/Carswell Head Comparison:

Two identical objects may appear very different from each other when viewed from slightly different directions or when illuminated from different angles. Notice that the same tramp's features seem to change when the photos are taken from different perspectives.

Top row (left to right): Blow up **P2**, "Dan Carswell", Blow up **P5** reversed.

Bottom row (left to right): Blow up **P3** reversed, Blow up **P7**, Blow up **P4** reversed.

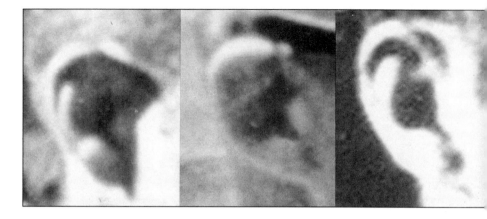

Oswald-like Tramp/Carswell Ear Comparison:

"Carswell's" ear and the Tramp's ear have the same proportions and matching internal helix structure.

Left to right: Blow up **P2**, "Dan Carswell", Blow up **P7**

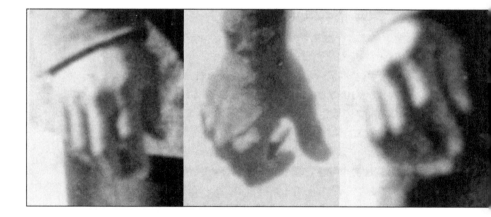

Oswald-like Tramp/Carswell Hand Comparison:

"Carswell's" hand has a large vein which can be seen in the Tramp's hand. Also, both men hold their hands with a distinctive gap between the index and middle finger.

Left to right: Blow up **P2,** "Dan Carswell", Blow up **P1**

Electronic photo-imaging on the blow up of **P5** shows what the Tramp looks like with "Carswell's" pipe and sunglasses

Recent dis-information releases have tried to identify Gedney, Abrams and Doyle as the Tramps photographed walking through Dealy Plaza. However, these arrest reports contradict the supervising police officer, D.V. Harkness, who found the Tramps on an open gondola car, and testified that they were released the same day . These reports show that the men were in a box car, and were held for four days.

The TV show "A Current Affair" featured a story in which they claimed that Harold Doyle is the "Carswell" Tramp. They showed a current picture of him instead of one from 1963.

Forensic Analysis and Reconstruction
166 Nathan Drive, Bohemia NY 11716
Day (516) 853-5325, Evening (516) 589-0132

January 6, 1992

Jeremiah S. Gutman
Levy, Gutman, Goldberg & Kaplan
275 Seventh Avenue Suite 1776
New York, N.Y. 10001

Your Re: A.J.
Our File: T920101

Dear Mr. Gutman,

The three negatives submitted for examination and comparison were developed and made into print 8"x10" photographs to assist in the analysis.

The following facial characteristics were noted in all photographs, and, in my opinion, are significant:

- The nose has a characteristic slope that terminates into a distinctive point.

- The nostrils are elongated as a result of the sloping nose.

- The opening in the right ear has a geometrical shape consistent in all photographs. Furthermore the ear lobe in all photographs is continuous and is attached to the face.

- Although the hair length differs the hairline appears to be consistent both horizontally and vertically with respect to the face line.

- Finally and most significantly there is a skin blemish on the right cheek noted in all three photographs. This blemish appears located in the same area of all the photographs. The blemish is located by fixing a horizontal parallel line along the right nostril following front to rear. Furthermore, the blemish can be located by fixing a vertical parallel line along the hairline, on the right side of the face, following top to bottom.

As a result of the above listed characteristics, specifically the skin blemish, it is my opinion that the same person appears in all of the submitted photographs.

I have enclosed all submitted negatives and copies of the prints for your reference.

I hope that this analysis will assist you in your case work. Please contact me if you require to discuss the analysis any further.

TASA. The invoice for services rendered will be forwarded to

Respectfully submitted,

Robert Genna

RG/lg
encl.

Robert E. Genna, Assistant Chief of the Suffolk County Crime Laboratory, holds a M.S. in Forensic Science, is Past President of the Northeastern Association of Forensic Scientists and a member of the International Society for Identification.

PETERE VERITATEM   PETERE INDICIUM

PHYSICAL EVIDENCE CONSULTANTS

VALLEY PARK PROFESSIONAL CENTER
2517 HIGHWAY 35
BUILDING J, SUITE 103
MANASQUAN, NEW JERSEY 08736
FAX: (908) 528-3312
(908) 528-5310

February 18, 1992

Levy, Gutman, Goldberg and Kaplan
275 Seventh Avenue, Suite 1776
New York, New York 10001

Attn: Jeremiah S. Gutman, Esq.

Re: A.J.

Dear Mr. Gutman:

As per your request, an examination of three (3) 8x10 black and white negatives were made. Three contact prints were made from the original negatives obtained from your office. These contact prints have been marked A, B, and C.

Photograph A depicts a white male wearing sunglasses with a pipe in his mouth. The subject has short, cropped hair and appears to be in an airport setting. Photograph B is an enlargement of photograph A depicting the previously mentioned white male. Photograph C depicts a white male in a street setting.

It is initially apparent in photograph C that there is a weight difference between the two subjects. Further, there is a time sequence delay in the photographs. This is obvious from the hair style and the hair length. Given those conditions, there are striking similarities in the facial features of both subject A and C. Upon examining the hair line, you will note that there is a high recessing forehead on the right-hand side. This is seen in both photographs. The shape of the ears are similar in both of these photographs. We are unable to make a determination of the eyes due to the presence of sunglasses in photograph A. The forehead shape and size are again similar between the two photographs. The nose and nostrils have similar characteristics. The subject in both photographs has a long, thin jawline. Although the lips are turned up in photograph A, one can see that the lips in photograph A and C are similar that being long thin lips. Examination under magnification indicates a mole of some type located on the right upper cheek of both photographs A and C.

As previously mentioned, there is a time delay between the taking of photograph A and C. Even given this time delay, both subjects have strikingly similar characteristics. Given those physical attributes as described and including the apparent mole as seen in all three (3) photographs, I would conclude that subject A and C appear to be one in the same.

If I can be of any other service to you regarding this matter, please advise.

Sincerely,

Dennis J. Fahey

DJF:dar

Enclosures: Negatives 8x10 three (3)
              Contact prints three (3)

Dennis J. Fahey, Executive Vice President of Physical Evidence Consultants, Inc., holds a M.S. in Criminal Justice from Rutgers University and is a member of the New Jersey State Identification Association.

Key to Footnotes Chapters 1-12

Warren Commission: 26 Volumes of Hearings and Exhibits

2 H 333		CE 000
Volume number of Warren Commission Hearings	Page number of Warren Commission Hearings	Commission Exhibit Number

000R—Warren Report—single volume summary of twenty-six volumes.

National Archives collection of Warren Commission evidence.
CD000—Commission Document number 000.
Entry # and Box #—refers to National Archives inventory of JFK record group, by Marion Johnson.

SS File # ⎫ cross reference file with CD and CE,
FBI File # ⎭ available at National Archives.
Commission memos, executives sessions.

NYT—New York *Times.*
N.O. *States Item*—New Orleans *States Item.*
Anderson—Jack Anderson syndicated column.
AP—Associated Press dispatch.
UPI—United Press International dispatch.
Pressina Latin—Cuban Propaganda and news agency.
Copies of all unidentified documents available free: 6 Bleecker Street, NYC 10012. Copies of documents, tapes, etc. also available.

Note: Footnotes often refer to ALL facts in paragraph.
References often refer to entire testimony.

Footnotes Chapters 1-12

Chapter Three
1. CD931
2. 8H303
3. 11H42—Entry 44-Oswald-Misc. Mil.
4. Washington **Star** 11/59
5. CD977
6. **News-American** 1/31/75
7. CE915
8. Washington **Post** 6/9/62
9. 277R; **Who's Who In CIA**-Mader
10. **Only One Year** by Svetlana Stalin, Harper-Row Publishers, page 308; 11H442
11. 11H442
12. Scoby: pgk Box 23, Entry 44; R326
13. CD294; 16H436
14. 11H193—Seeley
15. FBI File #CI62-2758; **The War Con spiracy** by Peter Dale Scott
16. 9H1
17. CD735; CD544; 8H355-George Bouche **Newsweek** March 6, 1967 **The Warfare State** by Fred Cook
18. CD1066 **Operation Paperclip**—Lasby—p. 265
19. CD531; 9H166
20. Chicago **Tribune** 2/2/75 p. 2
21. CD186
22. **Invisible Government**—Wise—p. 122 Surfeit of Spies—**Harper's** 12/74— James O. Goulden
23. CD60
24. 9H166; CD531; CD532
25. 9H166; CD533
26. **Undercover**—Hunt p. 55
27. **Day**—Hunt p. 19; 9H166
28. CD531; 9H166
29. Helms Test. to Senate Select Committee on Campaign Practices
30. CD1107—Willard Banker
31. Demohrenschildt Exhibit #6, #16 **Silent Syndicate**—Messick p. 28
32. CD208; CD214; CD849; **Ibid** 18
33. 9H169, 183-4; NYT 2/12, 20/75; 2H386; 433, 427, 284R

34. 10H167; CD75—p. 78
35. **Undercover**—Hunt, p. 222, 165; CD1124; 185R
36. 11H404; CD1124
37. 183-5R; 282R
38. Conference with Issac Don Levine, 5/28/64. Present—Dulles, Slawson; CD1245
39. CE1973; CD599
40. Undated Memo from Hoover to Rankin Copy available upon request. 189R; Willens Memo 2/28/64
41. **Portrait of the Assassin**—Ford
42. **Bremer's Diary**, p. 70
43. UPI Dispatch, 8/1/74
44. NYT 6/8/73
45. New York **Post**, 6/21/73
46. CD75; 726R
47. 729R; 407R
48. Barker Test. to Senate Select Comm. On Camp. Act.—Questioned by Guerny
49. **Ramparts**, June 1967—Bill Turner
50. **Undercover**—Hunt, p. 96, 97; **Day**— Hunt, p. 22
51. **Day**—Hunt, p. 26, 63, 202
52. Telephone conversation with Jim Garrison; CE1414; CD638
53. Interview with Mary Bannister—New Orleans District Attorney's office, 4/29-30/67 **Undercover**—Hunt, p. 67
54. New Orleans Police Dept. Report Item #K-12634-63; FBI File #89-69 (New Orleans); CD75
55. **Day**—Hunt, p. 44, 183
56. **Day**—Hunt, p. 46, 79
57. **Kennedy Conspiracy**, p. 96
58. **Plot Or Politics?**—James, p. 113 **Kennedy Conspiracy**, p. 96—Steve Plotkin
59. NYT 4/5/67; New Orleans **States Item** 4/25/67
60. **Kennedy Conspiracy**, p. 23; N.O. **States Item** 4/25/67

61. N.O. **States Item** 4/25/67; **Day**—Hunt, p. 182
62. N.O. **States Item** 3/22/67
63. **Day**—Hunt, p. 46; **Plot Or Politics**—James, p. 11
64. **Kennedy Conspiracy**—Flammonde, p. 100; N.O. **States Item** 4/22/67
65. Jack Anderson 8/15/74
66. 11H325; 325R
67. NYT 8/18/74—Roy Sheppard; NYT 1/5/75
68. Interview with V.M. Newhall 12/73; also **True** April 1975
69. **Le Devoir** 3/16/67; **Pasa Sera**, 3/4, 12, 14/67
70. NYT 7/1/59
71. **Ibid**; CD 1085
72. 10H32; **Day**—Hunt, p. 62
73. 728R
74. CE799; CD137; CD6
75. 408R—V.T. Lee
76. Recently declassified Hubert memo
77. **Ramparts** Nov. 1973—P.D. Scott
78. WH Tapes, p. 153
79. CD1214
80. **Day**—Hunt, p. 92, 93, 95
81. CE1414; 410R; 11H156
82. **Rev. Is My Profession**—Ed Butler
83. **Counterplot**—Epstein, p. 36—Capt. Neville Levy
84. Interview of David Ferrie by New Orleans District Attorney's office 2/20/67; **Plot Or Politics**—James, p. 45; NYT 1/14/73
85. Jack Anderson, 5/61
86. **Plot Or Politics**—James, p. 44, 46
87. New Orleans Police Dept. Record dated 8/30/61
88. **Day**—Hunt, p. 77—Knight
89. Los Angeles **Times** 9/4/70
90. **Counterplot**—Epstein, p. 36
91. **Comp. Spy**—Szulc, p. 96
92. FBI File #89-69 (New Orleans)
93. CD645
94. **Kennedy Conspiracy**—Flammonde, p. 181
95. **Kennedy Conspiracy**—Flammonde, p. 22
Heart Of Stone—Garrison, p. 128

96. **Kennedy Conspiracy**—Flammonde, p. 19
Miami **Herald** 2/22/67
97. **Superlawyers**—Goulden, Chapter 6
98. CD294
99. CD2; CD427
100. CD984B; 11H346; CD1349
101. CD984B—Ruperto Pena; CD1389A—Rodriguez
102. CD1203 report 12/5/63; 6/4/64; 6/64
103. 11H346; CD1203
104. Progressive Labor Party Newspaper, 2/6/75
105. CD1940; CE1941
106. **Undercover**—Hunt, chapt. 8, p. 194, 210
107. 734-5R; CD1216
108. **Day**—Hunt, p. 29, 40, 52
109. Rankin Memo to CIA, recently declassified documents
110. Rankin Memo 2/12/64; CD631
111. Slawson Memo GA1 CIA 3/12/64
112. NYT 1/14/75, p. 23; 477R
113. NYT 5/4/73
114. NYT 1/17/75
115. CD1479
116. Exec. Sessions; CD721
117. CD205, p. 453-62; Hubert Memo 3/19/64
118. **Ibid.**; Hubert Memo 3/6/64
119. London **Sunday Times** 6/3/74
120. 131R; 129-31R
121. 131-35R; 6H337
122. FBI File #DL 89-43 11/26/63—M.W. George

Chapter Four
1. 1H285-86
2. **Undercover**—Hunt p. 169, 223, 228
3. CD1245
4. Interview with Mark Lane 3/31/66 Arlington, Texas, cited in **Rush To Judgement**, p. 32; 1H284
5. 2H165
6. 24H522
7. 6H200-01; 6H191; 6H193
8. 6H239; 24H217; 22H833; 22H836; Winborn Murphy taped interview with Mark Galanor as cited in **Rush To**

Judgement, p. 40; CD205, p. 39
9. 6H321—Earl Brown; 6H284
10. 7H105
11. 7H284; WNEW-TV transcript 3/24/66
    p. 42—Dodd, Simmons
12. 7H531
13. 7H105
14. CD1095
15. **Undercover**—Hunt, p. 97
16. **Day**—Hunt, p. 39
17. NYT 9/8/73
18. NYT 10/31/74
19. CD81B
20. 6H205
21. CD291
22. 3H281—Mooney, Walters
23. 7H565—E.L. Smith
24. 14H515
25. 14H515—Curry Dep.; 5145—Player
26. CD354
27. 3H186
28. Dallas **Times Herald** 3/10/64
29. NYT approx. 12/6/73
30. INV 1-2; GA 3-1, Nov. 18, 1964,
    Rankin to Hoover
31. 156R
32. CD897, Sec. 1
33. 7H539; 253R—W.E. Barnett
34. 151-55R
35. 6H308
36. 6H277
37. CD81B
38. CD1108
39. Private, tape-recorder telephone call
    with D.V. Harkness, Dallas P.D.
40. Rec. Int. with Mark Lane 3/31/66
41. **Who's Who In America**
42. Dallas P.D. Yearbook 1963
43. "Kennedy's Last Hour"—Dallas
    Cinema Associates
44. Tape recorded conversation between
    Will Fritz and Canfield, 1/75
45. UPI Dispatch re: D. House 9/29/64;
    CE5323
46. CD1420
47. CE5323
48. FBI File #LA 105-15823
49. **Legacy of Doubt**—Noyes, p. 240
50. 7H507; 3H291—Mrs. Baker

51. CE358; 2H165
52. Memo from Rankin to Hoover re:
    Testimony of Arnold Rowland
53. 24H522
54. 6H200; 6H191
55. 147R
56. 21H p. 391-92—Harkness, Brewer,
    Batchelor
57. CD711; CD81B; 6H205
58. CD87; 2H190
59. 3H281—Luke Mooney
60. 19H492
61. 6H284
62. CD1036
63. 5H47
64. 9H102
65. **John Reed,** testimony to House Gov.
    Activities Subcom. headed by Jack
    Brooks
66. Washington **Post** 6/14/73
67. Jack Anderson 11/12/73
68. Dr. Roy Bohl
Chapter Five
1. **Undercover**—Hunt p. 370
2. **Harper's** Oct 74
3. Watergate File p. 41-43
4. **Undercover**—Hunt, p. 146
5. **Day**—Hunt, p. 37
6. **President's Men**—Woodstein, p. 23
7. **Day**—Hunt, p. 13
8. **Day**—Hunt, p. 27, 29
9. **Counteragent**—Tanner, p. 65—Lau-
    reano Batista; **Day**—Hunt, p. 47
10. **Day**—Hunt, 70
11. **Day**—Hunt, p. 75
12. **Day**—Hunt, p. 84. 88
13. **Day**—Hunt, p. 156. 220
14. **Day**—Hunt, p. 187
15. 7R246
16. **Day**—Hunt, p. 219; **Heroin In S.E.
    Asia**—McCoy
17. **Undercover**—Hunt, p. 132; NYT
    12/30/75
18. **Esquire** 2/74—Szulc
19. **Comp. Spy**—Szulc, p. 95
20. **Undercover**—Hunt, p. 132
21. **Plot or Politics**—James, p. 126
22. **Kennedy Conspiracy**—Flammode,
    p. 253; A.P. Dispatch 5/10/63

23. White House Tapes, p. 1022
24. **Castro**—Dubois—Bobbs Merrill 1959 **Newsweek** 5/18/73 P. 22
25. **True**—Andrew St. George, 8/74
26. NYT 1/23/75; **Undercover**—Hunt, p. 148
27. Senate Select Comm. on Camp. Activities testimony 3880
28. Canfield/Sturgis interview—taped
29. FBI File #Phil. 157-916
30. NYT 6/23/72—Szulc
31. CD1347—Prestly Walton
32. CE3067
33. CD395
34. **Day**—Hunt, p. 28
35. **Dagger**—Lazo, p. 236
36. **Day**—Hunt, p. 39
37. **Current Bio** 1970
38. **Ibid.** 18
39. Miami **Herald** 2/14/67, P. 10A
40. **Nixon**—Mazo, p. 38
41. Miami **News** 6/25/74
42. **Ibid** 18
43. **Hoover**—Messick, p. 120
44. **Heroin in S.E. Asia**—McCoy, p. 186
45. Penn. Central Hearing; Conversation with Prof. Peter Dale Scott
46. 9H102
47. Kefauver hearing Part 7—Ed Meyer, Index under Ed Myer
48. CD86, P. 537
49. 4H627
50. Bell Telephone records in New Orleans 9/24—Chicago, Ill. (312) WH 4-4970. Amount $3.85. Your #524-1047; CE2350
51. 7H289, 525
52. White House Tapes, p. 3, 1295
53. Nixon to Haldeman 6/23/72, 1:04—1:13 pm
54. Helms testimony to Sen. Select Comm. 3275
55. White House tapes 215, 196, 672-73, 242-43, 206
56. Sen. Select Comm. Hearing V8, Hunt testimony
57. Watergate Exhibits p. 3880
58. NYT 11/5/74
59. **Hoover**—Messick, p. 136
60. **Atlantic** 4/75
61. NYT Compilation of Watergate hearings, p. 732
62. Los Angeles **Star**
63. Conv. w/J.J.Wilson Sec. 3/75
64. Jack Anderson 11/10/71—Pauco/Pastor
65. Washington **Post** 11/22/74
66. Jack Anderson 8/9/74
67. **Harper's** Oct 74
68. White House tapes 880
69. **Ibid** 25
70. N.Y. **Post** 2/6/75
71. **Undercover**—Hunt, p. 220
72. **Ibid** p. 25
73. **Counteragent**—Tanner, p. 154
74. Canfield interview w/Sturgis
75. Anderson—6/12/60, Wash. **Post**
76. A.P. Dispatch 5/12/60; **Hoover**—Messick, p. 154
77. **Lansky**—Messick, p. 191
78. Watergate Ex. 9913; Caufield Ex 3; Miami **Herald** 1/19/71
79. **Time** 1/13/75
80. NYT 4/20/61; Anderson 5/61; N.Y. **Daily News** 4/20-25/75
81. Canfield/Sturgis interview
82. **Day**—Hunt, p. 98-101
83. Miami **News** 10/30/62
84. CD1179
85. CD59; CD1179
86. **Counteragent**—Tanner, p. 117
87. **Counteragent**—Tanner, p. 117
88. Miami **Herald** 12/5/62
89. CD1020—O'Connor 4/30/64—Zararis Acosta
90. NYT 4/3/63
91. NYT 4/29/63; 10/27/59; 4/27/63; 9/15/63
92. Anderson 5/4/63
93. **Syndicate Abroad**—Messick, p. 32, 137
94. CD984B; Wash. **Post** 8/1/63; CD984B, also "P72"
95. FBI File #MM8342, also report O'Connor, Miami, Fla., 12/31/63
96. NYT 6/21/63
97. NYT 8/11/63
98. NYT 9/15/63
99. Canfield/Sturgis interview 2/75

100. CD59
101. CD395
102. CD395
103. CD1020—VP Geraldine Shamma
104. CD810
105. CD1020
106. **Ibid**
107. Secret Service report CO234030
108. Miami **Herald** 3/9/75
109. CD657; NYT 9/27/60; 3/11, 12/61;
     10/22/60
110. CD561
111. CD961
112. CD1169
113. CD691
114. N.Y. **Journal American** 12/28/63
115. CD395—"Sanchez"
116. CD1020
117. CD1020
118. CD1020; CD916; CD395
119. CD59—Alan Courtney
120. FBI File #DL100-10461—Ray Carney
121. CD812
122. Anderson 4/16/74
123. Transcripts of People vs. Sturgis in
     Miami Federal Court, Florida
124. **$400,000 Pour Abattre Kennedy a
     Paris** by Cammille Gilles Julliard/
     1973/Paris; Dora Robineau
Chapter Six
1. Friends of Democratic Cuba, alias Citizens for Free Cuba (founded 1961)
   Records in New Orleans County
   Clerk's office
2. CD953; CD856
3. 10H369—Malcolm Price; 318R
4. CD7, p. 252, 236; 318R
5. 318R—Homer Wood; CD205, p. 122;
   CD1063
6. Dallas **Times Herald** 11/28/63; 315-6R;
   646R; CD996; CD1066, p. 197
7. CD7, p. 268
8. Mrs. Hall deposition
9. CE3071; CD567; CD179; CD71
10. 10H340
11. 3H140, 184, 211; CD329, p. 8
12. CD7, p. 252; 10H378
13. CD205, p. 122
14. CD1063

15. CE3071; 10H352; CD329, sec. 1, p. 77
16. CD7, p. 252-68—James Dale
17. CD1085D
18. NYT 4/6/63, 9/14/62, 10/11/62,
    4/1/63
19. Miami **Herald** 4/9/63; CD1085
20. FBI File #MM 89-35
21. **Ibid**—Marguerite Dignum;
    Miami **Herald** 4/11/63
22. NYT 4/11/68
23. NYT 5/24/68, 4/11/68
24. A.P. dispatch 5/26/75; Miami **Phoenix**
    10/2/74
25. NYT 10/30/74
26. NYT 11/16/68
Chapter Seven
1. CE3108; FBI File #44-1639
2. 364R
3. Reveille head of CID; 5H33; 327R; PC6,
   Memo for record from Willens
   dated 2/12/64
4. 11H367
5. **Ibid**; CE2943
6. FBI File #DL 100-10461; CD1553
7. CD1546
8. CE2907; CD854
9. Memo Rankin to Hoover, JCR, WDS,
   HPW 7/23/64; Undated Rankin
   memo
10. Undated Rankin memo; CE2943
11. CE2943
12. **Day**—Hunt, p. 55
13. **Ibid**, p. 91, 92, 215
14. **Ibid**, p. 140, 142, 153, 175
15. **Ibid**, p. 56, 188
16. NYT 5/24/61
17. CD1546; CD854
18. **Day**—Hunt, p. 71
19. **Counteragent**—Tanner, p. 97
20. **Pressina Latin** 11/74; CD1553
21. **Ibid** 1
22. 626R
23. CD854
24. CD946
25. CD453; SS report Miami 11/24-
    12/4/63
26. CE2943
27. Undated Rankin memo
28. CE3147

29. CE3148
30. **Glasshouse**—Freed, p. 172
31. Ex. 142, Watergate Hearings, 3850 (Senate)
32. Miami **News** 6/25/74
Chapter Eight
1. FBI File #105-15823
2. NYT 7/1/59
3. FBI File # PX 105-1529 CWE/utp
4. CD1563
5. **Ibid** 1
6. CD1553
7. Item 4—List of CD's
8. **Ibid**, p. 577, 117
9. CE1414
10. FBI inter. w/Lanusa—O'Conner 11/23/63; Unidentified document; CD897
11. **Undercover**—Hunt, p. 141
12. **Day**—Hunt, p. 13, 15
13. CD1546
14. CE3146
15. 5H100
16. Dallas **Times Herald** 2/13/75
17. Recorded interview w/Agent Kananskie 2/75
18. Chicago **Tribune** 12/13/73
19. **Oswald in New Orleans**—Weisberg, p. 256; CD897—Pasqual Goncona
20. CD1026—Mrs. Arensberg
21. FBI File #WFO 89-75—Daniel James
22. CD916
23. **Ibid** 21
24. **CIA Diary**—Agee, p. 619
25. CD349; CD295
26. FBI File #DL 100 10461
27. CD1214
28. CD378; **Nation** 5/9/66 **Ibid** 24, p. 611
29. Anderson 10/8/73; **Undercover**—Hunt, p. 134
30. 151R
31. **Jury**—Belin, p. 261-72—TSBD sec., Mrs. Reid
32. 163R
33. 14H330
34. 369R
35. CD1447; CD1465—Larry Crawford
36. Scobbey AS; mfd 7/27/64, Entry 44

Box 22
37. 6R
38. 17H471; CD868; CD993; CD1245; CE162
39. 7R; 176R;559R;180R
40. NYT 11/18/73, 11/22/73
41. 178R; CD1245
42. 4H253, p. 258-60; Letter of Hoover to Commission 6/2/64
43. 565R
44. **Harper's** May 1975
45. 566R; Notebook relating to witnesses and testimony—Latona summary
46. SS File #CO-2-34 030
47. 18H795
48. Transcripts KLRD Reel 9 30:57
49. 201R; 655R
50. CD1406
Chapter Nine
1. NYT 11/25/63; V. Riesel 11/30/63
2. NYT 11/25/63
3. **RFK**—DeToledano, p. 232
4. **Hoffa**—Sheridan, p. 408
5. Riesel 11/30/63
6. CD301, p. 172
7. Commission correspondence to CIA in author's possession.
8. Wash. **Star** 11/23/73
9. **Secret File**—Messick, p. 351
10. **RFK**—DeToledano, p. 237
11. CE2331
12. **Legacy of Doubt**—Noyes, p. 206
13. 25H244—Dusty Miller 25H246—Irwin Weiner
14. White House Tapes 675, 1280
15. NYT 9/18/74
16. **Hoover**—Messick, p. 182-87
17. **Harper's** 12/74
18. CE2979
19. **Hoffa**—Sheridan, p. 356
20. CD1152; 792R
21. CE1692
22. Kefauver hearings P5—Lt. Butler
23. CD1262
24. NYT 7/1/59—Dominick E. Bartone
25. CD360; CE3065
26. **True**—St. George 8/74
27. CD914; CD919;
28. **Sil. Syndicate**—Messick, p. 237, 272

Secret File—Messick, p. 205, 211, 222
29. CE3063
30. 5H181; 14H504
31. CE1688; CE3066
32. Warren Comm. Exec. Session—Item one, Nat'l Archives; 369R
33. CD856
34. CD1193
35. CE3061; CD799A,B; 14H330; CD1071; CD1178
36. **Syndicate Abroad**—Messick, p. 19
37. **Silent Syndicate**—Messick, p. 205
38. **Secret File**—Messick, p. 204
39. Kefauver hearings, P7, p. 1089
40. CE3061—Dick Cherry
41. **Rush to Judge.**—Lane, p. 279, 788; **Ibid** 35; NYT 4/28/71
42. CD1071; CD1178; CE3059
43. CE2943
44. **Counteragent**, p. 3
45. CE1546
46. **Silent Syndicate**—Messick, p. 272 Kefauver hearings P7, p. 607 **Lansky**—Messick, p. 175
47. **Syndicate Abroad**—Messick, p. 66
48. **Lansky**—Messick, p. 196
49. CE1697; CD1151B
50. N.Y. **Daily News** 4/25-30/75
51. NYT Obituary index, 1953
52. Hubert memo 3/19/64
53. FBI File #DL 44-1639 11/30/63
54. Recorded conversation with Carlos Prio
55. 5H181; 14H504
56. 14H429; 15H321
57. CE1691; CD86; **Ibid 55**
58. Canfield interview with Sturgis; **Ibid 37**
59. CE697
60. Kefauver hearings, part 12, p. 597
61. CE1690
62. Kefauver hearings—Cal Neva, P439, 548, 549, 1074, Part Ten—Bones Remmer
63. **Syndicate Abroad**—Messick, p. 89, 128
64. Anderson 1/25/71 **Hoover**—Messick, p. 176
65. **Atlantic** July 1973
66. **Parade** 4/12/64, p. 4
67. **Ibid 58**
68. Conversation with FBI record service

69. John Dean memo to Haldeman 1/26/71 Watergate Senate Ex p. 3370 **Hoover**—Messick, p. 237 NYT 7/2/74, 1/1/71
70. **Undercover**—Hunt, p. 141
71. **Comp. Spy**—Szulc, p. 98
72. CE1697
73. CE1546; CE1697
74. CE3012
75. Hubert memo re: Ruby and Cuba
76. CD7, p. 114; Hubert memo 3/19/64
77. Memo from Rankin to Hoover CD1409, declassified 2/1/71
78. Memo from Rankin to Hoover— Griffen; ju 6/16/64—A. Sayman Hubert memo, p. 8—Thomas Hill (declassified 2/1/71)
79. CE1729
80. Letter written by Jack Ruby **Ramparts** 2/67
81. NYT 2/27/66
82. CD735
83. CD806
84. Conference with Issac David Levine, Dulles, & Slawson, 5/28/64
85. NYT 12/30/75
86. CD1546
87. Memo from Sam Stern to Norman Redlich 2/18/64, p. 3
88. CD432; CD499; CD880
89. CD1546; CD887—Declan Ford, Peter Gregory

Chapter Ten
1. **Lansky**—Messick, p. 230
2. **Day**—Hunt, p. 15
3. White House tapes, 341
4. Eisenberg memo re: First Staff Conference 2/17/64
5. NYT 3/16/75—Retson
6. **Ford**—terHorst, p. 82; CD1431 **Newsday** 9/28/64
7. **American Opinion** 6/72; NYT 3/4/25
8. **Undercover**—Hunt, p. 66
9. **Undercover**—Hunt, p. 132
10. Atlanta **Journal** 9/28/64
11. NYT 1/22/71
12. Washington **Post** 1/21/75
13. Executive Hearings V4 Memorandum concerning Comm. PC8

14. NYT 4/19/72

15. Memo concerning Commission PC8
    Recorded conversation with City Desk
    of Philadelphia **Enquirer**
    NYT 12/6/73

16. Miami **Herald** 2/5/75

17. NYT 2/28/74, 5/4/70

18. NYT 10/31/74

19. NYT 4/28/71

20. Memo from S.R. Pollack to Rankin
    dated 7/28/64

21. Letter from Rankin to Miller 10/22/64
    re: Rowcotsky & Peter

22. Memo from Miller & Katzenbach to
    Commission dated 11/27/63

23. Letter from Hoover to Rankin 1/10/64

24. Presidential Comm. Admin. Recs Item
    20—bio of A. Goldberg
    NYT 6/16/63, p. 24

25. **Detente-Cold War Strategies in Transi-
    tion**—Praeger, 1965

26. 7H332; Manchester **Guardian** 1/9/74

27. **Who's Who in CIA**
    Press release from office of Waggoner
    Carr 12/2/63

28. Gerald Story Bio. Sheet—Special JFK
    document collection, Library of
    Congress; **Who's Who in CIA**

29. Phoenix **Gazette** 2/26/64

30. **Invisible Government**—Ross, p. 5

31. NYT 2/21/67

32. **Friendship and Frat**—Zeligs, p. 255

33. NYT 7/3/73

34. NYT 1/5/75

35. New Orleans **States Item** 2/25/67

36. **Legacy**—Noyes, p. 184, 206-07

37. 160R; 6H260

38. 6H220

39. Recorded phone conver. with R.
    Sprague, winter 1974

40. Recorded phone conver. with V.
    Salandria

41. NYT 12/27/67

42. **Kennedy Consp.**—Flammode, p. 203-5

43. NYT 11/8/63
    Tacoma **News Tribune** 11/22/68

44. New Orleans **Times Pic** 3/14/72

45. **Thousand Days**—Schlesinger, p. 200—
    General Stroessner

46. **Day**—Hunt, p. 61

47. **Thousand Days**—Schlesinger, p. 339,
    448

48. NYT 1/20/75

49. NYT 1/6/75

50. **Nation** 1/16/67

51. NYT 3/8/75
    Private phone conver. with William
    Snyder

52. NYT 12/25/74

53. NYT 3/2/75, 3/10/75, 3/11/75

54. NYT 3/2/75

55. Miami **Herald** 3/9/75

Selected Bibliography

Agee, Philip. *CIA Diary.* Penguin. 1975.

Bremer, Arthur J. *Artie Bremer's Diary.* Harper's Magazine Press, 1973.

Buschel, Jim. *Watergate File.* Flash Books, 1973.

Butler, Ed. *Revolution Is My Profession.* Twin Circle Press, 1968.

Committee of Concerned Asian Scholars. *The Opium Trail.* New England Free Press, 1972.

Cook, Fred. *The Warfare State.* MacMillan, 1967.

DeToledano, Ralph. *RFK—The Man Who Would Be President.* Putnam, 1967.

Dulles, Allen. *The Craft of Intelligence.* Harper and Row, 1963.

Epstein, Edward. *Counterplot.* Viking, 1968.

Flammonde, Paris. *The Kennedy Conspiracy.* Meredith Press, 1969.

Ford, Gerald. *Portrait of the Assassin.* Simon & Shuster, 1965.

Freed, Don. *The Glasshouse Tapes.* Avon, 1973.

Garrison, Jim. *Heritage of Stone.* Putnam, 1970.

Goulden, Joseph. *The Superlawyers.* Weybright and Tally, 1971.

Hunt, E. Howard. *Give Us This Day.* Arlington House, 1973.

————————. *Undercover.* Berkeley-Putnam, 1974.

James, Rosemary, and Jack Wardlaw. *Plot or Politics.* Pelican, 1967.

Lane, Mark. *Rush to Judgement.* Holt, Rinehart & Winston, 1966.

Lasby, Clarence. *Project Paperclip.* Atheneum Press, 1971.

Lazo, Mario. *Dagger in the heart.* Funk & Wagnalls, 1968.

McCoy, Alfred. *Heroin in Southeast Asia.* Harper and Row, 1973.

Mader, Julius. *Who's Who in the CIA.* 1066 Berlin W66/Maverstrausse, E., East Germany, 1968.

Messick, Hank. *John Edgar Hoover.* David McKay, 1972.

——————. *Lansky.* Berkeley, 1971.

——————. *The Secret File.* Putnam, 1969.

——————. *The Silent Syndicate.* MacMilllan, 1967.

——————. *The Syndicate Abroad.* MacMillan, 1969.

Marchetti, Victor. *The CIA and the Cult of Intelligence.* Knopf, 1974.

Mazo, Earl. *Nixon.* Avon Books, 1959.

New York *Times. The Watergate Hearings.* Bantam, 1973.

Nixon, Richard Milhous. *Submission of Recorded Presidential Conversations, April 10, 1974.* U.S. Government Printing Office, 1974.

Nixon, Richard. *My Six Crises.* Doubleday, 1962.

Noyes, Peter. *Legacy of Doubt.* Pinnacle, 1973.

Schlesinger, Arthur. *A Thousand Days.* Houghton, Mifflin, 1965.

Scott, Peter Dale. *The War Conspiracy.* Bobbs-Merrill, 1972.

Sheridan, Walter. *The Fall and Rise of Hoffa.* Saturday Review Press, 1973.

Szulc, Tad. *Compulsive Spy.* Viking, 1974.

Tanner, Hans. *Counterrevolutionary Agent.* G.T. Foulis, 1961.

terHorst, J.F. *Gerald Ford and the Future of the Presidency.* Third Press, 1974.

Weisberg, Harold. *Oswald in New Orleans.* Canyon, 1967.

Wise, David and Thomas Ross. *The Invisible Government.* Random House, 1964

Woodward, Bob and Carl Bernstein. *All the President's Men.* Simon & Shuster, 1974.

Youngblood, Jack. *The Devil to Pay.* Coward McCann, 1967.

Zeligs, Meyer A. *Friendship & Fratricide.* Viking, 1967.

Index to Chapters 1-12